☐ NATIONAL GEOGRAPHIC

GUIDE TO FAMILY
ADVENTURE
VACATIONS

NATIONAL GEOGRAPHIC

GUIDE TO FAMILY ADVENTURE VACATIONS

Wildlife Encounters, Cultural Explorations, and Learning Escapes in the U.S. and Canada

BY CANDYCE H. STAPEN

CONTENTS

Title page: Siblings check out giant Pacific sea stars at Mystic Aquarium in Mystic, Connecticut (page 204).

Venturing with Your Family

This *National Geographic Guide to Family Adventure Vacations* contains my favorite places for adventurous families to vacation in the United States and Canada. Throughout the book, I have used the word "family" in its broadest possible sense: In addition to trips designed for parents and their young children, I have included vacations for those with preschoolers, grade-schoolers, teenagers, and adult children. (Recommended age ranges accompany most write-ups.) My use of the word "parent" should be loosely interpreted, too; it is meant to encompass grandparents, favorite aunts and uncles, and other extended-family members or friends.

Packed with 327 entries, the book showcases a wide range of family adventures. After describing each activity in detail, I offer a section labeled "Tips" that is intended to spare you aggravation and enhance your enjoyment of a destination. These are the same sort of useful nuggets I share with friends who are headed for a place I've just visited—advice such as which parking lot is nearest the bathrooms at a sprawling living history museum, or crucial reminders such as the advisability of requesting a covered or air-conditioned jeep for a summer tour in Arizona.

The guide can be used in a number of ways. If you have wanted to break free of your traditional annual week or two at the beach or lake, you'll find suggestions in the following pages for all sorts of unique, innovative, and offbeat vacations. Among the possibilities: digging for dinosaur bones in Colorado or Alberta; watching whales in Baja California or Canada; and riding horses across the Cheyenne Reservation to gather Native American medicinal plants, then spending the night in a tipi.

Family Adventure Vacations can also be used as an instant on-site resource when the inspiration hits to break away from a resort stay or business trip with your kids. Rather than buying into the packaged diversions offered by a hotel in Maui, for example, why not hike across a million-year-old lava field? If the sponsor is Maui Eco-Adventures (see page 56), you can recoup those lost calories with a picnic lunch at a taro farm high in the mountains. If you're cruising Alaska's Inside Passage, the book tells you how to add a bear-watching trip (pages 46-48) or remotelodge stay (page 49) afterward. Or perhaps you simply like to hike the backcountry of Glacier National Park; in that case, the book offers side trips to a buffalo jump and sun-dance site in the company of a Blackfeet guide (pages 125-127).

In recognition of the busyness of both parents and children today, the book also profiles a number of one-day trips and overnights. These getaways provide a respite from ringing phones and undone house- and homework, giving you a chance to

Zuni White Buffalo Dance participants at Inter-Tribal Indian Ceremonial in Gallup, New Mexico

spend time with your kids. Such jaunts need not take you far from home. The guide's day trips can help you (re)discover the museums, aquariums, and zoos that lie just beyond your own backyard. You may not have known that you can kayak the Potomac River through the District of Columbia's Georgetown, learning some capital history in the process (page 233); that you can bed down next to "Sue," the world's largest *Tyrannosaurus rex* skeleton, on an overnight at Chicago's Field Museum (page 84); or that you can learn about the Underground Railroad by enacting the role of an escaping slave at Conner Prairie near Indianapolis (page 79).

WIDEN THEIR WORLD

Families crave a new kind of travel—a form of shared discovery that values insight over sights. That's why wildlife encounters, cultural explorations, and learning escapes such as the ones covered in this guide have become so popular with families. Although they are just plain fun to do, both you and your kids will also learn something from each type of experience.

On the wildlife encounters, families can savor the peace of natural places and the joy of being close to animals. On the cultural explorations, which focus on interactions with Native Americans, Hawaiians, and First Nations (the indigenous people of Canada), parents and children can explore unspoiled countryside while learning about the history, language, and beliefs of other cultures. And on the learning escapes, families share the pride of acquiring new skills and knowledge—as well as the sense of accomplishment that comes from tackling a task as a team.

The nature-based spirituality of Native Americans seems to hold special appeal for burnt-out city dwellers. "People are trying to get a different viewpoint on life," says Darrell Norman (page 129), a Blackfeet artist who lives in Browning, Montana. "They are trying to learn how to live better with the earth. They come here to the reservation to view another culture—to experience a different way of thinking and a different spiritual environment."

A week or even a weekend of riding horseback across open plains, hiking to the top of mesas, and listening to Native legends around a campfire may endow you with a "slot-canyon view." Like those Western chasms where a single shaft of sunlight provides a brilliant illumination, these cultural exchanges may give you a new way of looking at Native American lives—and, perhaps, your own.

If you decide to accept this book's invitation to explore one of the many Native cultures that continue to thrive in the United States, keep in mind that Native Americans welcome visitors, not tourists. Follow the same rules on a reservation that you would as a guest in someone's home: Be tactful, gracious, and helpful. Don't snoop. Be sure to share. Listen.

You should also be aware that many Native American societies consider it impolite to look someone in the eye when you talk to them. If people do not meet your eyes in conversation, they are not being rude—they are showing respect.

SOME LORE BEFORE YOU EXPLORE

The goal of any family adventure vacation should be quality time together, not induction into the Tourism Hall of Fame. Scheduling less will get you more: Rather than constantly hustling your kids off to the next "must-do," linger at the science museums's "Journey to Mars" exhibit, or indulge in an impromptu picnic. In short, be sure to underplan.

As part of that, go for the green—spaces, that is. Seek out parks where you can play catch or do a little inconspicuous people-watching. When traveling with more than one child, be sure to engineer some time alone—a morning walk, an afternoon swim in the hotel pool—with each one. Above all, keep your sense of humor. Attractions get crowded, cars break down, kids spit up. Remember why you sought out this adventure in the first place: to have fun with your children.

I welcome your comments and experiences at stapenc@aol.com. I promise to respond to you as soon as I can. Please understand, however, that I may be out of town on a new adventure, finding the next wonderful vacation to tell you about.

—Candyce H. Stapen

THE SOUTHWEST
AND PACIFIC

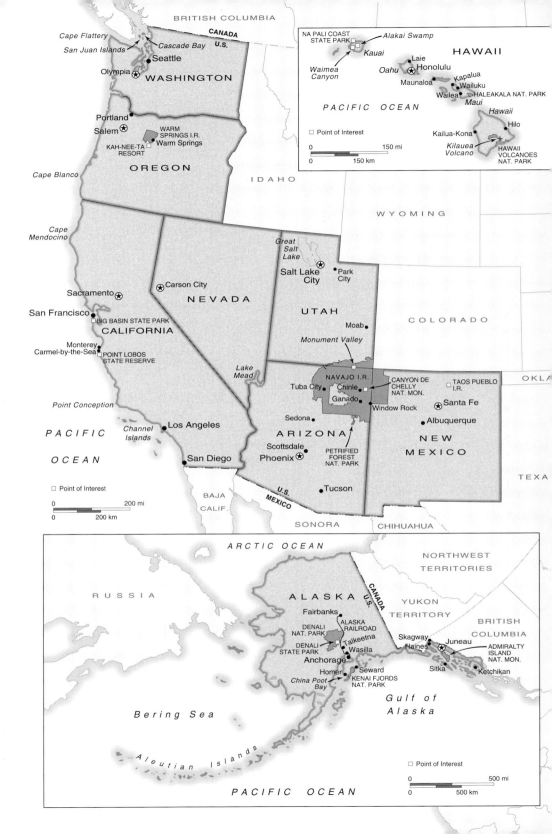

BRITISH COLUMBIA

Cape Flattery
San Juan Islands · *Cascade Bay*
· Seattle

CANADA
U.S.

Olympia ⊛
WASHINGTON

Portland ·
Salem ⊛
KAH-NEE-TA RESORT
WARM SPRINGS I.R.
Warm Springs

Cape Blanco

OREGON

IDAHO

Cape Mendocino

Sacramento ⊛
⊛ Carson City

NEVADA

Great Salt Lake
Salt Lake City ⊛
· Park City

WYOMING

San Francisco ·
□ BIG BASIN STATE PARK
CALIFORNIA
Monterey ·
Carmel-by-the-Sea ·
□ POINT LOBOS STATE RESERVE

UTAH

· Moab

COLORADO

Point Conception

Lake Mead

Monument Valley

□

NAVAJO I.R.
Tuba City ·
Chinle □
Ganado ·
Window Rock ⊛
CANYON DE CHELLY NAT. MON.
□ TAOS PUEBLO I.R.
⊛ Santa Fe

PACIFIC OCEAN

Channel Islands
Los Angeles ·

Sedona ·

· Albuquerque

ARIZONA

NEW MEXICO

OKLA

Scottsdale ·
Phoenix ⊛

PETRIFIED FOREST NAT. PARK

San Diego ·

□ Point of Interest
0 — 200 mi
0 — 200 km

BAJA CALIF.

· Tucson

U.S.
MEXICO

TEXAS

SONORA

CHIHUAHUA

NA PALI COAST STATE PARK
□ — *Alakai Swamp*
Kauai

HAWAII

Waimea Canyon

Oahu
· Laie
· Honolulu
Maunaloa ·
Kapalua ·
· Wailuku
Wailea ·
HALEAKALA NAT. PARK
Maui

PACIFIC OCEAN

□ Point of Interest
0 — 150 mi
0 — 150 km

Hawaii
· Hilo
Kailua-Kona ·
Kilauea Volcano
HAWAII VOLCANOES NAT. PARK

ARCTIC OCEAN

NORTHWEST TERRITORIES

RUSSIA

ALASKA

CANADA U.S.

YUKON TERRITORY

BRITISH COLUMBIA

Fairbanks ·
DENALI NAT. PARK
ALASKA RAILROAD
DENALI STATE PARK
Talkeetna ·
· Wasilla
Anchorage ·

Skagway ·
Haines ·
· Juneau ⊛
ADMIRALTY ISLAND NAT. MON.

Homer ·
China Poot Bay
· Seward
KENAI FJORDS NAT. PARK

· Sitka

· Ketchikan

Bering Sea

Gulf of Alaska

Aleutian Islands

PACIFIC OCEAN

□ Point of Interest
0 — 500 mi
0 — 500 km

Taos Pueblo

The Sangre de Cristo foothills unfolded before us, revealing a sweep of mesas, mountain passes, and gorges carved out by the Rio Grande. Against this majestic backdrop, **Taos Pueblo**—a multitiered adobe dwelling that is one of the oldest continually inhabited communities in the United States—exuded a simple dignity and a powerful spiritual presence.

The Taos-Tiwa Indians, or People of the Red Willow, have inhabited this region (now a part of northern New Mexico) for nearly a thousand years. Taos Pueblo is the largest existing multistory pueblo in the United States. When the Spaniards arrived in 1540, the Taos Indians enjoyed a flourishing culture—and the pueblo was already a well-developed structure. Today, about 50 families continue to live within the thick adobe walls of the pueblo. They draw water from the river and bake bread in outdoor ovens as their ancestors have done for the past 10 centuries. Most Taos-Tiwa families—some 4,000 people in all—live on the reservation in homes with modern conveniences.

Families find themselves drawn here by more than the snowcapped mountain scenery and the site's thousand-year-old heritage; the Taos pueblo also draws you in with its spirit. "You start feeling the power once you get through the pass after Santa Fe," says Blue Spruce Standing Deer, a Taos Indian artist who operates the reservation's Medicine Bird gallery. "When people come through the 'horseshoe' [the last turn] and suddenly arrive on top of the mesa, they say, 'Oh my God! I didn't know such a place existed!'"

The more time you spend in the pueblo, the more you may sense its power. On an initial visit, take the 30-minute guided tour of the village. The guide will explain the history of the pueblo and its system of government; afterward, you can browse the shops for pottery, leather goods, and drums. Children will be most interested if you visit on a feast day, when the pueblo comes alive with drumming and dancing by scores of American Indians in regalia. "The drum," Standing Deer informs a visitor, "is used to reach the destination of the spirit. It is a vibration of the power within."

One of my favorite ways to reach Taos Pueblo is on a guided horseback ride led by **Taos Indian Horse Ranch.** The horses walk or trot alongside ravines, through streams, up ridge tops, and across high mountain desert dotted with sagebrush. On past rides, our guide has pointed out ancient arrowheads, coyote tracks, and significant American Indian sites.

Page 9: Two Navajo girls in Monument Valley on the border of Arizona and Utah

 WILDLIFE ENCOUNTER    CULTURAL EXPLORATION   LEARNING ESCAPE

A modern occupant of ancient Santa Clara Pueblo

TIPS: If possible, plan your visit to coincide with the **Taos Pueblo Powwow,** held the second weekend in July, or the **Feast of San Geronimo,** held the last weekend in September. On both occasions, the pueblo holds dances, pole-climbing races, and foot races.

BASICS: **Taos Pueblo Visitor Information** *(P. O. Box 1846, Taos. 505/758-1028 or 9593).* For **guided horseback rides,** contact the Taos Indian Horse Ranch *(P. O. Box 3019, Taos 87571. 505/758-3212).*

Indian Pueblo Cultural Center Albuquerque

Stomping in rhythm to the drums, the dancers appeared to be a seamless swirl of feathers and headdresses, the silver bells on their ankle bracelets glinting in the sun. It was another New Mexico spring, and American Indian dancers were performing the Eagle Dance to honor and thank the eagle for his gifts to the Indian people.

The Eagle Dance is just one of many that families can witness during a visit to

PUEBLO ETIQUETTE

Visiting a pueblo is like visiting someone's home. The following tips will help you observe "pueblo etiquette":

✢ Call ahead to be sure visitors are welcome. Pueblos sometimes close for private ceremonies.

✢ Ask permission before taking any photographs or videos. Some pueblos ban cameras and videos; others charge a photo fee.

✢ Remain silent when watching dances. Do not applaud; dances are religious ceremonies.

✢ Do not approach or talk to the dancers before, during, or after a performance.

✢ Enter only those buildings that are open to the public.

✢ Stay in the immediate village area; do not wander about.

✢ Be aware that some pueblos have no bathrooms for the public.

For more information: Contact individual pueblos or the visitors bureau *(800/284-2282. www.abqcvb.org).*

Albuquerque's **Indian Pueblo Cultural Center,** which is owned and operated by the 19 Indian pueblos in the area: Acoma, Cochiti, Isleta, Jemez, Laguna, Nambe, Picuris, Pojoaque, Sandia, San Felipe, San Ildefonso, San Juan, Santa Ana, Santa Clara, Santo Domingo, Taos, Tesuque, Zia, and Zuni. The public is invited to join in the Friendship Dance at the end of each performance.

The museum building is the site of cultural events throughout the year. (The building itself is modeled on **Pueblo Bonito,** a well-known abandoned site in Chaco Canyon in northwestern New Mexico.) Museum displays use crafts and artifacts such as murals, contemporary pottery and drums, and ancient arts to trace the history and spoken traditions of the 19 pueblos.

At the **Pueblo House Children's Museum,** kids are encouraged to handle stone tools and weapons that were used by early nomadic hunters. They can also make their own pictographs. In the **Pit House,** children grind corn using a grinding stone, find out whether yucca fibers really feel yucky, and then learn the Pueblo technique for weaving those fibers into baskets and mats. Kids can also handle the tools and materials used to make contemporary pottery, as well as learn how to fashion beaded jewelry. At the Pueblo Restaurant, open for breakfast and lunch, visitors can sample such local specialties as a Tiwa Taco or a bowl of posole (dried corn, pork, and chile).

A new **Living Village,** scheduled to open in 2001, will show what life was like for people living in pueblos of the late 1800s. Interpreters will demonstrate home-building, breadmaking, weaving, and silversmithing.

TIPS: According to the **Albuquerque Convention and Visitors Bureau,** the preferred term for New Mexico's tribal members is "American Indians," not "Native Americans."

Visitors join a Friendship Dance at Indian Pueblo Cultural Center, Albuquerque.

The gift shop at the Indian Pueblo Cultural Center boasts the largest collection of authentic Indian jewelry in the Southwest, along with hand-carved kachinas, pottery, woven rugs, Indian sculpture, and ritual sandpaintings.

Try to visit during special festivals such as the **Children's Festival of Indian Dance** in February, **American Indian Week** in April, or **Night Under the Stars** (featuring bonfires and storytellers) in September.

BASICS: **Indian Pueblo Cultural Center** *(2401 12th Street N.W., Albuquerque. 800/766-4405 or 505/843-7270. www.indianpueblo.org)* Dances are held Saturday and Sunday at 11 a.m. and 2 p.m.

OTHER PUEBLOS

Many of New Mexico's 19 pueblos lie within a one-hour drive of Albuquerque. Call the Indian Pueblo Cultural Center, or contact the pueblos directly, to find out which ones will interest your family the most.

Here is a sampling of see-worthy pueblos north of Albuquerque. **San Juan Pueblo** *(505/852-4400)* is the largest of the six Tewa-speaking villages. **Santa Clara Pueblo** *(505/753-7330)* is known for both its trout fishing and its black-and-red pottery. **San Ildefonso Pueblo** *(505/455-2273)* is famous for its black-on-black pottery. **Nambe Pueblo** *(505/455-2036)* offers campgrounds, as well as trout fishing in Nambe Lake. **Pojoaque Pueblo** *(505/455-2278)* features the work of hundreds of local artists at its Tourist Information Center. **Tesque Pueblo** *(505/983-2667 or 505/455-2467)* offers campgrounds and a casino. **Taos Pueblo** *(505/758-1028 or 9593)* boasts the tallest adobe pueblo in the Southwest.

Fifteen minutes south of Albuquerque on I-25 you'll find **Isleta Pueblo** *(505-869-3111)*, whose grounds are home to the Church of San Augustin—one of the oldest mission churches (circa 1613 to 1630) in the Southwest. The pueblo operates Isleta Lakes Water Recreation Area, which has picnic grounds and camping.

TIPS: *Eight Northern Indian Pueblos,* published by the **Indian Arts & Crafts Association** *(122 La Veta N.E., Suite B, Albuquerque 87108. 505/265-9149)*, elaborates on the attractions above.

Albuquerque Biological Park

The **Albuquerque Biological Park** comprises an aquarium, a zoo, and a botanical garden. At the **Albuquerque Aquarium,** visitors can walk through a re-created cave where moray eels lurk in crevices or slither overhead. The aquarium traces the course of the Rio Grande from its source in the mountains of Colorado through Albuquerque to the Gulf of Mexico. The shark tank, holding 285,000 gallons of salt water and stretching from floor to ceiling, boasts an acrylic front that is 70 feet (21 m) wide. The coral reef tank is comparatively small—only the size of a wall—but still large enough to hold hundreds of brightly colored fish.

At the **Albuquerque Zoo,** visitors can watch from a special viewing area as polar bears swim underwater. The zoo also houses such exotic species as Mexican wolves, Komodo dragons, and other animals.

The **Rio Grande Botanic Garden**—specifically, **El Jardin de la Curandera**—is the place to go to learn all about the secrets of medicinal plants. The showcase of the botanical garden is a 10,000-square-foot (930 sq m) conservatory, whose **desert pavilion** displays cactus, yucca, and other plants native to the Mexican state of Sonora. The conservatory's **Mediterranean pavilion,** meanwhile, contains an array of colorful plants that are indigenous to Spain, Turkey, and Portugal. Plans are also in place for a new gallery, Tropical Americana, that will house rain forest birds and predator cats.

TIPS: At 7 p.m. on selected Fridays in June, July, and August, the zoo stages free concerts of country, bluegrass, light rock, or semiclassical music.

BASICS: Albuquerque Biological Park *(903 10th St. S.W. 505/764-6200. www.abqcvb.org/info/biopark)*

MORE NEW MEXICO MIND BENDERS

Albuquerque: The **New Mexico Museum of Natural History and Science** *(1801 Mountain Rd. NW. 505/841-2800)* explores 38 million years of the state's geologic history. View fossils and find out about the era when New Mexico was seacoast.

At the **National Atomic Museum** *(P.O. Box 5800, Kirtland Air Force Base. 505/284-3243),* kids can learn about robotics, rockets, and the Manhattan Project.

Explora! Science Center and Children's Museum of Albuquerque *(800 Rio Grande Blvd., Suite 19. 505/842-1537)* is ideal for younger kids: They can stage puppet shows at the Creation Station, play with bubbles at the Bubble Zone, and create art at Make-It-Take-It.

Navajo Nation Experience
Tsaile

Some of the most spectacular scenery in the Southwest lies on the 27,000 square miles of **Navajo Nation** land in Arizona, New Mexico, and Utah. The sun turns slot-canyon walls the color of flame. Red-rock buttes and mesas rise from the desert floor. Ribbons of cream, pink, and yellow weave their way through wind-sculpted sandstone ridges.

With little development, few tourists, and the sort of sweeping vistas that draw crowds to nearby national parks, the reservation is a special place to be. Two Navajo-owned companies—**Coyote Pass Bed and Breakfast** and **Largo Navajo Land Tours**—will introduce you and your family to this landscape. Both offer overnight stays at a reservation hogan (the traditional Navajo dwelling of logs and earth), and both design custom cultural tours.

Explaining Navajo culture comes naturally to Will Tsosie, the owner of Coyote Pass. His grandfather, an interpreter for the public health office, frequently brought nonnatives to the house to share Navajo traditions. "It's a different type of tourism," says Tsosie, "to share a taste of what our everyday life is like."

John Largo left a career in state tourism to launch Largo Navajo Land Tours, which specializes in tourism devoted to Navajo culture. On Largo's eight-day **Outdoor Adventure Indian Culture tour,** for example, visitors hike the east rim of the Grand Canyon, ride horses on the reservation, learn how to make cornmeal cakes, and take a jeep tour of **Canyon de Chelly** *(pages 19-20)* and **Monument Valley** *(page 20).*

Both companies also offer the option of lodging at an area hotel and taking day trips with Navajo guides. These tours give participants a chance to absorb local perspectives of such well-known attractions as Canyon de Chelly, the Painted Desert, the Petrified Forest, and Monument Valley, as well as lesser known sites such as Diné College *(page 18)* and Window Rock.

The best way to sample Navajo land, however, is to stay in a hogan for at least one night and have Tsosie or Largo tailor a program to your family's interests. Among many other activities, this will allow you to hike to mesas harboring ancient petroglyphs; walk dried riverbeds littered with petrified logs; ride horseback across pastel-painted valleys; climb to ancient cliff dwellings; listen to storytellers relate Navajo tales by firelight; try your hand at Navajo weaving; and learn about the medicinal powers of herbs and wild plants.

For one family, Tsosie created a week-long pottery workshop: Parents and kids hiked together to collect clay and pinyon pitch for the glaze, learned the lines of

Left: Rock of ages at Canyon de Chelly

Navajo design, and discovered the legends behind various pottery shapes. The adventure culminated in the crafting of a small Navajo pot.

For three sisters with an interest in food, Tsosie cooked up a day-long workshop in Navajo cuisine. The women spent the morning finding berries, digging for yams, wild celery, and wild onions, and picking vegetables from Tsosie's garden. In the afternoon, they ground corn. For dinner, the sisters cooked a traditional meal from the ingredients they had gathered: dumpling stew with wild vegetables and fresh corn bread with blue-corn tortillas.

For a third family group, Tsosie created a weaving workshop. Participants learned about the influence of traders and the legends of weaving, then carded and spun wool, collected plants to make a dye, and wove a simple pattern.

Tsosie's Coyote Pass uses the following accommodations: **Beauty Under the Tree,** in a forest of ponderosa and pinyon pine; **Green Canyon Meadow,** in a desert clearing opposite a painted mesa; and **Horse Line Cliffs,** high in the Chuska Mountains.

Logan uses a variety of hogans, some in the Chinle area and others in Utah's Monument Valley. On Largo's day tour of Canyon de Chelly, guests hike down the canyon for 3 to 5 miles (5 to 8 km), enjoy a box lunch, then depart in waiting jeeps, sparing themselves the task of hiking back up the canyon.

TIPS: To ascertain which aspects of Navajo culture intrigue them the most, interested families should do some research on the area and its people before asking either company to create a customized itinerary. **Arizona Tourism Alliance** *(1212 E. Osborn Rd., Phoenix 85014. 602/604-0632. www.arizonaguide.com)*

BASICS: **Coyote Pass Hogan Bed and Breakfast** *(P.O. Box 91-B, Tsaile. 520/724-3383. www.navajocentral.org).* **Largo Navajo Land Tours** *(Box 5373, Window Rock. 888/726-9084 or 505/863-0050. www.navajolandtours.org.)*

Navajo Arts
Diné College

Built in the shape of a hogan and situated amid sagebrush and juniper trees in the foothills of the Chuska Mountains about a 20-minute drive from Chinle, **Diné College** offers summer workshops on traditional Navajo arts taught by American Indian artists. Diné has the distinction of being the first tribally controlled community college in the United States. Students can choose a week-long workshop in weaving, pottery, painting, or silversmithing. Participants stay in a college dorm where every two bedrooms share a communal living area and a bathroom.

TIPS: The **Rainbow Inn** *(Box 128, Tsaile. 888/464-2648),* with a layout similar to that of the dorms, offers rooms at about $70 a night year-round.

Pass it on: two generations of weavers in Canyon de Chelly

BASICS: Diné College *(Ofc. of Continuing Education, P.O. Box 731, Tuba City 86045. 520/283-6321)* charges about $1,500 per person, double occupancy. The fee includes courses, meals, lodging, and art supplies.

MORE ARIZONA ADVENTURES

Petrified Forest National Park *(I-40 and US 180. 520/524-6228):* Walk along trails where quartz crystals formed in sunken wood, giving it the consistency of stone. Although vandals have diminished the park's grandeur, some trails are still worth the walk. On the **Giant Logs Trail** (a 0.3-mile loop behind the visitor center), for example, visitors can spot marbleized logs from 6 inches to 6 feet in diameter. The 0.75-mile **Crystal Forest Interpretive Trail** also leads to several petrified logs.

Hubbell Trading Post *(P. O. Box 388, Ganado. 520/755-3254):* Established in 1876, this is the oldest U.S. trading post still in operation. With its shelves piled high with buckskins and baskets, the trading post looks remarkably true to the period when it first opened for business more than 120 years ago. At the visitor center, a Navajo weaver practices her art and answers questions. The trading post also abounds with Navajo rugs for sale. All are handwoven, but some rugs are made from machine-spun wool; those from hand-spun wool are thicker.

Canyon de Chelly National Monument *(P.O. Box 588, Chinle 86503. 520/674-5500):* Thousand-foot-high sandstone walls ring the 84,000-acre Canyon de Chelly, located on the Navajo reservation (where it is known as "Tsegi"). Check out the canyon-history video at the visitor center, then take a tour with a Navajo guide to observe ancient cliff dwellings and petroglyphs of dogs, turkeys, and ducks.

The Navajo revere Canyon de Chelly: According to their legends, Navajo culture emerged from here. On occasion, it has sheltered here as well; the Navajo sought refuge in the canyon when the Spanish showed up in the mid-16th century. In 1864, Colonel Kit Carson and his troops attacked under the auspices of the territorial commander, killing many Navajo. Stories handed down for generations recount the whine of bullets ricocheting across the canyon and tell of bloody handprints left on the canyon walls by Navajo trying to escape.

Those who weren't killed set off on the Long Walk—a forced march of more than 300 miles to Fort Sumner, New Mexico, during which many Navajo perished. After four years of imprisonment, the Navajo were allowed to return home in 1868; they then began rebuilding their lives and their land.

Monument Valley Navajo Tribal Park *(P.O. Box 360289, Monument Valley 84536. 801/727-3353):* Plan to spend some time at this spectacular park, where sandstone mesas, canyons, buttes, and spires create a breathtaking interplay of red-rock formations and open spaces.

The first Navajo arrived in the Monument Valley area in the late 15th or early 16th century. In the 19th century, more Navajo fled here to escape roundups and forced marches perpetrated by U.S. Cavalry. The 30,000-acre park, straddling the Arizona-Utah border, lies within the 16-million-acre Navajo Reservation. **Goulding's Trading Post & Lodge** *(435/727-3231),* the only hotel in the park, features great views and minibus tours led by Navajo guides. **Largo Navajo Land Tours** (pages 17-18) arranges Navajo-led backcountry jeep excursions, as well as horseback trips and overnights in bed-and-breakfast hogans.

For more information, contact **Navajo Nation Tourism** *(520/871-6436 or 7371).*

Heard Museum
Phoenix

Kachina dolls, Navajo blankets, turquoise jewelry, and other traditional Southwestern crafts are all part of the **Heard Museum's** display of the best in contemporary Southwestern art. The museum's complex of buildings, replete with courtyards and fountains, is something of an oasis in downtown Phoenix. The artwork collected here gives kids a fascinating "avenue of approach" for understanding Native American culture.

Start with "Native Peoples of the Southwest," a slide show in which people discuss the pluses and problems of growing up in two cultures. An older woman tells

Right: Hoop dancer at the Heard Museum, Phoenix

Scorpion and cautious admirers at the Arizona Sonora Desert Museum

of going to school and being told to "forget your stories, forget the names of the mountains and the rivers, and just speak English."

The legends of Arizona's natives also come across in their art. The **Kachina gallery**—a favorite with kids—features carved kachina dolls, which served as ceremonial gifts. (The dolls, representing a wish or prayer for the recipient, were usually given to little girls.) Carved from cottonwood roots, the brightly painted Hopi kachinas, many adorned with masks and feathers, stand for the spirit essence of all the natural things in the world. Chanting music played in the background enhances the otherworldly quality of the figures.

Modern sculpture and painting grace the **main gallery**, a soaring space flooded with light. The galleries devoted to traditional crafts are lined with coiled Apache baskets, beaded cradleboards, buckskins, earthen-hued jugs and bowls, and Zuni squash-blossom necklaces blooming with turquoise nuggets.

A hands-on **learning room** was added in 1999. Although school groups often occupy the space, take the time to visit. The exhibits make it easy for children to design their own crafts—a simple way to learn about the art and culture of various tribes. In the Navajo section, kids fashion saddlebags, design a rug, and wrap a doll in a cradleboard. In the Hopi area, children use colored stencils to create pictographs and traditional patterns. And in the Yavapai section, kids can make (not draw!) stick figures from split twigs.

TIPS: For snacks or light lunches, order your food from the Ironwood Café located in the museum's courtyard and carry it outside for a picnic.

BASICS: Heard Museum (*2301 N. Central Ave., Phoenix. 602/252-8840. www. heard.org. Adults $7, seniors 65 and up $6, children 4 to 12 $3, members free*)

Desert Botanical Gardens *(1201 N. Gavin Pkwy. 480/941-1225)*: At this outdoor living museum, kids discover that many shades of green color the desert and learn what sort of vegetation thrives there. The 35-acre gardens are home to 20,000 plants representing desert flora around the world. Children especially enjoy the Sonoran display, with its saguaro forest, mesquite thicket, and stream.

Desert Storm Hummer Tours *(15525 N. 83rd Way, Suite 8, Scottsdale. 480/922-0020)*: In these suburban versions of the behemoth U.S. Army vehicles that saw service in the Middle East, naturalists transport visitors to Bureau of Land Management areas and to the Tonto National Forest for guided hikes. The Hummer is equal to the terrain: It crosses creeks, climbs the sides of ravines, and rolls down bumpy backcountry roads where burros roam among saguaro cactus growing 30 feet high. In summer, take the early-morning tour.

Sonora Desert Museum Tucson

Walk through a mountain woodland of mesquite and yucca that's home to mountain lions and black bears. Cross a grassland that shelters prairie dogs, burrowing owls, and rattlesnakes. Explore a cave eerily aglow with phosphorescent blue azurite, green malachite, and orange wulfenite.

You've been tricked into taking the survival portion of an Outward Bound program, right? Not quite: The setting is Arizona's **Sonora Desert Museum**—part zoo, part botanical garden—a site dedicated to presenting the habitats and inhabitants of the state's Sonoran desert. In addition to the animals mentioned above, this mostly outdoor living museum boasts a population of tarantulas, scorpions, vultures, bighorn sheep, coyotes, Mexican gray wolves, javelinas (also known as peccaries), and jaguarundis. The museum is world famous for its displays of such living desert animals as gila monsters and desert pupfish.

In the museum's **Pollination Garden**—the largest such open-space garden anywhere—children can watch butterflies landing on milkweed, hummingbirds heading for the ocotillo, and digger bees boring into a barrel cactus. The **coyote exhibit** was expanded in 1998.

On **Family Safari** day outings, museum naturalists lead hikes into the nearby canyons, where visitors can collect fossils and minerals and learn about the wildlife.

TIPS: In summertime, arrive early in the day, when the animals are more active.

BASICS: The **Sonora Desert Museum** *(2021 N. Kinney Rd., Tucson. 520/883-1380. www.desertmuseum.org. Oct.-Feb. 8:30-5:00, March-Sept. 7:30-6:00)*

San Diego
Wild Animal Park

Kids fall asleep to the not-too-distant rumble of lions on a **Roar and Snore** campout at **San Diego Wild Animal Park**, a 2,200-acre wildlife preserve where more than 3,200 rare and endangered animals roam in large herds. At "base camp" (beside the East Africa exhibit), naturalists explain animal behavior and guides tell campfire stories. Roar and Snore aims at parents with children ages 8 and up; **Beastly Bedtime**, in the same locale, is geared to families with kids 4 to 7.

If you can't spend the night but still want to get close to the animals, try a **Photo Caravan.** On this three-hour tour, you can pet a giraffe, pop apples in a rhino's mouth, and come within yards of gazelle, zebra, and Cape buffalo. Shorter rides are available too; the minimum age for both the caravan and the rides is 8.

The park's 30-acre **Heart of Africa** exhibit re-creates an African landscape. The trail winds through forest, savanna, and wetland inhabited by warthogs, bat-eared foxes, wattled cranes, okapi, cheetahs, and bontebok. From the island research station, Kikuyu colobus monkeys can be seen scampering through the trees.

If the new North American habitat known as **Condor Ridge** opens as scheduled in May 2000, patrons will be able to watch a California condor gliding through the air. Also housed here are desert bighorn sheep, western burrowing owls, black-footed ferrets, Harris's hawks, black-tailed prairie dogs, and aplomado falcons.

From the **Wgasa Bush Line Monorail** (a 50-minute ride), white rhino and antelope can be seen grazing in the East Africa area; blackbuck and sambar gather at the **Asian Waterhole** and **Plains** exhibits; ostrich and wildebeest move through the South African fields.

Hold a cup of nectar as you walk through **Lorikeet Landing** and brightly colored birds will drink from it. In **Nairobi Village,** youngsters can touch deer, antelope, and potbellied pigs. And at the **Mombasa Lagoon** play area, kids can hop over giant lily pads or crawl into an aardwolf cave (don't worry—it's vacant).

TIPS: Reserve Roar and Snore or Beastly Bedtime several months ahead—and bring proof of age with you. In summer, see the park in early morning or late afternoon, when the animals are more active. Take advantage of August's **Sunrise Safari,** which grants you early (7:30 a.m.) admission to the Heart of Africa exhibit.

BASICS: San Diego Wild Animal Park *(15500 San Pasqual Valley Rd., Escondido. 619/234-6541 or 760/747-8702. Adults $21.95, children 3-11) $14.95.* **Roar and Snore** *(800/934-2267 www.sandiegozoo.org; April-Oct. Non-member adult and child 12 or older $105, member adult and child 12 or older $80; non-member adult and child 8-11 $85, member adult and child 8-11 $70)*

Owl encounter during a "Roar and Snore" at the San Diego Wild Animal Park

San Diego Zoo

Small children overwhelmed by the San Diego Wild Animal Park may feel more comfortable with the small scale—just 100 acres—of the **San Diego Zoo.** Pride of place goes to the zoo's koala colony (the largest outside Australia), pygmy chimpanzees from central Africa, tree kangaroos from New Guinea, Komodo dragons from Indonesia, and two Chinese pandas—Shi Shi and Bai Yun—who became parents of a female in August 1999. (The infant was the first panda born in the Western Hemisphere in ten years.) Before visiting the zoo, check out the "Panda Cam" on its website.

The San Diego Zoo offers three special programs for getting close to the animals: On a summer **Nighttime Zoo** walk, watch nocturnal animals replace their daytime languor with jungle moves: The fruit bats fly, the lions pace, and the leopards and Indo-Chinese tigers prowl. From the end of June through Labor Day, take advantage of **Morning Zoo Rise;** this program lets you in the gates at 7:30 a.m., when the keepers start feeding the animals and interacting with them. On a **Safari Sleepover,** naturalists lead guests on a moonlit stroll, then conduct a themed animal workshop before everyone beds down in sleeping bags (BYOSB).

At the 4-acre **Ituri Forest,** a re-created central African rain forest, kids can stroll a path through dense groves of ficus trees. Along the way, they get to scope out hippos underwater through a glass-walled enclosure, see forest buffalo wallowing in mud, and spy monkeys swinging through the treetops.

In the **Rain Forest Aviary,** visitors walk through a southeast Asian jungle that is authentic in every detail, from its waterfalls and lush plants to its collection of more than 50 species of exotic and endangered birds. At the 2.2-acre **Polar Bear Plunge**—one of the largest polar-bear exhibits in the world—the bears display the grace of underwater swimmers.

Preschoolers may enjoy the **Children's Zoo,** where they can pet sheep, goats, and potbellied pigs or watch baby animals being cared for in the nursery.

TIPS: The zoo's Safari Sleepovers are so popular they should be reserved several months in advance. Many programs are geared toward two age groups: 4 to 7 years and 8 years and older. Spare small feet by taking the **Kangaroo Bus Tour;** it allows visitors to hop on and off at nine stops throughout the zoo.

BASICS: The **San Diego Zoo** *(2920 Zoo Dr., San Diego. 619/234-3153. www.sandiegozoo.org. Adults $18, ages 3-11 $8. Two-park package: adults $38.35, children $23.15)* is open daily from 9 a.m. to 4 p.m.

SeaWorld Adventure Park San Diego

At **SeaWorld Adventure Park San Diego,** you can sit in the "splash zone" and get drenched by Shamu the killer whale, then learn all about sea animals and conservation by viewing manatees, polar bears, and other live exhibits.

The most exciting programs are also the least known. On a 90-minute **Behind the Scenes** walking tour, for example, families can visit research areas with park naturalists. At the shark lab, kids touch a baby shark and find out about shark diets; at Shamu Stadium, they discover how the park's star performer is trained; and at the animal-rescue center they learn how beached animals are rescued.

Overnights provide an even more in-depth experience. On an **Ocean Exploration Sleepover,** campers bed down in the **Manatee Rescue** or **Shark Encounter** exhibit. Naturalists are on hand to explain the animals' behavior. SeaWorld also operates a range of summer camps for kids: At the **Dolphin Interaction Program,** for instance, participants attend a workshop and then get in the tank with the dolphins—a rare opportunity to touch and interact with these intelligent creatures.

Many of the exhibits and programs at SeaWorld San Diego are similar to those at SeaWorld Orlando. For a more detailed write-up of the latter site, see page 173.

TIPS: Register for a same-day Behind the Scenes Tour as soon as you arrive.

BASICS: SeaWorld Adventure Park *(500 SeaWorld Dr., San Diego. 800/732-9675 or 619/226-3901. www.seaworld.com).* **Behind-the-Scenes Tours,** not part of park admission *(adults $39, ages 3-11 $30),* cost $8 for adults and $7 for ages 3 to 11.

MORE SAN DIEGO VENTURES

The city's 1,200-acre **Balboa Park,** in the middle of the city, offers not only expansive green space but some cool interiors as well: the **San Diego Museum of Man,** the **Reuben H. Fleet Space Theater and Science Center,** the **San Diego Natural History Museum,** and the **Marie Hitchcock Puppet Theater. Balboa Park Visitor Center** *(1549 El Prado, San Diego. 619/239-0512)* offers a schedule of events, maps, and discounted passports to several area museums.

A 15-minute ferry ride will take you from **Seaport Village** to **Coronado,** famed for its beaches and family-friendly **Hotel Del Coronado** *(1500 Orange Ave. 800/468-3533 or 619/435-6611. www.hoteldel.com).*

Monterey Bay Aquarium

Peer through the world's largest window—the 17-foot-high, 56-foot-long, 39-ton acrylic panel that holds back the ocean at the **Monterey Bay Aquarium's Outer Bay** exhibit—and you'll find 200-pound sunfish, huge green sea turtles, and blue sharks staring back at you. The aquarium focuses on the marine life and habitats of Monterey Bay and the area about 60 miles offshore where the bay blends into the open ocean. Set right on the bay, the aquarium's location underscores its content. Families will appreciate California's coastal scenery even more once they have visited the aquarium and learned what lives in the water offshore.

Splash Zone, to debut in April 2000, is an innovative, hands-on gallery designed for families and kids from infants to 9-year-olds. A mix of interactive exhibits and live animals enables children and adults to discover the critters that inhabit such environments as coral reefs and rocky shores. Sitting in the bubble window, kids feel as if they are right inside the habitat of the black-footed penguin. Kids can climb inside a giant "clam" to see how mollusks grow, or crawl through a coral tunnel to discover sea horses, harlequin shrimp, ribbon eels, and other make-believe versions of a reef's inhabitants. At **Coral Cove,** for infants to 3-year-olds, even babies can get a sensory introduction to sea life by playing on a water-bed-style mat surrounded by the soothing sounds of bubbling water. At the **Rocky Shores** exhibit, learn how creatures cling to rocks despite being battered by waves. At the touch pool, kids can pick up sea stars, sea urchins, hermit crabs, and sea cucumbers.

Other highlights include the 28-foot-high **kelp forest,** one of the world's tallest aquarium exhibits. Sardines, leopard sharks, sea urchins, and wolf eels all thread their way through the towering kelp strands, which stay healthy thanks to bay water that circulates through them. **Monterey Bay Habitats** features sharks, rays, salmon, and bass. At **Sea Otters along the Coast,** California sea otters swim and splash. **Mysteries of the Deep,** on view until January 2002, is the world's largest deep-sea exhibit; here you'll find ratfish, sea whips, mushroom corals, eelpouts, and many sea creatures that have never been displayed in an aquarium. As you tour the facility, keep an eye peeled for the interactive learning stations beside the main galleries.

TIPS: Check the aquarium's schedule for its daily tidepool talks, puppet programs, and feedings at both the kelp forest and the sea otter tank. At certain times, kids can make crafts in the deep-sea craft room. From Memorial Day to Labor Day, the WAVE shuttle connects the aquarium with hotels and waterfront attractions in Monterey and Pacific Grove. It's a good idea to buy advance tickets to the aquarium.

BASICS: **Monterey Bay Aquarium** *(886 Cannery Row, Monterey. 800/756-3737 or 831/648-4800. www.mbayaq.org. Adults $15.95, ages 3-12 $7.95)*

MORE FAMILY ATTRACTIONS

Carmel: In nearby Carmel, take a walk in **Point Lobos State Reserve** *(State Route 1. 831/624-4909),* where hiking trails wind along the wave-splashed shore and through thickets of pine and cypress; along the way, you may spot sea lions, sea otters, and harbor seals. **Carmel Valley Ranch** *(1 Old Ranch Rd., Carmel. 800/422-7635),* a family-friendly resort on 1,700 rolling acres, offers horseback riding, hiking trails, golf, tennis, and swimming.

Zeum
San Francisco

Dancing critters made of clay are commonplace at **Zeum,** a San Francisco art-and-technology center for ages 8-18. Functioning something like a giant toy store for the visual and performing arts, Zeum encourages kids to play with the high-tech tools needed to create animation and movies. Assisted by teen facilitators, children learn how to design their own website, produce an animated cartoon, and develop a multimedia show.

In the **Production Lab,** teams of kids serve as actors, videographers, graphic artists, and sound engineers. Budding media gurus can operate video cameras, manipulate an audio mixing board, compose digital pictures, and add graphics to create a video that is broadcast on Zeum's website.

Stocked with 22 computers, the **Learning Lab** invites kids to experiment with 3-D modeling, video editing, and computer illustration. A favorite activity here is to turn yourself into a work of art: Take a digital photo of your face, load it into a computer, then manipulate the photo with the latest software.

At Zeum's popular **Artists Studio,** future cartoonists learn claymation—the craft that elevated the Raisinettes from cereal ingredients to cultural icons. Kids begin the process by sketching their comic "stars" on an electronic easel; they then fashion wire frames and flesh them out with modeling dough. Manning a video camera loaded with animation software, the young artists use stop-action—the

Right: Taking the sting out of a jellyfish encounter at the Monterey Bay Aquarium

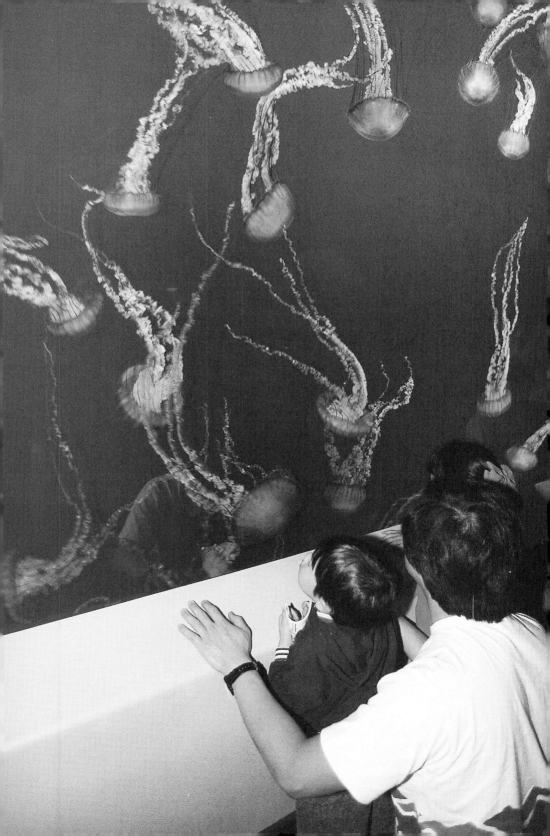

Tomorrow's stars cavort in today's video at San Francisco's Zeum.

technique of shooting a sequence of individual frames in which an object changes position very slightly—to create movement. The end result is a 10- to 20-second cartoon.

In the **Performing Arts Lab,** kids experiment with puppetry, props, and videos to create their own shows. A gallery on the first floor displays works created by Zeum students, some under the tutelage of local artists. If your kids show the slightest affinity for technology or the arts, they'll find their muse at Zeum.

TIPS: To avoid feeling overwhelmed by the rich opportunities available at Zeum, target just one or two projects per visit—you can't do them all!

BASICS: Zeum *(221 4th St., San Francisco 415/777-2800. www.zeum.org. Adults $7, kids $5)* is part of San Francisco's Rooftop at Yerba Buena Gardens complex.

Rooftop at Yerba Buena Gardens

Zeum (page 28) is the anchor for a block-long, $56 million San Francisco complex called the **Rooftop at Yerba Buena Gardens** (so named because it was constructed atop the underground Moscone South Convention Center). The Rooftop and Sony's Metreon, just across the street, have combined to make the city's 87-acre South of Market area something of an adventure mecca for vaca-

MORE BAY AREA FUN: THE EXPLORATORIUM

The king of hands-on children's museums is **The Exploratorium,** founded in 1969. Curious minds will be intrigued by the museum's 700 exhibits, which bring natural phenomena and scientific principles to life. Kids can "freeze" their shadows, use a tiny magnet to move a 400-pound pendulum, and visit a distorted room where nothing is as it seems. The popular **Tactile Dome** is a pitch-dark, crawl-through maze designed to put kids in touch with their senses besides sight; expect a few sensory surprises.

Tips: Make reservations in advance for the Tactile Dome, open to non-claustrophobic kids of 8 and older. An "escape hatch" lets kids bail out early if they want to before reaching the end of the experience.

Basics: **The Exploratorium** *(3601 Lyon St, San Francisco. 415/563-7337. www.exploratorium.edu. Adults $9, kids $5)*

tioning families. In addition to imagining their own worlds at Zeum, children can visit the Rooftop to skate on a regulation **NHL ice rink** or ride a **1906 carousel** that was hand-carved by Charles Loof. The views of San Francisco through the glass walls of the complex are something of an adventure in themselves.

Kids will probably lure their parents across the street to **Metreon,** Sony's first entertainment complex, which bristles with retail temptations: eight restaurants, seven stores, a 15-screen multiplex, and an IMAX theater. At the **Airtight Garage,** aimed at teens, participants vie with one another in networked virtual-reality games designed by French artist Jean "Moebius" Giraud. **HyperBowl** lets kids live out their Godzilla fantasies by rolling a giant ball down San Francisco streets to knock down landmark buildings.

For younger siblings, **Where the Wild Things Are** offers an interactive retelling of Maurice Sendak's classic fable. As Max's bedroom morphs into the enchanted forest, projected images of goblins—a story embellishment courtesy of Sony's SFX department—glower from a cauldron. The goblins will try to detain you, offering bribes that range from holographic ice-cream sundaes to "electric helium"—that is, machines capable of making you sound younger, older, or even canine. Upon emerging from the woods, players enter a landscape of mischief: Here you can make fake birds suspended from bungee cords "dive bomb" exiting guests, or jump on a giant button that prompts the 14-foot-tall Wild Thing puppet to roll his head, shrug his shoulders, and stick out his tongue.

TIPS: The nearby **W. San Francisco** hotel *(877/946-8357 or 415/777-5300)* usually targets business travelers, but the property's glass-enclosed swimming pool (not to mention its guest rooms with laptops and Web TV) gives it family appeal as well.

BASICS: Carousel *(221 Fourth St. 415/777-2800).* **Yerba Buena Gardens Ice Skating and Bowling Center** *(130 Third St. 415/243-4450. www.yerbabuena.org)*

Powwow Dancing
Warm Springs Reservation

Dancing, drumming, prayers, and performances characterize **Pi-Ume-Sha** **(Let's Celebrate),** a powwow that brings together many different nations each June on Oregon's **Warm Springs Reservation.** A powwow is part festival, part social gathering, and part dance contest.

Free and open to the public, Pi-Ume-Sha has the neighborly feel of a small-town country fair. About a dozen vendors sell jewelry, T-shirts, and beads from over-stuffed booths, while others hawk munchies such as nachos and Indian fry bread. Families chat in the bleachers ringing the grassy field behind the Warm Springs Community Center. Preschoolers play tag among the lawn chairs, and giggly pre-teen girls help each other with last-minute adjustments to their outfits. Teenage boys riding horses materialize in silhouette on a ridge top nearby.

At the powwow my daughter and I attended, the ceremonies began when a grand-father with a face furrowed like a dry creek bed walked onto the playing field with his 12-year-old grandson. "The grandpa's giving him his feather bustle," my daugh-ter excitedly reported. Some newfound friends explained that the transfer of these eagle plumes signaled a "joining"—the ceremony at which a young man, often fol-lowing his first deer kill, formally joins the traditions of his forefathers. My daugh-ter likened the rite to her own bat mitzvah—and immediately empathized with her peer's nervous pride.

The crowd quieted as a trio of men burned sweet grass to purify the arena. After a Warm Springs woman chanted a prayer in Sahaptin (her native tongue), the grand parade began. Scores of dancers were led by a tribal elder wearing traditional regalia; this included a roach, or crown, of brown and gray porcupine needles arching from his forehead down his back. The dancers moved slowly and rhythmically to a beat-ing drum, weaving a spiral of color as they coiled toward the center.

The cadences linked onlookers to performers—and participants to one another. Along with the Confederated Tribes, many other nations—Shoshone-Bannock from Idaho; Flatheads, Blackfeet, and Sioux from Montana; Navajo from Arizona and New Mexico—became joyfully connected by the music.

A Wasco tribe member (and Vietnam veteran) sitting behind us explained that one should never touch an Indian's eagle feathers unless invited to; the feathers are considered sacred. He also pointed out how to distinguish a traditional dance (look for measured movements) from a fancy one (note the exaggerated steps).

As one dance segued into the next, we marveled at the energy involved and felt privileged to observe these rituals, which have been a key part of Warm Springs cul-ture for generations. At the same time, we found ourselves searching for the proper response: Since no one clapped, applauding seemed out of place (see box on page

LEARNING TRIBAL HISTORY

Oregon's Wasco Indians were traditionally fishermen and traders, while the Warm Springs Indians were hunters. The two tribes spoke different languages and observed different customs, but their proximity brought them together frequently to trade and socialize. In 1855, leaders of both tribes signed the Middle Oregon Treaty, which ceded 10 million acres while retaining the 650,000 acres that became the Warm Springs Reservation. The U.S. Government moved 38 Paiute Indians to Warm Springs in 1875. The Paiute are known as skilled weavers today. In 1937, all three tribes—Wasco, Warm Springs, and Paiute—formed the Warm Springs Confederation.

Visitors can learn all about the Plateau Native Americans in the two large galleries of the **Museum at Warm Springs**, 11 miles from Kah-Nee-Ta. Kids will especially enjoy exploring the re-created traditional dwellings—a Warm Springs tipi, a Wasco plank house, and a Paiute family wickiup. (Be sure to ask for the children's materials, which explain such details of daily life as picture writing and how to capture a wild horse.) In summer, Living Traditions programs highlight antler carving, flute making, cedar-root basket weaving, and other traditional crafts.

Designs prized by Warm Springs tribes show up in the museum's architecture. The handles of the entrance door take the shape of an eagle-feather bustle—part of the men's regalia in the eagle dance. Similarly, the brickwork patterns on the building's exterior evoke the design of baskets used to gather huckleberries—a traditional tribal food.

Basics: **Museum at Warm Springs** *(Hwy. 26, Warm Springs. 541/553-3331. www.tmaws.org. Adults $6, children $3)*

13). Watching in silence, on the other hand, seemed an insufficient acknowledgment.

Feathers—symbolizing the breath of life—swirled everywhere. Men promenaded in regalia that included eagle-feather bustles, breastplates made of quills, and beaded vests. As they moved, they shook dance sticks, some decorated with eagle talons. Other dancers, their arms covered with bright orange-and-blue rosettes of dyed goose feathers, twirled like dervishes.

Some women danced in beaded buckskin. Others wore dresses adorned with elk teeth or conch shells, while still others sported beaded capes as they stepped in a staccato tiptoe. We liked the young girls in their "jingle" dresses best. When these dancers swayed, rows of silver cones (made from snuffbox lids) jangled like bells.

Children under the age of 12 competed in a dance festival. A young girl in a white buckskin dress rocked next to her mother, while a flurry of yellow fringes finally slowed down long enough for us to discover that it was a smiling boy, carefully mimicking his father's steps. Other children imitated turkeys or roosters. Without fail, their innocence and exuberance touched us.

As the sun set, spirits rose. Friends pulled friends out of their seats and into the drum beats. More and more families joined in. Whether they were wearing a ribbon shirt and headgear or jeans and a T-shirt, every dancer rejoiced and felt proud.

Caught up in the festive atmosphere, my daughter entered the circle and shed her teenage self-consciousness. As I watched her blend in and dance to the spirit of the powwow, I realized we had both received a special gift of friendship.

BASICS: The **Pi-Ume-Sha Powwow** is held the weekend closest to June 23 at **Kah-Nee-Ta Resort** *(P.O. Box K, Warm Springs 97761. 800/554-4786 or 541/553-1112. www.kah-nee-taresort.com or www.warmsprings.com).*

Kah-Nee-Ta Resort Warm Springs Reservation

A visit to the 600-acre **Kah-Nee-Ta Resort** in central Oregon lands you on a high desert plateau, dotted with sagebrush and juniper trees, where birds twitter by day and coyotes howl long into the night. The resort is run by the three tribes that make up the Confederated Tribes of Warm Springs.

Tribal dances take place on Sundays during the summer. Two children's programs—one for ages 6 to 8, the other for ages 9 to 14—operate from Memorial Day through Labor Day, giving kids a chance to bike and hike on the reservation, listen to some traditional storytelling, or fashion dream catchers and beaded key chains. Their parents can opt for golf, tennis, or swimming, or sign up for a learning adventure that includes hiking, horseback riding, and immersion in the culture of surrounding Warm Springs Reservation.

Visitors opt to stay in luxury suites or hotel rooms, or camp out in a family tipi. A tribal member is available during the day and evening to answer questions about the confederation, the history of its tribes, and life on the reservation today.

Families are welcome to participate in Warm Springs activities the rest of the year, too. These include a **New Year's Day Feast**, a **Fourth of July** celebration and bear barbecue, and an **arts-and-crafts show** in October. The biggest event of the year—the three-day **Pi-Ume-Sha Powwow** in June—is described on pages 32-34.

TIPS: Members of the Confederated Tribes of Warm Springs welcome questions from visitors on all topics except spiritual beliefs and ceremonies, which are considered private.

BASICS: The **Kah-Nee-Ta Resort** *(P.O. Box K, Warm Springs. 800/554-4786 or 541/553-1112. www.kah-nee-taresort.com or www.warmsprings.com. $130 to $145 per night)* is a two-hour drive southeast from Portland. If you plan to stay in a tipi *($70 per night),* bring your own sleeping bag.

Oregon Museum of Science and Industry, Portland

With six exhibit halls and eight hands-on laboratories, the **Oregon Museum of Science and Industry** (OMSI) is one of the country's top ten science museums. In the **Turbine Hall**, kids can erect a four-story building and then destroy it with a simulated earthquake, have a hair-raising experience with the Van de Graaff generator, or produce hydroelectric power on their own. The **Edison Corner** contains one of history's first light bulbs, while the **Laser Lab** shows children how holograms are created. In the **Chemistry Lab**, kids don goggles and work with their parents to discover the secrets of fireworks and glow-in-the-dark toys.

The **Earth Science Exhibit Hall** features one of OMSI's most popular attractions: The Earthquake Room re-creates the unsettling experience of being caught in a tremor registering 5.5 on the Richter scale. Nature's Fury lets you disrupt a simulated tornado by sticking your hand inside it, while visitors to the **Paleo Lab** can watch the excavation of a 65-million-year-old triceratops. In the **Watershed Lab,** create your own soil erosion at the stream table.

For those with strong stomachs, Bone Up on Bones in the **Life Science Exhibit Hall** offers the chance to watch bone surgery and virtual dissections. Everyone else assembles a skeleton puzzle or tries to extract a maximum number of calcium "rods" from a "bone tower" before it collapses. Baby chicks emerge from their shells in the chick hatchery; the 12-foot-long python, thankfully, is part of a separate exhibit. In the **Life Science Lab,** visitors experience what it's like to be pregnant by trying on an "empathy belly" and observing ultrasound equipment in action.

Electrons move through circuits to power computers in the **High Tech Exhibit Hall.** Armed with this knowledge, you'll be thoroughly prepared for the **Vernier Technology Lab,** where visitors test-drive computers and surf the Internet. In the **Electronics Lab,** surf a little farther out: Send a message into outer space.

For newborns to 6-year-olds, there's **Discovery Space**, where developmentally appropriate activities invite them to experience (if not always grasp) the fundamentals of science. Floating objects in water, playing with magnets, and making Flubber are all exercises in "stealth education."

At Busytown—an interactive math-and-science exhibit based on the children's stories of writer-illustrator Richard Scarry—ages 2 to 10 load groceries (or each other) onto a conveyor belt, turn the wheels of a factory pulley, talk on phones, deliver mail, and use a crane to move cargo in a shipyard. Although Busytown is not a permanent exhibit, it will remain at the museum until the summer of 2000, and possibly longer.

What's it like to live on a submarine? To find out, tour the U.S.S. *Blueback*. Launched in 1959 and decommissioned in 1990, the *Blueback*—the U.S. Navy's last diesel-powered sub—appeared in the 1990 film *The Hunt for Red October* before taking up permanent residence at OMSI in 1994. Your guide on the 45-

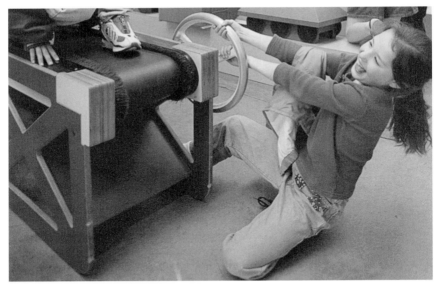

Small wheel, big fun: Oregon Museum of Science and Industry, Portland

minute tour of the vessel is likely to be an ex-submariner—and may even have served aboard the *Blueback* itself.

At the **Murdock Planetarium,** a Digistar II projector allows visitors to view ten times as many stars as they can see from Earth. It also creates three-dimensional space travel, giving viewers the sensation of moving through space. In addition to staging its regularly scheduled music and light shows, the planetarium hosts star parties on selected evenings in the parking lot. Although the planetarium charges a separate admission fee, the star parties are free. Also on-site is a five-story-high, domed-screen OMNIMAX theater.

TIPS: To take advantage of every precious minute at OMSI, visit the museum's website in advance of your visit to get a sense of which labs and exhibits your family wants to see. The website's rat and salmon-tank pages show a few OMSI residents in action.

For children ages 7 to18, OMSI sponsors **summer science and adventure camps,** as well as **family weekends** devoted to canoeing, fossil study, astronomy, hiking, swimming, and exploring. Prices average $90 for a two-night program, $320 for a week *(503/797-4662).*

BASICS: The **Oregon Museum of Science and Industry** *(1945 S.E. Water Ave., Portland. 503/797-4000. www.omsi.edu. Adults $6.50, children $4.50)* offers a planetarium *(503/797-4610),* music and light shows *(503/797-4646 for schedule),* and OMNIMAX theater *(503/797-4640).* An extra fee is charged for *Blueback* tours and the planetarium.

Pacific Science Center Seattle

Water-play sculptures in the courtyard of the **Pacific Science Center** herald the interactive fun on tap at the facility, where kids can shoot high-powered jets of water at kinetic sculptures or ride a high-wire gravity bike. The hands-on exhibits inside are equally intriguing—as are the two IMAX theaters (one boasting 3-D technology) and planetarium with laser-light shows.

If you visit in winter, start with the **Tropical Butterfly House.** This 4,000-square-foot oasis of warm, jungly forest comes as a welcome respite from the cold and rain outside. As you stroll its garden path, hundreds of colorful butterflies—including such exotic species as the Blue Morpho from Costa Rica and the Peacock Pansy from Malaysia—flit about you. Peer into the Emerging Room to see butterflies coming out of their chrysalises and moths leaving their cocoons. In addition to learning how to tell the two families apart, kids find out about insect metamorphosis and life spans (most moths and butterflies live just 7 to 14 days).

Next to the butterfly house is **Insect Village,** home to hissing cockroaches and honeycomb-building bees. Under the big top of **Insecta Sideshow,** kids learn that a flea jumping from a carpet onto a tall dog is the proportional equivalent of a person jumping from a sidewalk onto the top of Seattle's Space Needle.

In **Tech Zone,** children play tic-tac-toe with a 10-foot-tall robot and use a joystick and virtual-reality helmet to hang-glide over a city. Basketball fans can match rim shots against a member of the Seattle Supersonics in a virtual-reality basketball game. For the non-digerati, a kiosk version of Bill Nye the Science Guy explains how to navigate the Internet.

One of the center's most popular exhibits is **Waterworks.** Here kids can power a waterwheel by running hamster-style inside it, or spin a two-ton granite ball using the principles of water pressure. **Kids Works** offers hands-on exhibits for toddlers and up. Only those 44 inches or shorter, however, can gain access to **Just for Tots,** which provides a bubble tub, model car, and scale helicopter. Bubbles also pop up in **Water Play,** where older children can use them as building blocks to construct a giant, soapy wall. Young astronauts will gravitate to **Rocket Climb,** an exhibit in which they climb to the top of a 22-foot starship, then land the craft on Earth.

TIPS: Wear red to encourage butterflies at the Tropical Butterfly House to land on you. Special events include the **Bubble Festival** (August), **Gross Out Week** (Spring Break), and **Dino Days** (May).

BASICS: Pacific Science Center *(200 2nd Ave. N., Seattle. 206/443-2001. www. pacsci.org. Daily 10 a.m.-6 p.m. Adults $7.50, children 3-13 $5.50, members free)*

The Inside Passage

From our helicopter at 10,000 feet, Ruth Glacier in **Denali National Park** spread out below us in a massive river of blue ice. The glacier, slit with crevasses and dotted with turquoise pools, seemed to run on forever. Craggy cliffs and rugged brown slopes towered on either side. The closer we flew to Denali—the Great One, as North America's highest peak is known in native languages—the more jagged, menacing, and majestic the mountain became. Suddenly, within 2 miles of Denali's summit, the clouds parted and Denali's sharp, snow-covered pinnacle split the sky.

We took this glimpse of the top of the world as a great gift—and good omen. As our return flight hovered over **Denali State Park,** we spotted a family of grizzlies loping across the frozen tundra. This was the Alaska we had traveled so far to see.

A cruise up the Inside Passage and into the Gulf of Alaska is an easy way for families to explore Alaska's spectacular terrain of glaciers, mountains, and fjords. It's also an excellent way to see the region's wildlife and experience its Native American heritage. If possible, try to work in a side trip to Denali State Park or Denali National Park. You might also consider staying at one of the fishing or bear-watching lodges mentioned on page 49.

The Inside Passage is a protected, island-studded channel that begins at the U.S.-Canada border near Seattle. It then winds north past Victoria, Vancouver, and Ketchikan before skirting Admiralty Island to reach Juneau and the longer inlets of Glacier Bay and the Lynn Canal. The Gulf of Alaska stretches even farther north, into Prince William Sound and to Seward. Because so much of this region is still a vast and trackless wilderness, a cruise can simplify the challenge of experiencing Alaska's beauty and heritage.

A cruise can also take the guesswork out of trying to budget a family vacation: The up-front cost covers everything but shore tours, drinks, and tips. Each day brings a different port—and a new adventure. You can paddle a sea kayak through bays populated with porpoises, sea lions, and whales; search for eagles on a float trip; go fishing for salmon; dogsled atop a glacier; fly over ice fields and glaciers; or watch Native Americans carve totem poles. Indeed, a large part of the appeal is the chance to witness the wonders of this land through the eyes of those whose ancestors lived here for thousands of years.

TIPS: Consider the following caveats before signing up for an Alaska cruise:

Sitka is not St. Thomas. In cruise season—June to mid-September—highs hover around 70°F and lows are often in the 50s. Add some wind and rain and you'll be glad you packed a parka and long underwear. A sweater is fine for touring ports, but ski jacket and gloves are musts on a small boat seeking out porpoises and whales.

Even caribou seem impressed by Denali.

The National Park Service limits cruise-ship access to **Glacier Bay National Park and Preserve**. To cruise past the blue-white ice walls of Glacier Bay, reserve space on a ship that has been granted access to this gem of the Inside Passage.

It can be pricey to see the Alaska of your dreams. That's because the best way to navigate the interior is via raft, dogsled, floatplane, or helicopter. For a week-long trip that gets you close to backcountry wildlife, expect to spend several hundred dollars per person.

I recommend an adventure vacation in Alaska for families whose kids are not afraid of flying in noisy helicopters or floatplanes. It helps, too, if the children are old enough to paddle a sea kayak or sit still in a raft. This probably limits the "pool of applicants" to nature-loving kids ages 8 and up.

BASICS: **Denali State Park** *(HC 32 Box 6706, Wasilla 99654. 907/745-3975).* **Denali National Park** *(on AK Rte. 3. summer 907/683-1266; winter 907/683-2294. www.nps.gov/dena)*

SIDE TRIPS

Take a ride on the **Alaska Railroad** *(800/544-0552 or 907/265-2494. www.akrr.com)* if you want to leave your car in Anchorage and visit **Denali State Park** (three hours away) or **Denali National Park** (seven hours away). Cruise passengers from the Princess and Holland America lines ride in glass-domed cars; everyone else occupies the Alaska Railroad section, a series of ordinary but comfortable

Paddles and propellers in Glacier Bay National Park and Preserve

railroad cars. Still, the same engine pulls everyone past the same forests, towns, and mountains.

If your own cargo manifest includes younger children and teens, get off the train in **Talkeetna.** Not only is Talkeetna the gateway to **Denali State Park,** but it inspired the small town of Cicely, Alaska in the television series *Northern Exposure.* From Talkeetna, it's a 75-minute bus ride to the **Mt. McKinley Princess Lodge** *(Princess Tours, 800/365-5522),* whose deck faces mighty Denali. You can book raft trips, helicopter flights, and guided hikes from the lodge or from Talkeetna. Our favorite Alaskan outing was a flight-seeing tour of the **Ruth Glacier** with **Era Helicopters** *(800/843-1947 or 907/586-2030. www.era-aviation.com/alaska).*

MORE ADVENTURES ON THE COAST

Seward: On a wildlife-watching expedition into **Kenai Fjords National Park** *(907/224-3175. www.kenai.fjords.national-park.com)* southwest of Seward, you're likely to spot orcas, humpback and minke whales, sea lions, and puffins. **Kenai Fjords Tours** *(888/478-3346)* operates 150-passenger boats that navigate narrower channels than cruise ships can, getting you closer to the wildlife. On a half-day trip, the vessel passes within 100 yards of a glacier—near enough for visitors to hear the thunderous crack of icebergs being calved into the sea. (The full-day outing involves more wind and water than most kids—and many adults— can handle.)

TIPS: It's cold on deck, so bundle up. You can always take refuge in the heated cabin, but those susceptible to seasickness will want to stay out in the fresh (but

FAMILY-FRIENDLY ALASKAN CRUISES

Some Alaskan cruise ships welcome children more warmly than others. Be certain, therefore, to select a cruise line—and a vessel—that offers facilities and programs geared to your family. Carnival, Celebrity, Norwegian, Princess, and Royal Caribbean, described in more detail below, all feature comprehensive children's programs offering activities such as shipboard scavenger hunts, science experiments, and computer games.

Carnival Cruise Lines *(800/227-6482. www.carnival.com)* offers teens-only shore excursions in Alaska. On all ships year-round, Carnival organizes children's programs in the following age categories: 2 to 4, 5 to 8, 9 to 12, and 13 to 17.

Celebrity Cruises *(800/437-3111. www.celebrity-cruises.com)*, known for its sophisticated and relatively new ships, sponsors a summer children's program for five age groups: 3 to 6, 7 to 9, 10 to 12, 13 to 15, and 16 to 17.

Kids Crew, a year-round youth program offered by **Norwegian Cruise Line** *(800/327-7030. www.ncl.com)*, divides participants into four age groups: 3 to 5, 6 to 9, 10 to 12, and 13 to 17.

Princess Cruises *(800/774-6237. www.princesscruises.com)* operates some of the newest cruise ships on the water; many cabins are equipped with private balconies. Its children's program divides kids into groups aged 2 to 6, 9 to 12, and 13 to 16. In 2000, Princess will take more passengers into Glacier Bay National Park than any other line. Because Princess operates two lodges near Denali parks, it is able to offer land-sea tour packages as well.

Royal Caribbean International *888/950-8005. www.rccl.com)* offers youth programs year-round. In general, kids are divided into four age groups: 3 to 5, 6 to 8, 9 to 12, and 13 to 17.

Even though **Holland America Cruise Line** *(800/426-0327. www. hollandamerica. com)* offers shore excursions for kids only in Alaska, this cruise line is not as kid-friendly as its competitors. Club HAL offers intermittent activities–not a day-long children's program— for the following age groups: 5 to 8, 9 to 12, and teens.

The **Big Red Boat IV** *(800/990-7770. www.premiercruises.com)* will begin Alaskan voyages in July 2001. Children's programs will be offered for ages 2-4, 5-7, 8-10, 11-13, and 14-17.

frigid!) air. The nearby **Alaska SeaLife Center** *(Milepost 0, Seward Hwy. 800/224-2525. www.alaskasealife.org)*, devoted to marine mammal research and rehabilitation, is one of the few places in the United States to view Steller sea lions.

Skagway: The name of this town means "home of the north wind" in the native Tlingit language, and Skagway is indeed the northern terminus of the Inside Passage. As a gold rush boomtown in 1898, Skagway saw its population surge to nearly 20,000. To retrace the arduous path of those Klondike fortune hunters, board the narrow-gauge **White Pass and Yukon Railroad** *(800/343-7373 or 907/983-2217.*

SCENIC DRIVE: ANCHORAGE-SEWARD HIGHWAY

Cruise ships advertised as embarking from Anchorage actually leave from Seward, 127 miles to the south. Along the **Anchorage-Seward Highway,** you'll pass slopes green with spruce trees and purple with wildflowers. Those birds you see swooping across the Cook Inlet south of Anchorage are probably arctic terns, their wings flashing bright white against the mist and mountains. From the marsh boardwalk at **Potter Point State Game Refuge** (*Milepost 117.4*), you can spot Canada geese, trumpeter swans, and many species of ducks. At **Beluga Point** (*Milepost 110.3*), named for the whales who frequently swim nearby, you may witness Alaska's fearsome **bore tide**—a breaking wave of water up to 6 feet high. And at the drive-through game park known as **Big Game Alaska** (*Milepost 84; 907/783-2025*), moose, caribou, eagles, elk, ox, and bison are usually on hand.

www.whitepassrailroad.com)*; the locomotive climbs nearly 3,000 feet in a mere 20 miles of track. En route to Dead Horse Gulch—named for the 3,000 pack animals that died in the struggle to cross it—passengers are treated to trainside views of canyons, gorges, waterfalls, and rushing streams.

Haines: From mid-October to mid-December, thousands of bald eagles descend on the **Chilkat Bald Eagle Preserve,** forming one of the world's largest concentrations of these majestic birds. **Chilkat Guides** (*907/766-2491*) offers scenic half-day float trips through the preserve. The outfitter also stages a canoe outing that threads icebergs at the toe of **Davidson Glacier**—the summer home of 250 to 400 bald eagles.

TIPS: Bundle up, and don't forget the binoculars. Although the mere prospect of seeing bald eagles excites most adults, younger kids may get bored or disappointed when they discover that the cold weather often outweighs the action; for most of the day, the birds seem bent on sitting still and looking regal. **Haines Visitors Bureau** (*800/458-3579 or 907/766-3138*)

Juneau: About a 20-minute drive from Juneau lies the **Mendenhall Glacier,** a 12-mile-long river of white-blue ice. The best time to visit is often late afternoon, when the crowds and bright sun have both diminished. Take time to explore the trails alongside the glacier. **Photo Point Trail** near the visitor center, for example, is handicapped accessible and good for strollers; the scenic path is about one-third mile long. **Era Helicopters** (*800/843-1947 or 907/586-2030. www.era-aviation. com/alaska*) offers aerial tours, as well as a combined flight-seeing-and-dogsled tour: You can overfly several glaciers while listening to a taped narrative, then set out on a short dogsled ride around the bowl of a glacier. **Juneau Convention and Visitors Bureau** (*888/581-2201 or 907/586-2201. www.juneau.com*)

Sitka: When Sitka was the thriving capital of Russian America in the mid-1800s, its population reached about 3,000 (Alaska was transferred to U.S. hands in 1867).

Some of Sitka's buildings retain distinctive traces of traditional Russian architecture. About half a mile from town is 107-acre **Sitka National Historical Park** *(907/747-6281)*, where totem poles line a nature trail leading to the site of a Tlingit fort burned by the Russians in 1804. Also in Sitka are **Alaska Adventures Unlimited** *(800/770-5576 or 907/757-5576)*, which offers wildlife safaris in search of whales, eagles, sea otters, and puffins, and the **Alaska Raptor Rehabilitation Center** *(800/643-9425 or 907/747-8662)*, which heals wounded or sick birds of prey and returns them to the wild. The rehabilitation center gives youngsters extreme close-ups of eagles, hawks, and other raptors.

Ketchikan: Ketchikan is the hub of three Alaskan tribes: the Tlingit, the Haida, and the Tsimshian. Both Prince of Wales Island and Alaska's only reservation—the Tsimshian settlement of Metlakatla on Annette Island—lie within reach of the town. The **Totem Heritage Center** *(907/225-5900)* displays 33 totem poles retrieved from abandoned Tlingit and Haida villages. Two miles south of Ketchikan is **Saxman Native Village**, where dancers perform and carvers transform a cedar trunk into a totem pole. Saxman village is popular on the cruise-ship circuit, so kids may prefer the less crowded **Saxman Totem Park** nearby. Among the park's 28 decorated totems is one dedicated to Abraham Lincoln after his assassination.

Also accessible from Ketchikan is **Tongass National Forest**, which contains **Misty Fjords National Monument** *(907/225-2148)*, a 2.3-million-acre rain forest wilderness of waterfalls, fjords, and rugged granite cliffs rising 4,000 feet high. Several companies, including **Taquan Air Alaska** *(800/770-8800 or 907/225-8800)*, offer flight-seeing tours over Misty Fjords. **Ketchikan Visitors Bureau** *(800/770-3300 or 907/225-6166. www.ktn.net)*

FOR MORE INFORMATION Contact the **Alaska Public Lands Information Center** *(605 W. 4th Ave., Anchorage. 907/271-2737)* for a directory of 250 guides and outfitters offering adventure trips, nature tours, and remote-lodge accommodations.

Alaska Native Heritage Center, Anchorage

Outside the **Alaska Native Heritage Center** in Anchorage stands a 13-foot sculpture that sets the tone for the exhibits inside. The human face in the belly of **Raven, the Creator** (by Aleut artist John Hoover) represents Mother Earth; from his beak dangle the stars; from his wings are suspended the sun and the moon. The face on the back of Raven's head represents the transformations Raven underwent— into men, women, babies, and other beings—as he created the modern world.

The facility is the realization of a dream by the Alaska Federation of Natives to create a place where Alaska's indigenous people could celebrate, share, and per-

Riding high on a blanket toss at the Alaska Native Heritage Center in Anchorage

petuate their rich and diverse cultures. The 26-acre site features a welcome house and five traditional villages showcasing the five groups that comprise Alaska's 11 distinct native cultures: **Athapaskans** from the state's interior; **Yup'ik** and **Cup'ik** from the west coast; **Inupiaq** and **St. Lawrence Island Yupik** from the north; **Aleuts** and **Alutiiqs** from the north Pacific; and **Eyak, Tlingit, Haida,** and **Tsimshian** from the southeast. Although residents of the lower 48 often use the catchall term "Eskimos" to describe the Yup'ik, Cup'ik, St. Lawrence Island Yupik, and Inupiat peoples, these bands prefer to differentiate themselves by the names above.

In the **Welcome House**, a wall display highlights important firsts in Alaska native history: The emergence of the Bering Land Bridge around 23,000 B.C. (allowing migration from Siberia) and the appearance of copper arrowheads in A.D. 1300. The display also details "origin stories": how Raven gave light to the world, how snowshoes were invented, how the first ceremonies honoring the dead came about.

Reflecting the heritage center's focus on contemporary as well as traditional native life, a short film introduces visitors to the state's regions, landscape, and people. Video monitors show glimpses of Alaska's native peoples today, while kiosks provide information about travel to other parts of the state.

At the **Gathering Place**—a large, open, circular hall—storytellers, dancers, and musicians convey more about their cultures. Storytelling, an integral part of native culture, is a means of giving new generations an understanding of their people, history, values, and mythology. Visitors hear such tales as how Raven made land from the sea and how the crane got its blue eyes.

The **Hall of Cultures** has three separate areas: Feature Walls ("Stories from the Land"), Cultural Galleries ("Stories from the Heart"), and Studios/Workshops ("Stories from Our Hands"). The walls and galleries teach visitors about the natural environment and cultural identities of all five native groups. Photographs, short videos, and art objects relate details of modern and historic native life.

As the exhibits make clear, the nomadic Athapaskans relied on moose, caribou, salmon, and birch trees. A moose-heart bag, made from the pericardium of a moose, typifies the respect shown by the Athapaskans in using every part of the animal's body. Ivory carvings and seal-gut drums reveal that sea mammals were cornerstones of the lives of the traditional Yup'ik and Cup'ik.

Photographs document the whale's critical importance to the Inupiaq and St. Lawrence Island Yupik cultures, as do tools used for carving, drilling, and inscribing whalebone. Contemporary artwork by the Aleut and Alutiiq peoples, who also depended on the sea, includes Aleut basketry—some of the finest in the world. Exhibits show how the Eyak, Tlingit, Haida, and Tsimshian people used wood not only for practical items (houses, canoes, cooking utensils) but also for ceremonial objects such as their distinctive totem poles. Throughout the year, native artists demonstrate traditional crafts: They show how to sew skins, string beads and quills, carve masks, create drums, and fashion silver jewelry. They also exhibit contemporary works based on these traditions.

Enter the **Village Sites** surrounding Tiulana Lake and you step into Alaska's past. In the Athapaskan log cabin, a native staff member invites visitors to imagine scraping skins with a caribou shinbone—not to mention living in a cabin insulated with moss against the subzero winters. The Yup'ik and Cup'ik site features a *qasgiq*—a large earthen mound containing a fire pit for sweat baths.

Children especially enjoy the Inupiaq/St. Lawrence Yupik community house; its underground entryway lets visitors pop up through the floor. Wood frames covered with sod form the Aleut/Alutiiq site, where visitors enter at ground level but can also view the traditional roof entry. An Aleut interpreter shows off a sealskin in preparation, a kayak frame, and the notched ladder that was used to access the home. The Eyak, Tlingit, Haida, and Tsimshian carving shed and clan house sit side by side.

Kids should not miss the Alaska Native Heritage Center's terrific summer program. Called **Icu** (EE-shoe), which means "welcome" in the Eyak language, it offers children four years and older a chance to learn about native Alaskan culture through crafts, games, and storytelling. Kids make sealskin yo-yos, play a St. Lawrence game similar to jacks, have their faces painted in traditional tattoo designs, create masks, and hear elders tell stories about the first Alaskan people.

In winter, the Welcome House becomes the scene of dancing and storytelling; skating parties are held on the lake each Saturday. On weekends throughout the year (check for times), artists teach traditional and contemporary crafts. The theme for 2000—boatbuilding—spotlights the variety of vessels that native Alaskans used to negotiate these waters. For 2001, the theme is clothing; for 2002, it is traditional medicine.

TIPS: A native bazaar and craft fair are held the second weekend of each summer month. There is an all-Alaska-native juried art show in April, and a major Fourth of July celebration, complete with games, barbecue, and blanket tossing. To avoid large groups from cruise ships, visit on Saturdays.

BASICS: The **Alaska Native Heritage Center** *(8800 Heritage Center Dr., Anchorage. 800/315-6608 or 907/330-8000. www.alaskanative.net. Adm. fee)* is a ten-minute drive from downtown Anchorage *(Anchorage Convention and Visitors Bureau. 800/478-1255. www.anchorage.net).*

Watching Grizzly Bears
Homer

Chris Day—a petite blonde with a rifle slung over her shoulder—led our group of eight away from our lakeside floatplane, through an open meadow, and up onto a plateau. Looking down on the glittering river below, we spotted four grizzly bears, then 10, then 12. After a while, we walked down the hill, pulled on waders provided by Day, and forded the river. Walking along the far bank, we sang, clapped, and talked loudly; startling a bear, Day had warned us, is the last thing you want to do in the Alaskan wilderness.

We spied another bear—this one weighing a good 500 pounds and standing on the riverbank directly opposite—about a mile later. My heart skipped a few beats as Day's instructions raced through my head: If the bear charged, I was to drop into a squat and cover the back of my head with my hands.

Fortunately, this didn't happen—nor has it ever, reports Day, on one of her tours. As we continued to watch the extraordinary creature, however, it became clear that it meant to cross the ribbon of water and approach us. "Stand very still," Day calmly ordered us. We obeyed. About 30 feet away, the bear stopped to look us over. "If you do it slowly," whispered Day, "you can take a photo." With the bear patiently looking on, everyone in the group raised their cameras and fired away. After a few minutes, having had her fill of posing, the bear crossed back to the other bank and ambled on.

Day Trips—named after its owners, Chris Day and her pilot-husband Ken Day—is one of Alaska's best bear-viewing operations. The company flies groups of up to eight people to remote areas of Alaska, where they follow bear trails as long as 5 miles through the tundra and along fishing streams. At lunch on a riverbed or in a flowered meadow, you may glimpse caribou, moose, or the occasional wolf.

Having guided visitors through bear country for more than 12 years, Chris Day infuses her bear-watching trips with expertise and enthusiasm. Her mission is to entertain, but also to inform. In the latter role, she dispels myths such as the common notion that bears are predators out to get people. "That's not true at all," notes Day, "and that's one of the things people learn on our trips."

To counter such misconceptions, Day starts each trip by steeping visitors in bear facts. Rule #1: Don't back away slowly from a bear encounter. "Bears love to make things move," says Day. "It's a game to them. If they can move you one step, they'll try for 4 and then 12. They become exponentially aggressive as you step away. And the worst thing you can do when a bear is focused on you is run. At that point, nature takes over."

According to Day, bears have a strong sense of personal space—and they maintain it with guile. "Part of a bear's posturing with other bears is to ignore them," Day points out. "They'll act like they don't see you—they may even walk past you just 15 feet away—but they know you're there. And the first sign of anxiety in a bear is yawning."

Although females protect their cubs aggressively, Day has managed to safely

Worry if it yawns: an Alaskan grizzly

view such family groups; the key is to let the bear spot the observer. On one trip, Day's group sat on a bluff 40 feet above a stream, watching a bear and her four spring cubs. "She went out of her way to come up on the bluff," recalls Day, "then sat down about 18 feet from us, nursed those babies, and took a nap. She left them with us for about 15 minutes while she fished in the stream. When she caught a fish, she called the babies and they went down and ate with her."

Bears can also be so playful as to mug for the crowd. In one viewing area on the coast, says Day, "I've got one bear who loves to play with driftwood and fishing buoys—he puts on a heck of a show. Others will climb out on the branches of trees over streams and yo-yo the branches in and out of the water. If you laugh and they know they're entertaining you, some bears will keep doing it. A young bear glutted with salmon loves to toss the fish around. One group of young bears was flinging around so much salmon we had to duck for cover."

TIPS: Although Day accepts children 7 years and up, I recommend this trip for families with teenagers who can follow directions carefully. It's scary enough to face a grizzly without worrying about the effect on it of a frightened child's cries.

Day Trips also offers an **Alpine Lake Trip** at $300 per person that includes a flight over the shores, mountains, and ice fields of the Kenai Peninsula. After landing on a mountain lake ringed by snowy peaks and glaciers, participants hike around the lake, learning which plants and animals live at the ice's edge.

BASICS: **Day Trips** *(P.O. Box 635, Homer. 907/235-6993. daytrips@xyz.net)* offers eight-hour excursions departing from Kachemak Air Service on Beluga Lake in Homer *(late May-Oct. $500 per person)*.

Admiralty Island National Monument

Around 1955, a crusty Alaskan named Stan Price moved to Pack Creek (on Admiralty Island south of Juneau) and took a liking to the brown bears he found there. For the next 40 years, Price prohibited bear-hunting in the area. Whether the bears somehow spread the word of this "safe zone" or whether they just don't mind having people around, no one knows. What's certain is that **Admiralty Island National Monument**—now a part of Alaska's Tongass National Forest—is a great place for families with older children to see bears.

Pack Creek Brown Bear Viewing Area on Admiralty Island offers families an opportunity to view Alaskan brown bears in their natural environment (you must be accompanied by a park ranger or a guide). A charter provides transportation to and from Pack Creek, but no guide. A guide furnishes transportation and leads you to the bear-viewing spots. Even though Admiralty Island has one of the world's highest concentrations of brown bears, sightings are not guaranteed because the animals are spread out over one million acres.

There are two viewing locations; both can be visited in a day. The likelier place to spot bears is the viewing spit—a sandy mound with two log seats. From here, you can gaze across one of the bears' favored hunting grounds—a mile-wide tidal flat. About a mile away—and deep in the woods—is a viewing tower, prized somewhat less as a vantage point because the surrounding foliage can obstruct sight lines. Make noise as you walk the tower trail, alerting the bears to your presence.

TIPS: Warm, layered clothing is essential. Your family may be standing in a cold, driving rain all day long, or the weather may suddenly turn hot and sunny in the afternoon. Pack Creek offers no amenities besides the two viewing areas—no shelters, food, water, or bathrooms. Not even a floatplane dock is available; depending on the tides, you step from the plane's pontoons onto a muddy beach or into foot-deep water. In either case, wear high boots.

BASICS: **U.S. Forest Service Information Center** *(101 Egan Dr., Juneau. 907/586-*

KACHEMAK BAY WILDERNESS LODGE

At the tip of the Kenai Peninsula, **Kachemak Bay Wilderness Lodge** offers a forest refuge amid mountains and the clear waters of China Poot Bay. The lodge keeps families busy with sea kayaking, trout and salmon fishing, hiking, boating, and wildlife-watching. (It's not unusual to spot a humpback whale on the boat ride from Homer to the lodge.)

Younger kids can join the lodge staff for a tide-pooling session, where they find out about invertebrates and tidepool ecology. With older siblings, they can try their hand at fishing. For adults, the bay affords ample opportunity to catch salmon, rainbow trout, flounder, halibut, and Dollyvarden—an arctic char named for a Dickens character.

Diane and Michael McBride opened Kachemak Bay Wilderness Lodge in 1969. The couple added a sister accommodation, **Loonsong Mountain Lake Camp,** in 1986. Visitors may stay at either place: The lodge has private cabins for up to 12 guests, while Loonsong has a large, two-bedroom chalet suitable for one or two couples or a family. (Loonsong, however, is rented only to those who wish to extend a Monday-Friday stay at Kachemak Lodge into the weekend.) Kachemak's cabins are simply but beautifully furnished: exposed beams, antiques, quilts, and wood-burning stoves. Both sites have saunas.

The McBrides' commitment to their guests is equaled by their dedication to Alaska's environment. About 10 percent of the lodge's income supports conservation projects.

Tips: Book well in advance.

Basics: **Kachemak Bay Wilderness Lodge** *(China Poot Bay, P.O. Box 956, Homer, 99603. 907/235-8910. www. alaskawildernesslodge.com).* A Monday-Friday stay costs $2,500 per person, including round-trip coastal ferry from Homer. A weekend stay at **Loonsong Mountain Lake Camp** costs $1,500 per person, plus $250 per person for round-trip floatplane from lodge to Loonsong to Homer. Price includes all meals and incidentals. Some guided trips are extra.

8751. *www.fs.fed.us/r10/chatham/anm).* Both charter and guide services are available from Juneau; check the U.S. Forest Service website for details.

The Pack Creek viewing area is open June 1 to September 10. All visitors—every family member—must purchase a permit to view the bears; only 24 people are admitted each day. Permit applications for the peak season (July 5-Aug. 25) are accepted starting February 20; permit processing begins March 1, and all permits are awarded on a first-come, first-served basis. Permits for the periods June 1 to July 4 and August 26 to September 10 are less in demand; they need not be made in advance. Each viewing permit is for a period of one to three days. Peak season: Adults $50 per day, children and seniors $25 per day. Non-peak season: Adults $20 per day, children and seniors $10 per day. A one-day guided tour (includes floatplane transportation) costs about $400 per person. Charters (transportation, no guide) start around $100 per person.

BEST PLACES TO WATCH WHALES
ON THE WEST COAST

In addition to the whale-watching possible in Alaska, the following three sites are likely places to give your kids the sight of a lifetime: a whale swimming wild in its natural environment.

HAWAII: Humpback whales from Alaska travel 2,500 to 3,000 miles to winter in the warm waters of Hawaii. According to the Pacific Whale Foundation, the first whales arrive in late September, and some linger into April. The prime season for spotting these behemoths from shore or boat, however, is January through March.

Maui is an unusually good vantage point. Many humpbacks like to stay in the shallow channel separating Maui, Lanai, and Molokai, which forms part of the **Hawaiian Islands Humpback Whale Marine Sanctuary.**

In January, Maui's **Four Seasons Wailea** hotel *(800/334-6284)* hosts the **Celebration of Whales**—a multiday event that is open to the public. Also on Maui, **Lahaina**—a town with a whaling past—hosts **Whalefest Week** in March **(Maui Visitors Bureau,** *800/525-6284. www.visitmaui. com)*. On **Molokai,** the best whale watching is on the southern coast **(Molokai Visitors Association** *(800/800-6367 or 808/ 553-3876. www.molokai.com)*. On the **Big Island,** most sightings occur on the Kona-Kohala coast **(Big Island Visitors Bureau** *808/961-5797. www.bigisland.org)*.

SAN JUAN ISLANDS, WASHINGTON: A whale-watching cruise is becoming a summer tradition in the San Juans, where visitors are likely to spot orcas breaching in salmon season (May–mid-July).

Although whale-watching day trips depart from several of the islands, our favorite spot in the San Juans is laid-back **Orcas Island.** The island's **Rosario Resort**—a peaceful place offering good food and fine accommodations—juts out into Cascade Bay. From the deck of their room or a chair by the pool, guests can gaze out on a soothing waterscape of green peninsulas receding into a blue haze of sea and sky.

Tips: Climb the lookout tower of nearby Moran State Park for its panoramic views of the snowcapped Olympic Mountains.

Basics: **Rosario Resort** *(Orcas Island. 800/562-8820 or 360/376-2222)*. The resort runs a summer children's program for ages 5 to 12. Rooms start at $185.

MAGDALENA BAY, MEXICO. We spotted the telltale heart-shaped spray not 30 feet from our skiff. Within seconds, the black back of a 40-foot-long Pacific gray whale broke the surface. The whale then dived out of sight, only to reappear inches from our boat—so close that we almost could have patted her barnacled head.

When the gray whale's calf rolled gently near the bow of our boat, my teenage daughter and I could hear the rhythmic whistle of its inhaling. Both cow and calf then gracefully dived under the boat, only to circle back to our port side. The 1,500-pound calf—seemingly as curious about us as we are about him—slid over his mother in order to stay alongside our skiff for several minutes.

For decades, pods of Pacific gray whales have made the 5,000-mile journey from Alaska to Magdalena Bay in Baja California. The bay's protected lagoons provide safe havens for birthing and nursing.

Flukes of nature: close-up whale-watching from a kayak

Perhaps encouraged by the friendliness of local fishermen, the whales seek out human contact. A whale-watching trip in February or the first half of March will give you a chance to see these leviathans at close range.

We chose **Outdoor Adventure River Specialists** for their family-friendly trips. Twice daily, we left our camp on sandy, windblown Isla Santa Domingo to search the horizon for the heart-shaped spray. Twenty minutes or more often passed before we sighted a whale, and even then the creatures could always dive deep to elude us. At other times, however, we spied the long, gray backs of the whales rolling through the waters just yards away. One day a school of dolphins tailed us, leaping in and out of the boat's wake.

When we weren't yelling "Thar she blows!", we slid down sand dunes and sea kayaked through the mangrove estuary opposite our camp. The night sky was so brilliant with stars that only the wind and the thought of the island's roving coyotes made us bed down in our tent. Camping, unlike a day outing, gave us not only more "whale time" but also a chance to explore the landscape of sand, bay, and sea.

At times, ten or more boats cruise Magdalena Bay in search of whales. Although most of them respect the rules against chasing whales, the occasional overzealous day tour may be spotted pursuing a fleeing whale. If caught, the guides are fined.

Tips: You'll be camping on a sand dune, so expect sand to invade everything: tent, bedding, shoes, clothes. Bring layers, rain gear, and gloves; the weather varies from cold and rainy at night to warm and sunny by day. Pack lots of flashlight batteries for those midnight visits to the outhouse.

Basics: **Outdoor Adventure River Specialists** *(Box 67, Angels Camp, CA 95222. 800/346-6277 or 209/736-4677. www.oars.com)* runs 6-day trips in February and March for ages 8+ *($1,195 per person).*

ADOPT A WHALE

Kids who want to help endangered animals can adopt a wild whale through the **Pacific Whale Foundation** *(800/942-5311 or 808/879-8860. www.pacificwhale.org).* For $35, they receive a history and photo of the whale, a map of recent sightings, an adoptive parent ID card, and a newsletter.

Volcanoes National Park
Big Island

A tour of 230,000-acre **Hawaii Volcanoes National Park** lets kids feel the power of volcanoes—including **Kilauea,** still oozing lava—and helps them appreciate Hawaiian legends about these smoking, sputtering, occasionally exploding hot spots. For an unusually dramatic view, board a helicopter and peer down into the spewing caldera, or crater, of Kilauea itself. You may also be able to see lava flows on a driving tour, particularly at the end of **Crater Rim Drive—** an 11-mile circuit of the Kilauea caldera. To find recent lava flows, watch for rising clouds of steam, then check their location (and safety!) with park rangers. (The visitor center has information on the latest flows and road closings.) Never get too close to lava or steam (see sulfur-vent warning below), and always follow park regulations.

Like all national parks in the United States, Hawaii Volcanoes offers **Junior Ranger programs** for kids in the summer. After taking part in several activities *(adm. fee),* children receive a Junior Ranger badge—a nice memento of their trip.

Crater Rim Drive passes steaming sulfur vents, a grove of lehua trees, and several overlooks and short hikes. A favorite formation is **Thurston Lava Tube,** a cooled lava flow from a past eruption that is big enough to walk through. Visit early or late in the day to avoid the crowds that invariably gather at this popular spot.

From the park's main parking lot, a ten-minute walk takes you to **Halemaʻumaʻu Crater Overlook,** the site of another lava flow. **Devastation Trail,** a half-mile-long boardwalk, was built to show visitors the destruction and rebirth that have occurred along the path of a 1959 lava flow. That smell of rotten eggs—warn the kids— comes from the crater's steaming **sulfur vents;** those with asthma or respiratory problems should keep the windows closed when driving past them.

The **Thomas A. Jaggar Museum** couples exhibits of seismographs and scientific explanations of eruptions with displays about Pele, the Hawaiian goddess of volcanoes.

The best views of lava flows are often from the sea. It's frequently possible to spot an erupting volcano from the deck of ships operated by **American Hawaii Cruises,** which offers year-round sailings to the islands. If the event occurs at night and you have left instructions to be woken, the crew will summon you on deck for a lava-viewing party; there, in the company of other passengers clad in their robes and pajamas, you can watch red lava tubes, glowing like fire, snake their way down the mountainside. Years after they experienced this sight, my children are still talking about it.

Left: Braving the lava field at Hawaii Volcanoes National Park

TIPS: Before booking a helicopter tour, investigate the company's reliability and safety record. Talk to your hotel's concierge, the local tourist bureau, or the local FAA Flight Standards District Office.

Volcano House, across the street from the visitor center, serves lunch and dinner. Perched at the edge of Kilauea Crater, the restaurant has scenic views. To avoid its tour-bus crowds, arrive early—or simply get a sandwich from the snack bar.

Look and enjoy—*but do not sample!* Not only is it illegal to bring back bits of lava rock, but—according to Hawaiian legend—it's bad luck. The visitor center occasionally displays letters written by "cursed" tourists, shamefacedly returning chunks of rock in order to reverse their recent misfortune.

BASICS: Hawaii Volcanoes National Park *(P.O. Box 52, Big Island. 808/985-6000. www.nps.gov/havo/. $10 per vehicle)* is about 30 miles southwest of Hilo. **American Hawaii Cruises** *(Box 56729, New Orleans, La 70156. 800/513-5022. www.cruisehawaii.com)*

Pu'uhonua o Honaunau National Historic Park

This seaside refuge has been a place of peace since the 15th century, when—legend has it—its rock walls provided sanctuary for everyone from defeated warriors to violators of island taboos to women and children fleeing scenes of battle. At **Pu'uhonua o Honaunau** on Hawaii, outcasts sought absolution from priests. The centerpiece of the 182-acre park is now the restored **Hale o Keawe temple,** which holds the bones of ancient Hawaiian chiefs. Let your kids wander around the grounds, peering at carved idols and koa wood canoes or trying their hand at *konane*—an ancient form of checkers.

TIPS: Green sea turtles and humpback whales are sometimes visible from the picnic area in winter. The **Hawaiian Cultural Festival,** held every year on the weekend closest to July 1, features a royal court procession, hula, and crafts.

BASICS: Pu'uhonua o Honaunau National History Park *(Hwy. 160. 808/328-2326. www.nps.gov/puho)* is about 22 miles south of Kailua-Kona.

MORE HAWAIIAN CULTURE

The **Hawaiian EDventure Program** *(200 West Kawili St., Hilo, Hawaii. 808/974-7555. foxgolds@hawaii.edu. www.uhh.hawaii.edu/~confctr)* creates intensive hands-on cultural experiences, primarily for groups (including students). During Hawaiian EDventures' **Japanese Day,** for example, the group takes part in a sunrise fish auction and a formal tea ceremony; it also learns origami and haiku poetry.

Spectator solidarity: Girls watch hula dancing at Hawaii Volcanoes National Park.

On a **marine EDventure,** kids go snorkeling, watch for humpback whales and hawksbill turtles, and explore tide pools with a marine biologist. On a **volcano expedition,** they hike across craters, track lava flows, and read seismology measurements. Participants can also craft an outrigger canoe or learn Hawaiian quilting.

TIPS: Families are occasionally allowed to join existing groups. Alternatively, depending on cost, Hawaiian EDventures may be able to create a program for an individual family. Most programs take place on the Big Island.

The **Ka'upulehu Cultural Center** distinguishes the **Four Seasons Resort Hualalai** (*Kailua-Kona, Big Island. 800/332-3442, 888/340-5662, or 808/325-8000. www.fourseasons.com*) from Hawaii's other upscale properties. Located in an impressive room dominated by a large tropical aquarium and paintings by native artist Herb Kawainui Kane, the center organizes complimentary Hawaiian cultural activities. Here children (and their parents) can learn to play the ukulele, dance a traditional hula, understand Hawaiian place-names and words, and see the stars through the eyes of ancient Hawaiian seafarers.

TIPS: Among the hotel's five swimming pools are a 25-meter lap pool and **Kings Pond**—a 2.5-million-gallon pool, made from black-lava rock and stocked with 3,500 tropical fish, in which children can snorkel. Kids new to snorkeling will find it easier to learn in the current-free environment of Kings Pond. The complimentary **Kids for All Seasons** program, designed for ages 5 to 12, meets year-round.

Lava Peninsula Hike Maui

Lava rocks glinted in the sun as far as we could see, creating a striking contrast of silky black stone and fluid blue Pacific. With a thundering whoosh, white sea spray suddenly shot 20 feet into the air; the mist lingered long enough to arc into a rainbow.

We were standing beside the **Nakalele Blowhole,** whose fame is well earned among nature lovers. Few others, apparently, venture to this spit of land several miles north of Kapalua on Maui's west side. The solitude is one of the pleasures of hiking with **Maui Eco-Adventures,** which showcases spots off the beaten path. Adam Quinn, the company's co-owner and guide, dubs these places "a little bit of the true Hawaii."

The blowhole and its surrounding lava field are not readily visible from the road, so we never would have found them on our own. From a small parking area, we descended a grassy slope to reach the lava. Along the way, Quinn explained that volcanic lava had spewed across this end of the island more than a million years ago. Picking up a piece of lava known as *aa,* Quinn pointed out the telltale signs of quick cooling: a honeycomb structure pocked with bumps resembling peanuts in brittle. Farther along, he directed our attention to a blacktop-smooth section of lava called *pahoehoe*—the hardened remains of a slow-moving flow.

At the blowhole, fascinated by Nakalele's sheer power, we lingered on the rocks near the perimeter, getting good and soaked by the spray. Our route back to the van took us through a grove of tall ironwood trees, their wispy leaves floating in the wind.

After a snack of muffins and juice provided by our guides, we climbed back into the van and set off for **Kahakuloa Valley, Waihale,** about 8 miles east of Nakalele. Having secured the owner's permission in advance, Adam took a dirt road across some private land, then drove past a small sugarcane field and forded a streambed. The group hiked into the woods, walked across a rope bridge, and passed through stands of banana, java plum, and coconut trees before coming upon a taro *(karo* in Hawaiian) pond brimming with the broad-leaved plants. On the surface of the water, a white duck paddled between the stalks. Adam led us farther up the slope, where an *ahupua'a*—a traditional Hawaiian farming community—stretched from the mountains to the sea.

Just when it seemed things couldn't get more scenic, we passed 2,000-year-old stone terraces created by Hawaii's first farmers and found ourselves hiking beside a riverbank full of ferns. Ripe papayas hung from the trees. Red-and-yellow ginger blossoms scented the path. Not another visitor was in sight.

TIPS: The six-hour day includes two moderate hikes, with lots of rest stops on each hike and a van ride in between. I recommend this outing for kids 8 and older who like the outdoors (younger ones run the risk of getting bored or tired). Be sure to pack plenty of water.

BASICS: Maui Eco-Adventures *(808/661-7720. www.ecomaui.com)* charges $110 per person (including shuttle-bus rides to and from west Maui hotels) for its **Lava Peninsula Hike.** Additional tours run by the company include the six-hour **Ridgelines and Waterfalls,** which takes in a waterfall and bamboo forest, and the four-hour **Maunalei Arboretum,** which visits a private, 70-year-old botanical garden containing trees from all over the world. Private charters focusing on special interests are also available.

Time Travel
Kapalua, Maui

Well-known for its five-diamond service, the Ritz-Carlton Kapalua also offers a less heralded history tour called **A Sense of Place.** The free program starts with Elizabeth Lindsey's 30-minute documentary on Hawaii, in which she ties the loss of island culture to declines in its native population.

When Capt. James Cook landed on Kauai and Nihei in 1778, notes Lindsey, "there were more than 500,000 pure-blooded Hawaiians." By 1821, however—after the arrival of missionaries bearing religion, measles, and chicken pox—Hawaii's native population had dwindled to 230,000.

By the 1840s, Lindsey continues, hundreds of American whaling ships thronged Lahaina and Honolulu. Both the California gold rush of 1849 and the Civil War created a demand for Hawaiian sugar, vegetables, and meat. As sugar became king, the white plantation owners—many of them missionary descendants—brought Chinese, Japanese, Portuguese, and Filipino laborers to Hawaii to work in the cane fields. The missionaries, Lindsey notes, "came to do good—and they did well."

Upon King Kalakaua's death in 1891, his sister Liliuokalani became queen. Both rulers opposed annexation by the United States; the nonnative plantation owners, on the other hand, wanted stronger ties to the mainland. In 1893, prominent annexationists (many of whom owned plantations) formed a "Committee of Safety"; backed by U.S. sailors and Marines, the committee overthrew the Hawaiian kingdom and arrested Queen Liliuokalani. By then, the population of pure-blooded Hawaiians had declined to just 40,000.

President Grover Cleveland launched an investigation of the affair. The monarchy had been toppled by force, declared the investigative team: "A great wrong has been done to the Hawaiians." Cleveland promptly directed Congress to restore Queen Liliuokalani to the throne, but Hawaii's provisional government—backed by nonnative businessmen—refused to step down. The Republican Congress, for its part, failed to act. After Cleveland lost the November 1897 election, his successor—Republican President William McKinley—signed a resolution of annexation in July 1898. Hawaii became a U.S. territory less than two years later.

Early in the 20th century, Lindsey's documentary reveals, teachers regularly beat local schoolchildren for speaking Hawaiian. By 1922, the number of pure-blooded Hawaiians had dwindled to 22,000. As developers turned taro patches into resorts and military personnel swarmed the islands in the wake of Pearl Harbor, Hawaiians became a minority in their own land.

In 1959—the year Hawaii became the 50th state—pure Hawaiians numbered just 12,245. Hawaii's popularity as a tourist destination drove up the cost of land pricing many natives out of the market. The Homesteading Act, designed to enable Hawaiians with more than 50 percent native blood to own land, helped some families but denied others. By the time Hawaiians gathered in front of Iolani Palace in 1993 to protest the overthrow of their nation (for which the United States has issued an apology), the population of pure-blooded Hawaiians had dropped to 8,711.

After viewing Lindsey's documentary, visitors can take a tour of the property. A medicinal herb garden features *kukui* trees, aloe, *awa*, *awapuhi*, and taro plants. There is also an ancient burial site, located on a rise in front of the resort.

Unlike most resorts, the Ritz-Carlton sits well back from the ocean, behind an expanse of lawn. When excavations unearthed bones in the beachfront area, the resort and the community realized that the property contained an ancient burial site (the earliest bones dated to A.D. 850). Out of respect, Ritz-Carlton redesigned its planned building and facilities, moving them about 200 yards from the beach.

TIPS: In April the hotel stages a weekend-long **Celebration of the Arts** festival devoted to traditional Hawaiian arts. The property also offers **Ritz Kids,** a supervised, year-round activity program for ages 5 to 12.

BASICS: The **Ritz-Carlton Kapalua** *(1 Ritz Carlton Dr., Kapalua. 800/262-8440 or 808/669-6200)* offers its free **Sense of Place** tour each Friday morning year-round.

Mountain Biking Haleakala Volcano

At the summit of **Haleakala**—Maui's 10,000-foot-high dormant volcano— we gazed upon a moonscape of craters brown and red. Clouds hung in white wisps from the gray peaks of the lava cones. The earth inside the summit crater was a trail of black ashen pebbles.

It had taken our guide two hours to drive us up here along the 38 miles of pathways that snake their way to the top, but now we were about to take a different way down. In honor of my son's high-school graduation, we straddled mountain bikes and prepared to coast all the way down to sea-level sugarcane fields. Along

Bombing down the flanks of Haleakala

the way, we would come to understand the Hawaiian fascination with volcanoes.

It was cold at the top, so we paused just long enough to admire the shooting tendrils of a silver sword—a sunflower that grows only in the high, dry lava beds of volcanic peaks. Nearby, two rare nene geese, the Hawaiian state bird, peered back at us with a mix of curiosity and indignation.

As we set off downhill, it became clear that the weather moves in mysterious ways up here. At first, the sun coddled us; then, around the next bend, we were caught by the clouds that lace Haleakala's ridges, and visibility dropped to 3 feet. For a few moments, we could see nothing but the yellow dividing line on the pavement and the rain that was turning it slick. Just 300 feet farther on, however, the sun shot out, and a rainbow arced across a distant valley.

After a lunch of sandwiches and soft drinks at 7,000 feet, our guide warned us that the most difficult part lay just ahead: twenty-nine 100-degree turns in succession. Because of these sharp bends, we found ourselves biking blind around hairpin turns, straining for the sound of buses and carloads of tourists laboring up the volcano. The heady sequence of sharp rights and lefts simultaneously scared and energized me; my son negotiated the turns with an ease born of athleticism.

Halfway down the slope, I stopped worrying about my son—he was helping the guides by now—and began to feel a kinship with this mountain that transforms itself. The green of native koa trees began to replace the red-and-brown ash. The wind rippled the yellow-gold *pili* grass on the hillsides, and cactus dotted the black-top. Our final turn led us through a eucalyptus grove pungent with mint.

When we hit the straightaway, we caught our breath for the four knolls in front of us. Near Kula, a small town of rolling golden hills at 2,500 feet, we cycled by a pasture just after a cow had given birth. Our guide signaled us off the bikes to watch the newborn calf, wobbly-legged and sticky white, struggle to her feet.

Over the last 1,500 feet of our descent, as we pedaled through the sugarcane and pineapple fields on Haleakala's flanks, the sun burned steamy hot. We celebrated our arrival in Paia, the small town at the base of the volcano, with cups of shaved ice—a local favorite.

Biking down Haleakala was a special shared outing. While my son admired both the views and his mother's stamina, my own mountaintop epiphany was the realization that he was grown up and ready to go off on his own.

TIPS: The park's visitor center, about 11 miles from the summit, has a good collection of material, including children's books, on volcanoes. Kula Lodge *(Hwy. 377. 808/878-2517),* located on the slopes, serves moderately priced meals.

Dress in layers; temperatures at the summit range from 40°F to 65°F—considerably cooler than those at the base. Family members who don't want to bike down Haleakala should still visit the summit to experience the volcano.

BASICS: Haleakala National Park *(Crater Road, Maui. 808/572-4400. www.nps.gov/hale).* Because the bike trip can be dangerous, go with a reputable company. Check the safety record of an outfitter before signing on. Companies include **Maui Downhill** *(808/871-2155. www.mauidownhill.net),* **Mountain Riders Bike Tours** *(808/242-9739. mtriders@maui.net),* and **Maui Mountain Cruisers** *(800/232-6284. www.mauimountaincruisers.com).* Some outfitters also offer horseback rides into the crater and other adventures.

Maui Ocean Center
Wailuku

Sharks and spotted eagle rays star at the **Maui Ocean Center,** an aquarium devoted to the creatures found in Hawaiian waters. Although the 5-acre facility may seem small when compared with big-city aquariums, its focus on Hawaiian animals makes it an interesting stop—especially before snorkeling.

The **Living Reef** is a wall-size tank that will impress kids with its multihued corals, yellow tang, red Hawaiian squirrelfish, black-and-white-striped pennant butterfly fish, and other colorful creatures.

Make sure your children hold onto their brochures. The tanks don't identify

OF LUAUS AND LOCAL CUISINE

OLD LAHAINA LUAU: For kids and adults alike, the lures of a traditional luau are legion: fire dancers, hula, flickering torches, chants, and a "buried pig." We'd all like to believe such island magic still exists, but the reality is that most luaus are overpriced buffet lines of mediocre food, packaged with a hodgepodge of singers and dancers of varying talents and authenticity. Although your 9-year-old may come away wide-eyed, you're likely to find yourself grumbling about all the other ways you could have spent $200—the average cost of a luau for a family of four.

Happily, that's not the case at the **Old Lahaina Luau,** a very Hawaiian "dinner theater" that gives you your money's worth. Much of the pleasure comes from the locale: Outdoor tables face the setting sun, banyan trees sway in the breeze, an outrigger canoe floats near the shore. It's as tasteful a setting as a commercial dinner party for 400 of your closest friends can be.

The menu mixes traditional luau dishes (kalua pork, chicken long rice, lomi lomi salmon, taro-leaf salad, and poi) with entrees such as seafood salad, teriyaki sirloin, and guava chicken. Most kids fill up on the chicken and rice plus the fruit desserts.

The after-dinner show features choreography and chants detailing the Polynesian migration, ancient hula, the legend of Pele the fire god, tales of warriors and lovers, and a modern "hula" poking fun at missionaries. The dancers and singers are talented; a narrator provides a helpful summary; and the entertainment is delivered with cultural sensitivity.

Tips: Bring a sweater for the night breezes. Ask in advance about the possibility of special food for finicky eaters. Book several weeks ahead of time.

Basics: The **Old Lahaina Luau** (*1251 Front St., Lahaina. 800/248-5828 or 808/667-1998*) charges $65 for adults and $30 for ages 2 to 12 (drinks included).

HAWAIIAN REGIONAL CUISINE. Hawaiian regional cuisine blends elements of Chinese, Japanese, Polynesian, Thai, Portuguese, Vietnamese, and mainland American cooking with fresh local produce and Pacific fish to create some extraordinarily good food. Don't hesitate to enjoy these meals with your kids. Here are two of our favorite dining spots on popular Maui.

Hali'imaile General Store (*900 Hali'imaile Rd., Maui. 808/572-2666. Dinner entrees $17-32*): If you think you're irretrievably lost, you've almost reached the restaurant of noted chef Beverly Gannon. Set amid a pineapple plantation in the foothills of Mount Haleakala, this converted general store has a country-comfortable ambience that is welcoming to families. Voted one of Maui's best restaurants by *Honolulu* magazine in 1999, the General Store offers these signature dishes: Szechuan barbecued salmon; rack of lamb Hunan style; pina-colada cheesecake; and chocolate macadamia-nut fudge pie.

Sansei Seafood Restaurant & Sushi Bar (*The Shops at Kapalua, 115 Bay Dr., Unit 115, Kapalua, Maui. 808/669-6286. Appetizers $3-12, entrees $9-23*): Chef Dave Kodama serves a palate-pleasing blend of Japanese and Pacific Rim cuisine in a low-key setting that is one of Hawaii's top-ranked restaurants. The 130 appetizers are a great way to get kids to sample new foods. Try the crab and mango in a *mamenori* wrap; tempura shrimp rolls; Asian rock-shrimp cake; tea-duck rolls; or Japanese fried chicken. If all else fails, of course, you can always order a bowl of ramen noodles.

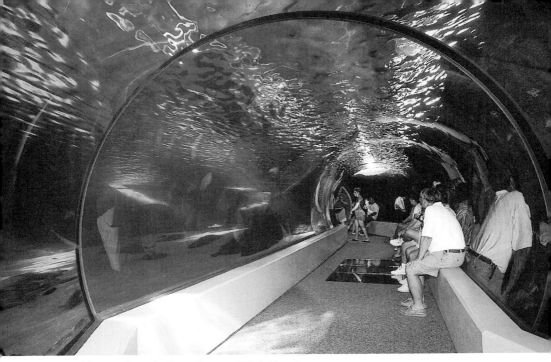

The view from the Open Ocean exhibit in Hawaii

the fish, so you'll need to consult the brochure illustrations to answer the inevitable questions of "What's *that* thing?" The exhibits nonetheless manage to capture kids' attention: "Cover your wrasse," for example, points out the advantages of camouflage as a system of defense for this tropical fish.

Outdoors, turtles laze in a lagoon, and a touch pool invites little fingers to pick up sea stars, helmet shells, and other tide-pool denizens. In the stingray cove, kids can watch these sleek gray creatures glide by, flapping their fins and revealing their white underbellies. At the daily "lunch," baby spotted eagle rays playfully suck up periwinkle mollusks fed to them by hand.

The **Whale Discovery Center** uses hands-on exhibits to teach kids about humpbacks and other leviathans. Listen to the rumbling vibrations of a blue whale or the louder, popping sounds of a fin whale. See what a whale looks like when it breaches, tail slaps, or dives. By matching the flukes to the correct creature, kids learn to distinguish one whale from another. They also find out how much food a male cetacean eats each day (answer: up to one ton).

At the **Open Ocean** exhibit, wall-to-wall sharks—tigers, gray reefs, and whitetip reefs—zigzag about you as you pass through a 54-foot-long acrylic tunnel that affords 240-degree views of the predators swimming in the surrounding tank.

TIPS: The Open Ocean exhibit is extra lively at 10:30 a.m. and 3:30 p.m., when a scuba diver feeds the sharks. The facility is located in Ma'alaea Harbor Village, near the spot where boats depart for popular snorkel trips to Molokini (page 63).

BASICS: Maui Ocean Center *(192 Ma'alaea Rd., Wailuku, Maui. 808/270-7000. www.coralworld.com)*

MORE FISHY BUSINESS

Molokini: Snorkel at Molokini, a partially submerged volcanic crater and marine preserve off the shore of Maui, and you'll find yourself swimming among hundreds of rainbow-colored fish—not to mention plenty of other snorkelers. This popular preserve is a mecca for day-trippers. In spite of the crowds, you'll see scores of parrot fish, blue-and-green wrasse, yellow tangs, black triggerfish, orangeband surgeonfish, and many others. For the viewing convenience of small children and nonswimmers, many dive boats offer "seeboards," which are equipped with built-in masks. These are popular items, so ask about them as soon as you get on board.

TIPS: Although half-day trips depart both in the morning and in the afternoon, the earlier voyage is a safer bet; the sea tends to be rougher in the afternoon—no fun for those prone to seasickness.

BASICS: Many boats leave from Ma'alaea Harbor. Good choices include the **Pacific Whale Foundation** vessel *Ocean Spirit (101 N. Kihei Rd., Kihei, HI. 800/942-5311 or 808/879-8811. www. pacificwhale.org)* and the *Wailea Kai,* operated by the **Ocean Activities Center** *(1847 S. Kihei Rd., Suite 203, Kihei, HI. 800/798-0652 or 808/879-4485).*

STARRY, STARRY SKI IN MAUI

Though initially skeptical that a chain hotel could create a quality stargazing program, we came away delighted from an evening on the roof of the **Hyatt Regency Maui** *(800/233-1234 or 808/661-1234. www.hyatt. com)* in Kaanapali. The resident astronomer showed us close-ups of Mars, Virgo, the Milky War, binary stars, and other heavenly bodies through "Little Blue"—a Meade LX200 reflector telescope. We also made use of the hotel's own star—"Big Blue," a 16-inch computerized prototype reflector. We simply clicked on what we wanted to see—birthday constellations were big hits—and Big Blue brought the object into focus. Never had the skies shone so brightly for us.

Tips: Reserve ahead for this one-hour program (adults $15, children $10). Maximum of 10 stargazers, with priority given to hotel guests.

Atlantis **Submarine:** Get a diver's-eye view of life in the sea aboard this recreational submarine with room for 40 passengers. From a depth of 150 feet—far enough beneath the waves to see black coral—you can watch schools of fish (and perhaps even a lazy sea turtle) float by. The minimum height for passengers is 3 feet, making this a suitable choice for most kids ages 4 and older.

TIPS: A boat departs Lahaina for the sub. While you're boarding, the sub bobs, causing some to get seasick. Take precautions if necessary.

BASICS: *Atlantis* **Submarine** *(800/548-6262 or 808/667-7816. www.goatlantis. com)* also offers dives from Waikiki on Oahu and Kailua-Kona on the Big Island. On Maui, submarine dives cost $79 per adult and $39 per child under 12.

Aloha, hombre: For Hawaiian cowboys at Molokai Ranch, never is "herd" a discouraging word.

Molokai Ranch

Rainbow-colored tropical fish surrounded us as we snorkeled at the base of jagged sea cliffs rising 2,000 feet above our secluded cove. We were the only boat in sight—but that's what we expected when we came to Molokai, least developed of the Hawaiian islands. Already that day, my husband had raced barrels and roped mock calves, my daughter had whizzed down a 40-foot zip line on a ropes course, and I had hiked to the site of a 14th-century Hawaiian temple.

Because we were staying at **Molokai Ranch,** we also could have sampled such adventures as mountain biking, sea kayaking past ancient fish ponds, net throwing, outrigger-canoe surfing, or weaving baskets from pandanus leaves. We also could have taken part in such *paniolo* (Hawaiian cowboy) practices as rounding up heifers on a cattle drive or riding horses along ridge tops with sweeping Pacific views.

Our adventures made us Molokai Ranch enthusiasts. A working cattle ranch on the dry west end of Molokai, the ranch covers 54,000 acres of elemental Hawaii—a rugged land of red-dirt hills, pine trees, and windswept beaches. This is the Hawaii of long ago, before the days of condominiums and trendy shopping centers. Visitors bunk at one of three campsites in a "tentalow"—a surprisingly comfortable permanent tent with a platform, plumbing, solar lights, ceiling fans, and maid service. The tentalows jibe with the ranch's overall goal: to provide eco-adventures along with an appreciation of Hawaiian traditions and culture.

Both children and their parents kids love the tentalows, which allow them to camp without roughing it. We never felt so good about bedding down "outside."

At Paniolo Camp (set on a ridge top of Cook's pines at 1,100 feet) and at Kaupoa Beach Camp (fronting a white-sand beach laced with swaying palms), each unit has two tentalows that share a deck and a roofless bathroom. That means you can shower under the stars and fall asleep with the trade winds wafting through the canvas flaps. The third campsite at Molokai Ranch is the more secluded Kolo Cliffs Camp set on a bluff; it accommodates couples in yurts furnished with queen beds.

Lawrence Aki, our guide on a cultural hike, showed us history in the stones. Those seemingly random rocks in the red dirt are an *aku*—a trail marker of a centuries-old path, created by King Lonopialani, that rings the island. A pile of coral and sandstone turned out to be the foundation of a 14th-century fishing shrine.

Aki also pointed out a smooth, oblong rock near the front wall. It was a *Ki'i pohaku ke akua kuula*—an image stone to the fishing gods. Before undertaking a fishing expedition, the men would place their hooks and nets on the *lele* (altar) and pray. In a clear, powerful voice, Aki gave us an example—he chanted a 1,500-year-old prayer that had been handed down to him—and we sensed the Hawaii of yore. When the ancient fishermen returned at day's end, they traditionally gave the gods their best catch—often a *kumu*, or red snapper (red being the color of sweetness).

About 40 yards away lay the remnants of a terraced wall. This, Aki revealed, had been the site of a house for a chief, his *kahu* (caretaker), and his *kahunas*, or lesser chiefs. Because *mana* (power) is believed to reside in old bones, Aki told us, only on a *po'okine* (a moonless night) can a chief's bones be buried by his *kahu*— who must then kill himself to protect the secret of their location.

Afterward, listening to the wind and surf from our deck, it was easy to envision ancient fishermen casting their nets into the sea below and kahunas, deep in prayer, walking the ridgeline. We felt close both to the land and to the spirit of the people who had lived here for hundreds of years.

To enjoy Molokai Ranch thoroughly, it helps to be a good camper who does not mind adhering to a rigid schedule of meals and activities. After breakfast (7 a.m. to 8 a.m.), there's just enough time to ride the shuttle bus to the site of your 9 a.m. activity. Guests then eat lunch at the nearest camp and tackle an afternoon adventure. The day ends with a shuttle ride back to your base camp and a rest before dinner. To make the day feel less regimented, we often skipped activities to lie on the beach, lounge in a hammock, or sit on our private deck and take in the view.

Evening entertainment at the ranch is sparse. One night we watched a film on volcanoes; another night we listened to a Hawaiian country singing group whose leader bantered with the audience. The idle evenings left us free to do the simple things we hadn't done in a while: We played marathon rounds of Chinese checkers with other families, rehashed the day's events, and talked to the children over hot chocolate.

Despite forgettable meals of mediocre chicken, steaks, and fish—not to mention the inconvenience of waiting for the shuttle bus to arrive—Molokai Ranch has become one of our favorite island places. There's no glitz at this true Hawaiian getaway—just adventure, spirit, and spectacular views.

TIPS: Try to book the most popular activities—outrigger canoeing and sea kayaking are two—ahead of time. If your family needs to be oceanside, choose Kaupoa Beach Camp. Because Kaupoa's dining pavilion is relatively small, however, lines form for meals, making the place feel crowded. Our favorite camp is Paniolo: The elevation keeps it cool, there's more space between units, the dining pavilion is large enough to accommodate all guests, and the views of the sea are unbeatable. Still, Paniolo is a 25-minute shuttle ride from the beach.

Active kids 10 and up—the minimum age for trail rides, mountain biking, kayaking, cattle drives, and many other outings—relish Molokai Ranch. Indeed, the ranch's rate for kids under 12—they're free—fills the site with families. Despite an ambitious children's program (tide-pool explorations, bug hunts, nature hikes, lasso lessons) for ages 5 to 12, children too old to be entertained by such activities but too young for the adventure trips will wind up frustrated.

BASICS: **Molokai Ranch** *(P.O.Box 259, Maunaloa, Hawaii. 877/726-4656. www. molokai-ranch.com).* **Kamalii Ed-Ventures,** a year-round program for kids 5 to 12, runs from 9:30 to 11:30 each morning and from 1:30 to 3:30 each afternoon. Half-day $25, full day $35.

Platform rates (including breakfast) start at $145 per night, single or double occupancy. Children ages 12 and under are free. Ages 13 and older on the same platform pay $40 per night. Activities range from $20 for half a day of mountain biking to $135 for a full day of sea kayaking and the ropes challenge course. The **Molokai Ranch Lodge** *(P. O. Box 259, Maunaloa, Hawaii. 808/660-2720)* in town has 22 traditional guest rooms (from about $300 per night) and an upscale restaurant.

Molokai Mule Ride

As the mule carried my teenage daughter down some of the steepest sea cliffs in the world on a narrow, 3-mile trail with 26 switchbacks, I asked Roy Horner—co-owner of **Molokai Mule Ride**—the name of the beast.

"It's *Kiawe*," Horner shot back without hesitation. "That means 'blind' in Hawaiian."

Horner's teasing broke the tension in our group of 18 people (including an 85-year-old grandmother) and five guides. Before sending us out to conquer the 1,700-foot-high cliffs above **Kalaupapa National Historical Park** on Molokai, he also serenaded us with Elvis tunes strummed on a ukulele.

Yet even that send-off could not prepare us for the steepness of the descent. The second switchback from the top rivaled the visceral thrill of any roller coaster: Suddenly we were on a ledge not much wider than a saddle, peering down nearly perpendicular cliffs at the Pacific far below. For the next 1-1/2 hours, we trusted our mules ("Good boy, *Kiawe!*") to pick their way down the narrow path. Despite a nerve-racking habit of stepping to the outside edge of the path before turning, the animals handled the windy trail with ease.

When we reached the black-sand beach at Kalaupapa and looked back at the fluted green cliffs above, they seemed impenetrable. Indeed, that was part of their original appeal. In order to prevent the spread of leprosy—now called Hansen's disease—King Kamehameha V authorized this isolated parcel of land to be set aside for advanced cases in 1865. Kalaupapa, with the sea on three sides and those towering cliffs behind it, became the "living tomb" for 8,000 sufferers of the disease, who were torn from their families and shipped to this valley settlement.

The first group—nine men and three women—were dumped offshore in January 1866; they had to fight their way through the surf to reach their own prison. Joseph de Veuster (later known as Father Damien), a pipe-smoking Belgian priest, arrived in 1873 and set to work building houses, tending the afflicted, and bringing order and hope to what had been a lawless and forsaken place. Mother Marianne Cope reached the colony in 1888. For the rest of their lives, she and Father Damien ministered to the terminally ill; both are being considered for sainthood.

Despite the spectacular setting, Kalaupapa seems tinged with sorrow. More than 8,000 graves line a dirt road on this 12-square-mile peninsula. Of the residents, Robert Louis Stevenson wrote: "They were strangers to each other, collected by common calamity, disfigured, mortally sick, banished without sin from home and friends . . . . In the chronicle of man there is perhaps no more melancholy landing than this."

Walking through the small church built by Father Damien and listening to the guide tell how the priest spent a lifetime making coffins and digging graves, we felt incredibly sad. The story of Kalaupapa is not an easy one to hear.

TIPS: The bag lunch provided by Molokai Mules Ride is modest. Hungry kids and picky eaters should bring their own food—as well as plenty of bottled water to get them through the 7-1/2-hour day. Mule riders must be 16 years or older.

BASICS: **Molokai Mule Ride** *(Box 200, Molokai. 808/567-6088. www.muleride. com)* charges $150 per person, which includes the ride, lunch, and park permits.

MORE MOLOKAI MUSTS

Molokai Horse and Wagon Rides *(P. O. Box 1528, Kaunakakai, HI 96748. 808/ 558-8380. www.visitmolokai.com/wgnride):* Take a guided ride on the back of a horse or the buckboard of a wagon through woods and mango groves to reach the ruins of an ancient Hawaiian *heiau,* or temple. Black volcanic rock covers the area, which is nearly the size of a football field.

Papohaku Beach: Stroll this 3-mile stretch of sand—one of the longest beaches in Hawaii and especially pretty at sunset—but *do not attempt to swim here.* The rough surf and riptides make the water dangerous.

Murphy's Beach: Families favor this narrow strip of sand on the east end of Molokai. You'll find it along Highway 450 between Mileposts 19 and 20.

Kanemitsu's Bakery & Restaurant *(79 Ala Malama St., Kaunakakai. 808/553-5855):* Join the "midnight bread run" at this popular bakery, a local legend for more than 65 years. From 9 p.m. to 1 a.m. every night but Monday, the smell of freshly baked bread draws locals down Mango Lane, behind the bakery, to line up for a loaf spread with butter, strawberry jam, or cream cheese. During regular hours *(Wed.-Mon., 5:30 a.m.-6:30 p.m.),* try the popular banana, mango, or raisin breads. The bakery's well-rounded French bread is aptly named *okole* (backside).

Polynesian Cultural Center Laie, Oahu

Learn how to throw a spear in Tahiti. Play bamboo drums in Fiji. Win at *tititorea* (a traditional stick game) in New Zealand. In Tonga, weave a fish out of palm fronds; in Samoa, play shuffleboard with shells. Or try your aim at Hawaiian bowling, then go to the Marquesas for a traditional tattoo.

This time travel to old Polynesia is possible at seven living history villages in the **Polynesian Cultural Center,** a 42-acre facility run by Brigham Young University, Hawaii. Costumed interpreters—many of them BYU students—deliver facts with a vaudeville pacing guaranteed to get giggles from grade schoolers.

"Villagers" demonstrating age-old crafts go out of their way to engage onlookers. Get ready to banter with artisans as they fashion tapa cloth from mulberry

bark, carve miniature tiki (religious statues), and create lauhala-leaf baskets.
Make a day of it here. At 2:30 p.m., scores of villagers in native attire take part in a daily canoe pageant featuring island songs and dances. The IMAX screen offers *Polynesian Odyssey*—a panoramic portrayal of 5,000 years of Polynesian history—*The Living Sea,* and *Everest.*

The pageantry continues at night with the 500-guest **Ali'i Luau.** Though not for everybody, the razzle-dazzle performance is usually a hit with kids. The luau kicks off with a conch-shell call to order, then continues with *hula kahiko*—ancient dances that retell stories from Hawaii's history. By the end, guests are swaying to tunes played on Hawaiian steel guitars. The menu includes roast pig, lomi lomi salmon, and other authentic dishes. Another spectacle is *Horizons: Where the Sea Meets the Sky.* Staged in a 3,000-seat amphitheater, the show features 100 performers, a fiery volcano, and crackling sound effects.

TIPS: Don't arrive too early; the center doesn't open until 12:30 p.m. Closed Sun.

BASICS: The **Polynesian Cultural Center** *(55-370 Kamehameha Hwy., Laie, Oahu. 800/367-7060 or 808/293-3333. www.polynesia.com)* is on Oahu's north shore.

WAIMEA VALLEY ADVENTURE PARK

Part botanical garden, part living-history facility, part adventure park, this facility occupies 1,800 verdant acres on the north shore of Oahu, not far from the Polynesian Cultural Center. Fragrant paths lined with hibiscus, ginger, and bougainvillea lead visitors to performances of old Hawaiian traditions: storytelling, hula dancing, and cliff diving from a 60-foot waterfall. Park patrons get to throw spears and fishing nets, drive all-terrain vehicles around a track, or explore mountain-biking and horseback trails with a guide.

TIPS: Some local hotels offer packages that include admission to the park. Overnight camping is available in summer.

BASICS: Waimea Valley Adventure Park *(59-864 Kamehameha Hwy. at Wei Mei. 808/638-8511)*

Bishop Museum
Kauai

The **Bishop Museum** boasts a first-rate collection of Hawaiiana—more than 20 million items, all told—but media-minded kids may find the display-case presentation tedious. For that reason, head for the more engaging exhibits: In addition to live demonstrations of hula, these include *Explorers,* a planetarium show that invites the audience to join in. Here you'll learn how star navigation enabled the first Hawaiians to reach the islands 2,000 years before Captain Cook, and how the constellation Scorpius came to be (a fishhook owned by the demigod Maui flew up into the sky). Virtual stargazers also help the planetarium narrator plot a seafaring course from Polynesia to Hawaii.

Kids may also be intrigued by the exhibit-hall displays of fierce carved masks and feathery orange-and-yellow capes worn by past kings and queens of Hawaii. Other exhibits detail the contributions to Hawaiian culture that have been made by Koreans, Japanese, Filipinos, Portuguese, and many more. The **Castle Memorial Building** occasionally hosts hands-on exhibits designed to appeal to children.

TIPS: The museum's gift shop has an excellent collection of Hawaiian material, including children's books.

BASICS: **Bishop Museum** *(1525 Bernice St., Honolulu. 808/847-3511)*

Cliff Hiking
Kauai

Less developed than Maui and more lushly green, **Kauai** still has pockets that represent the languid and less populated Hawaii of long ago. Nicknamed "the garden isle," Kauai is often captured in a trademark photograph showing the tunnel of towering eucalyptus trees that signals the turnoff from Koloa toward **Poipu,** a popular beach area. Bougainvillea, bird of paradise, ginger, and hibiscus all grow in profusion on Kauai, as do the ferns that feather the roadsides. Kauai is also the home of several natural wonders, free for the looking: **Waimea Canyon, Kokee State Park,** and the **Alakai Swamp.** Most impressive, however, are the fluted **Na Pali Cliffs.** You can reach these only by foot, boat, or plane.

KAUAI'S NATURAL WONDERS

Na Pali Coast State Park: Do the towering green Na Pali Cliffs shelter the bones of ancient Hawaiian kings? Legends say they do. Hike even a portion of the **Kalalau Trail**—an 11-mile clifftop path—and you will sense the power of these ancient mountains with their secluded caves, skydiving waterfalls, and dramatic sea views.

Only the hearty (and extremely physically fit) should attempt to hike the entire trail—a round-trip of 22 miles. Most hikers making the complete out-and-back route pack in their own provisions and camp overnight before returning. The weather here is notoriously fickle—sunshine giving way to thunderstorms with almost no notice—and services remain nonexistent. Still, even families with gradeschoolers can experience the natural majesty of these cliffs.

From the trailhead at **Ke'e Beach,** it's a half-mile climb past wild orchid and

Right: Hikers negotiate a waterfall on the Na Pali Cliffs.

kukui trees to the first lookout, a windswept patch of sand and sea. Preteens and teens may want to press on for another mile and a half to reach **Hanakapiai Beach,** an isolated and sandy cove at the base of the cliffs. No matter how hot and tired you may feel when you reach this point, however, *do not attempt to swim here;* riptides and an unpredictable surf make it much too hazardous. Hanakapiai Beach, on the other hand, is a pretty place to picnic before you undertake the trek back to Ke'e Beach. (Even Ke'e, by the way, can have rough surf and a strong undertow, so ask local authorities before swimming there; as a general rule, if you're not sure, don't swim.)

TIPS: A permit is required for overnight stays; ask park authorities about conditions and requirements. Allow at least eight hours to hike Kalalau Trail one way.

BASICS: Dept. of Land and Natural Resources *(808/274-3444)*

Flight-seeing: Flight-seeing on Kauai is a memorable experience. As you soar above the Alakai swamp, Waimea Canyon, and along the Na Pali coast, taro and sugarcane fields, waterfalls, and landscapes made famous by the movie *Jurassic Park* pass beneath your wings (or rotors, as the case may be). Check the pilot certifications and safety records of any outfit before you book a flight; the **Kauai Visitors Bureau** *(800/262-1400 or 808/245-3971. www.kauaivisitorsbureau.org)* keeps a list of companies.

Waimea Canyon: Dubbed "the Grand Canyon of the Pacific" by Mark Twain, Waimea Canyon—a mile wide and 10 miles long—is indeed a marvel to behold. A drive to the popular **Waimea Canyon Lookout** (elevation 3,400 feet) makes you privy to a dreamscape vista: pink-and-gray striated cliffs broken by the silvery streams of falling water.

Kokee State Park: Next to Waimea Canyon, **Kokee State Park** offers a variety of trails. Some are bordered by yellow ginger bushes and sandalwood trees; others wind through groves of koa and lehua trees. My family and I have hiked trails that stretched just a few miles from the park's roads, as well as trails penetrating the park's wild interior through a sliver of the vast **Alakai Swamp.** The swamp—one of the largest high-altitude wetlands in the world—is a designated wilderness reserve. It also happens to be simply a great place to enjoy scenery in serenity; we saw no other groups while we were there. Our moderate 2-mile hike passed through a muddy bog, where the waterlogged soil kept the lehua trees (recognizable by their spindly red flowers) at a dwarfed height of only 3 feet; normally they grow to 20 feet or more. Our return route took us downhill along the **Pihea Trail,** a path that leads through groves of lehua trees laced with hanging vines.

FOR MORE INFORMATION: For hiking in **Waimea Canyon, Kokee State Park,** or **Alakai Swamp,** contact the **Division of State Parks** *(808/274-3444).* For more Kauai information, contact the **Kauai Visitors Bureau** *(800/262-1400 or 808/245-3971. www. kauaivisitorsbureau.org).*

THE MIDWEST
AND ROCKIES

The Wilds
Cumberland

Endangered and threatened animals from Africa, Asia, and North America range across 10,000 acres of reclaimed strip-mining land at **The Wilds.** Visitors travel the 7-mile loop road through the game park on 90-minute bus tours led by naturalists knowledgeable in animal behavior. The giraffes, scimitar-horned oryx, rhino, sable, and other animals housed here give researchers the opportunity to study survival strategies for these dwindling creatures and breed them to create sustainable populations.

For that reason, you may spot a high percentage of babies during a visit to The Wilds—possibly the only place in the continental United States where seven white rhino can be glimpsed moving together in a herd. As we watched their big bodies in the tall grass, the guide informed us that rhino can run almost 25 miles an hour—not too shabby for three-ton animals—and that they typically eat more than 100 pounds of grass a day.

Cresting a rise, we met three Bactrian camels (two humps apiece) sitting by the road, fixing us with big brown eyes. Three Hartmann's mountain zebras—only 2,000 remain in Namibia—turned their heads to watch us pass. In the distance, a pair of giraffes stood silhouetted on a hilltop, munching leaves from black-locust trees. After a gestation period of 15 months, the guide related, a female giraffe gives birth standing up (this tidbit elicited a sympathetic moan from the mothers on the tour bus). Her newborn giraffe may be as tall as 6 feet (this time it was the kids on the bus who responded with a collective "Wow!").

Most of the 160 animals quartered at The Wilds maintain a respectful distance from the tour buses. On our trip, the exception to this rule was a herd of Przewalski's wild horses; these precursors to the modern horse were shorter than the windows of our bus, yet they kept trying to peer inside. Visitors can leave the bus behind and walk a short trail bordering a freshwater marsh that serves as a habitat for trumpeter swans; these big, graceful birds are slowly being reintroduced into Ohio's lake regions.

After your tour, get a snack at the Visitor Center café or find out more about Ohio wildlife at the education center. For example, the center taught us the difference between horns and antlers: Horns, extensions of the skull, cannot grow back once broken off, but antlers are shed each year to make room for new ones.

On page 73: Digging for dinosaur bones at a Dinamation family camp in Fruita, Colorado

 WILDLIFE ENCOUNTER    CULTURAL EXPLORATION   LEARNING ESCAPE

Southern white rhino get down and dirty at The Wilds.

TIPS: Bring binoculars so that you can observe the animals from a distance. Tours of the research facilities are planned for the summer of 2000.

BASICS: **The Wilds** *(14000 International Rd. off Ohio 146 between Zanesville and Cambridge, Cumberland. 740/638-5030; www.thewilds.org. May 1-Oct. 31)*

COSI Columbus

Ride a high-wire bicycle to learn about gravity and mass. Pitch a fastball to witness aerodynamics in action. Freeze your shadow to understand the properties of light.

These are just some of the hands-on activities that make the science museum known as COSI Columbus so much fun for kids—*and* adults. ("COSI" used to stand for "Center of Science and Industry"; now it is simply the museum's name.) Located on the banks of the Scioto River in a 320,000-square-foot (30,000 sq m) facility that opened in November of 1999, COSI boasts a 34-year tradition of challenging young minds (of any age) to understand science by manipulating and experimenting with it.

In the museum's seven **Learning Worlds,** visitors participate in activities dealing with exploration (**Adventure in the Valley of the Unknown**); the human mind, body, and spirit (**Life**); creatures of the deep (**Ocean**); inventions and timesaving tools (**Gadgets**); a time-traveling journey through the wonders of 1898 (**Progress**); a celebration of technology (**i/o**); and, opening in 2000, **Space.**

In addition, **COSI Camp-Ins**—themed to coincide with exhibits in one or several learning worlds—are offered throughout the year. During **Science Sleuth** (a favorite camp-in), families solve a mystery by using scientific techniques similar to those employed by criminal investigators.

Kidspace—a play area restricted to individuals 48 inches or less in height—encompasses **Babyspace,** which stimulates crawlers with mirrors in the floor and fabrics attached to the baseboards. **The Ball Tree,** featuring balls that float on a burst of air, gives toddlers a chance to experiment with cause and effect. At the **Water Table,** tots find out what happens when they cover a spurt of water with their hands. Through role-playing in the **Clinic,** preschoolers have fun playing with a pretend ambulance and helicopter while acting out some of their fears about visiting a doctor's office.

At **Adventure in the Valley of the Unknown,** families work together as archaeological detectives. Upon arriving at a tent in the middle of the valley, visitors are greeted by members of the Explorers Society (museum staffers who turn up periodically to help out with clues). The explorers explain that an ancient idol—the Spirit of Questions—has just been discovered. Not only that, but the idol promises to unlock the Observatory of Knowledge.

Part Indiana Jones and part Sherlock Holmes, Adventure also takes you on a search for gold figurines (these signal a nearby clue) through the Maze of Reason, which is constructed of cloth and rope; through the Temple of Inspiration, a room bathed in yellow light; and through the Cavern of Perseverance, where you must survive the Eyes of Scorn—crisscrossing laser beams that must be avoided in order to reach a clue (younger, shorter kids come in very handy here).

In the **King's Throne Room,** which tilts at an angle of 20 degrees, children can learn about some of the tricks played by perspective.

In **Gadgets,** those who are nimble of finger and mind can disassemble a car, VCR, or computer; position low-powered lasers using optics; stand inside a giant television to learn how it was manufactured; or use a "graviton" to build a burst of air. Shows featuring demonstrations of supergadgets take place at the **Gadgets Theater** throughout the day.

At **Ocean,** explore the inside of a two-person yellow submarine, then use it to maneuver around the sunken wreck of a 19th-century sailing ship. Or enter **Dreamscape**—a sound-and-light show. In **Life,** children enjoy watching what happens when mold and maggots are allowed to run rampant in a decomposing dinner. In **Progress,** museum visitors can stroll down a street straight out of 1898, then enter a time tunnel to 1962.

The **i/o** exhibit contains the first arcade game ever produced. Nope, it's not Pong—it's Computer Space. Free your inner rock star in the **Jam Room,** where computer technology enhances the musical talent you always suspected was there.

Finally, don't miss the **Mad Science Park** outdoors: Its Centripetal Generotor—a favorite old-fashioned carnival ride—features a cylinder that spins fast enough to stick patrons to the cylinder walls when the floor drops out. Another popular display, **Big Giant Lever,** enables a child to lift a 1967 Mercury Comet. Smoke and mirrors? Not at all—Newtonian mechanics.

Neptune points the way to the Ocean exhibit at COSI Columbus.

TIPS: If your daughter is interested in science, encourage her with the news that COSI's president and CEO—Kathryn Sullivan, Ph.D.—majored in geology and deep-sea research before turning to space. In 1978, Sullivan became a NASA Mission Specialist. Over the next 14 years, she flew three space shuttle missions and became the first woman to perform an EVA (extravehicular activity, or space walk).

BASICS: COSI Columbus *(333 West Broad St., Columbus 43215-2738. 614/228-2674. www.cosi.org)* offers overnights *($25 to $29)* that include meals and two days' admission to the museum.

Pioneer Reenactment Conner Prairie Museum

We made our way downhill in darkness, guided only by lantern light. Despite receiving directions from a reluctant farmer, some help from Quaker abolitionists, and a map from a family of free blacks, we couldn't elude the slave traders. They jumped out of the woods and grabbed us, shouting "You'll get down on your knees and stay quiet if you know what's good for you!"

This harrowing re-creation of the plight of runaway slaves is staged several times a year at **Conner Prairie**, a living-history museum where the year is always 1836. Called **Follow the North Star**—the advice given to slaves fleeing the South—the intensely realistic educational program drops visitors into the situations that runaways experienced as they traveled the Underground Railroad in the 1830s. Because the authenticity can be frightening to some, the program is recommended for children 12 and older. It provides a lesson in history that few will forget.

Follow the North Star is indicative of the quality of the Conner Prairie experience overall. Many of the museum's buildings, constructed between 1800 and 1840, were moved here from sites across Indiana. The clothing, food, customs, values, and dilemmas portrayed at Conner Prairie are all genuine to the period.

Stroll through **Prairietown Village** and you'll encounter townsfolk venting their views on current events or engaging in heated debate with their neighbors. When we asked the town doctor how he cures people, the weaver next door jumped in with a litany of the doctor's failures. (The weaver, no fan of newfangled medical science, also sells botanic medicines.)

At the smithy, children learn how to use a bellows. At the Baer family's pottery workshop, they watch jugs and bowls being made. At the William Conner Estate, kids may be surprised to learn that they live better today than the wealthiest man in town lived in 1823. Tours of the Conner house take visitors through the "best room" (parlor), kitchen, and bedrooms (furnished with trundle beds, wallpaper from China, and period rugs).

The **Pioneer Adventure Area** is a hands-on heaven: Kids are encouraged to milk a cow, dip a candle, use a spinning wheel, and lie down on a tick (straw mattress). They also get to watch their parents scrub clothes on a washboard or chop wood with an ax. There's even a barn dance where families can dance to fiddle tunes.

Conner Prairie's dozen or so **Family Weekends,** held throughout the year, are designed to educate and entertain. They present 19th-century forms of religion, health, horse racing, agriculture, and baseball (called "rounders" back then). Other special programs feature face painting, frontier food, and old-fashioned toys such as corn-husk dolls.

The museum's free **Nature Programs**—held on weekends from April through

October—include Legend of the Bear, Life in a Rotten Log, and Reading the Rocks: Indiana Fossils. **Prairietown Tykes** classes, geared for ages 2 to 5 (with accompanying parent or guardian), involve the littlest pioneers in milking a cow or searching for a beaver dam.

Grind coffee, churn butter, and clean vegetables for your **Hearthside Supper**, served January through March at the Conner house. After dinner, guests can opt to take part in 19th-century parlor games.

At **Conner Prairie by Candlelight**, museum visitors discuss the meaning of the holidays with villagers. Mrs. Zimmerman, proprietor of the Golden Eagle Inn, bakes cookies while awaiting the arrival of *Belznickel*—the German bearer of gifts.

In **Winter on the Prairie**, children receive a lesson at the schoolhouse while adults go to the store to trade for sorely needed items. The families then come together for an 1836 home-cooked meal that they all help prepare.

At the log-cabin **Trading Post on the White River,** slated for opening in April 2000, families will learn the mechanics of fur trading; in the **Delaware Indian Encampment** next door, they will find out what the activity meant to the Delaware Indian culture. The encampment will also give kids a chance to grind corn and prepare animal hides for use as shelter and clothing. At the **Quaker Meeting House,** planned for 2001, visitors will learn about the religious beliefs and values of this frontier Indiana population.

TIPS: In August, the Indianapolis Symphony gives evening concerts in the museum's outdoor amphitheater. Listening amid the moonlight and fireflies is a great way to introduce little ones to orchestral music.

BASICS: **Conner Prairie Living History Museum** *(13400 Allisonville Rd., 6 miles N of Indianapolis in Fishers. 800/966-1836 or 317/776-6006. www.connerprairie. org. April 1-Nov. 30).* The website offers a schedule of classes and events.

Children's Museum of Indianapolis

At 356,000 square feet of space on five levels, the **Children's Museum of Indianapolis** is the biggest in the world. It is also one of the best. Covering everything from ancient civilizations and contemporary construction sites to African-American culture and space exploration, the exhibits sparkle with enough appeal to engage kids. At the same time, they provide ample opportunities for children and parents to puzzle out solutions and play together.

Special family programming adds even more things for families to do together. In the **Science Works** gallery, for example, you can learn how to scale the museum's 20-foot climbing wall (right). Other displays invite you to investigate the struc-

Belay there, matey! Kids climb the walls at the Children's Museum of Indianapolis.

ture of crystals or find out what snakes, lizards, and turtles have in common. All this special programming makes the Science Works gallery the museum's most popular. In addition to the activities above, kids can move rubble with a bulldozer and peer into an Indiana pond. Young children favor the bubble-dome window, which lets them crawl up and see the pond from the inside.

Playscape, designed for infants to 4-year-olds, has a tree house to climb, a sand table for sifting, and a water area for splashing. The train exhibit, called **All Aboard!,** consists of a room-size model-train display complete with bells, whistles, crisscrossing tracks, and a pop-up window that puts you in the middle of the action. Although kids can't work the train, they can manipulate the switches and lights on the set. Little ones can also dress up as conductors, then climb aboard a real passenger car where the floor vibrates and a video makes the scenery go by.

At **CFAX**—the **Center for Arts Exploration**—preteens and teens get creative with arts technology. They can synthesize music or create their own videos, T-shirts, and photographs. At the **IWERKS CineDome** theater, a domed movie screen 76 feet high makes you feel like you're living out the film.

Other must-sees include the Victorian carousel with its carved horses, the antique-doll collection, and the **What If** gallery. Geared to ages 6 through 10, this hall is the place to explore fossils and bones at a dinosaur dig, dive to a coral reef, and wander through the tomb of an Egyptian mummy.

TIPS: **Rex's Lending Library** encourages children to continue exploring a topic long after they have left the museum; visitors can borrow books here and return them to many Indiana libraries. **The Ruth Lilly Theater** hosts productions of children's plays, many aimed at younger kids.

BASICS: **Children's Museum of Indianapolis** *(3000 North Meridian St. 800/208-5437 or 317/924-5431. www.childrensmuseum.org)*

The Eiteljorg Museum Indianapolis

The eye-catching design of the **Eiteljorg Museum of American Indians and Western Art**—home to one of the country's finest collections of Native American and Western art—evokes the adobe architecture of Taos, New Mexico. Indeed, the museum derives part of its collection from the artists' colony in that town.

The Eiteljorg is also a reminder that not all Native Americans made their homes in tipis on the plains. As Native American curator Ray Gonyea points out, that distinction is a key part of the Eiteljorg's mission. "We realize the general public has some misconceptions about Native Americans in general," says Gonyea. "They may not know anything about those who lived in this area."

For this reason, the Eiteljorg tells the history of various native cultures through the paintings and artifacts they produced. Museum displays of art from 10 regions of North America feature pottery, basketry, and clothing. The Eiteljorg also offers a chance to view in one place the works of such artists as Frederic Remington, Charles Russell, and Georgia O'Keefe, as well as contemporary Native American artists such as Jaune Quick-to-See Smith, Louis Gonzalez, and R.C. Gorman.

Hands-on carts scattered throughout the museum make the experience fun for younger children. Near *Trapper's Bride* by Alfred Jacob Miller, for instance, a cart holds a beaver pelt, a hat made from badger skin, and the kind of coat a mountain man would have worn. Other carts offer lassos, chaps, and cowboy hats. (Lasso twirling in the main hallways only, please!)

The Old West of legend is memorably portrayed in the action-packed paintings of Frederic Remington, whose renderings of cowboys and Native Americans hunting and warring seem ready to rise off the canvas. Also worthy of note are the early 19th-century Native Americans portrayed by artist-historian George Catlin.

Every June on the weekend following Father's Day, the Eiteljorg hosts the largest **Indian market** in the Midwest. Craftspeople must meet the museum's high standards in order to be included. As Ray Gonyea explains, "We control not only the quality of work—that is, the quality of the art—but also the quality of the cultural tradition. The art must come from the historic traditions of each individual artist's tribe." (Dream catchers being a Chippewa tradition, for example, the only dream catchers you'll see at the market are those made by a Chippewa craftsperson.)

The Eiteljorg also encourages the work of new artists through its fellowship program, which each year awards $20,000 to five fellows; their work is then displayed in the museum.

TIPS: At press time, the museum was undergoing a renovation that will double its size by 2002. On weekends when artists demonstrate their work, kids can learn about such methods as lost-wax casting. Contact the museum for scheduled events.

BASICS: The **Eiteljorg Museum of American Indians and Western Art** is located in **White River State Park** *(500 W. Washington St., Indianapolis. 317/636-9378. www. eiteljorg.org).*

MORE INDIANAPOLIS ATTRACTIONS

Indianapolis Motor Speedway Hall of Fame Museum *(317/481-8500. www.indyracingleague.com):* For race-car fans, a visit here is akin to a pilgrimage—even if the closest they come to driving the famous track is a ride on a tour bus. The museum contains a collection of the sleek and shiny speedsters that were driven to glory by Hall of Famers and past Indy winners.

Indianapolis Zoo *(317/630-2001. www.indyzoo.com):* This well-landscaped, 64-acre cageless zoo blooms with black-eyed Susans, daylilies, and lilacs in spring. The stars of the facility are the dolphins, who perform—er, exhibit their behaviors—at daily shows.

Sports Facilities. Because Indianapolis hosts so many sporting events and serves as the headquarters for so many amateur sports organizations, the city boasts a bevy of first-class sports facilities that are open to the public. (Call first, however, to make sure that no venue is closed because of a competition.) Visitors can swim at the **Indiana University Natatorium** *(317/274-3518),* jog at the **Indiana University Track & Field Stadium** *(317/274-3518),* work out on top-quality equipment at the **National Institute for Fitness and Sport** *(317/274-3432),* ice-skate at the **Indiana World Skating Academy** *(317/237-5565),* or play tennis at the **Indianapolis Tennis Center** *(317/278-2100).*

The Field Museum
Chicago

At the **Field Museum,** kids can wander through an Egyptian tomb without worrying about the mummy's curse, sit on buffalo robes and listen to Pawnee songs, and meet Sue, the world's largest Tyrannosaur skeleton. The Field Museum is located on **Museum Campus,** an area that is also home to the **John G. Shedd Aquarium** and the **Adler Planetarium.**

Don't miss Sue. Discovered near Faith, South Dakota, in 1997, the dinosaur skeleton is scheduled to be unveiled in mid-May of 2000. With 90 percent of her bones intact, Sue is the most complete *Tyrannosaurus rex* ever found. To learn more about the era when dinosaurs like Sue roamed the planet, head for the exhibit entitled **Life over Time**—an exploration of the history and evolution of life on Earth. Find out how the appearance of a single-celled DNA molecule more than 3.8 billion years ago ushered in the age of dinosaurs. Additional dino displays feature a 72-foot-long (22 m) *Apatosaurus* and an *Albertosaurus* preparing to devour its prey. Outside on the museum's terrace is a four-story-high, 75-foot-long fiberglass *Brachiosaurus* that reigned as the world's largest mounted dinosaur until Sue came along.

Another favorite exhibit is **Inside Ancient Egypt.** Here kids wend their way through a life-size Egyptian mastaba (a tomb that prefigured the pyramids), climb to the tomb's roof to see the mummy hidden below, then descend into the actual chambers. Learn to read hieroglyphics, watch your face acquire "Egyptian" features, and discover the secrets of mummification—a process with an admirably high gross-out factor (it required extracting the brain of the deceased through his or her nostrils).

In **Underground Adventure,** a journey beneath the surface of the earth, children get to find out what it must feel like to be the size of a bug. After winding through a warm, dark, tunnel-like jungle full of tree roots and fungi, visitors come face-to-face with animatronic creatures such as a 4-foot centipede and a wolf spider twice their size.

For a close-up look at some "charismatic megavertebrates," visit **Animal Biology.** Here kids can stare into the (preserved) eyes of lions from Tsavo, a very large polar bear from the Arctic, and "Bushman"—a 6-foot-2-inch, 550-pound lowland gorilla who has been a favorite attraction since he was presented to the museum in 1953. For more than 20 years before he died, Bushman was one of the favorite attractions at Chicago's Lincoln Park Zoo.

In **Native Cultures of the Americas,** visitors sit in a Pawnee earth lodge and listen to traditional Pawnee songs and drumming. In **Plants of the World**—the world's largest museum exhibit devoted exclusively to plants—five ecosystems

The Illinois answer to Indiana Jones: Exploring at the Field Museum of Natural History in Chicago

beckon: an Illinois woodland in the spring, a Rocky Mountain alpine meadow in the summer, the seacoast of Maine, water lilies in the Amazon River, and the Namib Desert of Africa.

A dazzling display of precious stones awaits museumgoers at the **Grainger Hall of Gems.** The collection, totaling more than 500 specimens, began with a purchase from Tiffany & Co. in 1893. Although children can leave here knowing how gems are cut, they will probably be much more interested in which of the jewels supposedly carry curses.

TIPS: At **Family Overnights,** children and their parents can participate in workshops while getting a behind-the-scenes look at the museum's exhibits. After lights out, take a flashlight tour of the Egyptian tombs (above), then unroll your sleeping bags next to a polar bear or a lowland gorilla. Reserve well in advance by calling 312/665-7400 or checking the museum's website (below).

BASICS: **The Field Museum** *(1400 South Lake Shore Dr., Chicago 60605. 800/343-5354 or 312/922-9410. www.fieldmuseum.org. Adm. fee)* is open daily from 9 a.m. to 5 p.m.; it is closed on December 25 and January 1.

The Shedd Aquarium
Chicago

The largest of the country's 42 aquariums comes with a bonus: The **John G. Shedd Aquarium** occupies a beautiful setting on the shores of Lake Michigan in the heart of downtown Chicago. On display are more than 8,000 aquatic animals, which represent 650 species from North America, the Caribbean, Asia, Africa, Australia, and—with the scheduled opening of **Amazon Rising: Seasons of the River** in the summer of 2000—both land and aquatic creatures from South America.

The Amazon exhibit shows how the mighty river moves from dry, low levels to high water, creating floods that nourish the region's fragile ecosystem. This exhibit features land animals—a first for the Shedd Aquarium—in order to portray how land and river animals interact. You'll see pygmy marmosets, sloths, iguanas, an anaconda, and an emerald-green boa, not to mention insects and caimans.

At the 90,000-gallon **Caribbean Reef Tank**, green moray eels slither out of crevices, hawksbill turtles float lazily by, silver barracudas zigzag through the current, and schools of tropical fish swim past in a rainbow of colors. If possible, time your visit to coincide with feeding time, when the fish reach a frenzy of activity. See pregnant males—sea horses, pipefish, and sea dragons—at **Seahorse Symphony,** a special exhibit continuing until 2002.

In the **Asian River Habitat,** waterfalls and lush plants create a familiar environment for such stars as gourami. These large Asian fish have "trailers"—string-like appendages that help them explore their habitat.

Despite its Midwest setting, the Shedd Aquarium boasts a wing that re-creates the coastline of the Pacific Northwest. At behavioral presentations held in the **Oceanarium,** visitors can watch beluga whales and Pacific white-sided dolphins leap, tail walk, and use sonar to locate objects. The Oceanarium's glass walls face out on Lake Michigan—thus the facility's nickname, "ocean on the lake."

A family overnight lets you get close to the animals while leaving the crowds behind. Participants in these special programs learn about marine life at naturalist-led workshops and fall asleep to the soothing sight of hundreds of tropical fish. The next morning, **Breakfast with the Belugas** lets you talk to the animal trainers and watch the whales start their day; kids then get to make a whale-related craft. In summer, the Thursday-night program **Jazzin' at the Shedd** is distinguished by smaller crowds, good music, and dinner at the Oceanarium.

TIPS: Aquarium admission is discounted on Mondays. From the Shedd you can take a water taxi to the Navy Pier, home to the Chicago Children's Museum.

BASICS: **The Shedd Aquarium** *(1200 South Lake Shore Dr., Chicago. 312/939-2438; www.sheddnet.org).* For family overnights, call 312/692-3160.

MORE CHICAGO SHENANIGANS

Art and Architecture

Art Institute of Chicago *(111 South Michigan Ave. 312/443-3600. www.artic.edu):* This prized collection spans world art from the Mayan to the modern. Highlights include canvases by Degas, Monet, and Renoir. Don't miss the contemporary exhibits or the Mrs. James Ward Thorne collection of miniature rooms.

Outdoor Art: The famous painted cows were auctioned off in 1999, but you can still walk along the Loop and admire outdoor sculptures by Picasso, Dubuffet, Miro, Chagall, and Calder. Contact the Chicago Office of Tourism *(312/744-2400. www.ci.chi.il.us/Tourism/)* for a guide.

Museum of Contemporary Art *(220 East Chicago Ave. 312/280-2660. www.mcachicago.org):* The museum's large post-1945 collection features works by Jasper Johns, Jeff Koons, Andy Warhol, and Alexander Calder.

Skyline Boat Tours: Forget the traffic and take a relaxing waterborne cruise of Chicago's landmark buildings. Whether or not your kids are budding architects, they will at least enjoy the boat ride. Boat-cruise companies include **Chicago's Skyline Cruiseline** *(SW corner of Michigan Ave. & Wacker Dr. 312/332-1353),* which also offers a **Pirate Cruise for Kids,** and **Chicago from the Lake** *(435 East Illinois St. 312/527-1977).*

Science

Adler Planetarium and Astronomy Museum *(1300 South Lake Shore Dr. 312/322-0304. www.adlerplanetarium.org):* Take a computer-animated 3-D ride through the Milky Way galaxy and fly through 15 million years of galactic history in the high-tech shows offered by this planetarium.

Museum of Science and Industry *(57th St. & Lake Shore Dr. 773/684-1414. www.msichicago.org):* Where else can you explore a coal mine, walk through a German U-boat captured in 1944, see a dollhouse containing 1,000 miniature furnishings, and watch eight model railroads chug through re-created U.S. landscapes?

Economics

Chicago Mercantile Exchange *(30 S. Wacker Dr. 312/930-8249. www.cme.com):* Find out how to make money on pork bellies or currency options by watching the deals go down from the visitors' gallery.

Untouchable Tours *(610 N. Clark St. 773/881-1195. www.gangstertour.com):* Chicago's Prohibition-era gangsters were a special kind of economic force. This two-hour tour invites kids and adults to scope out the "hot spots, hit spots, and hideouts" of such gangland legends as John Dillinger, Al Capone, and Bugs Moran.

Dogsledding
North Woods

Have you ever wondered why Sergeant Preston of the Yukon was always smiling—even in perilous pursuit of some nefarious Canadian bandit? Maybe it was because driving a dogsled across snowy fields is such grand fun. Ever since, as a little girl, I saw this debonair television Mountie zipping through the woods pulled by a team of loyal huskies, I've wanted to go too.

What kept me and my daughter Alissa away was the thought of sleeping in an ice yurt. At both **Gunflint Lodge** and **Wintergreen Lodge,** however, you can dogsled by day and come back to hot showers, hot food, and a warm bed at night.

Dogsledding is easy to learn. The jubilation of the dogs delights us, as does the chance to be more than mere passengers, savoring the wilderness without the noise of snowmobiles or the exertion of cross-country skiing. The rules of dogsledding are similar to those for parenting: praise, patience, and no yelling. To keep the gang line taut (that's the long chain linking dogs to sled), we had only to shout "Good, Raspberry!" or "Tighten up, Sheba!" Hearing those words, our huskie-shepherd-malamute mix instantly ran faster and in better formation.

As you might expect, these are great trips for dog lovers. Each lodge offers a different family-friendly adventure, however, so read on to find out which one is best suited to the experience you seek.

GUNFLINT LODGE, GRAND MARAIS

The blue-white expanse of iced-over Gunflint Lake seemed borrowed from a fairy tale. Framed by rocky cliffs and towering pines laced with snow, **Gunflint Lodge** appeared magical. The sun glinted off the lake's glassy surface and the windows of the woodsy cabins beside it, while the only sounds were the thin, steady humming of the wind and an occasional muffled boom as ice blocks shifted deep within the frozen lake.

At Gunflint Lodge, situated adjacent to the **Boundary Waters Canoe Area** in Minnesota's North Woods, you can opt for a dogsled outing, day trip, or mushing package; the last lets you harness the dogs yourself and handle your own sled. We opted for the mushing package, which made us overnight experts in canine psychology. Alissa and I took turns sitting in the sled. Swaddled in comforters and sleeping bags and lulled by the rhythm of the runners, we often fell asleep with the sun on our faces. Off the sled, we tried our hand at ice fishing and cross-country skiing, went snowshoeing to a frozen waterfall, and hiked across fields in search of moose antlers.

Although far from designer chic, our "super cabin"—two bedrooms, two baths, a living room, and even a sauna—proved spacious and modern. At dusk, we got

IF YOU WANT TO RUN WITH THE WOLVES...

Howl into a North Woods night and a pack of gray wolves just might howl back at you. (The wolves respond about 50 percent of the time.) Even if the creatures keep their distance, a weekend at the **International Wolf Center** in Ely brings you closer to understanding these much-maligned mammals, which have been unfairly pigeonholed in the varmint category.

During a typical wolf weekend, naturalists teach you how to locate the animals using radio telemetry. Citing members of the center's resident pack as examples, the guides also explain wolf behavior. Evening **Wolf Howls** are also offered. The minimum age for these outings is 6 years old. Participants stay in four-bedroom cabins with shared bathrooms.

Tips: Programs operate regardless of weather, so pack rain gear; you could be howling into a downpour.

Basics: 1396 Hwy. 169, Ely. 800/359-9653 or 218/365-4695. www.wolf.org. $275 per adult, $195 per child.

almost nose-to-nose with the deer that stood before our cabin's picture window, lured by the corn we had left out for them. After dinner, we admired the night sky with its popping stars and northern lights. Gunflint Lodge also serves good food—some of the best in northern Minnesota.

Gunflint Lodge attracts couples as well as families. A mushing adventure can be enjoyed by families with children as young as 4; the preschoolers we met sat happily in the sled, enjoying the sun and the scenery. You can sample as much dogsledding as you like, mix dogsledding with other winter activities, or just loll about your private cabin. In short, the days are as rigorous or as relaxed as you want them to be.

TIPS: In case your cabin is equipped with a VCR, bring some videos. The lodge does not serve lunch in winter, so you'll have to bring your own lunch fixings; soup, bread, peanut butter and jelly usually work well.

BASICS: Gunflint Lodge *(143 South Gunflint Lake, Grand Marais. 800/328-3325 or 888-486-3546).* A cabin for two starts at $195, including breakfast. Mushing packages cost $230 per adult per night *($170 for children 12 or under)* and include cross-country skiing, snowshoeing, breakfast, and a full dinner.

WINTERGREEN LODGE, ELY

Owned by well-known musher-adventurer Paul Schurke, **Wintergreen Lodge** offers four- and five-day dogsled trips more strenuous than those at Gunflint Lodge. Some of the outings are family oriented; others—especially the trips to upscale inns—are aimed at couples. Hoping to avoid couples on romantic getaways and perhaps even meet some other teens, my daughter and I chose the basic inn package.

Gateway North's Lori Houle and daughter mush across Burnside Lake near Ely, Minnesota.

We enjoyed the challenge of leading our own team of eight dogs through woods and across frozen lakes and marshland on daily routes of 11 to 14 miles. Schurke's guides are good: While one stays with the main group of several dog teams and their mushers, a second plays "rabbit"—cross-country skiing ahead of the first team. The Inuit dogs are large, friendly, and (for the most part) hard workers. We fell in love with Beauford, our strong, copper-coated, good-natured wheel dog.

Schurke makes his own sleds, which carry gear, not people. That means you'll be on your feet for up to six hours a day, holding onto a sled in the chilling Minnesota winds. With snow covering the ground and fallen trees, we remained standing even during lunch—a short break for hot soup and handfuls of trail mix. Given the stamina required, I recommend these dogsledding ventures for outdoor-oriented kids ages 8 and older.

A high point of the trip was our interaction with the dogs. We harnessed the team, learned the dogs' personalities, and kept them under control—or tried to—before heading out. My daughter held onto Sisu, our lead dog, until I yelled "Ready hike!"—the signal for our team to move. Alissa then hopped aboard the moving sled, a maneuver she soon perfected. The easiest stretches took us across frozen lakes, the hardest through hilly woods. In places where the snow cover was light or the trail worn, the dogs jumped nimbly over the exposed roots and rocks; unless we held tight at such moments, we flew off the sled and landed on our behinds in the snow. More than one dog team crested a hill with its mushers running along behind.

Some of the lodging on the basic inn trip proved too basic for our liking. In White Pine Cabin at **Timber Trail Lodge,** for example, the bedrooms lacked heat and the bathrooms were not especially clean. We were also unpleasantly surprised to discover that we had to share a room with a stranger—information that had been withheld when we paid for our "double room."

Wintergreen Lodge, owned by Schurke and his wife, is more comfortable. Its warm rooms are graced by the clean lines of Scandinavian furnishings—and lots of blankets. Although no bedroom has a private bath, sinks in the hallway keep the waiting time down. For those who want to try winter camping, an outdoor tipi or igloo is a nightly possibility. On our basic trip, the food was, well, basic—think spaghetti and lasagna—and plentiful (except at lunch). After-dinner conversations were lively.

TIPS: Come prepared. Expedition-weight long underwear is a necessity. You can also rent or buy parkas and boots at the Schurkes' store in Ely—we rented warm, waterproof boots that were worth every penny. If your kids are not big fans of granola and trail mix, ask ahead of time for sandwiches for lunch.

BASICS: **Wintergreen Lodge** *(1101 Ring Rock Rd., Ely. 218/365-6022. www. dogsledding.com)* stages three-night dogsledding trips that cost $725 per adult and $625 for children ages 8 to 12.

Minnesota Science Museum
St. Paul

Dinosaurs, 3-D laser multimedia shows, and a DNA fingerprinting lab—not to mention its dynamic location atop the bluffs of the Mississippi River—make the $100-million, 370,000-square-foot **Science Museum of Minnesota** a winner. Boasting a fossil collection begun in 1907—when the museum opened its doors as the St. Paul Institute of Science and Letters—as well as the first convertible-dome omnitheater in the United States, the museum spans the gamut from the prehistoric era to the present.

The dinosaurs are both formidable and fun. The Triceratops mounted in the **Dinosaurs and Fossils Gallery** is one of only four in the world; it is also the largest complete specimen of its kind on display. Kids can operate the jaws of a Tyrannosaur and crawl through the stomach (a modified 500-gallon tank) of an 82-foot-long *Diplodocus*. Drop rice cakes down the dino's esophagus, then use your hands to pump his stomach and grind the rice cakes, simulating *Diplodocus* digestion.

In the **Experiment Gallery,** visitors can play with a 17-foot-high tornado, make waves by raising and lowering the floor of a wave tank, try out enormous magnets, and generate electricity by pedaling a bike. Children who constantly ask "How do they *do* that?" at magic shows will find some answers at the **Perception Theater** in the **Human Body Gallery.** The theater explains how the brain processes information to convince us we're seeing something we are not. Kids will be riveted or repulsed—or both—by the **Body Hotel,** which displays preserved specimens of the wide variety of parasites that have been found living in some human bodies. Which family member has the most blood? Probably Dad; to find out for sure, take turns standing on the platform that calculates how much blood is in your body.

In the **Mississippi River Gallery,** the **Virtual River Pilot** lets you steer a barge through the gantlet of bridges in downtown St. Paul. From there, step into the pilothouse of the *Charles E.*—an authentic, 1940s-vintage Mississippi River towboat—and enjoy the view of the river 75 feet below. **The Collections Exhibit,** containing "greatest hits" from the museum's 95-year history, features an Egyptian mummy, an entire Hmong house, and the trunk of a Douglas fir tree 7 feet in diameter.

To make sense of all these stimuli, take time to stroll around the Science Museum's 10 acres of outdoor parks.

TIPS: The **William L. McKnight 3M-Omnitheater** fills up fast, so purchase your timed tickets early. Because the sound track can be loud and the footage intense, prepare young kids who might get frightened. Ask someone at the information desk which shows are best suited for small children.

BASICS: Science Museum of Minnesota *(120 West Kellogg Blvd., St Paul. 651/221-9444. www.smm.org)*

Owl Prowl
St. Louis Zoo

Crawl through a cave, canoe an Ozark stream, or go on an owl prowl during a naturalist-led overnight sponsored by the **St. Louis Zoo.** In addition to telling the global story of animals and their environments, the St. Louis Zoo hosts inexpensive family trips that explore Missouri's **Ozark Mountains.** Many of the outings are held at **Reis Biological Station** *(314/977-3902),* which is affiliated with St. Louis University. (Be prepared to use a bathhouse and sleep in a bunkhouse.)

The zoo also stages on-site after-hours camp-outs that let kids observe the animals in the absence of crowds, getting a true view of nocturnal creatures. By day, the somnolent lions and tigers, their white bellies soaking up the sun, can seem to be little more than overfed house cats. On a flashlight walk through the zoo's jungle habitats, however, kids watch the big cats stalk with the slinky precision of predators. After a box dinner, children get to view the koalas and other animals before bedding down for the night. The next morning, campers awaken to the screeching of peacocks and the barking of sea lions. After breakfast, they shadow the keepers on their rounds, watching them feed the animals before the zoo opens for the day.

Even without the overnights, the 90-acre St. Louis Zoo is one of the city's most popular attractions. If you have young kids in tow, head straight for the **Emerson Electric Children's Zoo** *(adm. fee).* At this modern facility, opened in 1998, kids learn about animals by mimicking their behaviors through a clever combination of exhibits and play. Visitors can feed nectar to lorikeets, slide down a see-through chute in the otter pool, climb a spider web made of rope, and view koalas without any barriers.

Older children relish the **Living World Educational Center**—two halls of high-tech gadgets that encourage kids to explore a wide range of life. The center's computer games and exhibits trace animal life from one-celled creatures to mammals. Here kids can learn about everything from honeybees and the chambered nautilus to extinct animals and even "Lucy"—the first known primate to walk upright. The **Animal Hall,** a favorite, has a dazzling display of four viewing levels: tanks of coral, screens that flash images of spawning salmon, live animals such as quail, and computers that define terms and display videos.

The **Monsanto Insectarium** shows kids why critters that buzz, chirp, sting, and chomp on your food are crucial threads in the fabric of life. In **Not Home Alone,** you are free to open kitchen drawers, lift lids, and look under a front porch for ants, cockroaches, and other real live creepy crawlers; in the process, you discovering what makes these "pests" prime recyclers. **Architects without Blueprints** focuses on the engineering skills of spiders, bees, and other insects.

An endangered King Cheetah (note the dorsal stripes) at the River's Edge exhibit, St. Louis Zoo

New in 2000 is the first phase of **River's Edge,** an "immersive exhibit" whose concealed barriers make you feel close to the cheetahs, hyenas, and Asian elephants. When the exhibit is completed in 2001, you'll be able to view warthogs, black rhino, and underwater hippos, as well as the animals of a Missouri wetland.

At **Jungle of the Apes,** chimpanzees, orangutans, and a family of gorillas climb, care for each other, and stare back at visitors. Fred—a 330-pound silverback gorilla—is still the king of this particular jungle. Birds swoop and chatter as you walk through the free-flight cage, one of six aviaries at the zoo. Other enclosures house bald eagles, red-billed toucans, and other colorful birds.

TIPS: The Painted Giraffe, located in the Living World Educational Center, is the zoo café with the best assortment of sandwiches and salads for lunch. A miniature train *(fare)* picks up and drops off passengers at four stops throughout the zoo, making it possible to see most of the exhibits without walking kids into the ground. Warn little ones, though, of the short ride through a dark tunnel.

BASICS: The **St. Louis Zoo** *(Forest Park. 314/781-0900. www.stlzoo.org)* is free except for a $3 fare to ride the miniature train and a $3 admission to the Emerson Electric Children's Zoo (neither charges admission for kids under 2). **Ozark Overnights,** for families with kids in grade 3 and up, cost $40 for Zoo Friends and $44 for nonmembers. **Camp-Out at the Zoo** *($25 per child or adult for Zoo Friends, $28 otherwise)* has two sessions—one for families with kids in kindergarten through grade 3, the other for families with kids in grades 4 and up.

Virtual Reality
St. Louis Science Center

Virtual reality rules at **Cyberville,** the high-tech gallery of the **St. Louis Science Center.** Tapping into user-friendly programs, kids can build a robot, pilot a riverboat down the Mississippi, design a website, learn binary code, or create a virtual fish and see how it fares against predators—the digital kind, of course!

Consistently rated one of the country's top 10 science facilities, the St. Louis Science Center (dubbed "the playground for your head") updates its exhibits on a regular basis. That explains why the **McDonnell Planetarium**—a St. Louis icon for decades—is closed until 2001 for a $10-million overhaul that is transforming it into a "space station." In the reopened planetarium, you'll be able to view night constellations all day long in **StarBay**—the facility's domed atrium—and stroll through exhibits detailing what it's like to live and work in space. Using interactive computers, kids will be able to monitor the health of their space-station crew, discovering details as seemingly mundane as how low the crew is on groceries.

Another reality check—this one guaranteed to get a giggle—will be the toilet bolted to the space station's ceiling. Because space has no "up" or "down," such a design would be perfectly serviceable. At the very least, it's sure to get kids thinking about how people wash, eat, dress, and get through the day in a world devoid of gravity. (How *do* astronauts spit out toothpaste, by the way?)

The **MedTech Gallery,** too, is designed to spark some family discussions. While scanning the latest medical equipment and advances, kids are encouraged to express their views on ethical questions. When I undertook this exercise with my daughter and son, it led to some heady talks—on cloning, euthanasia, and using fetal tissue for medical research—that far exceeded the scope of the exhibit.

In the **DNA Zone,** listen to a "talking" cell, learn how the police use DNA matching, and find out how dominant and recessive traits show up by mixing and matching the characteristics of styrofoam critters. Explore perception and how the brain processes sensory information in **Human Adventure.** Discover how a black-and-white wheel makes you see colors when it spins, and how pretzel shapes in your ears help you hear.

Even getting from one building to another is fun. The connecting tunnel is a coal mine, complete with shoveling noises and canary songs. From the connecting bridge, you can check the speed of passing cars below with a radar gun.

Nor does the Science Center overlook small children. In the **Discovery Zone,** for example, kids can handle skeletons, play in sandboxes, crawl through an earthen woodland Indian home, and explore a Plains Indian tipi.

The museum also has **Family Camp-Ins** for those with children in grades 3 to 6. These allow you to investigate the center after hours, going on a scavenger hunt, watching an OMNIMAX film, and sleeping next to two robotic—and roaring—dinosaurs (one of them a *T. rex).*

CITY MUSEUM

You expect surprises from a building with a three-story praying mantis and a log cabin out front, and the **City Museum** in St. Louis delivers. The brainchild of a popular animal sculptor—check out the whale's head and the sea lion—the City Museum exists in that borderland where controlled chaos turns into art. Parents may not know what to make of the museum's far-out combinations of recycled mouse cages, mosaic tiles, watchbands, airplane panels, and other discarded items, but their children certainly will. A trip here recharges the batteries of young imaginations.

No sooner have they arrived than kids are crawling around in the fanciful aerie known as the **Sky Tunnel.** Children can also take part in a dog circus, examine gargoyles and other salvaged architectural items, and watch jewelers, potters, glassblowers, and other studio artists ply their crafts. For a fee, they can even create their own art and then take it home.

Basics: The **City Museum** *(701 N. 15th St., St. Louis. 314/231-2489. Adm. fee)* is best for ages 5 and up.

TIPS: The Family Camp-Ins are popular, so book them well in advance. Allow time to stroll through family-friendly **Forest Park,** enjoying the outdoors.

BASICS: St. Louis Science Center *(5050 Oakland Ave. in Forest Park. 800/456-7572 or 314/289-4444. www.slsc.org. Mon.-Thurs. and Sat.-Sun. 9 a.m.-5 p.m., Fri. 9 a.m.-9 p.m.)*

MORE FUN IN ST. LOUIS

Magic House *(516 S. Kirkwood Rd. 314/822-8900. www.magichouse.org):* At this top children's museum—geared to infants through 9-year-olds—kids zoom down a three-story slide, explore a multilevel children's village, produce television news, tap out Morse Code, and lots more. There is even a peekaboo play area for babies.

Sophia M. Sachs Butterfly House*(15193 Olive Blvd. 314/361-3365):* Wear articles of red clothing, and one of the hundreds of rainbow-colored butterflies at this informal insectarium might just land on your shoulder.

Forest Park *(5600 Clayton Ave. 314/289-5300):* Besides being the site for the St. Louis Zoo and the St. Louis Science Center, Forest Park—a 1,300-acre urban oasis 15 minutes from the Gateway Arch—is home to the **St. Louis Art Museum** and the **Missouri Historical Society.** You will also find an ice-skating rink, bicycle paths, tennis courts, a pond, and picnic spots.

Bob Kramer's Marionettes *(4143 Laclede Ave. 314/531-3313):* Little kids love the Saturday Puppet Follies at this longtime St. Louis attraction.

SeaWorld Adventure Park San Antonio

Like its sister facilities in Orlando, Cleveland, and San Diego, **SeaWorld Adventure Park San Antonio** offers much more to experience than Shamu, the killer whale. Families learn about animals and conservation by viewing sharks, penguins, dolphins, birds, and other animals.

The programs that get you closest to the animals, however, are among the least known. On a 90-minute **Behind the Scenes Tour,** park naturalists accompany visitors into several research areas. At the **Animal Care Area,** for example, you can watch lab technicians perform checkups on the animals. At the **Breeding Pools,** see dolphin mothers and their young; at **Shamu Stadium,** discover how the star performer is trained. Finally, the **Bird Adventure Tour** lets you pet a penguin and feed tiny lorikeets from cups of nectar you hold in your hand.

SeaWorld San Antonio offers two interactive programs—one with sea lions, the other with beluga whales. The **Sea Lion Interaction Program** starts with a classroom session on sea-lion anatomy; participants then act as apprentice trainers, requesting behaviors of the animals and rewarding them with rubdowns and handfuls of squid. The **Beluga Interaction Program** also starts with a workshop on physiology; then it's time to climb into the tank with the whales, where you can touch, feed, and (via hand signals) communicate with them.

Many of the exhibits and programs at SeaWorld San Antonio are similar to those at SeaWorld Orlando; for a detailed description of them, see SeaWorld Orlando on pages 173-175.

TIPS: Register your family for a same-day Behind the Scenes Tour as soon as you arrive at the park.

SeaWorld and the nearby **Hyatt Regency Hill Country Resort** *(9800 Resort Dr. 800/233-1234 or 210/647-1234)* offer a three-day **Family Animal Adventure** program in December, when the park is closed to the general public. Families attend workshops on whales, sea lions, walruses, sharks, and penguins.

BASICS: **Sea World Adventure Park** *(10500 SeaWorld Dr., San Antonio. 800/423-8368 or 210/523-3000. www.seaworld.com).* The **Behind the Scenes Tour,** in addition to the regular park admission of $32.95 for adults and $22.95 for children, costs $8 for adults, $7 for ages 3 to 11, and is free for children under 3. The interactive in-water programs cost $125 per participant and $42 for one observer (both fees include park admission). Participants in the sea-lion program must be at least 10 years old and 48 inches tall; those taking part in the beluga program must be at least 10 years old and 52 inches tall. Reservations required.

Fossil Rim Wildlife Center
Glen Rose

We fell in love with Ichabod the reticulated giraffe when he strode over, stuck his head in our lap, and let us pet his nose. Later on, as Ichabod trotted along behind our jeep, we marveled at his fist-size brown eyes and foot-long purple tongue. Also trailing the vehicle were groups of addax, a North African antelope, while on either side stood herds of kudu, zebra, and blackbuck. Cheetahs ran through the bush, black rhino sunned themselves in the mud, and an ostrich pair with wings outspread swayed slowly like ballerinas in a love duet.

A game park in East Africa? No, but **Fossil Rim Wildlife Center** in Glen Rose is the next best thing—and a lot easier to get to. At this wildlife conservation and education center about 60 miles southwest of Fort Worth, more than 1,000 animals roam free on 1,500 acres. The facility, accredited by the American Zoo and Aquarium Association, is dedicated to the survival of 32 endangered, vulnerable, or threatened species.

Among the animals you'll see in the multi-acre enclosures are emu, Grevy's zebra, gemsbok, greater kudu (Africa's second largest antelope), Arabian oryx (almost extinct in 1972), sable, blackbuck (fewer than 500 remain in Africa), and scimitar-horned oryx (captive populations keep the animal from becoming extinct). Fossil Rim participates in breeding programs designed to reintroduce the offspring of these creatures into the wild.

The ranch's wooded hills and grasslands, reminiscent of the African savanna, are divided into several large, gated pastures. Families can drive their own car along the 9½-mile path; take a naturalist-led jeep trip that features behind-the-scenes viewing of cheetahs, rhino, and wolves; or stay overnight. You can opt to bed down in a deluxe tent complete with private bath at the **Foothills Safari Camp** or in a guest room at the **Fossil Rim Lodge.** Either way, you'll be eligible to take part in a private outing before the park opens to day-trippers.

As we fed them nutritional pellets purchased at the Visitor Center, animals such as Ichabod viewed us as their "meals on wheels." My daughter—a purist—felt uncomfortable feeding the animals by hand, but I savored the chance to lure Ichabod within petting range. In the end, we both enjoyed coming within inches of creatures that we had once admired only from a distance. On a trip behind the scenes, we got so close to a white rhino that we were able to stroke his horn.

We also fed an apple to Mupani, a 4-month-old, 500-pound black rhino. Mupani is one of three black-rhino calves born at Fossil Rim since 1994 (the wild population fell from 60,000 in 1970 to 2,700 in 1990). Watching Mupani waddle happily behind her three-ton mother, kids and adults gain a newfound wonder for wild creatures—and a firsthand sense of the urgency of protecting endangered animals.

Staying overnight at Fossil Rim gave us more time with the animals and made it feel more like a safari. Driving to the dinner pavilion around sunset, we listened

Please *do* feed the animals: Fossil Rim Wildlife Center

to the landscape come alive with sound and noted how nocturnal animals such as the European red deer blend into the tall grasses at night. Dining in a glass-walled pavilion overlooking a water hole, we watched deer step around the cottonwoods to drink, saw stars pop and glow in a purple sky, and heard the not-too-distant howl of wolves. For animal-loving families, Fossil Rim Wildlife Center is indeed a peaceable kingdom.

TIPS: Kids love the heated and air-conditioned tents, which also boast private baths and showers. The compact units have room for only two beds, but a young child can use a sleeping bag on the floor. With two children, however, you will need to book two tents. In June, the fields of Fossil Rim bloom with wildflowers as well as animal babies.

BASICS: Fossil Rim Wildlife Center *(P.O. Box 2189, Hwy. 67, Glen Rose. 888/775-6742 or 254/897-2960. www.fossilrim.com).* Self-guided drive: adults $15, ages 4 to 11 $10, under 4 free. Guided tours: adults $27, children $20. Lodge rooms cost $125 and up per night for two, including breakfast. Tented camps (tents are heated and air-conditioned) cost from $150 per night for two with breakfast.

Cattle, Koalas, and Cowboys
Fort Worth

Fort Worth features its own brand of wildlife—**Texas longhorns**. Each day at 11:30 a.m. and 4 p.m., weather permitting, cowboys in period clothing drive about 15 head of cattle through the heart of the city's **Stockyards National Historic District,** re-creating a scene that was a staple of life in the Old West. Arrive early to talk to the hands, who accurately reflect the ethnic mix of men on the range circa 1870. Wearing brush cuffs and a vest (pants of the time had no pockets), African-American interpreter Chester Stidham informed us that in the aftermath of the Civil War a good drover could earn a year's worth of wages by rounding up wild herds of longhorn cattle in south Texas and then driving them along the Chisolm Trail through Fort Worth to Kansas.

The **Fort Worth Zoo** *(1989 Colonial Pkwy. 817/871-7050. www.fortworthzoo. com)* is known for its natural habitats and family-friendly layout of benches, shade trees, and snack carts. Be sure to see the bison and Mexican wolves, as well as the Komodo dragons, African penguins (also called black-footed penguins), and young Asian elephant named Blue Bonnet. The Fort Worth Zoo also happens to be one of only 10 facilities in the United States with an exhibit of koalas.

For more Western ambience, you can take in a rodeo at the **Cowtown Coliseum** *(121 E. Exchange Ave., Fort Worth. 888-269-8696 or 817/654-1148),* held on weekends year-round, or visit the world's largest honky-tonk, **Billy Bob's Texas** *(2520 Rodeo Plaza, Fort Worth. 817/624-7117).* Along with live country music and plenty of Texas two-step dancing, Friday and Saturday nights at Billy Bob's feature live bull riding. For the cowboys trying to hold tight to a bucking bull, it's a lo-o-o-ng eight seconds—the minimum time for a successful ride.

With grade-schoolers, try to catch a tour at **The Movie Studios at Las Colinas** *(6301 N. O'Connor Rd., Irving. 800/914-0006 or 972/869-7752. www. studiosatlascolinas.com),* a moviemaking facility in nearby Irving. The high-spirited, kid-oriented walk-through reveals the magic of movie sounds, blue screens, and other SFX (special effects). Our enthusiastic guide—and sometime actor—escorted us to the **Addams Family Values** set, which showcases props and instructs child volunteers in the rudiments of sound engineering: Scene necessities such as creaky stairs, bouncing balls, and Pubert baby gurgles are all taught here. In other exhibits, children can find out about blue-screen tricks by becoming instant weather forecasters, or learn more about special effects on the bridge of a starship.

At the **Legends of the Game Baseball Museum and Learning Center** *(1000 Ballpark Way, Arlington. 817/273-5099),* located in the Ballpark in Arlington, children learn not only about the hometown team (the Texas Rangers) but also about the history of baseball in general. Fans of the sport will appreciate the displays of vintage baseball cards, exhibits on women's baseball and the Negro Leagues, and memorabilia such as the jerseys that once belonged to baseball legends Babe Ruth,

Feeling right at home in Texas, African (black-footed) penguins chill out in the Fort Worth Zoo.

Cy Young, and Lou Gehrig. At the **Learning Center** (designed for grade-schoolers) on the third floor, an interactive exhibit lets you put your hand in a baseball glove to feel the sting of catching a Nolan Ryan fastball. Museum visitors can also use math to figure out the area of a baseball diamond (it's 800 square feet, in case you were wondering) and use computers to look up players and learn about the history of the game.

TIPS: For travel packages that combine hotel rooms with admission to the Fort Worth Zoo, a child's admission to Fossil Rim Wildlife Center, and a daytime entrance to Billy Bob's Texas, contact 800/433-5335 or www.traveltotexas.com. For more information, contact the **Fort Worth Convention and Visitors Bureau** *(800/433-5747. www.fortworth.com).*

Cherokee Heritage Center Tahlequah

The first thing grade-schoolers like about the **Cherokee Heritage Center** in Tahlequah is its 44-acre parklike setting. It's pleasant to meander the tree-lined paths leading to the center's two outdoor living history areas: **Adams Corner Rural Village** is a cluster of buildings that re-create an Indian Territory community from the period 1875-1890, while the **Tsa-La-Gi Ancient Village** portrays a Chero-kee settlement from the 1600s. The small scale of the villages and their lack of com-mercialization enhance the site's realism and give it a low-key ambience.

Tiny Adam's Corner has the frontier-weathered look of old wood. Its authen-tic general store, one-room schoolhouse, smokehouse, and church were moved here from sites in other parts of Oklahoma. In the summertime, costumed interpreters gather on the front porch of **Smith's General Store,** and a schoolmarm occasion-ally holds forth.

Young children also like **Heritage Farms,** where guinea hens, roosters, and chick-ens scratch about, and the corrals hold a Cherokee pony and pineywoods cattle—a breed brought to the New World by the Spanish.

Tsa-La-Gi represents a typical woodland village of the Cherokee in their origi-nal home, the Tennessee River valley. Based on archaeological finds, the Heritage Center has constructed three typical houses. The domed mud *osi*—the single-room winter sleeping quarters—easily retains a fire's heat all day. The longhouse on site, typical summer sleeping quarters, accommodates six people. The large, seven-sided council house was the venue for bigger meetings and ceremonies. In summer, inter-preters demonstrate bow-making, flint-knapping, basketry, pottery, and the fash-ioning of dugout canoes from burned-out walnut and poplar trees.

Deferring to Our Elders, a permanent exhibit at the **Cherokee National Museum,** pairs photographs of contemporary Cherokee men and women with first-person accounts of their life in two cultures. The purpose is to emphasize that Cherokees are not just historical figures—they are real people living today.

In 2000, the museum was being redesigned to serve as the terminus for the **National Historic Trail of Tears.** The new exhibit, scheduled for completion by June 2001, focuses on the 1,200-mile-long forced march that was endured by the Cherokee, Choctaw, Chickasaw, Creek, and Seminole bands between 1830 and 1850. These groups are often referred to as the Five Civilized Tribes because they had tried to appease the U.S. government by acceding to its campaign to "civilize" them with Christian religion, mission schools, and sedentary farming.

The Indian Removal Act, passed by Congress in 1830, authorized the president to negotiate with Native Americans living between the original states and the Mis-sissippi River. Gold had recently been discovered in Georgia, and the U.S. wanted their land for development. The tribes were to be relocated in Indian Territory—a frontier that spread from the Mississippi to the Rocky Mountains. Although the other tribes signed treaties and moved west, most of the Cherokee refused to budge. (A few, led by Major John Ridge, opted for relocation as the answer to their struggle for survival.)

At New Etocha, Georgia, in 1835, the U.S. government signed a treaty with 20 Cherokee tribal members; regrettably, none of them represented or had been elected by the Cherokee Nation. The treaty stipulated that the Cherokee cede their land rights in exchange for a payment of $5 million and a new homeland in what is now northeastern Oklahoma. Despite the protests of 15,000 Cherokee, the U.S. government—eager to obtain the Cherokee lands that occupied parts of North Carolina, South Carolina, Georgia, Tennessee, and Kentucky—formally recognized the treaty.

Although the treaty gave the Cherokee two years to move west, most tribal members believed they would never be forced to leave their homeland. In May of 1838, however, federal troops and state militia began rounding up the Cherokee. In the ensuing chaos, children were separated from their parents, families were split apart, and people were forced from their homes with few or no possessions. Looters often followed, stealing, burning, or claiming the newly vacated land.

Among those who participated in the removal was John G. Burnett, a U.S. Army private in Captain McClellan's company: "I saw the helpless Cherokees arrested and dragged from their homes," wrote Burnett, "and driven at the bayonet point into stockades. And in the chill of a drizzling rain on an October morning I saw them loaded like cattle or sheep into six hundred and forty-five wagons and started toward the west."

The lack of food and water, the winter cold, and the weariness of the forced trek all took a heavy toll. No one knows for certain how many Cherokee died on the Trail of Tears, as their route west became known, but estimates put the loss at more than 4,000—nearly one-fifth of the Cherokee population.

When the survivors reached Oklahoma in March of 1839, the town of Tah-

---

BEST BURGER IN OKLAHOMA: MEERSBURGERS

It's an incongruous coupling: The last of the old Wichita Mountains mining hamlets—virtually a ghost town except for the **Meers Store and Restaurant** *(580/429-8051)*—is a magnet for devoted hamburger aficionados, who drive here to devour the Meersburger, an oversize patty of beef ground from the meat of the restaurant's own herd of longhorns.

Housed in a 1901 building, the Meers Restaurant has the ramshackle feel of the Old West: The floors tilt, the ceiling is made of tin, and the walls are adorned with horseshoes and mounted elk heads. The restaurant, about 4 miles from the **Wichita Mountains Wildlife Refuge Visitors Center,** also serves steak, chicken, ribs, grilled-cheese sandwiches, and breakfast.

lequah became the tribal headquarters of the reconstituted Cherokee Nation.

Meanwhile back east, some 1,000 Cherokee had managed to escape the roundup and forced march. They sought refuge in the mountains of Tennessee and North Carolina; in 1868, they established a tribal government in Cherokee, North Carolina, becoming known as the eastern band of the Cherokee.

In light of this poignant history, the Cherokee Heritage Center's new exhibit on the Trail of Tears should be a moving portrayal of the march and its aftereffects.

TIPS: The museum's Tsa-La-Gi outdoor amphitheater is closed for renovation; no date has been set for its reopening. The gift shop, though small, has some nice children's books on Cherokee and Native American culture.

BASICS: Cherokee Heritage Center *(P.O. Box 515, Tahlequah. 918/456-6007. www.leftmoon.com/cnhs)*

Washita Battlefield
Cheyenne

It may be called **Washita Battlefield National Historic Site,** says Cheyenne peace chief Lawrence Hart of the 315-acre federal historic site he helped to create in 1997, but Washita was in fact more massacre than battle. "The charge through the village on November 27, 1868," Hart points out, "resulted in indiscriminate shooting of women and children. For that reason, we object to the word 'battle.' Custer and his forces attacked when people were still asleep. They shot into the lodges—it didn't matter at whom. Later, when warriors joined the struggle, it had elements of a battle."

Cheyenne peace chief Black Kettle and his band of 51 lodges had been forced to camp that November along the Hooxeeohe (the Cheyenne name for the Washita River) outside the main Cheyenne village because Black Kettle had sought peace—something opposed by the Cheyenne Dog Soldiers. This militant group of warriors sought to avenge the 1864 massacre at Sand Creek in eastern Colorado, where Chief Black Kettle and his camp—awaiting the signing of a promised peace treaty with the government—had been brutally savaged by troops under Col. John M. Chivington. The dawn raid on the peaceful village killed more than 270 Cheyenne—200 of them women and children. Having survived Sand Creek—and in the face of duplicity by the federal government—Black Kettle and other chiefs continued to seek peace as the best solution for their people.

A year before the Washita massacre, Cheyenne and Arapaho chiefs had signed the Treaty of Medicine Lodge. The agreement gave them a reservation in Indian Territory—lands in north-central Oklahoma to which they were ill suited. Seeking an area with more abundant game, the nations moved southwest to land near the

Traditional tipi pitched near Washita Battlefield National Historic Site

Washita and Canadian rivers. Rather than relocate the Cheyenne and Arapaho on the land designated by the treaty, President Ulysses S. Grant initiated a peace policy: In March 1868, he created the Cheyenne and Arapaho Reservation. It was on these lands that the Cheyenne were camped when Custer and his troops attacked them.

Drawn to Washita by gunshots and screams, the Cheyenne Dog Soldiers arrived on the scene (as did warriors from the Kiowa, Comanche, and Plains Apache tribes) to find that Black Kettle's village had been burned—and that many women and children had been killed. After slaughtering 875 Cheyenne horses and taking 53 Cheyenne prisoners (most of them women), Custer claimed that his forces had killed 103 warriors. The Cheyenne, according to a plaque at the site, tallied the deaths at 13 men, 16 women, and 9 children. Twenty-two U.S. soldiers also died in the melee.

"Washita, along with Sand Creek, is an important part of our history," says Chief Hart. "They are in our psyche. For some of us, we've worked our way through bitterness and distrust to reconciliation."

Washita and other sites constitute "sacred geography" for the Cheyenne. To drive home this point when he was lobbying Congress to declare Washita a national historic site in 1996, Hart recalls, he "compared Cheyenne respect for the Washita site to the revered Murrah site in Oklahoma City, explaining that the ground is

SEQUOYAH STATE PARK
WAGNER

Situated on a peninsula jutting into 20,000-acre Fort Gibson Lake, Oklahoma's **Sequoyah State Park** is a family-friendly base for exploring the area that includes the Cherokee Heritage Center (which is 18 miles away). This resort park offers golf, horseback riding, hayrides, boating, and swimming. The **Western Hills Guest Ranch** *(P.O. Box 509, Wagner, 74477. 918/772-2545)* has plain but moderately priced motel-style rooms. In summer, rooms range from $70 to $75 per night—as do the ranch's one-bedroom cottages with kitchens. Two-bedroom cottages cost $110.

considered holy because so many died there." Congress responded to the analogy, dedicating Washita as a national historic site in 1997.

It's important to know all this history before you arrive at the Washita historic site—especially if you plan to visit at a time of year other than summer, when park rangers are present. At the one-acre overlook of the rolling fields—which now belong to the **Black Kettle National Grasslands**—nothing conveys the lasting bitterness that the massacre engendered. (Indeed, the site could be mistaken for an insignificant picnic spot overlooking a prairie.) A historical marker identifies the site only as the locus of "a major engagement in the Plains Indian War" for westward expansion; it then hints at the differing interpretations of history by citing discrepancies in the number of people killed. In addition, there is a small monument. A trail about 1½ miles long leads from the overlook to the river.

TIPS: Guided tours are available in summer; to schedule one, contact the **Black Kettle Museum** *(Okla. 47 at US 283. 580/497-3929)* in Cheyenne. More detailed information about the site may soon be available to visitors as part of the proposed **Cheyenne Tribal History Tour,** which would also include visits to **Fort Reno, Fort Supply,** and the **Cheyenne Cultural Center.** Although the tours (scheduled to begin in the summer of 2000) will be tailored primarily to bus groups, they may also be made available to individual families.

Tornado season in Oklahoma, especially in the western part of the state, runs from April through June. Plan your trips accordingly.

BASICS: The **Washita National Battlefield** *(580/497-2742. www.nps.gov/waba)* is located on Okla. 47, about 25 miles north of I-40.

MORE LOCAL HISTORY

Black Kettle Museum *(Okla. 47 at US 283, Cheyenne. 580/497-3929):* This small museum, redesigned in 1999, presents Cheyenne history from prehistoric times to the present. Plans are in the works to include a tipi, a mural of the Washita battle site, Cheyenne bead-and-quill work, Cheyenne stories, and exhibits on the Cheyenne language.

Roll One-Room Schoolhouse *(Cheyenne City Park, US 283 S, Cheyenne. 580/497-3318. By appt. only):* A schoolmarm holds forth in this 1910 one-room school-house, located 1½ blocks from the Black Kettle Museum. The 1½-hour program will charm families with young grade-schoolers by showing kids that suffering through a school day is a universal experience: Back when William Howard Taft was president, schoolkids had to memorize the state capitals—all 46 of them—and perfect their penmanship by writing "Silence is golden." They also learned vocabulary words such as "victuals" and "nictation" (hint: though both sexes could eat the former, only men were allowed to do the latter). After lessons, grab your lunch tin for a snack before enjoying a recess of playing stilts, rolling hoops, and jumping rope.

Cheyenne Cultural Center *(2250 NE Rte. 66, Clinton. 580/323-6224):* Although the newly constructed center had only an artists' gallery in 1999, its educational building—dedicated to helping local children learn the Cheyenne language by computer—should be open by the summer of 2000. Performances and festivals are planned as well.

Horseback Riding Cheyenne

Set on 480 acres of red hills and rolling grasslands, the **Coyote Hills Guest Ranch** provides a convenient base for exploring Cheyenne country. It also offers a family-friendly Western experience of horseback riding and hiking. Although the ranch gets its fair share of tour groups, it has a laid-back feel. The 20 rooms (each with private bath) in the two-tier, motel-style bunkhouse are decorated in the "cowboy comfortable" scheme: pine beds, quilts, and dried-flower wreaths. You can also choose to camp in a tipi.

Be sure to go on a horseback ride—that's when you get to appreciate the land. Our ride wound up hills, through thickets of scrub oak full of quail, and past ridges where coyotes howled, before reaching the Cheyenne burial scaffold that commemorates the Washita massacre. The heart of ranch life is the social barn: Here meals are served, evening entertainment takes place, and families relax by playing board games.

TIPS: For one week in July and another in August, the ranch transforms itself into a camp for kids ages 10 to 13—no parents allowed!

BASICS: The **Coyote Hills Guest Ranch** *(P.O. Box 99, Cheyenne. 580/497-3931. coyotehr@logixnet.net)* charges from $49 per person for lodging to $95 per person for lodging, three meals, and all activities.

Tombstone Tales
Fort Reno

Established as a military fort in 1875 to protect Cheyenne and Arapaho agency personnel and tribal members, **Fort Reno**—now a part of the Department of Agriculture's **Grazinglands Research Laboratory**—is a storehouse of fascinating history. This becomes clear, however, only if you schedule your visit to coincide with **Tombstone Tales,** a reenactors' event held the last weekend in September. At all other times of the year, the historic barracks look like just another bunch of old buildings—only the exteriors are visible—and the cemetery will strike kids as just another burial place.

During Tombstone Tales, by contrast, the fort comes alive with costumed interpreters re-creating the lives of some of the frontierspeople buried here. Pvt. Clark Young—an African-American "Buffalo Soldier" stationed at Fort Reno in the 1880s—explains his motivation for joining the U.S. Army. (The Buffalo Soldiers got that designation from Native Americans, who admired the men's bravery in battle.) "The 9th U.S. Cavalry were all ex-slaves," Young informs visitors. "We got $13 a month, the chance to wear the blue uniform, three squares a day—and dignity." In reality, as Young also points out, the Army paid each Buffalo Soldier only $10 a month. "For the black man, they withheld $3 for the uniform, and we were only paid sometimes. We were given second-rate horses too—but we had the lowest desertion rate."

Ben Clark, a scout for Custer at the Washita massacre, tells how he became a Pony Express rider at age 18. "I answered an ad for 'young, unmarried orphans willing to face death every day and ride a horse 100 miles as fast as you can.' They paid $25 a week—10 times what I was making."

In an unnerving moment, Chalk—an Arapaho scout for the U.S. Cavalry against Dull Knife's Cheyenne in 1881—recounts the fierce fight with an avenging Cheyenne warrior that killed him.

TIPS: Because markers at the site offer scant information, you'll want to read up on the history of Fort Reno before you visit.

BASICS: **Fort Reno** *(7107 W. Cheyenne St., El Reno. 405/262-3987. www.3ctn.canadian.co.ok.us/fortreno)* is located about 30 miles west of Oklahoma City.

BEYOND THE TIP!

Indian City USA *(2.5 miles SE of Anadarko on Okla. 8. 800/433-5661 or 405/247-5661):* Grade-schoolers probably won't mind the commercialism of **Indian City USA,** where the first building you enter is a gift shop crammed with T-shirts and plastic tomahawks. They'll also be intrigued by the rich variety of dwellings they discover as they walk through this outdoor village of seven replicated Plains Indians homesites. The Pawnee, being hunters and farmers, constructed permanent homes of log and sod; the nomadic Chiricahua Apache, on the other hand, built wickiups—hutlike temporary dwellings of twigs and branches. Indian City also gives children the chance to learn how the Navajo, Caddo, Wichita, Kiowa, and Comanche lived. Native American dances are performed at selected times.

TIPS: Give your kids a spending limit for the gift shop, and don't miss the guided tour; you'll learn much more that way.

Geronimo's Jail
Fort Sill

Established in 1869 as a cavalry outpost in Indian Territory, **Fort Sill's Old Post**—constructed in 1872 and 1873 by the Buffalo Soldiers of the Tenth U.S. Infantry Regiment—is a National Historic Landmark. The troops held "hostile Indians" in the stone guardhouse, whose prison cells now showcase Native American history and artifacts. The most famous prisoner was the Chiricahua Apache warrior Geronimo, who was confined to Fort Sill from 1894 until his death from pneumonia in 1909. Although Geronimo was allowed the liberty of living on a small farm north of Old Post, he was never permitted to revisit his cherished homeland in Arizona.

Geronimo's grave site, on the eastern range of the Fort Sill grounds, is marked by an eagle with outspread wings. Among those interred on **Chiefs' Knoll** in the **Old Post Cemetery** are Quanah Parker, a Comanche chief who died in 1911; Set'-Tainte (White Bear), a war chief of the Kiowa; and Tene-Angopte (Kicking Bird), a fellow Kiowa chief. Although I found it unsettling to walk among the graves of warriors at an active military base, other buildings at Fort Sill portray more traditional military history: the weapons, uniforms and tools of the frontier army.

BASICS: **Fort Sill's Old Post** *(437 Quanah Rd., Fort Sill. 405/442-6570)*

MUSEUM OF THE GREAT PLAINS

The skull of an imperial mammoth—a creature that stood 14 feet high at the shoulder—is part of an exhibit on the Plains environment from the Pleistocene era through the 1800s at the **Museum of the Great Plains** in Lawton *(601 NW Ferris Ave. 580/581-3460. www.museumgreatplains.org)*. The best part of the museum— a replica of an 1839 fur-trading post—stands outside, surrounded by a stockade fence. At selected times in summer *(call ahead for schedule)*, a reenactor describes swapping tobacco, coffee, sugar, and bolts of cloth for buffalo hides and beaver pelts. At the picnic area, scurrying prairie dogs provide entertainment while you snack.

POWWOWS AND FESTIVALS

Powwows and festivals are the best times to visit Native America. Both are social gatherings that show pride in Native American traditions, with dancers wearing traditional regalia of feathers, shawls, bells, and rainbow-colored beads. The contestants swirl to the rhythms of drums, moving in syncopation with ancient steps as they perform dances labeled traditional, jingle, dress, grass, friendship, and fancy.

A powwow is also a traditional event—something in the spirit of a ceremony—and as such it has a prescribed order. Powwows start with a grand parade that is somewhat weightier than the pageantry of a festival. The parade—called *daanniiluua* in the Crow language—symbolizes the moving of the camp for the Crow; for this reason, the parade marshals are akin to the leaders of old, whose task was to scout new locations.

Powwows and competitive dances also include giveaways and honor dances; festivals do not.

Despite these and other distinctions, both powwows and festivals are celebrations of Native American culture to which others are invited. At both events, you'll find food booths selling authentic Indian fare: fried quail, roasted ears of corn, and Indian tacos—fry bread wrapped around meat, beans, grated cheese, jalapeño peppers, and picante sauce. Whichever type of occasion you and your family attend, you will enjoy the dancing, drumming, and overall feeling of friendship.

CROW FAIR: A sea of white tipis meets the eye as you pull into the parking lot in Crow Agency, Montana, for **Crow Fair**—one of the largest powwows in the United States. The campers have traveled a long way to get here—and they are prepared to stay for the duration of the fair. Linda Moss, a Crow Fair participant I met, had been drawn by the chance "to celebrate Crow culture and Plains Indian culture, to visit family members, and to participate in traditional culture through dance contests, parades, and rodeo."

Arrive in time to watch the dancers make their grand entrance into the arbor or arena. The different troupes stepdance, circling the arbor as they wind toward the center and transforming the arena into a swirl of color. Outside the arbor, vendors sell food while

Dancer in motion at the Red Earth Powwow

A woman congratulates her grandniece on a competition victory at Taos Pueblo Powwow.

craftspeople sell silver-and-turquoise jewelry, carved boxes, and beaded earrings.

Basics: Contact the Crow Agency (*P.O. Box 159, Crow Agency, MT 59022. 406/638-2601*) for the exact mid-August date of the **Crow Fair.**

RED EARTH FESTIVAL: Held early each June in Oklahoma City, the Red Earth dance festival boasts 1,500 competitors, making it one of the largest Native American performances in the country. The participants—bright with fiery colors, breastplates, quilled arm bands, fringed leggings, or beaded moccasins—come from more than 100 northern and southern tribes.

In addition to the dancers, storytellers are on hand to weave heroic sagas and creation tales. More than 250 juried artists present paintings, silver jewelry, beadwork, photography, and other crafts. At arts-and-

crafts booths, kids can make Native American items such as beaded necklaces and rain sticks. Films by American Indian artists are screened throughout the day. The festival usually kicks off with a parade of more than 2,000 Native Americans in regalia.

Basics: The **Red Earth Festival** (*2100 NE 52nd St., Oklahoma City. 405/427-5228*) will be held June 9 to 11 in 2000.

POWWOW ETIQUETTE

✦ If you want to know more about a dance, ask questions of those standing nearby. Be respectful; expect some religious customs not to be discussed.

✦ Ask permission before taking photos.

✦ Dance with tribal members, if you'd like to, when the emcee announces a "round dance" or "friendship dance." Women should wear shawls or cover themselves with a blanket when dancing.

NATIVE CULTURES DRIVING TOUR
FOUR CORNERS

Grandtravel's 11-day **Canyons and Native Cultures** trip is designed just for grandparents and grandchildren. A teacher-escort explains Indian dancing and pottery, guides you in sandpainting, tells Native American tales, and organizes other activities for grandparents to share with their grandchildren.

On other trips throughout the Southwest, grandparents and their charges can ride the **Sandia Peak Tramway** in Santa Fe, attend a chuck-wagon dinner in **Durango,** take a **narrow-gauge railway** to Silverton, go on a Navajo-guided jeep tour of **Canyon de Chelly,** or float down the **Colorado River.**

Basics: **Grandtravel** *(800/247-7651 or 301/986-0790)* has 38 departures to 20 domestic and international destinations, including Australia. Trips are scheduled for grandparents and grandchildren ages 7 to 11 and ages 12 to 17; prices range from $3,880 to $8,890 per person double occupancy.

SOUTHERN PLAINS INDIAN MUSEUM AND CRAFTS CENTER

Although the permanent one-room gallery features a display of colorful regalia and artifacts, we found this facility—which we had long looked forward to seeing—a bit disappointing. The war-dance bustles, fringed and painted buckskins, bear-claw pendants, rawhide drums, and beaded cradleboards pique the curiosity of kids, but not for long: The explanatory material is limited to brief explanations, and there are no children's guides or interactive displays. Another gallery hosts changing art exhibits.

The beaded earrings, pins, pouches, and bracelets in the gift shop did not live up to their advance billing as exceptional, high-quality crafts. **Southern Plains Indian Museum** *(715 E. Central Blvd., Okla. 62 E of Anadarko. 405/247-6221. www.tanet.net/community/anadarko/spmuseum.htm. Adults $3, children ages 6 to 12 $1, under 6 free. June-Sept. Mon.-Sat. 9 a.m.-4:30 p.m., Sun. 1-4:30 p.m.; Oct.-May Tues.-Sat. 9 a.m.-4:30 p.m., Sun. 1-4:30 p.m.)*

Wichita Mountains Wildlife Refuge

The rolling grasslands of the 59,000-acre **Wichita Mountains Wildlife Refuge** support a herd of almost 600 bison, members of which can be spotted (along with the occasional elk) from the road that winds through the refuge. There's no need to stay inside your car, however: Fifteen miles of hiking trails lace the refuge's prairie, woodlands, and hills.

At the refuge Visitor Center, simple but satisfying exhibits will answer younger kids' questions about the land. Press a button to hear the call of a bugling elk or the clicking sound of a diamondback rattlesnake. The **Night Shift** exhibit, housed in a darkened room with stars and silhouetted trees, quells first-time campers' fears about night noises: Those snorts you may hear in the dark, explains a comforting voice, are produced by nothing more ferocious than a white-tailed deer. The rustling noise, meanwhile, is probably an armadillo moving through the grass, while the hoot is the call of a great horned owl.

BASICS: The visitor center for the **Wichita Mountains Wildlife Refuge** *(Route 1, Box 48, Indiahoma. 580/429-3222)* is located at the intersection of state highways 115 and 49.

Wolf's Heaven
Anadarko

At **Wolf's Heaven**—a 10-tipi encampment on 640 acres outside the town of Anadarko—Edgar and Margot Edringer combine camping with Native American culture. The Edringers first became interested in Indian culture in their native Germany; they now work with tribal members to provide a personalized experience for guests. Melvin Kerchee, a Comanche, leads guided hikes into the Wichita Mountains, painting a vivid word-picture of Comanche culture along the way. Other activities focus on medicinal herbs, pottery, beadwork, storytelling, and horseback riding.

Wolf's Heaven is designed for adults ages 18 and older. Families with adult children interested in camping or Native American culture will find Wolf's Heaven to be an interesting respite.

TIPS: The tipis are fitted with mattresses and blankets, but bring your own sleeping bags with you for the guided overnight in the Wichita Mountains. Non-campers may attend the Tuesday-evening dances and storytelling; call ahead for details *(adm. fee).*

BASICS: Wolf's Heaven *(P.O. Box 1425, Anadarko. 405/247-3000. May-Oct.),* located about six miles west of Anadarko, charges $75 per person per night, including meals and museum tours.

Wagon Train Trip
Bayard

Lead a covered wagon across Nebraska's grasslands, learning how the hopeful and the hearty trekked west in the 1850s. Whether you opt for the overnight journey, called **24 Hours of 1850**, or the four-day **Oregon Trail Wagon Trip**, you will experience the pace and scenery of the legendary migration across the prairies to the gold mines of California and Oregon.

Kids like the authenticity of walking in the wheel ruts of the real Oregon Trail. Participants in the four-day journey pass **Chimney Rock,** the landmark that signaled the western edge of the prairie. (It also reassured pioneers they were headed in the right direction.) If there is time, take advantage of the chance to explore **Chimney Rock National Historic Site** by hiking a short trail or paddling a part of the North Platte River.

Along the way, you will learn such wagon survival techniques as how to grease the wheels and how to hitch up the horses. On some evenings, wagon-train members gather around a campfire to hear a historian relate true tales of the settlers and their prairie schooners. On another evening, you can grab your pardner and do-si-do at a square dance. The trip harbors a few surprises, too: The Pony Express delivers mail, friendly Sioux share folktales, and soldiers recount the hazards of patrolling the territories.

There's a leisurely pace to this trip, making it a good pick for younger gradeschoolers enamored of the Old West—but not yet old enough to crave whitewater thrills. The wagons cover a reasonable 11 miles per day. You can sit next to the teamster, ride horseback, or walk—or a combination of all three—meaning this trip is suitable for everyone from kindergartners to grandparents.

Nor do you have to cook. Ranch hands serve up steaks, flapjacks, cowboy coffee, and other tin-plate fare. Afterward, you can unroll your sleeping bag next to the wagon and sleep beneath the stars, or bunk in the wagon or a tent. (The overnight trip also features a rustic cabin option.) Sleeping bags and towels are furnished by the outfitter.

TIPS: Despite extra cushioning for comfort, those authentic wooden wagon wheels make for a bumpy ride. Bring a pillow to absorb the bumps.

Read up on (or play the popular computer game about) the Oregon Trail before you hit the dusty trail.

BASICS: Oregon Trail Wagon Train *(308/586-1850)* offers **24 Hours of 1850** (noon to noon) at $175 for adults and $150 for kids under 12. The 4-day trip, which can take up to 40 people, is $479 for adults, $379 for children (minimum age: 3).

Lighting out on the Oregon Trail in Nebraska, circa 1999

DAY TRIPS NEARBY

Scotts Bluff National Monument *(5 miles SW of Scottsbluff on Neb. 92. 308/436-4340):* Rising 800 feet above the North Platte River, the bluffs afford scenic views of the surrounding valley. You can drive to the top and walk a short way to the overlook, or follow the 1½-mile trail from the Visitor Center to the summit.

Agate Fossils Beds National Monument *(301 River Road, Harrison. 308/436-4340):* Exposed fossils from the Miocene epoch (13 to 20 million years ago) are visible along the trails in this 2,700-acre park. The Visitor Center displays Native American artifacts donated by James Cook—a 19th-century rancher and naturalist who gave the site to the Park Service and was a friend of Sioux chief Red Cloud.

Fort Robinson State Park *(US 20, 3 miles W of Crawford. 308/665-2919):* Fort Robinson, now part of a Nebraska state park, was established in 1874 as a way of controlling and limiting conflicts with the Sioux under Chief Red Cloud. In May 1877, lured by promises of peace with the U.S. government, Lakota chief Crazy Horse was arrested and imprisoned here; four months later, he was killed by a soldier. The Fort Robinson Museum contains artifacts from that period. In season at the park, you can swim, hike, ride horses, or take a bison-viewing tour.

Buffalo Safari
Custer State Park

As our jeep crested the hilltop, we suddenly spied hundreds of bison below. Some lumbered along, trailed by calves who seemed to hop after them. Others kept their curly brown heads fixed on the business at hand (or mouth), munching the prairie grass in **Custer State Park.** Except for a few other jeeps, there was no one around. With the bison silhouetted in the sunset over the sweeping plains, we were momentarily transported back to the era when buffalo were plenty and Plains Indians roamed the land.

Buffalo safaris, held just before the October roundup, reward you with this and other scenes that seem to have been transplanted from Western movies. Approximately 1,400 head of buffalo—one of the largest herds in the nation—roam the 73,000 acres of Custer State Park. In addition to sighting smaller concentrations of bison, you may spot some of the deer, elk, pronghorn antelope, and bighorn sheep that inhabit the park.

During the weekend before the Monday roundup, Custer State Park hosts a festival with arts and crafts, face painting, and games for kids. On roundup day itself, try to reach the viewing area before 7:30 a.m., when many park roads close. Except for noted wranglers and special friends of the governor, the public is not permitted to participate in the actual roundup. You can, however, watch the herds thunder by as the wranglers drive them past the viewing area. To guarantee themselves a prime spot, some visitors arrive in line by 6:00 a.m.

Wranglers on horseback and cowboys in pickup trucks equipped with walkie-talkies push the buffalo from pasture to pasture. (Though bison may attack a horse, they shy away from charging a Ford.) The pickup drivers funnel the buffalo into corrals, where they are sorted and then vaccinated; in addition, wranglers brand the new calves.

Park visitors are invited to witness the proceedings and to party. The festival features free country music and a lunch of—what else?—buffalo sandwiches.

TIPS: Other than during the roundup, you'll have to go off-road to see buffalo in large herds—a sight possible only on guided jeep tours such as those offered by **Buffalo Safari Jeep Tours** *(HC 83, Box 74, Custer. 800/658-3530 or 605/255-4541).*

BASICS: **Custer State Park** *(HC 83 Box 70, Custer. 800/710-2267 [for camping] or 605/255-4515. www.state.sd.us/sdparks/)* has several lodges and campsites. The **State Game Lodge and Resort** offers comfortable motel rooms and cabins, as well as a restaurant.

Annual bison roundup in Custer State Park, South Dakota

Jewel Cave
National Monument

Crawl through the wild areas of the world's second longest cavern, **Jewel Cave National Monument,** and you see some of the rarest formations on Earth. Balloon-like clusters of hydromagnesite—documented in only six caves in the world—shine silvery white in the beam of your spelunker's helmet. Rarely seen scintillites—chert coated with quartz crystals—glow sparkly red.

The guided tour of Jewel Cave takes three to four hours. There are no lights and no pathways. At one point, the passage narrows to an opening just 24 inches wide and 8½ inches high; to demonstrate that you can wriggle through the real thing underground, park rangers require you to creep through a similar-size cement practice block before the tour.

Two other regularly scheduled cave tours are the **Scenic Tour**—a 1½-hour walk through wide and well-lit passageways—and the **Candlelight Tour,** a slightly longer walk that conveys the caving experience without bringing you to your knees.

TIPS: Practice crawling by stretching a string across a doorway 8½ inches off the floor. Wear rugged clothes and dress in layers; the cave is a constant 49°F.

BASICS: The special tour of **Jewel Cave National Monument** *(RR 1, Box 60 AA, Custer. 605/673-2288. Mid-June–mid-Aug.),* whose minimum age is 16, costs $18 and can be reserved one month in advance.

SPIRIT OF THE BUFFALO

The buffalo was life—clothing, shelter, and food—to Native Americans of the Plains. Buffalo hides became robes and tipis; buffalo flesh became meat; buffalo sinew became thread.

The animal commanded such respect that it represents the north—a place of wisdom, renewal, and power—on the medicine wheel.

Unlike visitors in 1900, when the West's bison population fell to 300, modern families can witness the awesome sight of a teeming buffalo herd. Yellowstone National Park has the largest herd on public lands, followed by Custer State Park, So. Dak. Other herds graze in the Wichita Mountains National Wildlife Refuge, Okla., and the National Bison Range, Montana.

The Journey
Rapid City

The Journey is a museum that tells two versions of Great Plains history. The scientific explanation presents a geologic cross section of the Black Hills: fossils from the bone beds of Cretaceous dinosaurs, teeth from a Tyrannosaur, and other finds. The mythological explanation presents a Lakota Sioux creation story in which Inyan (stone) gives life to Wi (the sun); together they become Winyam (woman), from whom all life is created. By developing these two threads through exhibits in different galleries, the Journey respectfully and appealingly conveys both Native American and Western culture.

My family liked the Native American exhibit best. In the tipi exhibit, we learned that the point "where the tipi poles join reminds us that when we die we go through that vortex into another world." Although kids may not be ready to contemplate the hereafter, the here and now—in the form of a hologram—rivets their attention: Against a background of moving clouds and a Lakota melody, a laser projection of a woman suddenly appears in the tipi, explaining how the Sioux used dog travois to move their camps from site to site.

Another nice touch is the discovery boxes—drawers beneath the glass display cases that contain items for kids to touch. You can feel a parfleche container, turkey feathers, deer antlers, or sinew (used for thread). Part of the fun lies in the constant surprises; stand on a certain spot before an exhibit, for example, and sounds of that era—a train whistle, a fur trader crowing about his booming business—greet your ears. In the saloon where Wild Bill Hickok holds a winning hand, you hear the gunshot blast that killed him.

TIPS: If you're not an extreme motorcycling fan, avoid the Black Hills area during the first week in August, when nearly half a million bikers descend on Sturgis for an annual rally whose festivities are far from family-oriented.

BASICS: **The Journey** (*222 New York St., Rapid City. 605/394-6923. www. journeymuseum.org*)

Lakota Pony Rides
Pine Ridge Reservation

As we rode horseback along a creek bed laced with cottonwoods and oaks, the distant mesa looked yellow in the morning light. Soon we were moving up the brown hills, past ravines and hollows. On the opposite bluff, we caught sight of two antelope.

Alex White Plume—owner of **Lakota Pony Rides,** located on the **Pine Ridge Reservation**—pointed to Bad Bear Hill. From there, he told us, you can see Kicking Bear's homestead, the place where he received his vision of the ghost dance. White Plume, a descendant of Crazy Horse's band, then led us up the steep slope of an even higher butte, the sure-footed horses working hard to make the climb. From the top, we savored sweeping views. The purple line floating in the distance on one side was the badlands; on the other side loomed peaks of the Black Hills, which Alex referred to as Paha Sapa.

Horseback riding on the reservation transports you to the kind of wide-open spaces that appear only in dreams—undulating landscapes of flatlands broken by ridges and washed with wind. There is a sense of freedom and power on these Lakota lands. (Although the majority of outsiders use the term "Sioux," the people call themselves *Lakota*—a term that translates as "allies" or "friends." The word "Sioux" came about when French traders took it upon themselves to abbreviate the Chippewa designation for the Lakota of *Na.Joweisiweg,* which means "Lesser Snakes.")

About 25,000 Lakota live on four reservations in South Dakota. The Pine Ridge Reservation is best suited for visitors—and the best way to see these lands is to embark on a tour with a Lakota outfitter.

Alex White Plume, for one, started offering free rides to visitors in 1982. He wanted to educate outsiders both about the Lakota and about the Black Hills. "Your Supreme Court," says White Plume, "ruled in June 1980 that the taking of the Black Hills in 1868 was supposed to be for just 100 years." The Fort Laramie Treaty of 1868, which established the Great Sioux Reservation, stipulated that the Black Hills were to be part of that reservation—and that no white person could settle there (or even pass through) without permission of the Indians.

But in 1874, an expedition led by Lt. Col. George Armstrong Custer confirmed the existence of gold in the Black Hills, starting a gold rush. Prospectors and pioneers, followed by fur traders and homesteaders, headed for the region in droves.

Custer's attack at the Little Bighorn River on June 25, 1876, was part of a larger Army plan to remove Native Americans from the path of the gold seekers and settlers. Although the Native American warriors won that battle, wiping out Custer and all 262 of his troops, the victory was short-lived.

When South Dakota was granted statehood in 1889, the pressure for white development intensified. That same year, the government divided the Great Sioux Reser-

Erosion channels show the effects of wind, rain, and ice on a Badlands butte.

vation into four smaller reservations: Pine Ridge, Rosebud, Standing Rock, and Cheyenne River. After allotting 320 acres to every head of family (single people received 80 acres apiece), the U.S. government threw open the rest of the land for settlement. The Great Sioux Reservation had been cut in half—yet another violation of the Treaty of 1868.

In 1974, as a result of tribal lawsuits, the United States Congress awarded $17.5 million (plus $85 million in back interest) to the Sioux. When the Justice Department objected, the U.S. Court of Claims stepped in to review the case; six years later, it awarded the Sioux $105 million—a ruling that the Supreme Court has since upheld.

The Lakota refused the settlement; instead, they want the Black Hills returned to them. "The Black Hills are not for sale," explains White Plume. "Our origin stories tell us we came from the Black Hills. If we lose the Black Hills, we lose our identity."

Lakota Pony Rides offer both day trips and cultural overnights. Accommodations are in a tipi, or you may supply your own tent. On extended programs, guests are responsible for saddling, unsaddling, and grooming their horses, as well as washing their dishes. Options include spending a night on the prairie, taking a workshop on quillwork and beading, or listening to Lakota stories. In one of these, White Plume tells how Wa mni tu, the first horse, came to the Lakota:

GHOSTS OF THE PLAINS: WOUNDED KNEE

The town of Wounded Knee is on the Pine Ridge Reservation, just off BIA 28. Atop a rise there is a small church, a graveyard, and a stone monument that reads "erected by the surviving relatives and other Ogallala [sic] and Cheyenne River Sioux Indians in memory of the Chief Big Foot Massacre, Dec. 29, 1890. Big Foot was a great chief."

That simple tableau is the sole reminder of the massacre that took place here. Big Foot and his people were on their way to peace negotiations on Pine Ridge Reservation when soldiers caught up with them and ordered them to camp by Wounded Knee Creek. More than 350 Sioux were surrounded by 450 soldiers, who entered the camp to disarm them. Someone fired a shot, and the killing started. When it was over, every member of Big Foot's camp had been slaughtered. For the next two days, a great blizzard covered the plains, freezing the bodies in contorted shapes. They were buried in a mass grave.

In 1973, Russell Means, Dennis Banks, and Leonard Peltier—leaders of the radical American Indian Movement—led more than 300 protesters in occupying the site. They demanded that the United States government investigate the Bureau of Indian Affairs and honor treaties signed with Native Americans.

Wa mni tu was real ugly. He was small, and nobody wanted to hunt him or eat him. But one day a warrior followed him. He tracked him for years and then, one day, the warrior rode back into the land on a horse. But the tribes were doing bad things, committing atrocities against each other—incest, murder. They had lost their ways.

To punish the tribes, the Great Spirit took away the horse, and the people had to get about on foot for 400 years. Then, around the 16th century, the horse reappeared. "That's how we got the horse," says White Plume, "not because we stole them from Europeans. Everyone who comes here goes away with a better understanding of our beliefs."

TIPS: It's best to visit Pine Ridge Reservation as the guest of an authorized outfitter rather than on your own. A guide enables you to see and understand more, and ensures that you'll be welcomed.

BASICS: **Lakota Pony Rides** *(P.O. Box 76, Manderson. 605/455-2155. lakota1@gwtc.net. Mid-March–mid-Oct.)* are staged about two hours southeast of Rapid City. The rides cost $275 per person per night for tours that can last from three to six days. Day rides are also available. Children 10 and older should be accompanied by an adult; children under 10 ride horses only in the corral.

Crazy Horse Monument

All four presidents immortalized on Mount Rushmore would fit inside the head of the **Crazy Horse Monument,** the world's largest sculpture in progress. That suits the outsize dreams of Chief Henry Standing Bear, a Lakota leader, and Boston-born sculptor Korczak Ziolkowski. When Mount Rushmore was being developed in 1939, Standing Bear invited Korczak to create a counterpart to that monument: "My fellow chiefs and I would like the white man to know that the red man has great heroes, too."

Since Korczak detonated the first dynamite charge in June 1948, more than eight million tons of granite have been blasted away. Korczak, a storyteller in stone, chose a stance for Crazy Horse that was designed to evoke the Lakota leader's encounter with an arrogant white trader: With the Lakota having been forced onto reservations, the trader mockingly asked Crazy Horse, "Where are your lands now?"

Pointing over his horse's head, the proud warrior answered, "My lands are where my dead lie buried."

Although Korczak died in 1982, his family continues the project. On the 50th anniversary in 1998, Crazy Horse's head—87½ feet high—was unveiled. When completed, the sculpture of Crazy Horse astride his stallion will measure 641 feet long and 563 feet high.

TIPS: Also on site here are the **Indian Museum of North America,** which houses a collection of Native American artifacts, and the **Native American Educational and Cultural Center,** where craftspeople demonstrate—and sell—their art. There is a restaurant as well.

For an extreme close-up of the sculpture, visit during the annual **Volksmarch** the first full weekend in June, when you can walk along what will be Crazy Horse's arm. To help your kids appreciate the significance of the site, tell them a bit about Lakota history (see pages 119-121) and mention that Mount Rushmore (see below) is carved into a mountain that the Lakota still claim.

BASICS: Crazy Horse Monument *(Avenue of the Chiefs, Crazy Horse. 605/673-4681. www.crazyhorse.org)*

MORE GOOD IDEAS IN THE BADLANDS

Mount Rushmore National Memorial *(P. O. Box 268, Keystone. 605/574-2523. www.mountrushmore.org):* The 60-foot-high faces chiseled into Mount Rushmore—George Washington, Thomas Jefferson, Abraham Lincoln, and Theodore Roosevelt—are carved into the American psyche as well. After viewing the carv-

Right: After 50 years, the head of Crazy Horse emerges from a cliffside in South Dakota.

FOUR WINDS RANCH

Although Tom Steuer grew up in Germany, his interest in Native Americans ultimately led him and his wife, Christine, to open **Four Winds Ranch,** a tipi camp in the Black Hills. "Our dream is to bring people together from around the world," says Steuer, "in an exchange of ideas and cultures." During one-week programs at the ranch, you can watch powwow dancers, listen to storytellers and Native American flute players, or go hiking and horseback riding. Steuer also leads guests on tours of Wounded Knee, Custer State Park, Wind Cave, and other area sites.

Basics: A 7-day program at **Four Winds Ranch** (*R. R. I, Box 75H, Custer. 605/673-5176. www.fourwindsranch.com*) costs $840 for adults and $420 for ages 6 to 16 (meals, tours, and horseback riding included). The family rate is $1,800 for 2 adults and 1 child, or $2,020 for 2 adults and 2 children.

ing from a distance, walk the half-mile Presidential Trail for a closer look.

TIPS: John Gutzon [de la Mothe] Borglum, the sculptor of Mount Rushmore, crafted the presidents' features to appear most dramatic in the morning light. Try to tour the site between sunrise and 10:00 a.m.

The Mammoth Site *(1800 Hwy. 18 Truck Route [or P. O. Box 692], Hot Springs. 605/745-6017. www. mammothsite.com):* Many of the Columbian mammoths who roamed the Black Hills some 26,000 years ago became mired in a sinkhole, where their bones lay buried until a housing developer discovered them in 1974. The site turned out to be one of the richest mammoth finds in North America; today it is the only one where the bones still lie in situ, or as found.

At the indoor site, visitors walk on ramps built around the mammoth skeletons, some of which are almost intact. It's a fascinating look at archaeology and its quarry.

TIPS: Earthwatch sponsors a week-long dig at the site each July for participants 6 years or older. No experience necessary.

Black Hills Wild Horse Sanctuary *(Hot Springs, about 14 miles from the Mammoth Site. 800/252-6652 or 605/745-5955. www.gwtc.net/~iram):* A classic image of the Old West—wild horses running free over a sweeping grassland prairie—still greets the eye on this 300-acre sanctuary. "The horses and I," says sanctuary founder Dayton Hyde, "have been partners in trying to save the land." Guided bus tours that overlook the range are held at 10 a.m., 1 p.m., and 3 p.m. each day in season (May to September). Chuck-wagon dinners are also available.

Badlands National Park *(605/433-5361):* Erosion—by wind, water, and ice—designed the badlands, carving the landscape into jutting cones and peaks, twisting gorges and canyons. Do more than just drive through here; take the time to get out of your car and walk about the unusual formations. The **Fossil Exhibit Trail,** for example, is one-quarter mile long and accessible by strollers.

Blackfeet Tours
Northwest Montana

You could hike the trails, take a boat trip on **Two Medicine Lake,** and drive scenic Going-to-the-Sun Road through **Glacier National Park** without ever realizing that these jagged mountains, dense pine forests, and rolling grasslands were once the stronghold of the Blackfeet. (Indeed, they are still sacred to the Blackfeet nation, whose 1.5-million-acre reservation adjoins the park.) Take a tour with **Sun Tours** (page 130) or with Curly Bear Wagner's **Blackfeet Historical Tours,** however, and you'll discover some of the legends of *Mokakinsin,* or the Backbone of the World—the Blackfeet name for the land that became **Waterton-Glacier International Peace Park.**

With his elastic jowls, rubbery mouth, and deadpan delivery, Curly Bear Wagner comes across as the Blackfeet version of Walter Matthau. Once a week, Wagner delivers an informative talk on buffalo hunts, tobacco offerings, and sweat lodges to guests at **Glacier Park Lodge** in East Glacier. His braided hair falling to his waist, Wagner sprinkles his talk with just enough shtick to keep even casual listeners and grade-schoolers interested: "You go into a sweat lodge to pray," he told our group, "and since it's 125 degrees in there, you pray to get out!" Asked to give an Indian war cry, Wagner responds by impishly shouting "Bingo!"

A cultural adviser to the Blackfeet, Wagner began his day-long tours in 1984 as a way of educating visitors to the area. "You had people taking these bus tours, going up in the mountains, and exploring Glacier National Park without learning anything about the Blackfeet," says Wagner. "The reservation is right next door, and these are our sacred mountains. We didn't want to sell them, but we had to. We still fast and gather our roots for medicine up there."

Wagner's guided hikes combine storytelling with easy walks along forested trails appropriate for kids as young as 7. On a trek to Barren Falls, we learned how the beaver bundle came to the Blackfeet. On the path to St. Mary's Falls, for example, we listened to Wagner relate the antics of Napi, the legendary folk hero and sometime bad boy.

A typical tour begins at **Goat Lick** on Mont. 2 between East and West Glacier, where the natural mineral licks along the Middle Fork of the Flathead River attract mountain goats. At the **Museum of the Plains Indian** (page 130) in Browning, Wagner fleshes out the facility's limited explanations with tribal tales. He recounts how the buffalo hunt dominated traditional life, why women set up and decorated the lodges (the Blackfeet term for tipis), and how a dog travois was used to move a band's belongings before the Plains Indians had horses.

Wagner enlivens the stop at **Marias Pass** (or **Bear Pass,** as the Blackfeet call it)

A member of the Blackfeet nation arrives on horseback for the annual Blackfeet Powwow.

with details of how the Blackfeet used the spot—at an elevation of 5,216 feet, the lowest pass in Montana on the Continental Divide. At **Cut Bank Creek,** the Blackfeet crossed the mountains to trade hides for shells from west coast nations—and to steal horses from the Salish, Pend d'Oreille, and Kootenai in the southwest. Warriors posted atop the surrounding peaks guarded the Blackfeet hunting grounds from invasion by other nations.

In the absence of Wagner's explanations, there would not be much to see here besides the mountain peaks and a statue to Capt. Meriwether Lewis, who dubbed the river Marias in honor of his cousin, Maria Wood. There is one unassailable reason to pause at this place, however: Basic bathroom facilities are available.

Standing by the rubble of a late 19th-century church, Wagner describes the mission system in terms likely to be uncomfortable for children to hear. Missions—many of them established by the Catholic Church—provided food, clothing, and a basic education for Native American children, many of whom lived in poverty. In return, however, the mission students were forced to live away from their parents for months at a time. Some children were victims of child abuse; many suffered cruel punishments. Wagner remembers his uncles' stories of being forced to kneel on broom handles for hours at a time—the penalty for speaking their native language.

"They took our language from us," says Wagner, "and they took our children. We had to let our kids go to these schools; otherwise, we lost our rations." Like many members of the First Nations—a term he prefers to Native Americans—Wagner traces much of the despair and alcoholism on reservations to the family breakups caused by the mission system.

From the church, it's a bumpy off-road drive in Wagner's van to the **Buffalo Jump.** At the top of the 60-foot-high cliffs, Wagner explains the complexities of driving a herd of bison over the edge. This hunting practice represented a significant advance in safety over the technique it replaced—that of spearing buffalo while on foot.

At the site of a former **Sun Dance,** Wagner highlights the importance of the ritual. Like the skeleton of a circus tent, 28 birch-tree trunks create a round enclosure devoid of its original covering branches. Colored prayer cloths tied around a center pole flap in the wind. From a rise nearby, a badger peers down at the visitors to this ghostly site, while a prairie dog scampers across the yellowing field to its burrow. The rim of Glacier's mountains loom purple in the distance.

For families traveling with children, the advantage of taking a trip with Wagner is the opportunity to see the land—including Glacier National Park and its mountains, rising in the background as our tour ends—through the eyes of the Blackfeet. The journey becomes one of personal interchange—one that your kids are likely to remember for a long time.

"People want to know how we struggled," says Wagner, "and what makes us tick. Our elders always say, 'Teach the people who you are and what you stand for.' Well, we are a real people. I share our traditions so that we can educate people our way—a kind, civilized way."

TIPS: The best way to enjoy a trip with Curly Bear Wagner is to book a custom outing—for either half a day or a full day—of sites that will interest your family. The alternative is a long group tour, where your kids may find themselves stuck in the back of a 12-person van for hours. Bring your own picnic lunch, water, and binoculars for wildlife viewing.

The **Blackfeet Powwow** is held in Browning during the second week in July. The **North American Indian Days Celebration** takes place in Heart Butte during the second week of August.

BASICS: From the town of St. Mary—the eastern gateway to Glacier National Park and the entrance to the Blackfeet Reservation—the land changes dramatically: The park's serrate peaks and thick forests give way to rolling hills and scrub grass dotted with horses and cows. Browning, 32 miles south of St. Mary, serves as the hub of the Blackfeet Reservation. The town comprises the tribal headquarters, a hospital, a high school, the **Museum of the Plains Indian** (page 130), a gas station, and a smattering of stores.

Blackfeet Historical Tours *(406/338-2058)* charges $50 per adult *($25 for ages 6 to 15, free for kids under 5)* for its day-long group trips. Customized half-day tours start at $100 for adults and $25 for ages 6 to 15. For information on **Sun Tours,** see page 130.

Blackfeet Territory
Glacier National Park

Glacier National Park occupies United States territory. Its counterpart, **Waterton Park,** consists of land across the Canadian border. Both parks sit on the traditional hunting grounds of the Blackfeet—a confederacy made up of the Piegan, Blood, and Blackfeet tribes.

The history of the Blackfeet is both tragic and contentious. The Fort Laramie Treaty, signed in 1851, gave the Blackfeet and other tribes the right to roam parts of Montana north of the Missouri River and east of the Continental Divide. Treaties and negotiations in 1855, 1865, and 1868 further reduced the boundaries of the Blackfeet territory; in 1873 and 1874, President Ulysses S. Grant took back more Blackfeet land.

Deprived of their traditional grounds for hunting buffalo, hundreds of Blackfeet starved to death in the winters of the 1880s. Blackfeet leaders had no choice but to negotiate the Sweetgrass Hills Treaty, ratified in 1888, which exchanged land for desperately needed equipment and cattle. In 1891, the Blackfeet sacrificed even more land to the **Great Northern Railway.**

But the concessions had not ended yet. Around 1900, the federal government became convinced that the mountains on Blackfeet territory held rich lodes of precious minerals. They therefore pressured the Blackfeet into again selling land; according to the new treaty, however, the Blackfeet retained the right to log, hunt, and fish in these mountains. When the land turned out to be barren of minerals, conservationists led by George Bird Grinnell—editor of *Forest and Stream* magazine and a government negotiator for the Sweetgrass Hills Treaty—lobbied to preserve Glacier as a national park. Although the former Blackfeet territory became Glacier National Park in 1910, the Blackfeet maintain to this day that they hold treaty rights to the land.

Swiftcurrent Lake reflects the glory of Grinnell Point in Glacier National Park, Montana.

EXPLORE BLACKFEET CULTURE

Blackfeet artist Darrell Norman creates **customized Blackfeet cultural programs.**
Stay overnight in a tipi just down the hill from his house, or take part in a day program. In Norman's craft seminar, for example, you can learn enough about working with buckskin to turn out a fetish or fringed bag. On a longer stay, Norman
will teach you to make moccasins; he also arranges seminars in music, dance, and
other arts. Dinner is berry soup and roast buffalo or fried trout, followed by an
evening of conversation with Norman and the many locals who drop in.

TIPS: Most kids enjoy sleeping in tipis, but not all of them relish eating buffalo
meat; if such is the case with yours, request a kid-friendly meal ahead of time.

BASICS: Tipi stays at Norman's **Lodge Pole Pine Gallery and Tipi Village** *(P.O.
Box 1832, Browning. 406/338-2787)* cost $40 for the first person and $10 for each
additional person. Meals and seminars are extra. A six-hour art seminar for two
adults and two children costs $100 to $125. Other seminars by arrangement.

MORE MONTANE MONTANA

Glacier National Park *(406/888-7800. www.nps.gov/glac)* is one of the last strong-
holds of the grizzly in the conterminous states. About 300 of these giants roam the
park, along with 500 black bears. Consult park rangers before hiking; on the trail,
make noise to signal your approach. **Family programs** include summer nature hikes
led by guides from the **Glacier Institute** *(137 Main St., Kalispell. 406/755-1211.
www.digisys.net/glacinst)* on a moderate, 2-mile trail. The institute also sponsors
three- and five-day overnight ecology camps for ages 9 to 18.

MUSEUM OF THE PLAINS INDIAN, BROWNING

This relatively small museum has two main attractions: an exhibit of raw-hide shields, beaded saddle bags, and other clothing decorated with quills and beads and painted with pigments, and the **Northern Plains Craft Shop.** In addition to such child-friendly collectibles as dream catchers and buffalo pendants, the store sells some of the highest quality Native American work in the area.

"Everything in this shop has to be handmade by an Indian," says director Jackie Parsons, a Blackfeet member. "The pieces are bought outright from the artists, not sold on concession. This shop is about trying to entice younger people to keep their culture alive through their art."

The store represents some 150 Northern Plains artists, including Cheyenne, Sioux, Cree, Blackfeet, and Shoshone. It sells sculpture, hide paintings, parfleche bags, coup sticks, Blackfeet dolls, war shields, silver jewelry, and contemporary willow baskets, among other items.

Basics: **Museum of the Plains Indian** *(Hwys. 2 & 89, Browning. 406/ 338-2230. Adults $4, children 6-12 $1)*

Allow at least 2½ hours to drive the scenic 52 miles of **Going-to-the-Sun Road,** which crosses the Continental Divide. Other possibilities include splashing in **Lake McDonald**—the park's warmest and calmest lake—and taking a one-hour cruise on **Lake McDonald** or **St. Mary Lake.**

BASICS: Glacier National Park offers a variety of accommodations in addition to its campsites. **Glacier Park Lodge** in East Glacier, completed in 1914, boasts a three-story atrium lobby supported by pillars of centuries-old Douglas firs. Recent renovations have restored some of the lobby's grandeur; many of the rooms, though serviceable, remain plain. **Glacier Park Inc.** *(602/207-6000. www.glacierparkinc. com)* handles the lodge and other park accommodations.

The **St. Mary Lodge and Resort** *(Mont. 89 and Going-to-the-Sun Rd., .25 mile from St. Mary Visitor Center. 800/368-3689 or 208/726-6279)* offers motel rooms, cabins, modern cottages, a restaurant, supermarket, and gas station. Motel rooms cost about $115 at the height of the summer season. The **West Lodge** rooms *($108 double occupancy)* have heat only; the **East Lodge** rooms *($100 double occupancy)* have heat and air-conditioning. Each **Pinnacle Cottage** *(about $285 per night in summer)* features a kitchen, a living room with gas fireplace, two bedrooms, a bath, and a porch with views of the park. Don't miss the huckleberry pie at the restaurant, a favorite since Margaret Black opened the original Curly Bear Café (now defunct) in 1932.

Sun Tours *(800/786-9220. Adults $35 to $45, children under 12 $15),* a Blackfeet-owned company, offers bus tours of Glacier National Park. During the trips of six to eight hours, Blackfeet guides explain their history and traditions. Though informative, the outings do not include enough stops or activities for most kids.

Buffalo Tour
Moiese

The **People's Center** is a small museum with a big idea: Under the auspices of the center's Native Ed-Ventures, local guides offer tours of the **Flathead Reservation**—home to the Confederated Salish, the Kootenai, and the Pend d'Oreille tribes.

Like many other big ideas, this one is still being perfected. Our step-on guide—one who joins your car as a passenger—knew his history cold, and he escorted us to some family-friendly spots; in spite of all our protests, however, he insisted on showing us sights that held no interest. Be crystal clear, therefore, in specifying what you would like to see—or avoid. If grade-schoolers or teens are part of your group, request some activities; Native Ed-Ventures can arrange mountain biking, rafting, hiking, and fishing trips.

At the 1891 **St. Ignatius Mission,** we appreciated our guide's honest discussion of the mission system, which fed Native children food but starved them of their culture. We could have dispensed with the tour of bare and boring buildings, though. A compromise solution: Discuss mission schools in the car en route to the 18,500-acre **National Bison Range** in nearby Moiese. The advantage of going with a guide is that he or she can tell you buffalo tales while you admire these massive beasts of the plains. The guide will also answer questions.

If you visit the bison range on your own, you'll discover that there are two ways to see the almost 500 head of buffalo. With young children who are marginal car riders, drive the short loop (about 20 minutes), which gives glimpses of a few buffalo in pens. With older children, take the 19-mile-long, one-way drive through the range (about two hours). Along with buffalo roaming free, you'll see elk, antelope, and deer. The best times to sight bison are first thing in the morning (around 7 a.m., when the refuge opens) or on a summer evening around 7 p.m. The refuge closes at 9:30 p.m.

With advance notice, the center can arrange tours devoted to arts and crafts tours, mountain biking, hiking, or fishing.

TIPS: Doug Allard's **Indian Museum and Trading Post** *(US 93)* is cute, kitschy, and kid-friendly. We liked the huckleberry muffins and jam that Allard sells during the August huckleberry harvest.

BASICS: **Native Ed-Ventures** *(People's Center, Box 278, Pablo. 800/883-5344 or 406/883-5344. www.peoplescenter.org. tours@peoplescenter.org).* Price of a three-hour tour for a family of four averages $30 per person. **National Bison Range** *(132 Bison Range Rd., Moiese. 406/644-2211)*

Cheyenne Trailriders
Ashland

The sweet smell of burning tobacco mixed with the sound of ancient prayers being offered up to *Maheo Cheyenne*, the creator. Sitting in the shade of a pine tree and gazing at the pink buttes on the far side of the Tongue River, we could easily imagine the generations of women who came to these hills to forage for plants, their babies cooing in cradleboards set among the high grasses. Unspoiled by development, the land of the Cheyenne Indian Reservation has looked this pristine for centuries.

"The tobacco offering is for balance," explained Bently Spang, one of our guides (and a well-known artist; see pages 134-135) on this **Ethnobotany tour** sponsored by **Cheyenne Trailriders**. "We always give something back when we take something. This shows respect and shows we do not take too much."

After a few moments' searching, ethnobotanist Leo Spang—Bently's uncle—returned with a handful of plants. He passed around a root called Indian turnip, then peeled back the bark to show us the white meat inside. The Cheyenne eat the root raw, or boil it for use as a salve. Mint-scented man sage, normally used in sweat lodges, can be tossed in a campfire to ward off mosquitoes. Obeying Leo's directions to rub dry yellow flowers of the western yarrow between our fingers, we marveled at its camphor-like smell. (The Cheyenne use a mixture of yarrow flowers and leaves to stanch blood from a wound.) Warning us not to swallow, Leo next asked us to chew on black root—a natural echinacea that soothes toothaches. Leo learned this centuries-old lore as a boy, when he would accompany his grandmother on her medicinal walks through these hills.

As we rode back to the Spangs' house, the setting sun turned the brown hills crimson. A wild turkey flapped through a nearby grove, deer raced over a ridge, grasshoppers danced around the horses' hooves. This 440,000-acre reservation in southeast Montana, home of 6,000 Cheyenne, is a peaceful and healing place.

Cheyenne Trailriders is operated by Bently's parents, Zane and Sandra Spang. The outfit specializes in cultural workshops and personalized rides like the one described above. "There are so many stereotypes about Indian people," says Sandy. "We want others to see us as we are and what we are like today. We want to get away from images like the noble savage, the TV Indian, and drunken Indians."

Cheyenne Trailriders achieves this through its cultural programs—and through the good old-fashioned expedient of time spent together. After dining on Indian tacos, we sat on the patio watching the hills turn black and listening to melodies trilled by Jay Old Mouse, the flutemaker for the Cheyenne people. Taught by his grandfather Black Bear, Old Mouse today carves his own flutes from aromatic cedar.

"In the old days," Old Mouse recalled, "flutes were used for prayers and courting. The men would sit in the hills and play music from their heart." Old Mouse recounted the Cheyenne story of how the flute came to the Indian people:

All in the family: Bently Spang *(right)* and his cousin Bernice Anderson of Cheyenne Trailriders

Years ago, the way a young man gained recognition from his tribe was to hunt and fish. There was a young man who struggled in these areas. He was lonely. He wounded a bull elk but lost track of him. Sitting around the campfire, feeling down on himself, the man heard music. That calmed him. The next day he went hunting, killed the elk, and took the elk to his people.

The young man fasted and prayed in thanks. A woodpecker came to him and told him to follow. The man followed the woodpecker to an old tree with a hollow branch. The woodpecker was a carver. As the wind blew, the woodpecker spread his wings over the branch and played music. The woodpecker told the young man to take the wood back with him.

The tunes played by Old Mouse sounded rich and haunting in the night air. We felt connected to the surrounding woods and mountains. Despite a long day of travel, riding, and hiking, our group felt at peace in the moonlight, soothed by ancient melodies.

Old Mouse is typical of the artists, elders, and craftspeople who share their traditions with guests at Cheyenne Trailriders. "I want people to know that we are real," explained Old Mouse, "and that we live in two worlds. We have to provide and work—I'm a carpenter by trade—but we hang on to our traditions. I want people to respect and to learn—and, hopefully, to understand."

The Beginning of the End for the End of the Trail by Bently Spang, 1994

Admiring an intricately beaded Sioux buckskin dress, my daughter, Alissa—then just 6 years old—said to me, "I can't believe you get to wear something so beautiful every day." Through the dress, my daughter connected to a world in which the ordinary is extraordinary. She felt the spirit of a society in which, as she put it, "You could wear a party dress to the playground and use the good bowls every day."

For Alissa—as for many children—the first reaction to traditional Native American art is bedazzlement at the craftsmanship of ordinary objects. Taking time out to enjoy local works of art during your own family travels through Native America can therefore be richly rewarding.

Vines of blooming flowers adorn Salish cradleboards used to carry infants; rows of tiny porcupine quills delineate a warrior astride his horse on a Lakota storage bag. On the dress of a Seminole woman, strips of orange, green, pink, and blue patchwork alternate with bands of yellow, black, and red. A Crow belt is laced with rows of turquoise beads; a Cherokee split-cane basket is woven with stripes of green- and red-dyed reeds; a Pueblo pot features geometric black and white swirls.

Intriguingly, the Cheyenne and Blackfeet languages contain no special word for "art." According to Blackfeet artist Darrell Norman, "Art was an integrated part of your life. Everybody taught these art forms because art is a reflection of the world around us. It was a deep spiritual connection. In American and European traditions, art is for people who have money. As a Blackfeet, everything you did, you did in an artful way. When we needed things, we decorated them to be in harmony with the beauty of the earth. Respect for the earth and for objects translates into the care and craftsmanship of everyday objects."

A familiarity with Native American art can give kids and adults an understanding of modern issues as well as ancient ways. Bently Spang, a Northern Cheyenne sculptor whose works are on display in the Eiteljorg Museum of Indianapolis and the Heard Museum in Phoenix, sees art as a

Horse by Charles McLaughlin, 1992

healing tool: "It's restorative in terms of who you are as a Native person. Art can heal the grief that exists in the community over the genocide. Art helps rebuild self-respect in the community."

Some artists are raising the current resurgence of traditional art forms to a contemporary level. "Native art today is a complex field," says Spang. "Artists are expressing them-selves in everything from tradi-

Controlling Buffalo Territory by Al Chandler, 1997

tional beadwork and animal hides to highly contemporary forms utilizing video and cyber art. The unifying force is that they are all Native people expressing the experience of Native cultures in today's world. As such, Native-made artwork provides a unique opportunity for the viewer to gain accurate and profound insights into the Native expe-rience."

Three accomplished artists are profiled below, along with their thoughts on the works pictured here:

BENTLY SPANG *(P.O. Box 206, Ashland, MT 59003. bently@wtp.net):* "This piece uses the format of the Fisher Price busy box to teach people about Native stereo-types and contemporary Native issues. Each of the areas of the piece deals with a different stereotype or Native issue: The area titled 'Hand Out' speaks of the mis-conception that many people have about government support of Native people. I have been asked how much I get for my 'Indian check' numerous times—people assume I and other Indians get a check every month for 'being Indian.' The ques-tion gives me a chance to explain the treaty obligations of the U.S. government. The objects hanging at the bottom are scalps,

addressing the issue of scalping, introduced to Indians by Europeans. The 'Trinkets' area refers to the mainstream art world's opinion of Native art. I have heard contem-porary museum curators refer to Native art as 'just beads and trinkets.' I use the context of the child's toy to show just how ridiculous these stereotypes are."

CHARLES MCLAUGHLIN *(P.O. Box 295, Selfridge, ND 58568):* "*Horse* is a contem-porary version of a horse-dance stick. Tra-ditionally, horse effigies were made to show honor to a special horse—a horse who had been in battle and did great deeds with its owner, or a horse known for its special qualities such as running and endur-ance. Each stick was marked the same way the honored horse was marked."

Having grown up with horses, McLaugh-lin develops each piece using feelings he has for various horses in his life. He sees his art as a modern form of "special honoring."

AL CHANDLER *(Good Strike, P.O. Box 1038, Hays, MT 59417):* "I have my own styles and designs. I use bone paintbrushes, natural earth paints, and hide-scrapings for glue. By using this part of our culture, we are keeping it alive."

After the music, we headed back to our tipi, lay down on the earth, and fell asleep looking at the stars.

TIPS: The Spangs customize packages for individual families, so discuss your interests with them in advance. Minimum age for horseback rides is 8 years old. Wagon rides are also available. Programs are open to day guests who lodge elsewhere.

BASICS: Cheyenne Trailriders *(P.O. Box 206, Ashland, MT. 406/784-6150. cheytrider@mcn.net).* A typical overnight ride costs $250 per adult (horse fee, tent or tipi lodging, guide, and six meals included). The ethnobotany course on the trail is an additional $75 per person. Ask about family rates.

Little Bighorn Battlefield Crow Agency

For those with an interest in impartial accounts of Native American history, this National Park Service site may seem to lag a bit behind the times. Although protests prompted President George Bush to approve changing the name of the national monument from Custer Battlefield to **Little Bighorn Battlefield** *(406/638-2621)* in 1991, the place still overwhelmingly lauds and laments the lost cavalry—a curiosity, given that Lt. Col. George Armstrong Custer initiated the attack.

Neither the Native American guided tour of the battlefield nor the one led by park rangers can be considered kid-friendly; both tend to bog down in details of troop movements and battle tactics that appeal more to military historians than they do to families on vacation. Fortunately, visitors can get a poignantly clear idea of the action on that June day in 1876 simply by driving through the battlefield themselves.

About 267 cavalrymen died at Little Bighorn, says park superintendent Neil Mangum. "That number includes about 210 of Custer's men," he notes, "as well as those under Major Marcus Reno and Captain Frederick Benteen." On the battlefield today, 253 white marble markers (pages 138-139) identify the spots where these men fell in battle, but only two official markers—both made of red granite—honor the death sites of Custer's opponents. One marker, showing where Southern Cheyenne warrior Lame White Man was wounded, resulted from a lobbying campaign waged 82 years later by his grandson, John Stand In Timber. The second Native American marker stands where Noisy Walking, a Northern Cheyenne warrior, was killed in battle.

"Probably fewer than 40 [Native American] warriors died in this battle," estimates Mangum. Still, many visitors find it odd that a government historic site commemorates only one side of such a pivotal event. The disproportionate treatment is slated to be addressed with the dedication of an Indian memorial that will rec-

PROPHECY AND BATTLE: CHEYENNE HISTORY

Cheyenne prophet Sweet Medicine foretold the coming of the white man—and with him, the end of the buffalo and the start of deprivation. Several battles seemed to confirm his vision of struggle.

By the 1850s, the Cheyenne Nation had split into two tribes, easing the task of gathering sustenance from the land. The Northern Cheyenne roamed the Black Hills north of the Yellowstone River and the Bighorn Mountains, while the Southern Cheyenne settled along the Arkansas River in Colorado and into Oklahoma.

In the winter of 1864, a band of Southern Cheyenne led by Chief Black Kettle camped near Sand Creek, Colorado, awaiting the signing of a peace treaty. U.S. Cavalry troops under Col. John M. Chivington attacked the camp and killed more than 270 Cheyenne, the majority of them women and children. The Sand Creek massacre and another one four years later are defining events in the Cheyenne view of non-Natives.

Although the Fort Laramie Treaty of 1868 called for the government to respect Northern Cheyenne hunting grounds in exchange for building a railroad through Cheyenne lands, the 1874 discovery of gold in the Black Hills caused an influx of non-Natives. The Cheyenne and Lakota retaliated by raiding settlements. In December 1875, the commissioner of Indian Affairs ordered the tribes to return to the reservation before January 31, 1876—or be treated as hostiles. The Northern Cheyenne refused to go.

Lt. Col. George A. Custer set out to force the tribes to comply. On June 25, 1876, Custer attacked camps of Northern Cheyenne and Lakota under the leadership of Sitting Bull, Crazy Horse, and other war chiefs. The Battle of Little Bighorn—the best-known battle of the Plains Indian wars—wiped out Custer and his men.

"The Indians won a dramatic victory at the Little Bighorn," states a Park Service exhibit at the site, "but . . . within less than a decade they voluntarily returned to reservations or were forced to do so by the military. The Battle of Little Bighorn was their 'Last Stand' too."

ognize all the Native Americans—including the Crow scouts on Custer's side—who fought and died at Little Bighorn. The monument will feature a circular plaza surrounded by an earthen wall open to the four directions. From this Spirit Gate, battlefield pilgrims will be able to spot the U.S. Cavalry obelisk, gaining a clear view of the suffering that occurred on both sides.

Apsaalooke Tours *(406/638-2229)* offers one-hour guided bus tours of the battlefield that include frequent stops to walk this hallowed ground. Although the Apsaalooke guides are Crow Natives and students from nearby Little Bighorn College, the tours focus on battle logistics to the exclusion of Native perspective. (Sev-

Death-site markers indicate where U.S. Cavalry soldiers fell at the 1876 Battle of Little Bighorn.

eral Crow warriors served as scouts for Custer in the battle—a survival tactic for the Crow people at the time.) Tours may be reserved on site or in advance.

Custer's Last Stand Reenactment *(888/450-3577 or 406/665-3577. www.mcn.net/ ~custerfight. custerfight@mcn.net):* Every year on the weekend nearest the June 25th anniversary of the Battle of Little Bighorn, the town of Hardin presents a reenactment—complete with horses, soldiers, and warriors—narrated by a Crow tribal historian.

MORE CULTURAL TOURS

Museum without Walls, an outreach program of the Western Heritage Center in Billings, offers a variety of cultural day trips. On the **Deer Medicine Rocks Petroglyph Tour,** for example, participants view petroglyphs on Northern Cheyenne lands near Lame Deer. On a bus tour of the Crow Reservation, you can learn about Crow culture. The **Clark's Fork Bottom Rendezvous Camp Tour** allows you to travel back in time: Costumed interpreters show you how to make bows and arrows, set up lodges (tipis), and tan leather. (You might want to warn your kids that this last task involves urine and gobs of smashed brains.)

BASICS: **Museum without Walls** *(2822 Montana Ave., Billings. 406/256-6809. heritage@ywhc.org)* offers its tours at selected times from spring through autumn.

Little Bighorn College/Institute for Micro-Business and Tourism *(P.O. Box 370, Crow Agency, MT. 406/638-7211. Call for reservations):* The college offers an irregular schedule of cultural tours with Native guides to several Native American sites in the area, including Rosebud Battlefield and the Bighorn Mountains.

Custer Battlefield Museum: Frontier photographer David F. Barry's photos of Native Americans, on display in this small museum, put faces to such famous names as Sitting Bull and Buffalo Bill, making history more real for children. Barry traveled throughout the West in the 1870s and 1880s, taking candid and posed photos of Native Americans. The Lakota dubbed him *Icastinyanka Cikala Hanzi*—Little Shadow Catcher. In an 1884 photo, Sitting Bull wears a Western shirt, black braids, two feathers in his hair, and a look both regal and wise. The Custer Museum also has a good collection of artifacts, including Sitting Bull's only extant signature (it appears on the 1884 contract he signed to appear in Buffalo Bill's *Wild West Show).*
    BASICS: The **Custer Battlefield Museum** *(406/638-2000. May-Sept.)* is located on the site of Sitting Bull's camp, in the one-building town of Garryowen.

Wildlife Encounters
Yellowstone National Park

Track wolves, observe grizzly bears in their natural habitat, or travel through the canyons of Yellowstone National Park on a summer field course or horsepacking seminar sponsored by the **Yellowstone Association Institute.** Led by a naturalist guide, families can tour Yellowstone National Park while completing courses on everything from mammal tracking to photography. The institute even lets you visit paleontological sites to examine plant and animal fossils.

A guided family packhorse trip (beginning riders are welcome) generally covers three days and two nights. Riders travel the canyons and trails of Yellowstone while learning about the natural and human history of the area, including the record of the Native American tribes who first settled here. Kids enjoy the independence of packing their own horses and helping set up camp.

TIPS: These courses fill up fast, so reserve when registration opens in January. Unless you enroll in an overnight program, accommodations must be reserved separately.

BASICS: Field courses at the **Yellowstone Association Institute** *(P.O. Box 117, Yellowstone Nat'l Park. 307/344-2293. www.YellowstoneAssociation.org. dkline@Yellowstone. June-Aug. Minimum age: 8)* cost $30 to $60 per person per day.

ARE WE THERE YET?

Buffalo Bill Scenic Byway (US 14/16/20): President Theodore Roosevelt called this stretch of road—which runs from the east entrance of Yellowstone National Park to Cody, Wyoming—the "most scenic 52 miles in the United States." Because the landscape on either side of the highway has changed little since then, Roosevelt's sentiment is as true today as it was when he uttered it a century ago.

The drive parallels the Yellowstone River as it threads the **Shoshone National Forest** and the **Wapiti Valley.** Cottonwoods line the riverbanks and steep granite walls reflect the sunlight in **Shoshone Canyon,** where the road cuts through gorges surrounded by yellow and pink mesas, buttes, and bluffs with a range of evocative names: **The Slipper, Laughing Pig, Chimney Rock.** This is the West of pioneer treks and movie vistas, so keep an eye peeled for bison grazing along the road or bighorn sheep and elk clattering over the boulders.

Once you reach Cody, you can learn more Western lore at **Old Trail Town** *(US 14/16/20, 2 m. W of Buffalo Bill Historical Center. May-Sept. 307/587-5302),* a collection of more than 20 authentic late 19th-century log buildings. Inside, the weathered wood and simple furnishings create a haunting feel, recalling the West as it really was. You can also tour saloons, stores, and hideaways—including the

Hole in the Wall cabin where Butch Cassidy and the Sundance Kid plotted their escapades—as well as the **Trail Town Cemetery**, final resting place of pioneers and mountain men.

BASICS: Park County Travel Council *(836 Sheridan Ave., Cody. 800/393-2639 or 307/587-2297. www.pctc.org)*

ROLLING ON THE RIVER

Great blue herons, eagles, and moose are some of the wildlife you're likely to see on a dinner float trip down the Snake River through Grand Teton National Park. At day's end, sit down to a hot meal in camp and watch the sun set over the Tetons. **Barker-Ewing River Trips** *(Box 3032, Jackson, Wyo. 800/365-1800 or 800/448-4202. www.barker-ewing.com)*

GET BUFFALOED!

In Yellowstone, an excellent place to spot bison is the section of **Grand Loop Road** from Old Faithful to Mammoth Hot Springs—especially the area around **Gibbons Meadows.**

Afterward, experience the true Yellowstone by leaving your car behind and venturing into the wilderness. A hike or horseback ride of even half a mile will get you deep into the backcountry that has made Yellowstone world famous.

Basics: For Yellowstone activities, lodging, and tour information, contact **Amfac** *(307/344-7311. www.travelyellowstone.com).*

Buffalo Bill Center
Cody

This is the place to touch a bear claw, see a Winchester pearl-handled rifle, hear tall tales told by a U.S. Cavalry soldier, or sit on the floor of a Hidatsa earth lodge and listen to origin stories. For families interested in Western culture, the **Buffalo Bill Historical Center** in Cody is a must. The center's four museums, described below, feature interactive displays; in summer, live presentations occur throughout the day.

The **Whitney Gallery of Western Art** contains paintings, sculptures, and prints by "cowboy artist" **Charles M. Russell,** whose experiences as a wrangler brought such authenticity to his painting. Also included are works by **William Tylee Ranney,** whose depictions of everyday life on the American frontier formed the basis of public perception of the West in the early 1800s. An entire wing of the Whitney is devoted to the work of **Frederic Remington,** known for his active depictions of bucking broncos and the dangers of the open plains. After visiting Remington's studio, which was moved here from New Rochelle, New York, you can embark on a treasure hunt to find studio items in Remington's paintings.

The **Cody Firearms Museum** boasts the world's largest collection of American guns, as well as European arms dating back to the 16th century. In summer, muse-

Remington bronze, Buffalo Bill Cody Museum

um docent Joe Desson assumes the identity of Lt. William Winer Cooke, a 19th-century U.S. Cavalry soldier who died at Little Bighorn. In addition to discussing his weapons, Desson re-creates the world of the "blue shirts": He describes his uniform—an 1872 junior officer's fatigue blouse with mounted trousers and cavalry-style boots—and recounts some of the battle action he witnessed during the Civil War and the Indian Wars.

The third museum, dedicated to **William Frederick "Buffalo Bill" Cody,** brings to life not only the hunter, scout, and showman but the times in which he lived. On display are Cody's saddle, buffalo-hide coat, and a printing press he gave to the eponymous town of Cody in 1896. In summer, a master printer demonstrates the press in action—kids get to turn the wheel—while a saddler helps children design saddles and a cowgirl describes her life on a ranch in the late 1800s.

The **Plains Indian Museum** is home to one of the largest—and finest—collections of Plains Indian art and artifacts in the country. After renovation, the museum will reopen in June 2000 with interactive displays, Native story-tellers, and an earth lodge designed to show people how the non-nomadic Plains Indians lived. Also on display will be the museum's extensive collection of blankets, bow cases, clothing, banners, and other trappings of day-to-day existence.

TIPS: The Buffalo Bill Historical Center sponsors many special events. In April there is the **Cowboy Songs and Range Ballads** festival. June brings the **Plains Indian Museum Powwow** featuring drummers and dancers, while the **Frontier Festival** in July celebrates authentic frontier skills with a packhorse race and camp cook-off.

Pick up a copy of *Women in the Galleries* at the information desk; the guide is a great way to teach children about the critical roles women played in the West.

BASICS: Buffalo Bill Historical Center *(720 Sheridan Ave., Cody. 307/587-4771. www.bbhc.org)* is 52 miles from Yellowstone National Park's east gate.

Dinosaur Camp
Fruita

In the course of a **Family Dino Camp** hosted by the **Dinamation International Society,** campers get to examine real dinosaur fossils and learn what it's like to work a dig. They might even experience the thrill of unearthing a treasure that is millions of years old!

That's not such a remote prospect: During a Dinamation dig in the Colorado Canyon, a 13-year-old girl uncovered a rare dinosaur egg. This part of Colorado is rich in such finds because many dinosaurs once roamed the area, which was later buried in volcanic ash that preserved their bones as fossils. Afterward, the region underwent geologic uplift and erosion that exposed the fossil beds.

Even if they don't strike a bonanza in bones, dinosaur-loving youngsters will learn a great deal during one of these camps. On the first day, campers hike through Colorado's **Split Rock Dinosaur** area—probably a gigantic watering hole, at one time—to examine an *Apatosaurus* thigh bone as big as a man, plus the partial skull of a *Stegosaurus.* (Children can make rubbings of the bones.) The next day at **Cactus Park,** budding paleontologists get a vivid sense of the monstrous size of Jurassic-period meat eaters by walking in their footprints, left here 180 to 190 million years ago.

The **Dinosaur Discovery Museum** in Fruita features robotic dinosaurs that raise their heads to emit fierce roars. A favorite is the 20-foot-long *Dilophosaurus,* which spits out a stream of water. Kids can also examine a re-created dino heart or make dino tracks and rubbings.

During the camp's Lab Day, paleontologists show how to remove rock from bones and how to stabilize specimens using solvents and glues. Junior scientists create casts of dinosaur claws and teeth, which they can take home at week's end. On the final day of camp, adults dig for real fossils at the **Mygatt-Moore Dinosaur Quarry** while kids work nearby on buried replicas of finds.

Other expeditions, suitable for ages 13 and older, take dinosaur hunters on a two-day dig in the Colorado Canyons or a five-day dig in New Mexico.

TIPS: No special skills or background are required for these trips other than patience and curiosity, says paleontologist James Kirkland, a frequent trip leader. He encourages campers to read *Dinosaur Lives* by Jack Horner before arriving.

BASICS: Family Dino Camps *(800/344-3466. www.digdino.org. Adults $975, children 6 to 12 $575)* covering five nights and four days are available June through August. Canopies over the dig site provide a degree of shade, while fans help relieve the heat. Lodging is at the Grand Junction Holiday Inn.

History Mysteries
Crow Canyon

It takes patience to unearth an artifact buried for thousands of years, but kids usually prove equal to the task. Working calmly and carefully in the Colorado sun, they use centuries-old pottery shards to unravel history mysteries. Added to the thrill of touching something no one else has for 1,000 years is the excitement of solving puzzles from the past: How did the ancient Puebloans live? And what happened to them?

Every summer, dozens of families join the research team at **Crow Canyon Archaeological Center** at Shields Pueblo, a site that dates to A.D. 750. There, in the dramatic red-mountain landscape of the Mesa Verde region, parents and children in grades seven and above take part in a week-long excavation of ancient Anasazi communities.

Dedicated to longterm archaeological research on the Anasazi—or Ancestral Puebloans, as they are increasingly known—Crow Canyon digs have uncovered homes, public buildings, cooking vessels, and eating utensils. Few items are retrieved intact, but as Crow Canyon staff are fond of reminding volunteers, "It's not what you find—it's what you find out." On these programs, what parents and children find out together often amounts to quite a lot.

Crow Canyon's **Family Excavation Program** begins on Sunday evening with dinner and an introductory program. Families settle into their Navajo-style log cabins, or hogans, and meet other participants. Most days begin with a 7:30 breakfast; the programs get under way an hour later. Lunch is in the field or on the center's campus. Participants return to the campus by 5 p.m.

On Monday, the entire group learns basic archaeological concepts and tours the excavation site (about 15 miles from campus). The activities of the next three days, by contrast, are geared to specific ages:

On Tuesday, adults and high-school students spend the day in the lab, learning to identify ceramic pot shards, stone tools, and other artifacts likely to be encountered in the field. They are also taught how to wash recently excavated items, then analyze and catalog them. Middle-school students (ages 11 to 14) take part in a simulated dig to learn excavation techniques.

Adults and high-school students begin their field work on Wednesday. Archaeologists instruct class members in the proper use of a trowel and the best way to ensure a level digging space with plumb walls. Armed with a whisk broom (for dusting around large pieces), clipboard (for recording details of found objects), mesh tray (for sifting sand), and bucket (to catch excavated dirt), each participant is assigned a patch of 10 square feet. It's hot work—temperatures may rise into the 90s—but there's plenty of water on hand and a shaded area for resting.

Left: Driving home a point during a Family Dino Camp run by Dinamation International Society

If you uncover an item, the staff archaeologist puts it in a paper bag labeled with the date, site number, patch location, and level at which the piece was found. At day's end, the bag and others like it are taken to Crow Canyon's laboratory, where technicians wash and analyze the item, then enter its details into a database for further analysis. Eventually, your small discovery becomes part of the site's larger record, expanding our understanding of the people who inhabited the pueblo.

For middle-school students, Wednesday starts with half a day's lab work, followed by half a day in the field with the other students. "Middle-school kids learn a lot more and enjoy themselves more when they're only spending half a day at a time at the dig," explains research archaeologist Kristin Kuckelman.

On Thursday morning, families reunite for an ecology hike in the surrounding area—a chance to learn how the Ancestral Puebloans used plants for food, shelter, clothing, medicine, and religious ceremonies. Visitors tour a replicated pit house and find out how the Puebloans used juniper trees to build houses.

Staff archaeologists lead the group on a site tour of **Mesa Verde National Park** on Friday. With these knowledgeable professionals on hand, you'll be able to discover why people built there, how they lived, and what forced them to migrate, leaving it all behind. Friday evening's "graduation" ceremony features presentations of commemorative gifts to participants, giving the Crow Canyon staff a chance to thank families for their participation in the dig. Families curious about how their dig turned out can look up the reports on Crow Canyon's website.

For families with younger children or those unable to take a multiday trip, Crow Canyon has day programs every Wednesday and Thursday from June through September: Families with children 5 and older participate in an introductory program about archaeological excavation and the Ancestral Pueblo culture, then visit the dig and have lunch.

To savor the visual and archaeological wonders of the Four Corners region without going anywhere near a trowel and sieve, **National Geographic Expeditions** and Crow Canyon offer the **Four Corners Family Adventure:** This eight-day summer excursion, led by Crow Canyon's Kristin Kuckelman and her son Levi, includes rafting, riding horses on the buttes of Monument Valley, visiting Hopi mesas, and exploring cliff dwellings.

TIPS: Participants need to be in good physical condition for all trips. Those who register early—generally by the December before the program—may qualify for a discount. For the **Four Corners** trip, children must be at least 9 years old.

Throughout the week, evening programs focus on rock art (pictographs), stargazing (bring your own scope), and taking in the quiet grandeur of the desert canyon. If your family likes its nightlife well, livelier, the town of Cortez is 4 miles away.

BASICS: The **Crow Canyon Family Excavation Program** *(23390 Road K, Cortez. 800/ 422-8975 or 970/565-8975. www.crowcanyon.org)* costs $875 for adults and $675 for ages 12 through 18, plus a $75 family membership. Day programs cost $50 for adults and $25 for ages under 18.

Sling meets arrow: A student learns to use an atlatl to throw a spear at Crow Canyon Center.

Artistic Adventure
Anderson Ranch Arts Center

This might be the place where your 6-year-old discovers her gift for making masks or your 12-year-old finds out that photography can be a way to express what he's feeling. At the **Anderson Ranch Arts Center,** children ages 6 to 15 get hands-on experience in a wide range of studio arts: sculpting, painting, and making everything from pottery to toys to puppets. Adults, meanwhile, can draw on their own artistic side by painting or by creating collages, silk screens, prints, or digital photographs.

Self-expression and exploration are encouraged, and commitment is a necessity. Though children need not be artistic prodigies to attend, they must be willing to try hard. "Creative, flexible thinking is a skill our students will need all their lives," explains Susan Casebeer, Children's Program Director at Anderson Ranch. "For us, the process is far more important than the product. What does creativity mean? Where does it come from? Even very young children like to talk seriously about artists: What was the artist trying to say within this painting or sculpture?"

Despite these sobersided expectations, there is still lots of room for kids who just want to have fun. Young grade-schoolers learn how to make and illustrate their own books. They also discover the art of other cultures and are challenged to find parallels between seemingly disparate worlds: Can you imagine Mona Lisa

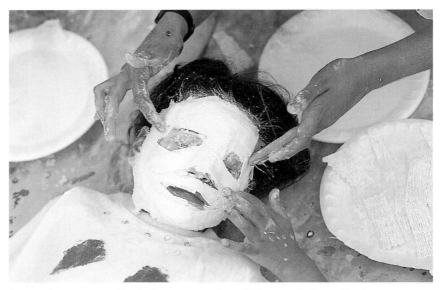

Face masks—not mummification!—are among the activities at an Anderson Ranch arts camp.

wearing braces? Which objects would an Egyptian mummy be buried with today?

Nor are students confined to classrooms. In a class devoted to making stick furniture, for example, teens spend their first day in—where else?—the forest, sitting on logs and sketching designs. The students gather the materials they will need to make a stool, chair, or small table. Back on campus, they learn to master the handsaws, drills, pruning shears, and other tools required to assemble the pieces.

TIPS: Anderson Ranch is also known for its **summer workshops** (for both children and adults) taught by noted artists. Families stay in condominiums near the campus. Parents can enroll in classes or—while their kids enjoy half-day or full-day art sessions—they can skip summer school to hike, fish, mountain bike, or river raft in the area surrounding Snowmass Village and Aspen.

Anderson Ranch also offers programs for children with special needs. Working with other nonprofit organizations such as Challenge Aspen, Anderson Ranch provides an environment where children with physical and/or emotional disabilities are able to express themselves through collages, photography, and word games. This is a morning program, coupled with afternoon activities such as horseback riding provided by Challenge Aspen.

BASICS: Students at Anderson Ranch are divided into three age groups: 6 to 8, 9 to 12, and 12 and older (the age groups vary with the subject of each class). The two younger age groups attend half-day classes only, while the teens attend full-day sessions. Classes are limited to 14 students and are staffed by a faculty member and a full-time adult assistant.

The **Anderson Ranch Arts Center** *(P.O. Box 5598, 5263 Owl Creek Rd., Snow-mass Village. 970/923-3181. www.andersonranch.org)* charges $100 to $200 tuition for children's workshops. Tuition for one- or two-week adult workshops ranges from $400 to $1,000.

Denver Museum of Natural History

On a walk along a creek bed from the Cretaceous period at the **Prehistoric Journey** exhibit of the **Denver Museum of Natural History,** crickets chirp, water flows, and dinosaurs roar in the background. Known for its "enviro-ramas"—dioramas that create an immersion experience—the museum eliminates glass barriers and creates multisensory experiences in their place.

Real fossils, dinosaur skeletons, and a reconstruction of "Lucy"—otherwise known as *Australopithecus afarensis,* the human ancestor believed to represent the transition from apes to *Homo sapiens* approximately 3.2 million years ago—add to the exhibit's effectiveness in portraying the evolution of life on Earth. Prehistoric Journey ends at a working fossil lab: Here a camera projects magnified images of specimens onto a television monitor, allowing visitors to watch scientists prepare fossils.

In two of the six dioramas depicting the wildlife of Botswana, zebras, water hogs, baboons, and a greater kudu cluster around a Savuti watering hole, while a cheetah pursues fleeing antelopes. At **Edge of the Wild**—an enviro-rama devoted to Colorado wildlife—visitors can listen to an elk bugle, a bison grunt, and a mountain lion cry. Young children can stand toe-to-toe with the latter creature; older ones can use computers to learn about wildlife management.

Inside the **Egyptian Mummies** exhibit, CAT scans reveal secrets of the mummification process as well as details about the skeletons of cats, birds, and human beings inside. Learn how CAT scans and x-rays led experts on the museum staff to conclude that one mummy is that of a rich woman while another had lived a life of poverty.

At the **Hall of Life,** plug your magnetic Life Card into various stations to create your own personal health profile containing statistics about your height, weight, blood pressure, flexibility, and endurance. With a simulator that shows how perception and coordination become impaired as the alcohol content of blood goes up, Hall of Life also gives parents an ideal opportunity to introduce teenagers to the negative effects of drinking.

Other highlights of a visit to the Denver Museum of Natural History include the facility's IMAX theater, its collection of about a dozen dinosaur skeletons, and its array of 2,500 gems and minerals—among them "Tom's Baby," a 102 troy-ounce nugget that is the largest piece of gold ever discovered in the state.

An *Allosaurus* attacks a *Stegosaurus* at the Denver Museum of Natural History.

The museum offers several programs for families to enjoy together. Half-day **Parent-Child Workshops** center on such museum specialties as anthropology and health sciences. In **Awesome Amazon,** for example, families with children in grades one through five can take an imaginary trip to the Amazon River basin, witnessing the sights and sounds of the people and animals who live in the world's largest tropical rain forest. **Family camp-ins,** held on weekends, offer crafts and mini-classes followed by a special tour of an exhibit or a visit to the **Denver Zoo** next door. Each family bunks down in the museum, then awakes to breakfast and an IMAX show.

TIPS: Use the museum's website to plot your visit in advance: Key in the number of people in your family, their ages and interests, and how much time you have, then print out a detailed plan of where to go and what to do based on your family profile. The **Gates Planetarium** is closed for renovation until 2001.

BASICS: The **Denver Museum of Natural History** *(2001 Colorado Blvd. 800/925-2250 or 303/322-7009. www.dmnh.org)* is located in Denver's City Park, next to the Denver Zoo. **Parent-child workshops** range from $25 to 36 per person, while **family camp-ins** cost $25 per person.

Ocean Journey Denver

Turn a corner and meet two Sumatran tigers, or watch an archerfish knock insects out of the air by spitting a jet of water from its mouth. These are some of the creatures on hand at **Ocean Journey**—a $93-million aquarium, opened in 1999, that traces the paths of rivers on opposite sides of the world. The two watercourses in question are the Colorado River, which starts out as meltwater streams high in the Rocky Mountains before winding its way to Mexico's Sea of Cortez, and the Kampar River in Sumatra, which rises in an Indonesian rain forest and flows 300 miles to the South China Sea.

Ocean Journey's strategy is a long way from static tanks of fish: Instead, the facility aims to immerse visitors in the aquarium experience by re-creating various watery environments. To accomplish this, Ocean Journey has installed floor-to-ceiling acrylic windows in 90 percent of its exhibit space. It presents land animals as well as aquatic ones, and it has barred high-tech, hands-on gadgets from its galleries on the principle that computers sitting in tropical rain forests are not the height of realism.

You can start your visit at either of the two river journeys. Before setting out, however, request a copy of the *Field Guide* in the lobby of the aquarium; the guide's beautiful illustrations and simply stated text come in handy as you stroll.

The **Colorado River Journey** begins with **Birthplace of Rivers** (the Continental Divide), an open area featuring a waterfall and 50-foot-high ceilings with skylights. Aquariums on both sides of the path feature native varieties of trout—among them the greenback cutthroat, the state fish of Colorado.

The air grows warmer as you enter the exhibit titled **Where Land and Water Meet**; in addition to trout, perch, and sunfish, you'll probably spot North American river otters and ducks. Children can touch replicas of animal skulls and see a beaver dam.

Canyon River takes visitors through cinnamon-colored canyons of sandstone containing tanks of humpback chub, Colorado pike minnow, and razorback sucker, not to mention tiger salamanders and boreal toads. More amphibians can be found at **River Discovery**, an interactive table where video microscopes give visitors a close-up view of leopard frogs.

The waters of the Colorado River pool into a deep lake in **Wild River Tamed**, the place to examine fossilized sea creatures such as the mosasaur—a prehistoric marine reptile—embedded in the walls of Glen Canyon. Turn the corner into **River of Life**, where the Colorado River meets the desert, and you'll find yourself face-to-face with a 2,500-gallon flash flood caused by a violent rainstorm.

Finally, the Colorado flows into the **Sea of Cortez**: On a beach bearing the bleached bones of a gray whale, turtle eggs incubate in the sand and shorebirds such as the American avocet forage for food. A walk through the exhibit's acrylic tube surrounds you with spotted eagle rays, moray eels, and many schooling fish. (Check for daily feeding times.)

To take the virtual **Indonesian River Journey,** aquarium visitors enter a cave and emerge in the **Endless Emerald Forest**—a re-creation of the Barisan Mountains of Sumatra, home to such exotic marine life as tiger barbs and the red-tailed shark. The aquarium could not acquire a living specimen of the endangered Malaysian rafflesia, the largest flower in the world, so it fabricated one on the spot: You'll find it "growing" on the forest floor, replete with blossoms 3 feet in diameter and the flower's distinctive fragrance of rotting meat.

The **Jungle Oasis** exhibit houses a pair of Sumatran tigers, named Bali and Java to honor two subspecies of Indonesian tiger that are now extinct. (The third subspecies, the Sumatran, is critically endangered.) **River's End** boasts a mangrove tree—the only variety that can live in salt water—and the upside-down jelly, whose top lies on the sandy river bottom while its tentacles reach toward the sunlight. Look for archerfish among the mangrove roots.

The **Coral Lagoon** features hermit crabs, blue-spotted jawfish, princess damsel, and scores of other fish. **Depths of the Pacific,** where the Kampar River reaches its journey's end in the South China Sea, contains a dazzling variety of fish and other marine life.

Bring your own journey to an end at **Sea Otter Cove,** where a pack of otters unable to survive in the wild have found a new home. The otters use rocks to crack open abalone and other shellfish—an advanced use of tools that few other marine animals have mastered. At the **Otter Cart,** kids can examine casts of the mammals' webbed and clawed feet, and feel their dark brown fur.

TIPS: Family overnights are likely to start by summer 2000.

BASICS: Ocean Journey Aquarium *(US West Park, 700 Water St., Denver. 303/561-4450. www.oceanjourney.org)*

MORE DENVER DOINGS

Black American West Museum and Heritage Center, the Dr. Justina Ford House *(3091 California St. 303/292-2566; www.coax.net/people/lwf/bawmus.htm)*: Discover African-American contributions to the West through oral histories of black wranglers, miners, and entrepreneurs.

United States Mint *(320 W. Colfax Ave. 303/844-3582. www.usmint.gov)*: Find out how those pennies in your pocket were shaped and stamped. The free tours are popular, so join the line in the morning.

Denver Zoo *(2300 Steele St. 303/376-4800. www.denverzoo.org)*: See primates, penguins, Komodo dragons, and more than 680 additional species at this 75-acre zoo. The **Children's Kraal,** open in warm weather, has pygmy goats to pet and performances by storytellers and musicians.

ILLINOIS

INDIANA

OHIO

PENNSYLVANIA

MISSOURI

MD.

WEST
VIRGINIA
• Elkins
⊛Charleston

Arlington• ⊛■ Washington, D.C

VIRGINIA

BERKELEY & SHIRLEY
PLANTATIONS

WINTERGREEN ■

Louisville•
⊛ Frankfort

KENTUCKY

Richmond■ Williamsburg
Petersburg• ■□YORKTOWN
JAMESTOWN Norfolk

OKLAHOMA

OZARK FOLK
CENTER ■ •Mountain
STATE PARK   View

Nashville• ⊛

GREAT SMOKY MTS.
NAT. PARK

Weaverville•
Asheville•

NORTH
CAROLINA

⊛ Raleigh

ARKANSAS

TENNESSEE

Bryson City•

⊛Charlotte

Cape
Hattera

Memphis•

Chattanooga•

CHEROKEE I.R.

CHIMNEY
ROCK PARK

⊛Little Rock

• Huntsville

BILTMORE
ESTATE

Columbia
•

Cape Fear

TEXAS

□CRATER OF
DIAMONDS
STATE PARK

MISSISSIPPI

ALABAMA

• Birmingham

⊛ Atlanta

GEORGIA

SOUTH
CAROLINA

Charleston
•

LOUISIANA

⊛ Jackson

Montgomery ⊛

Savannah
•

OKEFENOKEE
NATIONAL
WILDLIFE
REFUGE

Baton Rouge ⊛

• Mobile

STEPHEN C.
FOSTER
STATE PARK

• Folkston

ATLANTIC

• New Orleans

Mississippi
River Delta

Cape San Blas

⊛ Tallahassee

FLORIDA

Jacksonville

OCEAN

Orlando
•

Cape Canaveral

St. Petersburg•
• Tampa

GULF OF MEXICO

Tampa Bay

Lake
Okeechobee

W. Palm Beach
•

Clewiston•

Palm Beach
•

CORKSCREW SWAMP
SANCTUARY ■

□ BIG CYPRESS SEMINOLE I.R.
■ MICCOSUKEE I.R.

COLLIER-SEMINOLE STATE PARK ■

• Miami

EVERGLADES
NAT. PARK

Homestead
•

BAHAMAS

Duck Key
•

Florida Keys

□ Point of Interest

0   100 mi

0   150 km

MEXICO

CUBA

Colonial Life
Williamsburg

With an air of importance, the bewigged gentleman wearing a waistcoat rushed past my daughter Alissa, then 6. He nodded politely, peering at her from behind his spectacles; she smiled, a bit perplexed. She giggled when a woman in a bonnet and hoop skirt broad as a barn wished us "G'day" and asked if we had stocked up on candles. We came upon a group of girls wearing long cotton dresses and playing quoits (a version of horseshoes) on the **Palace Green.** Alissa watched excitedly, then begged for a dress like theirs. In negotiations that seemed as protracted as the ones preceding the Boston Tea Party, my husband and I persuaded her to settle for a white cap with a ribbon, sealing wax, and a gingerbread cookie. After all, a shilling saved was a shilling earned—especially in these uncertain times of British taxation and trade blockades.

The setting was **Colonial Williamsburg,** a 173-acre living history museum with 88 original buildings and hundreds of homes, businesses, and public buildings (many constructed on the original foundations). At the time of the Revolutionary War, Williamsburg was the capital of Virginia—England's oldest, largest, and richest colony. In the 1770s the town bred independent politics and attracted radicals such as Thomas Jefferson and Patrick Henry. You can get to know these important personages and other townspeople by paying a visit to the area. The clash between their 18th-century world and ours makes for a lively, always interesting trip through time. As a result, Colonial Williamsburg is a place you will want to visit often; what you do there will depend on the time of year and on the ages and interests of your children.

The best way to make the most of a visit and to see beyond the area's commercialism is to take part in special programs. More than two dozen programs, some of which are available only in summer, are designed especially for children and their families. Check the "Visitor's Companion," available at the ticket outlet, for schedules and locations.

Enslaving Virginia is a program that offers parents an opportunity to talk with their children about racial prejudice and the injustices of slavery. Reenactments occur throughout the town: You might observe a free African American speaking out against slavery, watch slaves being forcibly returned to their masters, or hear masters discussing slavery and the economy.

On page 153: The U.S. Space Academy in Huntsville, Alabama, gets a thumbs-up from a camper.

 WILDLIFE ENCOUNTER    CULTURAL EXPLORATION   LEARNING ESCAPE

Don't fire 'til you see the whites of their uniforms: Historical reenactors at Colonial Williamsburg

Alissa, on a visit at age 9, found the idea of enslaved children too frightening to think about. When she was 13, however, she was willing to spend a morning at **Carter's Grove,** a 17th-century plantation 8 miles from the historic area. The tour of the manor house bored us, but the re-created slave quarters gave us insight.

Especially recommended for families with children younger than 12, Colonial Williamsburg's **Remember Me** is an evening spent with an older slave named Paris, who recalls his home in Africa, his enslavement, and the ways that he and his fellow slaves preserved their culture and their spirit.

Visitors may also follow several African-American characters through their day, sharing their experiences. (Some parts of the program may be too harsh for very young children.) For more information, ask for the "African-American Program Schedule" at the ticket outlet.

Also powerful is a visit to the **Geddy House.** On a rare break from cooking, weeding, scrubbing, washing, and spinning, Grace—one of Miz Elizabeth's slaves—had time to chat when we were there. When we asked about her husband, Grace said, "Will and I jumped the broom, but he ran away out west because the master was going to sell him south." When we inquired about her children, she replied that she worried the master might sell Christopher, age 9. She hoped to convince Mr. Geddy of Christopher's usefulness in Geddy's foundry. Then Grace leaned toward me, telling me Miz Elizabeth demands rosemary be sprinkled on the floors to get rid of odors. "But that's a waste of good rosemary. So after I sweeps up the floor, I use the rosemary to make Miz Elizabeth's tea," she confided with a sly smile.

With **Order in the Court,** take part in reenactments of county and city sessions held at the Courthouse. Only white Protestant males who are over 21 and own land may be jurors, but other people can join the fun as plaintiffs, defendants, and witnesses. **The Subject Is Murder: Williamsburg's Most Wanted,** an evening program held in the candlelit courthouse, relives some of the most dramatic cases of colonial history.

Girls and boys alike are welcome at a **Military Encampment,** where they learn to lunge with a bayonet, present arms (with sticks, not muskets), and assist in cleaning a cannon. In **Bill & Betsy's Pirate Adventure,** kids help Bill, Betsy, and the gang rescue Granny Epps from a band of pirates. Families can help brickmakers knead clay, which is molded into bricks at the brickyard, and join a bucket brigade for a demonstration of Williamsburg's 18th-century fire engine.

For daughters who have a Felicity doll from the American Girls Collection, the **Felicity in Williamsburg** tour is a must. Mothers and daughters learn "courtesies" (curtsies), and a visit with Miss Manderly, Felicity's teacher, includes sewing, dancing lessons, and tea.

WINTERGREEN RESORT

A Blue Ridge mountain ski area sprawled across nearly 11,000 acres, Wintergreen offers summer nature programs for children, along with activities such as rock climbing, golf, boating, and horseback riding. In **Q.U.E.S.T** programs, a nature camp for ages 6 through 14, naturalists take kids creek stomping, animal tracking, and hiking to look for bees, beavers, snakes, frogs, and other woodland creatures. With **Junior Explorers,** an outdoor adventure day camp for ages 9 through 14, preteens and teens hike, canoe, rock climb, and rappel.

Basics: Two-bedroom condos begin at $250 per night. *(800/266-2444. www.wintergreenresort.com)*

If you have only a weekend, be sure to dine the first night at one of the **colonial taverns** to get into the spirit of the place. (Make your reservations when you book your lodging.) Even though the entrees are more adequate than memorable, the wooden, candlelit tables and the costumed wait staff helped transport us back 200 years. Sampling such 18th-century southern staples as spoon bread, Carolina fish muddle (a stew), and peanut pie is fun. For the less adventuresome, kids menus offer hamburgers, fried chicken, and other familiar fare.

Find time to walk along **Duke of Gloucester Street,** where you'll meet historical characters, shopkeepers, and tradesmen. The **Governor's Palace** is the place to see colonial life at its most elegant, while on the Palace Green kids may take part in hoop rolling, lawn bowling, and other games.

TIPS: Ask about packages. In summer, Williamsburg often offers special lodging and admission fares in combination with other area attractions. **Learning Weeks in Archaeology** *(800/603-0948)* is a program that offers participants hands-on experience in excavating important sites in and near the Historic Area.

BASICS: Colonial Williamsburg *(Williamsburg. 800/447-8679 or 757/220-7645. www.colonialwilliamsburg.org)*

Jamestown Settlement

It's only about a 10-mile drive along the Colonial Parkway from Colonial Williamsburg to **Jamestown: the Original Site** (formerly known as Jamestown National Historical Park). Make the drive, though, and you travel back to 1607, when the first permanent English settlement in the New World was established. You can see the ruins of the original colony, view excavated objects in the Visitor Center, and learn about current projects to unearth more artifacts. With **Pinch Pot**—a 20-minute, ranger-guided summer program—children make their own pots while learning about the importance of pottery to both the English settlers and the area's Powhatan Indians.

At neighboring **Jamestown Settlement,** a living history museum, you can visit a re-created **Powhatan Indian Village,** replicas of three ships—including the *Susan Constant*—which brought early settlers to the area, and **James Fort.** Aboard the *Susan Constant,* try reading latitude with an astrolabe, see what "crowded quarters" really means, and learn about the harrowing 144-day journey that colonists once made across the Atlantic Ocean.

TIPS: **Jamestown Landing Day** is celebrated in May with sailing demos and food.

BASICS: **Jamestown Settlement** *(888/593-4682. wwwhistoryisfun.org)*

Yorktown Battlefield and Victory Center

At **Yorktown Battlefield,** the 1781 site of the last significant battle of the Revolutionary War, sign up for one of the popular ranger programs, such as **Artillery Demonstrations.**

Among the most lively exhibits for children at the **Yorktown Victory Center** are the **Children's Kaleidoscope,** discovery room, and the **Witnesses to Revolution** gallery. In the children's area, kids can try on 18th-century clothing, copy from a hornbook, and make rubbings of woodcuts. In the gallery, "eyewitness" accounts of war stories rivet young listeners: Hear an American soldier from Rhode Island complain about the deep snow and his constant hunger, or listen to Mohawk chief Tigoransera counsel his people to stay out of a white man's war.

TIPS: On October 21-22, 2000, Yorktown celebrates the October 19th victory over the British, with Revolutionary War reenactors holding a weekend encampment.

BASICS: **Colonial National Historical Park** *(757/898-2410. www.nps.gov/colo)*

Two barques at Jamestown, the *Susan Constant* (left) and *Godspeed,* evoke early Atlantic crossings.

includes **Jamestown: The Original Site** *(757/229-1733),* **Yorktown,** the **Colonial Parkway,** and the **Cape Henry Memorial,** which marks the place where settlers first landed near Yorktown. **Yorktown Battlefield** *(757/898-2410)* is located at the easternmost point of the Colonial Parkway. **Yorktown Victory Center** lies 12 miles from Williamsburg *(Old Rte. 238 and Colonial Parkway. 757/253-4838).* Contact the **Jamestown-Yorktown Foundation** *(888/593-4682 or 757/253-4838. www.historyisfun.org).*

JAMES RIVER PLANTATIONS

The waterfront plantations along the James River reveal how some of the most prosperous people lived in the English colonies of the New World. Children are frequently awed by the long, tree-lined drives and the landscaped terraces with their expansive views of the river. The houses are worth seeing, but a little bit of "Don't touch the antiques!" goes a long way with most kids. For families who are pressed for time but want to visit at least one of the plantations, the best bets are the following:

Berkeley Plantation was the home of Benjamin Harrison, a signer of the Declaration of Independence, and William Henry Harrison ("Tippecanoe"), the ninth president of the United States; the site of the distillation of the first bourbon whiskey in America; and the place where "Taps" was composed while Union troops occupied the property during the Civil War. The gardens in the spring and summer are especially beautiful. Find the 1726 date stone over a side door; it shows the original owners' initials, separated by a heart.

SOLDIERING IN THE CIVIL WAR

Listen to the words of a Civil War soldier—your new buddy—via a compact disc player at the **National Museum of the Civil War Soldier** in **Pamplin Historical Park,** Petersburg. Learn how difficult it was to fight on foot during the war. A 13-year-old drummer boy serves as the "soldier comrade" for kids. As you visit the gallery, the boy's own words, taken from diaries and letters, add emphasis to the artifacts and the re-created settings.

In **Trial by Fire,** a simulated battle, you're assaulted by the sound of bullets piercing the air and by the screams of the wounded. **A Soldier's Fate** includes a video about amputation on the battlefield, and it is perhaps much too realistic for children under the age of 7. At the **Military Encampment** find out how soldiers cleaned their guns; watch a cook prepare a meal for several hundred men; or ask the camp's doctor how he performed surgery while a battle raged.

Special programs are available for children. At supervised **day camps** held every Wednesday in summer, kids drill like real soldiers, try on kid-size uniforms, and learn more about the soldier's life. With **See the Civil War & End with a Rebel Yell,** kids tour the museum and the park, visit **Shirley Plantation** (*see below*) for lunch, and end the day with a run on the Rebel Yell roller coaster at **Paramount's Kings Dominion.**

Basics: **Pamplin Historical Park** *(6125 Boydton Plank Rd. 877/726-7546 or 804/861-2408. www.pamplinpark.org)* is located 30 miles south of Richmond.

BASICS: Berkeley Plantation *(12602 Harrison Landing Rd., Charles City. 804/829-6018. www.berkeleyplantation.com)*

Shirley Plantation, the oldest plantation in Virginia, was founded in 1613, but construction of the present house wasn't begun until 1723. Robert E. Lee's mother, Ann Hill Carter, was born and raised here, and the plantation has played host to eight U.S. Presidents over the years. The current residents are direct descendants of the original families (Hill and Carter); occasionally the owners can be seen about the place, overseeing the farm chores.

BASICS: Shirley Plantation *(501 Shirley Plantation Rd. Charles City. 800/232-1613 or 804/829-5121. www.shirleyplantation.com)*

Additional information on the James River plantations can be obtained at the **Hopewell Visitor Center** *(201-D Randolph Sq., Rte. 10, Hopewell. 804/541-2461. www.jamesriverplantations.org or www.jamesriverplantations.com)*. Contact the **Petersburg Visitor Center** *(Old Market Square, Petersburg. 804/733-2400)* for more information about the Civil War.

Qualla Boundary Cherokee Reservation

Although the town of Cherokee can seem overcommercialized, the reservation near the southern entrance of Great Smoky Mountains National Park includes some of the most beautiful scenery in the United States. You'll discover woods, mountains, and three rivers—the Oconaluftee, the Tuckasegee, and the Nantahala—cutting through about 56,000 acres.

Visitors take advantage of plentiful fishing opportunities: Some 30 miles of streams are stocked with brown, brook, and rainbow trout. (In 1990, the state record for a brown trout—15 pounds, 2 ounces—was set on this reservation.) There are also three trout ponds located on **Big Cove Road.**

Hike along mountain trails through lush forests to scenic overlooks and waterfalls. If you prefer an easy woodland walk, try the path from the boundary line along the **Oconaluftee River** for about 1.5 miles to the **Mountain Farm Museum,** a sample pioneer farmstead. Another easy hike leads from Big Cove Road about 6 or 7 miles from downtown Cherokee to 200-foot-high Mingo Falls, one of the state's loveliest waterfalls. **Smokemont Riding Stable** offers a horseback ride to the falls, as well as a variety of guided rides lasting from an hour to all day. You can float down the river from the campgrounds to Cherokee, a 6- or 7-mile trip, using tubes or inflatable kayaks called funyaks. Mountain bikes are available through **Queen's Trading Post & Outfitters.**

When the Spanish explorer Hernando de Soto arrived in 1540, the Cherokee were a unified nation of about 25,000 people whose territory included the Great Smoky Mountains, an area of approximately 135,000 square miles. Over the next 300 years, the Cherokee tried to coexist peacefully with their neighbors but lost parts of their land through one treaty after another. Finally, in 1838, 16,000 people were forcibly removed to Oklahoma along what came to be known as the **Trail of Tears** (pages 102-104).

Under orders from Gen. Winfield Scott, men, women, and children were transported in wagons, steamers, and keelboats. The 1,200-mile journey lasted between 104 and 189 days and took the lives of at least 4,000 people through disease, starvation, and other hardships. Some Cherokee stayed behind, hiding in the mountains; their descendants came to be known as the Eastern Band of Cherokee Indians.

A good time to visit the reservation is during a **powwow** or a festival. You should start at the Visitor Center, where the staff has information on local activities, housing, and food. The public is invited to powwows over the Memorial Day and Labor Day weekends and on the Fourth of July. Enjoy watching dance competitions, eating traditional foods, and looking at local crafts. In October, the **Cherokee Indian Fair**—an event that has been held for more than 80 years—draws craftspeople from all over the reservation. Authentic Cherokee baskets, masks, wood sculpture, finger weaving, pottery, and beadwork are available all year at the **Qualla Arts and Crafts Mutual.**

TIPS: Fishing on the reservation requires a tribal fishing license. Children under 12 do not need a license if they are accompanied by a licensed adult, but their catches are counted as part of the adult's total. You can rent fishing gear at **One Feather Trading Post** *(828/497-3113)* or through **KOA** *(828/497-9711).*

BASICS: The **Cherokee Visitors Center** is at US 19 and Business Route 441 in downtown Cherokee *(800/438-1601 or 828/497-9195. www.cherokee-nc.com).* You can also contact **Smokemont Riding Stable** *(828/497-2373);* **Queen's Trading Post & Outfitters** *(828/497-4453);* and **Smoky Mountain Tubing** *(828/497-5453).* **Qualla Arts and Crafts Mutual** *(828/497-3103)* is located at the eastern entrance to Great Smoky Mountains National Park.

OCONALUFTEE INDIAN VILLAGE

Set among the pines and peaks of the Great Smokies and located only a few miles from downtown Cherokee, **Oconaluftee Indian Village** is a re-creation of a Cherokee village in the 1750s. Led by present-day Cherokee who dress in the manner of their 18th-century ancestors, the tours of the village last about an hour and a half and give visitors an introduction to the crafts and culture of the Cherokee of North Carolina.

Homes in the village are built from notched logs chinked with mud, and they have earthen floors and stone chimneys. In a home devoted to making pottery, women create ornately decorated vessels without using a potter's wheel. Clay is shaped into a 14-inch-long, breadlike form, which the women pound and knead with their hands and then build up from coils of clay. After the shaped vessel has dried, designs are impressed upon it with a carved wooden paddle. The finished pot is polished with a smooth wet stone and fired over an open flame.

Finger weaving calls for another kind of manual dexterity, as does the ancient art of beadwork, and both are demonstrated by Cherokee women using techniques passed down for untold centuries. Visitors can also find out how to pound corn and use it in cooking.

Some men demonstrate ceremonial mask carving, blowgun hunting, dartmaking, and flint chipping to create arrowheads. Others show how to use fire and a primitive ax to fashion a dugout canoe from a giant poplar tree. Basketmakers weave river cane and white oak splits—from saplings they soaked in a stream to make pliable—into beautiful patterns; to add color, they use vegetable dyes made by boiling yellow and blood roots and the bark of butternut and walnut trees.

Inside the seven-sided **Council House,** a villager tells visitors about traditional Cherokee customs and dances, treaties, territories, and language. The center of religious and political life, the Council House was the site where the people kept their sacred fire; from it, all fires in the village were relighted once a year in the

SOUTHERN SAFARI: UPSCALE CAMPING IN THE CAROLINA WOODS

Forget beef jerky, bedrolls, and cat holes. **Southern Safari,** with its five-course dinners, platform tents, real bathrooms, and guided adventures, is reminiscent of the upscale camping lodges of Africa. Instead of participating in big-game hunts, you go whitewater rafting, canoeing, mountain biking, hiking, and llama trekking, while enjoying the birds, deer, and other critters of the beautiful Blue Ridge Mountains.

The camp has attracted mostly couples who want woodsy getaways without the do-it-yourself work. With the opening of its **Lower Base Camp** in spring 2000, however, Southern Safari is actively seeking families. Couples stay at the **Upper Base Camp** in two-person tents, while families sleep four to a walk-in canvas tent lodge. You can choose from a menu of family-friendly activities at the Lower Base Camp. It also has a kids program for little ones who can't paddle through rapids or hike **Cold Mountain.**

Tips: On request the camp can arrange special evening events, such as dulcimer playing and storytelling.

Basics: **Southern Safari** *(Asheville. 800/454-7374 or 828/626-3400. www.southernsafari.com)* At **Lower Base Camp,** $245 includes lodging, dinner, and continental breakfast for two; $81 for ages 3 to 10; under 2, free. Children ages 10 and younger can choose from a kids menu. Activities such as llama trekking and mountain biking are extra.

"new fire ceremony." At the **Ceremonial Grounds,** visitors learn about Cherokee dances, masks, terrapin rattles, feathers, and the roles they played in the various ceremonies that took place here.

MOUNTAINSIDE THEATRE

Not far from Oconaluftee Indian Village is the **Mountainside Theatre,** where you can see *Unto These Hills.* First presented in 1950 as a project of the newly formed Cherokee Historical Association, this outdoor drama unfolds on three stages in a wooded setting. Seen by more than five million people, it depicts the history of the Eastern Band of Cherokee Indians. Some one hundred actors tell the story, from the arrival of Spanish explorer Hernando de Soto in 1540 to the tragedy of the Trail of Tears—or *Nunahi-duna-dlo-hilu-i,* as the Cherokees refer to the forced relocation of their people to Oklahoma. The event, which lasted from June to December of 1838, cost the lives of 4,000.

Authentic dress, the dramatic Eagle Dance, a mountain square dance, and a compelling narrative told with humor and honesty combine to make this play interesting to both adults and children. The theater's forested location is in the same area where many Cherokees hid to avoid removal to Oklahoma. Many of their descendants are among the actors in the play.

Keeping Cherokee traditions alive, a woman weaves a belt at Oconaluftee Indian Village.

MUSEUM OF THE CHEROKEE INDIAN

Completed in 1998, a $3.5-million renovation added a 12,000-square-foot exhibit to the **Museum of the Cherokee Indian**. The exhibit combines computer-generated imagery and special effects with an extensive artifacts collection to tell the story of the Cherokee people from 12,000 years ago to the present.

"*De tsv ya da ni lv ga!*—Welcome. I want to tell you a story, a very old story!" So begins the self-guided tour, prefaced by an opening video program in a three-screen theater that utilizes computer animation to relate the Cherokee creation story (how the buzzard made the mountains) and introduce visitors to the museum. The exhibits take families through a chronologically arranged history enhanced by ancient artifacts and unique special effects, such as shapes that form and dissolve in the smoke from a fire as a shaman talks to visitors.

The seven clans of the Cherokee—the Wolf Clan, Deer Clan, Bird Clan, Paint Clan, Blue Clan, Wild Potato Clan, and Long Hair Clan—are all represented in the museum's exhibits, as are the stories of the Cherokee. Listen to a Cherokee child tell about the day that soldiers came to take her family to the stockade before forcing them to walk the Trail of Tears. Learn about the Cherokee concept of *duyukta*—a way of living by seeking balance—and find out how to play the butter-bean game, a centuries-old Cherokee game of chance.

TIPS: Click on the museum's website for a detailed map of the Trail of Tears and for many interesting facts about the places the Cherokee passed through on their way to Oklahoma.

BASICS: On the **Cherokee Indian Reservation** (pages 161-162): **Oconaluftee Indian Village** *(828/497-2315 May 15-Oct. 25, and 828/497-2111 rest of the year. www.oconalufteevillage.com);* **Unto These Hills** at **Mountainside Theatre** *(828/497-2111. www.untothesehills.com. Mid-June–late Aug. Mon.-Sat. evenings);* **Museum of the Cherokee Indian** *(828/497-3481. www.cherokeemuseum.org)*

Swannanoa Gathering
Asheville

In the Blue Ridge Mountains, the melodies and myths of Appalachian, Scottish, and Irish songs, dances, and stories come alive for families at **Swannanoa Gathering, Warren Wilson College,** about a 30-minute drive from Asheville. Three of the seven weeks in this music festival host classes for adults and separate sessions for kids ages 6 through 12. In 2000, favorite family sessions are **Celtic Week,** July 9-15, and **Old Time Music and Dance,** July 23-29 and July 30-August 5. Each session is divided into four adult and children's class periods of an hour and 15 minutes daily. Families gather in the evening for performances and spontaneous jam sessions.

To get the most from the music classes, adult participants should have basic skills, but beginners as well as experts are welcome in the dance classes. Kids with skill levels from never-evers and up are also welcome. Families can perform together or with their groups during Friday's student showcases. Two evenings a week enjoy toe-tapping tunes at the mini-concerts.

During Celtic Week, kick up your heels *River Dance* style with lively step dancing. Try ceilidh *(kay-lee)* dancing, an Irish form of square dancing, or sing folk songs. Learn to play the flute, tin whistle, tenor banjo (a four-string banjo), and bodhran, an Irish drum that's something like a tambourine without the jingles. You can also try the Uilleann pipes, called Irish bagpipes; these strap around your waist so you can pump the bellows with your left arm. Children in separate classes learn how to play the fiddle or mountain dulcimer. They also create crafts, chomp down watermelons during an eating contest, and end their daily sessions with a supervised swim at the pool. Kids still have plenty of time for making music, as well as dancing and singing with mom and dad.

During **Old Time Music and Dance Week,** practice tunes for the fiddle and banjo, learn clogging, and do some square-dance swings. At the nightly dances, step lively while a caller tells you the moves to make; during the day, join in the fun as the musicians play impromptu tunes. Stomp your feet and clap your hands to such classics as "Wrassled with a Wildcat"—feel free to sing along—and "Maggots in the Sheep Hides."

TIPS: Instead of taking four different courses, participants are encouraged by instructors to register for just one or two different classes so that they will have plenty of time to practice and enjoy new techniques and skills. During **Sing, Swing, and Strings,** children 3 to 12 can enjoy supervised craft and nature activities.

BASICS: Swannanoa Gathering, Warren Wilson College *(P.O. Box 9000, Asheville. 828/298-3434 or 828/298-3325 ext. 426. www.swangathering.org).* Each student pays $320. For dorm housing and meals, adults pay $240 ($85 for children in same room). Meal tickets for children are $34.

MORE ASHEVILLE ACTION

Chimney Rock Park *(800/277-9611 or 828/625-9611):* From Chimney Rock—the 1,200-foot-high natural rock ledge that is the centerpiece of this 1,000-acre park— you get a panoramic view of the Blue Ridge foothills. Hearty types can hike to the top, but others prefer taking the elevator—something that makes the park especially nice for little kids who like the views but not the long climb. Our favorite easy nature walk is the one-hour, round-trip stroll to the bottom of **Hickory Nut Falls,** a 404-foot-high waterfall.

Biltmore Estate *(Biltmore Ave. 800/543-2961 or 828/255-1700):* Built in 1895 by George Vanderbilt, this 250-room mansion is one of America's great homes. The house, furnished in period antiques, is also crowded and filled with roped-off rooms, making the place difficult for young children to tour. Take interested preteens and teens inside, but with younger ones enjoy the grounds—including acres of formal gardens that are especially beautiful in late April and early May, when the azaleas bloom.

Nantahala Outdoor Center *(13077 US 19 W, Bryson City. 888/662-1662 or 828/ 488-2175. www.nocweb.com):* Learn canoeing, kayaking, and mountain biking at classes geared for adults, women only, and kids. Families can opt for private lessons, then put their newfound skills into practice on a group trip.

Right: Molly Medrano, daughter of Scottish-fiddle instructor Bonnie Rideout, plays at Swannanoa.

PARENT/CHILD SPACE CAMPS AND PILOT/COPILOT TRAINING

Team up with your child for a mission to the stars or train to be a fighter pilot with hands-on programs developed by the **U.S. Space and Rocket Center.** The three-day programs are for teams of one parent (or grandparent, aunt, uncle, etc.) and one child 7 to 11 years of age.

At **Space Camp,** offered in Alabama, California, and Florida, you and your child work with four or five other parent-and-child pairs to repair broken satellites, do scientific experiments, and perform other tasks. You train on equipment similar to that used by real astronauts: Bounce in a microgravity chair to replicate walking on the moon; "float" in the five-degrees-of-freedom simulator to learn how difficult it can be to work while weightless; and take a spin in the multi-axis trainer that simulates tumbling in space. You also get to build a rocket and launch it, and you can taste space cuisine specialties such as freeze-dried ice cream. All the meals, however, are typical earthbound cafeteria fare.

With **Pilot/Copilot,** offered only in Alabama and California, you train to be a top aviator in a fighter squadron. A fighter simulator gives you the feel of a dogfight, and from the cockpit of your jet you can watch for enemy aircraft. You learn E & E (escape and evasion) techniques that help you defend a landing base and "eliminate" the enemy before he or she gets you. You practice water-and-land survival techniques that include sliding down a zip line into a lake and swimming out.

Before or after camp, allow some time to explore a site's facilities. The U.S. Space and Rocket Center in Huntsville, Alabama, is often called the showplace of America's space program. Kids like the many hands-on exhibits and the grounds that bloom with aircraft. The **Space Museum's** two stars are the 43-foot, full-scale Hubble telescope and Space Shot, a 150-foot tower that catapults you to the top with more than three times the force of gravity. The result: For about two seconds, you are weightless—an extraordinary feeling. **Rocket Park** features rockets all in a row. See the 363-foot-tall Saturn V that launched 27 men toward the moon, and take a look at the SR-71 "Blackbird," a 99-foot-long jet that streaks through the skies at three times the speed of sound. The **Spacedome Theater** puts you into the action with its 67-foot domed screen and IMAX films.

Titusville's **Kennedy Space Center** features the **Astronaut Hall of Fame.** See space suits and memorabilia from the astronauts, and squeeze into a Mercury spacecraft. The bus tour takes you to a site overlooking the launch area and to the **International Space Station Center,** where you can view space modules and exhibits. When it's time to sit down, take in the panoramic views at the IMAX theater.

The California facility, located at the **NASA Ames Research Center** in Silicon Valley, does not have a museum. Your weekend comes with a special tour of Lockheed Martin Missiles & Space and a look at a wind tunnel. You also get time at the IMAX theater and on the vertical motion simulator used to train astronauts.

Tips: Only in Alabama can teams of males and females (mothers and sons, fathers and daughters, etc.) room together. In California and Florida, such pairs would be required to bunk separately in male or female dorms, an uncomfortable situation

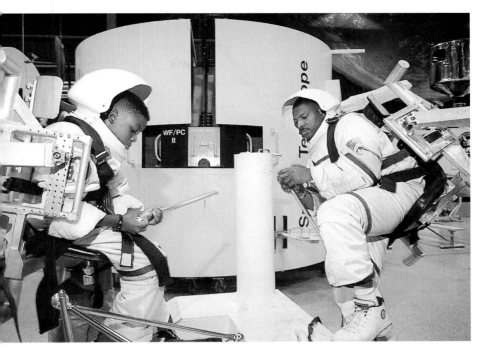

Father and son undertake a mission together at Space Camp in Huntsville, Alabama.

for a younger child. California offers special parent/child Space Camp sessions.

Basics: **U.S. Space and Rocket Center** *(800/637-7223. www.spacecamp.com)* charges $658 for the adult/child team in either **Space Camp** or **Pilot/Copilot.**

MORE ALABAMA SITES

Early Works *(400 Madison St., Huntsville. 800/678-1819):* This living history museum of federal period buildings commemorates 1819, the year that Alabama became the 22nd state to join the Union. Costumed interpreters man the printing press, cook in an open-hearth fireplace, and build furniture while you watch. The best times for visits by young grade-schoolers are during special events, such as the **Mother Goose tea parties** and the **spring demonstrations of fleece-shearing.**

At **Alabama Constitution Village,** which is part of Early Works, children can walk inside a log cabin, "shop" at an old-fashioned drugstore, and sit under the "talking tree" to hear stories about notable Alabamians.

Tips: Take some time to stroll the grounds of the 35-acre **Botanical Garden** *(4747 Bob Wallace Ave. 256/830-4447).*

Alabama's Black Heritage Trail: This driving tour highlights key sites in the civil rights struggle. At the **Birmingham Civil Rights Institute,** learn about freedom riders. In Selma, follow the route that marchers took in 1965 for integration and equal rights. In Montgomery, visit the **Civil Rights Memorial,** which lists the names of those who died in the 1955-68 struggle for racial equality. For brochures, contact the **Alabama Bureau of Tourism and Travel** *(800/252-2262. www.touralabama.org).*

Okefenokee National Wildlife Refuge, Folkston

Steady rain made dancing circles on the dark brown surface of the headwaters of the Suwannee River. We glumly tugged at our ponchos, and my daughter shot me a look that said "You've *got* to be kidding!" as she contemplated the gray February day and the canoes at **Stephen C. Foster State Park.** We had come to the west entrance of the **Okefenokee National Wildlife Refuge,** about 17 miles east of Fargo, to experience the swamp. We wanted slider turtles, white ibises, river otters, and hundreds of alligators—not rain.

The Okefenokee National Wildlife Refuge, the largest national wildlife refuge in the eastern United States, occupies 396,000 acres and is a slow-moving river of water that comprises lakes, marshlike prairies, and islands. The refuge was established in 1937 to preserve the swamp's unique ecosystem; 354,000 acres in its interior were designated a National Wilderness Area in 1974.

As we paddled into the first large body of water, **Billy's Lake,** we forgot about our soaking jeans, and my daughter's grumpiness disappeared. In its place, a sense of wonder took over. Spanish moss draped the gnarled branches of cypress trees, which rose in thickets from dense beds of peat called houses. Walk on them and the land quivers—a phenomenon that led Indians to call this place *Okefenokee* ("land of the trembling earth").

We practiced maneuvers in a thin fog, stopping to watch a family of otters catch fish near the shore. After hours in the rain, we were especially thankful for the comfortable cabin with its two bedrooms, two bathrooms, screened porch, fully equipped kitchen, and heat. We warmed ourselves with hot chocolate, hot showers, and hot food.

The next day, the sun transformed the swamp. "Look!" Alissa yelled breathlessly, pointing at two half-submerged snouts and four bulging eyes peering from the reeds. We marveled at these two critters, and admired another perched on a log—a bony, 4-foot-long stretch of crooked mouth and tail basking in the warmth. Hawks and herons swooped by, and the sun turned the dark water into a smooth mirror, magically reflecting the thick swamp growth.

Fifteen miles into the swamp, we pulled up at Billy's Island for a hike and a picnic lunch. Although the air here once buzzed with loggers' saws, we heard only the wind in the pines. **Minnie's Lake Run,** a favorite stretch, came next. A canopy of cypress branches closed over us, and we had to paddle around knobby cypress stumps called knees. Green patches of lichen added color to the trees' fluted gray trunks. In the **River Narrows,** a windy stretch where cypress trees gave way to Ogeechee limes, wispy lichen—aptly named "old man's beard"—dangled from branches like tinsel. A few golden clubs—spiky yellow flowers—foretold the spring.

The waters of Okefenokee National Wildlife Refuge beckon canoeists.

Come May, the refuge waters would be carpeted with white and yellow water lilies. On warm days, hundreds of slider turtles live up to their names, splashing from the shore into the water, and thousands of alligators bask on logs along the 107 miles of canoe trails. In spring, the swamp resounds with the bellowing of breeding gators and the exuberant trilling of frogs.

Despite the March cold, we were reluctant to leave the Okefenokee. Alissa and I enjoyed paddling in tandem through this remarkable world. We learned about the landscape and ourselves as we met the added challenge of bad weather. As we crossed the sill—an artificial dam—Alissa spotted two hearty alligators that quickly slithered under water. After telling me that she wanted to return in spring to see more wildlife, she added: "But I'm glad we came now. It was different and peaceful, and I never thought I wouldn't mind paddling in the rain."

TIPS: The refuge is best in winter, spring, and fall. In summer it's too hot and buggy. As we learned, it can be cold and damp in winter, so bring waterproof jackets and pants—and lots of layers.

Camping and canoeing permits are available 60 days before your arrival. To protect the refuge, each canoe trail for campers who overnight on raised platforms is limited to one party daily, with a maximum of 10 canoes or 20 people. No permit is required for day use of the canoe trails.

BASICS: There are two main entrances to the **Okefenokee National Wildlife Refuge** *(912/496-3331)*: The east entrance—the **Suwannee Canal Recreation Area**

(912/496-7836)—is approximately 7 miles southwest of Folkston, Georgia. Guided boat tours as well as canoe and motorboat rentals are available through the concessionaire *(912/496-7156)*. The west entrance to the refuge is **Stephen C. Foster State Park** *(912/637-5274)*, located 17 miles east of Fargo, Georgia. This park has 9 cabins for rental and 66 campsites. Boat tours and canoe and motorboat rentals are available as well.

For more information on Georgia's parks, contact the **Georgia Department of Natural Resources** *(205 Butler St. S.E., Suite 1258, Atlanta. 800/342-7275 in Georgia or 800/542-7275 outside Georgia)*. **Sea Kayak of Georgia** *(888/732-5292)* sometimes offers guided canoe trips for families who wish to paddle through the Okefenokee swamp.

GATEWAY ATTRACTIONS: SAVANNAH

Although Jacksonville, Florida, about 80 miles away, has the closest major airport to the Okefenokee, we prefer to use scenic **Savannah** as a gateway. It's about a two-hour drive or 110 miles to the Okefenokee's west entrance at Stephen C. Foster State Park. That way we can add an overnight or two in Savannah, a historic city with lots of southern charm.

Stroll streets shaded by live oaks that are draped with Spanish moss past numerous parklike squares. The city boasts many historic homes, but a tour of one or two is enough for most children. As a grade-schooler and Girl Scout, my daughter enjoyed touring the **Juliette Gordon Low Girl Scout Center** *(10 E. Oglethorpe Ave. 912/233-4501)*. The founder of the Girl Scouts was born at this site on Halloween night in 1860. Even though the 1818 Regency-style house isn't particularly posh by Savannah standards and the room tour can get boring, simply being in the house is exciting for most Girl Scouts. Reward yourself with a merit badge from the gift shop.

Browse the city's waterfront, where historic buildings now house cafés and boutiques. River Street is a prime souvenir shopping area. For a restful interlude, board either the *Savannah River Queen* or the *Georgia Queen* for a one-hour cruise. Little kids like riding the carriages pulled by the big Percherons. **Carriage Tours of Savannah** depart from the **Visitor Center** *(10 Warner St. 912/236-6756. Reservations suggested)*. Older kids enjoy the **Ghost Talk Ghost Walk** *(127 E. Congress St. 912/233-3896)* and the history tours led by **Hospitality Tours** *(135 Bull St. 912/233-0119)*.

Another Savannah tradition involves having lunch at **Mrs. Wilkes' Boarding House** *(107 W. Jones St. 912/232-5997)*. It's worth getting in line early for the family-style, ten-to-a-table platters of fried chicken, stew, rice, beans, biscuits, collard greens, and sweet potatoes. Lunch is served between 11:30 a.m. and 3 p.m. No reservations are taken.

BASICS: For more information, contact the **Savannah Area Convention and Visitors Bureau** *(101 E. Bay St. 877/728-2667 or 912/644-6401. www.savcvb.com)*

SeaWorld Adventure Park Orlando

Discovery Cove, SeaWorld Orlando's new 30-acre park within a park, opens in the summer of 2000 and gives families two things they've wanted: more opportunities to swim with the dolphins and a less hectic theme park experience. With a maximum daily attendance of a thousand people and a snorkeling cove surrounded by a sandy beach, families will be able to have their close encounters with wildlife and a relaxing day at the beach, too.

The heart of Discovery Cove's experience is the program that lets people swim with dolphins. It's a new version of the park's former Dolphin Interaction Program, which is no longer available in SeaWorld's main area. Discovery Cove provides a chance to spend some quality time with dolphins. Park visitors learn about dolphin physiology and habitats before getting into the water with these intelligent and agile mammals. During their time in the tank, people can touch the dolphins' rubbery skin, hang on to a dorsal fin for a ride, and communicate with a friendly "Flipper" through hand signals that give commands to flip, spin, and demonstrate other interesting behaviors.

All of the SeaWorld parks offer close encounters with sea creatures and well-done wildlife exhibits. Mammals such as manatees, sea lions, polar bears, walruses, and beluga whales, all swimming among schools of fish in unforgettable underwater habitats, are fascinating to watch. You can feed the stingrays at **Stingray Lagoon** and find out about endangered sea turtles at **Sea Turtle Point.** At **Terrors of the Deep,** see the world's largest collection of eels, barracudas, sharks, and other dangerous sea creatures. Watch **Shamu,** everybody's favorite killer whale, jump and fluke-hop at Shamu Stadium. At **Penguin Encounter,** look for hundreds of penguins.

For traditional theme park thrills, which are on the rise at the SeaWorld parks, ride **Kraken,** the new megacoaster, and hop aboard **Journey to Atlantis,** the park's water coaster. Preschoolers and little kids can climb and splash in play areas at **Shamu's Happy Harbor.**

So far, Discovery Cove is available only at SeaWorld Orlando. But if you don't want to spend the fee for Discovery Cove, you can take advantage of the many special programs available at **SeaWorld Adventure Park Orlando** and at the other SeaWorld Adventure parks. With few exceptions, the parks have similar programs.

In the **Trainer for the Day** program, you can find out what it's like to work with sea animals by assisting with food preparation, feeding, and training sessions—including getting in the water with the dolphins.

Sign up for a **SeaWorld Sleepover** and sleep with the resident sharks or manatees. Along with bedding down next to the big glass tanks, participants go behind the scenes with instructors to learn more about these creatures. Sometimes special

A dolphin encounter brings smiles to many faces at SeaWorld Adventure Park.

mother-and-daughter or father-and-son programs are offered; call or check the website for a schedule of upcoming events.

Among the bargains are the 60-minute group tours called **Behind the Scenes.** People of all ages can sign up for them. **To the Rescue** takes you to the rehabilitation area for rescued animals and to the surgical room where they are treated. On **Polar Expedition,** you get to touch a penguin while touring the **Avian Research Center.** You can even touch a shark and often see an egg case with an embryo inside at **Sharks!**

Adventure Express, a five-hour program, is for people who want a special encounter but hate to stand in lines. A guide escorts you to the front of the line for all rides (not to mention reserved seats at shows) and will also take you on a Behind the Scenes tour, usually to touch a penguin. There's a maximum of 16 people per group. For large families or families traveling together, consider a private Adventure Express tour. For a flat fee, you go behind the scenes at several areas; these may include the habitats for penguins, sharks, or polar bears.

Camp SeaWorld offers one- and five-day classes for kids who are dropped off by their parents and picked up later in the day. In the five-day **Photography Class,** preteens in grades six through eight learn how to take animal shots at SeaWorld and at **Busch Gardens** in Tampa Bay (pages 187-88).

With **Splash Attack**—great on a hot summer day—you can get splashed at numerous places throughout the park. The soakings are provided courtesy of Shamu as well as by the dolphins, the **Journey to Atlantis** water coaster, and by others. You can sign up for these popular programs at the guided tour counter.

TIPS: For all the special programs, except for the Behind the Scenes tours, register well in advance.

BASICS: SeaWorld Adventure Park Orlando *(7007 SeaWorld Dr. 800/327-2424 or 407/351-3600. www.seaworld.com)* offers interaction with dolphins; age 10 minimum or 52 inches tall. The fee is $179 per participant or $89 for a companion who just wants to watch; it includes admission to the park. Reservations are required. **SeaWorld Sleepovers** are $40 through **Camp SeaWorld** *(800/406-2244 or 407/370-1380).* **Adventure Express** is $55 per person or $50 for ages 3 through 9. The fee does not include park admission. The Adventure Express private tour is a flat fee of $200 for up to 25 people. Park admission is extra.

Animal Kingdom Orlando

We liked **Disney World's Animal Kingdom** for the very reasons that some families do not. This park, the fourth in the Walt Disney Company's Orlando collection, features animals and a less frenetic pace than Disney's other parks. Recreated animal habitats radiate from the Tree of Life, the park's 145-foot-tall central symbol. Although you'll see far fewer animals here than you would at zoos or animal parks, the Disney touch is apparent in cleverly designed exhibits, whimsical rides and shows, winsome fake creatures, and interesting real ones.

Action-oriented teens and even preteens might be bored here, but most gradeschoolers won't be. For visitors who want the joy of a wild ride before the thrill of a nature adventure, the ride to take in the Africa area is **Countdown to Extinction;** in Asia, try **Kali River Rapids.** Although lots of people love Countdown, the place where lifelike dinosaurs attack guests, we found it jerky and predictable—nothing like the creative rides we've come to expect from the Imagineers. Kali River Rapids, on the other hand, gets you wet and is lots of fun on a hot afternoon.

In the 18-minute **Kilimanjaro Safaris** ride, you weave through a landscape designed to look like the Kenyan savanna. The moats and barriers dividing the sections are cleverly disguised to convey a sense of sweeping plains. With luck, you'll spot marabou storks, giraffes, Egyptian geese, rhino, crocodiles, ostriches, antelope, elephants, and lions. Although some of the grazing areas are built on rises to maximize the chances of spotting game, other habitats provide necessary cover. No sooner had we caught sight of a lioness, for example, than she responded to our "oohs" by jumping off her rocky perch and out of sight. Live animals, unlike the cartoon kind, are unpredictable; the numbers of critters you see will vary.

Take the time to walk Africa's **Gorilla Falls Exploration Trail,** a path lush with bamboo and ferns and dotted with observation blinds. A highlight for us was the sleeping mother gorilla just inches from the viewing wall, cradling her napping baby. A glass-walled pond lets you see the massive, submerged bodies of hippos whose snouts are the only things visible above the water. The **Conservation Station**'s interactive computers inform you about the animals, some of which can be seen "live" on the "animalcam," a video camera. If veterinarians are performing procedures, you can watch through a glass-walled examination room.

Except for an aviary and some decorative flocks of flamingos, the rest of the park concentrates on extinct or exotic animals. **Boneyard,** for example, is a playground with rope bridges, slides, and fossils to uncover.

Like Africa's Gorilla Falls Exploration Trail, **Maharajah Jungle Trek** takes you to a cleverly designed landscape. This time it's the mythical village of Anandapur. In the rain forest setting, gibbons swing from the ruins of a Nepalese-style temple, and giant fruit bats fly above cliffs. Komodo dragons lounge around and Bengal tigers pace. In **Flights of Wonder,** parrots, macaws, ibises, Indian Runner ducks, Abyssinian ground hornbills, toucans, owls, cockatoos, and other birds demonstrate behaviors linked to tricks; the show is entertaining and educational, and you get to sit down. Plan this one for midday, when everyone is tired.

TIPS: To help spot the animals in Kilimanjaro Safaris, which doesn't stop for photo opportunities or viewing, teach your kids ahead of time to use clock directions to call out animal locations. A cry of "Cheetah at eleven o'clock!" is much easier to follow than "Look over there, just beyond that third tree!"

BASICS: Animal Kingdom *(407/824-4321. www.disneyworld.com)*

Orlando Science Center

Young Arthur—the future king—challenges Merlin the Magician, who has just dazzled you with magic tricks, declaring that "everything you call magic can be explained with scientific facts." Merlin sputters while Arthur commands you to "go throughout the center and find the exhibits I have marked explaining Merlin's magic." So, afraid of being turned into a toad, you and your child go forth into the ten exhibit halls of the **Orlando Science Center.** This is a plot for **Dreamscapes,** the museum's overnight program for families with children in grades one and up. Along with a pizza dinner, the "journey" gives you time with hands-on items, a CineDome movie viewing, and breakfast.

Other programs (not overnights) for families are **Li'l Explorers Workshops** and **Drop-In Discovery Labs,** both of which explain "science magic" through demonstrations and hands-on activities. In the 45-minute Li'l Explorers classes, work with your 2- to 5-year-old kids on such basics as turning wheels and pushing levers. At the Drop-In Discovery Labs, held for no extra fee from 1 p.m. to 3 p.m. on the first and third Saturdays of every month, spend as much time as you want learning to surf the Internet, solve crimes through forensic science, and program robots.

Check the schedule for performances at the **Darden Adventure Theater,** where the Einstein Players present plays focused on cleverly disguised scientific facts: In *Mysterious M,* detective L. D. Bug tries to find out who killed Honey Bee; in the parody *X and Y Files*, kids learn about genetics. A paleontologist's dinosaur daydreams come to life in the musical *Prehistorock*. Productions change, but old favorites do return. The free performances take place at least once a day—and sometimes more often, depending on the crowds.

The center also holds impromptu demonstrations and shows designed to make kids think about the exhibits. In **NatureWorks,** for instance, the Pied Piper Troupe leads visitors around the exhibit hall, using animal prints in the floor to demonstrate how different creatures move and walk. **Power Station** features a magnetic cannon that shoots small balls across the room and an electric motor whose parts kids can handle to see how they work.

LION COUNTRY SAFARI, WEST PALM BEACH

Even though the enclosures lack landscaping and the animals look a bit bored, it's fun to drive through gated pastures where the animals roam free and the people are locked in their cars. Go eyeball to eyeball with a curious ostrich that bends down to stare into one of your windows (keep them rolled up); see lions sleeping in the sun; observe blackbucks and buffalo roaming about; and watch African elephants grazing. *(On Southern Blvd., 15 m W of I-95. 561/793-1084)*

Studio Two stages larger science demonstrations. To simulate the power of a tornado, "Florida's Fury" uses compressed air to shoot a pencil through plywood. You can also get a good explanation of what causes lightning.

In **Dr. Phillips' CineDome,** the world's largest combined domed theater and planetarium, the surround-sound system and the images projected above you make you feel as if you're part of the film; the show gets really exciting when you feel you're stepping into a volcano or flying through the universe.

At the **123 Math Avenue** exhibit, kids use recipes, baseball statistics, and games of chance to learn arithmetic. The **Cosmic Tourist: Earth and Beyond** guides tourists on imaginary vacations to other planets. Preparation for the journey involves figuring out how much you'll weigh when you get there and visiting the **Planet Wall,** which lets you experience the greenhouse effect on Venus. You can also sample the powers of nature on Earth, including a shaky lesson on earthquakes.

BodyZone lets you choose which food item you'd like to be on an excursion through the digestive tract. In **TechWorks,** you can compose music with a laser harp. You can also learn about creating special effects for movies: Simulate hanging from a 20-story building or spin a table to form a hurricane's eye.

TIPS: The center has a nice cafeteria for light lunches and snacks.

BASICS: **Orlando Science Center** *(777 E. Princeton St. 888/672-4386 or 407/514-2000. www.osc.org)*

Miami Metrozoo

The nearly 300-acre **Miami Metrozoo** is friendly both to animals and to kids. Living in natural environments, the animals are confined by moats and landscaping rather than cages. Children are allowed to touch some of the animals, and kids can watch feeding sessions and ask questions of interpreters available throughout the zoo. As zoologist Ronald Magill explains, "We try to create opportunities for the public to become a little more personal with the animals. We believe it's important that people develop some kind of connection with the animal."

Like many other cutting-edge facilities, Miami's zoo is moving toward exhibits that go way beyond point-and-look shows; for example, **Dr. Wilde's World,** which opens in March 2000, provides cultural information about the regions the animals come from. The 5,000-square-foot space features exhibits based on the explorations of the imaginary Dr. Wilde. **Tropical America,** the first exhibit, features not only an aquarium with Amazonian fish but also headdresses, arrows, bows, and a spear from Central and South America. An ethnobotany section contains rain forest plants that are used in everyday medicine. Hidden among the plants are reproductions of many animals, which younger children have fun trying to find with a checklist and binoculars.

Kids under 5 years of age like **PAWS,** a children's zoo with a barnyard and sometimes a hand-raised antelope or deer. A variety of reptiles and birds are kept for the children to touch.

If you go to one of the **Keeper Feedings** scheduled throughout the day, you can watch how keepers feed the critters. At the daily **Wildlife Show,** you'll observe natural behaviors. The **Zoo-In** sleepovers on Friday and Saturday nights provide pizza, popcorn, and a chance for kids ages 6 and above to get up in the middle of the night to feed the animals. One of the highlights is helping a keeper feed a carrot to a hungry rhinoceros.

If you're more of a morning person, arrive at the zoo early to watch keepers feed the animals at **Breakfast with the Beasts.** This is a good time of day for a visit: The animals are more active during the early morning, and the air temperature is much cooler than it is at midday. Both you and the animals will be more comfortable. Reservations are required.

Find it awkward to talk with your older teens about sex? Start with **"Sex and the Animals,"** a slide show for ages 18 and up. The popular and entertaining program is usually held around Valentine's Day, and it describes the unique, fascinating, and sometimes humorous mating behaviors of wildlife.

Animals you won't want to miss include the pair of Komodo dragons, which in 1999 managed to produce a clutch of 27 baby Komodos—the largest clutch born outside Indonesia. The zoo is also home to a pair of black rhino, a family of lowland gorillas, and three African elephants. **Asian River Life** re-creates an exotic jungle setting complete with mist, bamboo, Asian small-clawed river otters, and a

Eyeing its observer, a Bengal tiger relaxes at the Miami Metrozoo.

six-and-a-half-foot-long Malayan water monitor—one of the largest lizards in the world.

Handcrafted ceramic pictographs posted next to each exhibit use pictures to describe where the creature normally lives, what it eats, what time of day it is most active, and what the survival status of its species is. These sources of information are easily understood by children if they use the guides at the bottom of the zoo map (available at the Information Booth).

TIPS: Save little feet by using the Zoofari monorail. This air-conditioned train stops every 20 minutes at four stations in the zoo, and it is free with admission. For an additional fee, families can get an overview of the zoo on the personalized tram tour—a 45-minute, in-depth guided tour of the zoo. Reserve the popular Zoo-Ins at least six months before you plan to visit.

BASICS: **Miami Metrozoo** (*12400 S.W. 152nd St. 305/251-0401. www.miamimetrozoo.org*). **Zoo-Ins** cost $35; **Breakfast with the Beasts**, $15; **"Sex and the Animals,"** $15.

POSE WITH MACAWS: PARROT JUNGLE, MIAMI

Parrot Jungle is a Florida classic. It can be hokey and is far from EC (Environmentally Correct): Cockatoos riding tricycles and macaws racing chariots are not exactly natural behaviors. Still, the place is undeniably fun for kids. The cages are low, making it easy for children to see the parrots and other tropical birds, and the

Two macaws make the most of a photo op at Miami's Parrot Jungle.

photo opportunities are classic. Catch your kids with oh-my-gosh grins as they hold a brightly colored macaw on each arm. Currently the Parrot Jungle consists of landscaped gardens near Coral Gables, but a new $47-million property on Watson Island should be ready by 2001.

BASICS: **Parrot Jungle and Gardens** *(11000 SW 57th Ave., Miami. 305/669-7037 or 666-7834. www.parrotjungle.com)*

Everglades National Park

As our tour boat moved slowly along a channel lined with red mangroves, the guide pointed to an alligator snoozing in the shade of a mangrove, almost imperceptible among the gnarled, fingerlike roots. The creature's bulging eyes had given it away. An osprey glided on a wind current, and a pelican swooped low over the boat, checking us out.

Encompassing three counties, **Everglades National Park** is a 1.5-million-acre subtropical wilderness of mangrove swamps and saw-grass prairie. Cut by watery channels, these rivers of grass harbor many species of birds, including ospreys, herons, pelicans, and eagles; the endangered American crocodile and the manatee live here as well. Florida panthers slink through the wetlands, but only on rare occasions have people seen them.

Shark Valley, about an hour's drive west on US 41 out of Miami, is on the park's northern boundary, near the **Miccosukee Indian Reservation.** Open-sided trams depart from the Shark Valley Information Center for two-hour **narrated tours** of the grasslands. Winter is particularly nice for riding a bicycle (bring your own) along the 15.5-mile loop, which is closed to all vehicles except the trams. Though no sharks inhabit the region (the area takes its name from the Shark River), plenty of alligators snooze in the sun. You're also likely to see raccoons, deer, and maybe a few river otters. Atop the 65-foot-high observation tower, you can enjoy a sweeping view of the seemingly endless grasslands.

Narrated **boat tours** are available from the park's gateways at **Everglades City** (about 50 miles from Shark Valley and an hour and 45 minutes from Naples) and **Flamingo,** which is located on Florida's southern coast. **The Flamingo Lodge, Marina, and Outpost Resort,** 38 miles southwest of the Flamingo entrance, rents kayaks and canoes and also offers a variety of guided cruises.

One of the best places for birding in the Everglades is along the **Anhinga Trail,** where in winter it's relatively easy to spot alligators, turtles, and sometimes otters. We also recommend the two-hour backcountry cruise that takes you far into a mangrove forest. Depending on the season in which you visit, you may be able to see hawks and manatees.

Because of urban development and water-diversion activities, the ecosystem at Everglades National Park is threatened. A visit to the park can give kids an appreciation for the environment, showing them how large areas of Florida may have looked before condos and hotels were built on them. The contrast between the rivers of grass and the seemingly endless, red-roofed developments that line many of the state's highways often impresses children with the need to conserve the wild lands of the Everglades.

TIPS: The best time to visit is during winter, the park's dry season *(Dec.–mid-April).* The park is open all year, but during the other seasons it's frequently hot and filled with mosquitoes. Be sure to wear a hat and put on sunscreen and insect repellent. Bring binoculars.

Although many operators offer airboat tours of the Ten Thousand Islands on the outskirts of the Everglades, the activity destroys plants and wildlife. Try to resist.

BASICS: Information about **Everglades National Park** *(40001 State Rd. 9336, Homestead. 305/242-7400. www.nps.gov/ever/)* can be obtained from the **Flamingo Visitor Center** *(Flamingo. 941/695-2945)* and the **Gulf Coast Visitor Center** *(Everglades City. 941/695-3311).* **Flamingo Lodge, Marina, and Outpost Resort** is managed by Amfac Parks and Resorts *(800/600-3813 or 941/695-3101).* Boat tours can be arranged with **Everglades National Park Boat Tours** *(800/445-7724)* at the ranger station in Everglades City.

MORE EVERGLADES EVERGREENS

Corkscrew Swamp Sanctuary *(375 Sanctuary Rd., about 20 miles N of Naples. 941/348-9151):* Owned by the National Audubon Society, Corkscrew Swamp Sanctuary is an 11,000-acre preserve that is part of the Everglades ecosystem but not part of Everglades National Park. The preserve features what may be the world's largest stand of bald cypress trees, which flank a 2.5-mile-long boardwalk. Corkscrew Swamp is also a major nesting place for North American wood storks.

Collier-Seminole State Park *(20200 East Tamiami Trail, about 17 miles S of Naples on US 41):* Also part of the Everglades ecosystem, this state park offers canoe trips on the **Black Water River** and through mangroves. A boardwalk cuts through the mangroves. The park has a Visitor Center *(941/394-3397).* **Boat trips** can be arranged through **Collier-Seminole State Park Boat Tours** *(941/642-8898).*

Seminole Tribe of Florida Big Cypress Reservation

In the interior of Florida, on the edge of the Everglades, the **Big Cypress Reservation** has rivers of grass, mangrove forests, and islands of hardwoods. It is a region harboring alligators, turtles, snakes, a variety of birds, and Florida panthers. The Seminole tribe, whose members descend from survivors of the Seminole Wars, has opened 2,000 acres of its reservation to tourism.

One of the best ways to see the land and learn something about the Seminole culture is to book an overnight **Billie Swamp Safari.** You'll start out by taking a four-hour ecotour, which can also be purchased as a day package. In swamp buggies you'll wind through hardwood hammocks, pine forests, and cypress domes while the guide describes Seminole traditions and food staples such as hearts of palm. You'll also learn about natural medicines, such as the aspirinlike substance made from the leaves of willow trees.

Although wild panthers do inhabit the Everglades, the ones you spot here are held in a lair. You will also see alligators—in a show, unfortunately—as well as bison and southern razorback hogs. A highlight of the overnight safari is the ride through the dark swamp, followed by Seminole stories told around a campfire. You then bed down in a *chickee*—a traditional rustic dwelling.

Some parts of the safari can seem hokey, but it's a unique experience to explore Seminole land and discuss Seminole culture with members of the tribe. "Sometimes people think we're just bingo-playing Indians," says Seminole spokesperson Lee Tiger, who is a Miccosukee, a tribe related to the Seminole. "The truth is we're taking those bingo dollars and converting the money into nature and ecotourism. This allows us to retain nature and give people jobs. It also creates friendships between Indians and non-Indians. It's good public relations."

The ancestors of the Seminole came from many tribes. When the Spanish and the British invaded the territory in the 17th century, many tribe members were killed or died of disease. The Seminole tribe estimates that 200,000 Native Americans were living in Florida in 1500; by 1708, that number had dwindled to fewer than 20,000. The survivors roamed free, earning them the Spanish name *cimarrones* ("renegades"), which in time became "shim-i-no-les."

Right: Kayakers paddle through Everglades National Park.

Great blue heron in Everglades National Park

When the Indian Removal Act was passed in 1830, many people were forced to migrate west (pages 102-104), but the Seminole refused to go. So began the Seminole Wars of 1835-1842 and 1856-1858, during which the U.S. government spent $40 million, evicted 3,000 people, and killed about 1,500. A relative handful (the Seminole put the number between 2 and 300) found refuge in the dense swamps and hammocks of the Everglades.

On a 60-acre site in the heart of the Big Cypress Seminole Reservation, the tribe's **Ah-Tah-Thi-Ki Museum**—the name means "to learn"—details the culture and history of the tribe. Dioramas and a multiscreen film relate the group's history and its struggles against early settlers. Through the exhibits, you learn about tribal life, including the story behind the Seminole's distinctive rainbow-colored patchwork clothing. You'll also come to understand the importance of the green corn dance.

"The green corn dance celebrates the harvest of corn in May or June," says Lee Tiger. "The whole tribe comes together for this annual renewing of spiritual values. It's like Christmas, Easter, and all the non-Indian holidays rolled into one. Plus it's like going to church." These festivities are closed to the public.

The collection of artifacts on view in the museum catches the interest of kids, who can browse through moccasins, leggings, turtle-shell rattles, medicine baskets, and bows and arrows. Also on view are rare swords from the Seminole Wars, plus a noteworthy collection of southeastern beaded shoulder bags. Kids also like the **folklore theater,** which presents the traditional beliefs and legends of the Seminole.

TIPS: The 2000-acre site has camping for recreational vehicles. Call 800/437-4102.

BASICS: Highlights at the **Big Cypress Seminole Reservation** include the **Ah-Tah-Thi-Ki Museum** *(Clewiston. 941/902-1113. www.seminoletribe.com/museum)* and the **Billie Swamp Safari Wildlife Park** *(Clewiston. 800/949-6101. www.seminoletribe .com/safari),* which offers overnight and day packages.

MICCOSUKEE RESORT & CONVENTION CENTER

The Miccosukee tribe was originally part of the lower Creek Nation, an association of Hitchiti-speaking clans on lands that became part of Alabama and Georgia. Settlement by Europeans devastated the Miccosukee. After the third Seminole War ended in 1858, the surviving Miccosukee settled in the Everglades. In 1962 the government recognized them as an individual tribe.

Opened in 1999, the **Miccosukee Resort & Convention Center** is just 15 minutes west of Miami on the Tamiami Trail. It offers an **Everglades Family Adventure** package that includes a tour of the **Miccosukee Indian Village,** 18 miles west of the resort. The fee includes lodging and a rental car. From 10 a.m. to 2 p.m., **Club Egret** stages supervised activities for infants and kids to age 12. The resort also has a gambling casino.

BASICS: Miccosukee Resort & Convention Center *(500 S.W. 177th Ave., Miami. 877/242-6464 or 305/221-8623).* Winter rates start at $250; summer rates begin at $105. Packages are available. Child care at **Club Egret** is $5 an hour.

Hawk's Cay Resort
Duck Key

The dolphin jumped so high out of the water that its flipper was level with my daughter's arm, making a handshake easy. The female bottlenose dolphin then swam close enough to the dock that my daughter could pat its rubbery back and scratch its white abdomen.

The dolphin interaction program at **Hawk's Cay Resort** is one of the best in the country. This 60-acre island resort is located on Duck Key—90 miles south of Miami and 60 miles north of Key West—between Islamorada and Marathon in the center of the Florida Keys.

At the **Dolphin Connection,** co-owners Cheryl Messinger (a marine biologist) and husband Doug Messinger foster an in-depth understanding of dolphins by creating hands-on programs that get you into the water with these intelligent and friendly creatures. "This kind of experiential learning, through touching and playing, is enhanced with using questions," says Cheryl. "We'll ask people what makes a mammal, and someone will answer 'a live birth.' So then we'll roll the dolphins over onto their backs, let people hold them on their laps, and show people the dolphins' belly buttons." The Messingers also let you look inside a dolphin's mouth, pointing out the little fringes along the edges of the tongue; these create a watertight seal that helps young dolphins suckle underwater. "When people see these things," says Cheryl, "they learn and they remember. And of course they have a lot of fun. We hope that creates a positive impact so that people will be more careful with the dolphin's environment."

Hawk's Cay offers different programs aimed at different ages. **Dolphin Discovery**—a 45-minute program for people at least 4 feet 6 inches tall with a clear understanding of English—starts in an outdoor classroom overlooking the enclosed saltwater lagoon where the Atlantic bottlenose dolphins live. After a brief introduction, participants (wearing life jackets) stand or sit on submerged platforms and feed, pet, and play with the dolphins. A professional photographer using a digital camera takes photos that can be purchased later on. Participants learn about dolphin diet, their behavior patterns, and how they interact with other marine life. The fee is $80 for resort guests or $90 for nonresort guests.

Dockside Dolphins is a 40-minute program for families and people who cannot participate in the Dolphin Discovery program, including young children (ages 12 and younger must be accompanied by a paying adult), non-English speakers, and pregnant women. Sitting on the dock next to the lagoon, participants feed, pet, and play with the dolphins; they also learn how to take blood samples and do an ultrasound. Children especially enjoy handling the apparatus used to listen to a dolphin's heartbeat. The fee is $40 for resort guests or $45 for nonresort guests.

For children ages 5 and up, there's **Dolphin Detectives.** This junior training program involves measuring the dolphins' food, teaching dolphins to play games, and learning how to tell if the animals are healthy. The program lasts about 30 minutes, and parents need not accompany their children. The fee is $30 for resort guests or $35 for nonresort guests.

Although dolphins are the big draw, Hawk's Cay offers many other activities, and you can stay in comfortable rooms, suites, or two-bedroom villas. With the Atlantic Ocean on one side and the Gulf of Mexico on the other, water activities are plentiful—and lessons are available for most of them. (Not all are available to younger children, however.) **Fly-fishing lessons** are for ages 16 and up, while the **diving programs** require that students be no younger than age 10. Snorkeling, diving, and tennis are available, and golf can be played nearby.

Glass-bottom boats go out Monday through Sunday for two-hour cruises around the Keys. These trips are especially nice for children who are too young to snorkel. With luck you'll see snappers, mackerels, and stingrays.

The supervised kids programs at Hawk's Cay include activities that focus on marine ecology. In the **Little Pirates Club** (ages 3 through 5, from 9 a.m. to 1 p.m. daily), kids take lessons in very small kayaks called tikis, or they board a boat where they learn to take the wheel and lower the sails. In **Island Adventure Club** (ages 6 through 12, from 9 a.m. to 4 p.m. daily), older children bicycle around the five islands that make up Duck Key, board the five-story-tall pirate ship, and fire water cannon. The **Paint Your Own Pottery** program in the pool hut lets kids decorate pieces shaped like dolphins and manatees. **Kids Night Out,** for children ages 5 through 12, is from 7 p.m. to 10 p.m. on Wednesday through Saturday evenings (or Friday and Saturday evenings during the fall months).

TIPS: The programs fill up quickly. Try reserving your place three months or more in advance.

BASICS: **Hawk's Cay Resort** *(61 Hawk's Cay Blvd., Duck Key. 888/443-6393 or 305/743-7000. www.hawkscay.com).* The **Dolphin Connection** *(888/814-9154 or 305/743-7000, ext. 3570. www.dolphinconnection.com)* offers hands-on programs. Nightly room rates are $230 *(Jan.-April)* and $190 *(May-Dec.).* Packages include the five-night **Family Island Explorer,** which starts at $615 for two adults and two children.

Busch Gardens Tampa Bay

The rides were great at **Busch Gardens Tampa Bay,** but we found the animal encounters—especially **Serengeti Safari** and the park's **VIP tour**— even better. On Serengeti Safari, we got as close to a giraffe as possible without going to Africa—or to Fossil Rim Wildlife Center in Texas (pages 98-99). As soon as our flatbed truck came into view, Claudia, a 14-foot-tall giraffe with a fondness for carrots, strode over to us. When our naturalist guide handed us the edibles, Claudia, accustomed to treats, lowered her boomlike neck to the truck bed, stuck out her seemingly endless purple tongue, and munched the goodies from our hands. It was a thrill for both the adults and the kids. Claudia happily let us pet her nose and neck; the kids stood amazed at her rough hair and sweet disposition.

Molly, the bongo, and a group of ostriches, whose names we didn't catch, waddled over. On cue from the naturalist, we proffered romaine lettuce and kept track of our fingers in the event an overly enthusiastic ostrich decided to peck at a pinky or two. But none did. We felt as if we were having hors d'oeuvres with Big Bird. These encounters were just some of the unforgettable moments on the 30-minute tour of Serengeti Plain for ages 5 and older (a bargain at $20 per person).

For more animal close-ups, book the VIP tour at $60 per person. This four-hour tour includes the Serengeti Safari experience, but it comes with a personal escort who takes you to the animal nursery, arranges for priority seating at shows, and gets front-of-the-line privileges for you at all of the park's roller coasters.

Myombe Reserve: The Great Ape Domain gets you close to gorillas and chimpanzees. This lush, walk-through exhibit has several shaded areas, benches, and thin (but strong!) glass. When we visited, a teenage male named Simsim grinned while snacking on red hibiscus just inches away from us. Kishina somewhat sloppily munched oranges to the delighted squeals of some grade-schoolers who said she ate just like their friend Dave. Should the animals be napping out of view, you can see them live via the videocam monitors.

Edge of Africa, another walk-through, uses glass walls to create a sense of proximity. The cutaway of the hippo pond let us see the rotund bathers resting their huge legs on rocks and occasionally bouncing their toes. Getting within inches of a lioness, snoozing belly up in the sun, was equally memorable.

Getting nosy, a giraffe checks for handouts during a Serengeti Safari at Busch Gardens Tampa Bay.

On a visit to the animal nursery, we saw blue and gold macaws, just a few days old, and baby koalas—fuzzy gray wonders with dark snub noses. Nearby was the petting zoo, a nice place to go with little kids. Huge tortoises that looked like rocks were in pens, and a small herd of baby goats stood ready to be groomed. At **Lorikeet Landing,** an aviary, kids attracted the colorful birds by holding a cup of nectar. The tiny creatures fluttered over, hovering above the cups to drink the nectar.

At the **Busch Gardens Tampa Bay Family Fun Adventure Camp,** families serve as assistant zookeepers, helping to set up animal habitats, preparing meals for creatures that range from monkeys to iguanas, and learning about some of the park's 290 species. Afternoons consist of roller-coaster rides and swimming at **Adventure Island,** a nearby water park. The overnights are for adults and children (the latter at least 8 years old).

Busch Gardens Tampa Bay also comes with the requisite **theme-park thrills.** Montu, the largest inverted coaster (your legs dangle) in the Southeast, zooms you through 4,000 feet of track at speeds up to 60 miles per hour. Kumba, the steel coaster, flips you seven times; Scorpion and Python feature dizzying loops. Debuting in 2000, Gwazi consists of dueling wooden coasters that roar up to 50 miles per hour while almost—but not quite—smashing into each other.

TIPS: Book the popular **Serengeti Safari** as soon as you arrive in the park. Visit **Myombe Reserve** early or late in the day; the chimpanzees and gorillas are less active at midday.

BASICS: Busch Gardens *(800/423-8368. www.buschgardens.com)*

Museum of Science and Industry, Tampa

The two 85-foot-long, 3-story-high *Diplodocus* dinosaur skeletons—the largest ones ever assembled—dominate the lobby of the **Museum of Science and Industry (MOSI).** A 70-acre scientific playground, this museum houses an IMAX theater, a planetarium, and more than 450 wide-ranging and engaging exhibits. Here you can climb inside a space shuttle, tour the human body, walk through a 3-D postcard, feel the fury of a hurricane, and enjoy the quiet of an urban nature center.

Two programs to check for are the **Family Camp-Ins** and **Great Escapes.** Bring your own sleeping bags to the overnight camp-ins, which feature special science shows and come packaged with dinner, breakfast, and an IMAX movie. Great Escapes take families (and others) on off-site trips led by MOSI scientists. You may visit the Kennedy Space Center or take a boat to explore the area's marine biology.

In **Welcome to Florida,** learn what it's like to be the size of a bug, watch lightning strike, and find out what causes thunder.

In the **Amazing You** program, video projection creates the illusion of being in an operating room while surgery is performed; a wheelchair course lets you experience what it's like to use a wheelchair; and a piano illustrates the infinite number of potential DNA combinations. Depending on your kids' ages, you may also want to view the human-development film that ends with a live birth. This may be the opportunity you're looking for to help them begin to understand the process.

As a memorial to the crew of the space shuttle *Challenger,* which exploded seconds after its launch in January of 1986, the families of the crew members have established an international network of more than 25 **Challenger Learning Centers,** one of which is at MOSI. The center features a simulated shuttle environment that can be entered through a light lock. Together, families complete assignments at workstations.

In **Space Station L1,** see what it's like to live and work in space, and plan a mission to Mars using a touch-screen monitor. In the flight simulator *(extra fee)*, experience space travel in a five-minute, motion-simulated flight.

At **Kids in Charge,** a hands-on gallery for ages 5 and under, preschoolers and parents explore basic science concepts by pulling levers, touching fossils, and driving child-size paddle-wheel boats. At 11 a.m. on Fridays, the KIC Club *(extra fee)*, offers a half-hour program with a MOSI educator; it can include science experiments, songs, crafts, and dances. **Little Explorers** (Tuesday at 10 a.m. and Saturday at 9 a.m.) is a preschool science class with in-depth demonstrations and activities lasting about an hour. The **Coleman Science Works Theater** is a daily 30-minute science show that combines show-biz dazzle with audience participation. This popular presentation, typically geared toward grade-schoolers, fills up fast, so check the schedule when you arrive.

TIPS: Explore the **Science Library** at MOSI, where you can check out books, CD-ROMs, a globe, or an "Ecology to Go" toolbox that contains headsets, binoculars, microscopic viewers, field guides, and identification cards to take with you when you go exploring in MOSI's **Back Woods.**

BASICS: **Museum of Science and Industry** *(4801 E. Fowler Ave., Tampa. 813/987-6300. www.mosi.org.)* is located 1 mile northeast of Busch Gardens Tampa Bay (pages 187-188). **Family Camp-Ins** are $28 for children and $12 for adults.

MORE TIME OFF IN TAMPA

The Florida Aquarium *(701 Channelside Dr. 813/273-4020):* The aquarium traces Florida's waters from their origins in underground springs through wetlands, bays, and coral reefs, and then out to sea. It also presents more than 4,300 animals and plants that represent 550 species native to the state. There's more than just fish in the cleverly created habitats: Wood ducks, stilt birds, and alligator hatchlings inhabit the wetland gallery. At the **Florida Bridges** exhibit, pilings are encrusted with corals, sponges, and barnacles. As you pass by, you hear the simulated rumble of cars and trucks overhead and see crabs, oysters, and shrimp.

In each of the four galleries on Florida—**Wetlands, Bays and Beaches, Coral Reefs,** and **Florida Offshore**—there are "wet labs." Some of them have computers, which families can use to find out more information.

Florida Coral Reefs, the largest gallery at the aquarium, features tanks of queen angelfish, parrotfish, blue tang, and schools of other rainbow-colored beauties. This gallery also lets you peer into caves to get a diver's-eye view of such hard-to-spot sea creatures as lobsters and eels.

Adventure Island *(10001 McKinley Dr. 813/987-5600. www.adventure island.com):* Splash and swim at this 22-acre water-play park, which is open from mid-March through Labor Day. Young ones like the kiddie-size slides, water jets, and gentle wave pool at **Fabian's Funport.** Older ones cool off by swirling down the **Caribbean Corkscrew,** a four-story tower, and twisting down **Runaway Rapids,** a 34-foot-high series of water-filled flumes.

Located a quarter mile from Busch Gardens Tampa Bay (pages 187-188), Adventure Island is part of Busch Entertainment Corporation. If you're planning to get wet at the park, consider a reduced-price combination ticket to Adventure Island and Busch Gardens Tampa Bay.

Paddle and Pedal: For more outdoor adventures, you can canoe along the Hillsborough River with **Canoe Escape** *(9335 E. Fowler Ave. 813/986-2067).*

Right: Tampa's Museum of Science and Industry offers sleepovers and a world of fun.

Tennessee Aquarium Chattanooga

Most aquariums attract viewers by displaying colorful species of fish that normally live among the ocean's coral reefs—a saltwater environment. The **Tennessee Aquarium** is different: It is the world's largest freshwater aquarium, with 9,000 specimens representing more than 350 species.

The facility traces the waters of the Tennessee River from their source in the mountains all the way to the Mississippi Delta and the Gulf of Mexico (by way of the Ohio and Mississippi Rivers). You can also see exhibits on other great rivers of the world, such as the Amazon in South America and the Congo in Africa. As a result, you not only look at fish but also view other animals that live in river environments. You'll encounter frogs, boa constrictors, yellow anacondas, river otters, alligators, snapping turtles, and other creatures you might not expect to see in an aquarium. Rattlesnakes, copperheads, blacksnakes, and other snakes indigenous to the Southeast are not forgotten; you can see them too.

The aquarium has a 60-foot central canyon that gives visitors the impression of following a river's path. A large tank called **Nickajack Lake** lets people watch 80-pound catfish swimming gracefully and alligator gar hovering motionless.

Not all of the creatures here are freshwater denizens, however. The facility also includes an exhibit about the **Gulf of Mexico:** Peer into its wall-size tank and you will spot toothy barracudas and sharks, loggerhead sea turtles, hogfish, squirrelfish, large stingrays with flapping fins, and hundreds of other species that swim in the Gulf.

At the **Environmental Learning Lab,** parents and kids can look at plant specimens under a microscope, use an interactive computer game to trace the path of litter in a stream, and connect to the Internet to find more information on a topic of interest. The aquarium has an IMAX 3-D theater, with a six-story-high screen that drops you into the action.

Venom: Striking Beauties debuted in March of 2000. On display are lionfish, black widow spiders, bullet ants, Gila monsters (24-inch-long lizards), stinging catfish, and lots more.

TIPS: Avoid the midday crowds: Arrive early or at 5:30 p.m. Although the doors close at 6 p.m., visitors who are already inside can stay until about 8 p.m. Check out the family-events schedule for walks among wildflowers and talks on animal colors and senses.

BASICS: The **Tennessee Aquarium** *(1 Broad St., Ross's Landing. 800/262-0695 or 423/265-0695. www.tennesseeaquarium.com)*

MORE CHATTANOOGA CHILD'S PLAY

Creative Discovery Museum *(321 Chestnut St., Ross's Landing. 423/756-2738. www.cdmfun.org):* This place is good for preschoolers and young grade-schoolers. Children make rubbings, dig at a full-size reproduction of a *Tyrannosaurus rex*, and drum their own tunes. Toddlers make a splash by floating boats in their own play area.

Lookout Mountain Incline Railway *(827 E. Brow Rd. 423/821-4224):* This old railway goes to the top of Lookout Mountain, which towers above Chattanooga. Making the climb each day are historic railcars that have been taking people up the 72.7 percent grade for more than a hundred years.

Some visitors take the railway up so they can tour **Rock City Gardens** (see next item), 14 acres of unusual rock formations. Lookout Mountain was a critical strategic objective during the Civil War, and many Civil War enthusiasts board the railcars to the top as part of a pilgrimage to the **Chickamauga and Chattanooga National Military Park,** one of many Civil War sites in the area.

MOUNTAIN CULTURE

Learn wood carving, broom making, quilting, blacksmithing, and other traditional crafts at the **Ozark Folk Center State Park in** Mountain View. Craftspeople demonstrate these old Ozark skills and teach one-day to one-week classes. In the **Young Pioneer Program,** kids join a workshop or team up for a one-on-one session with a craftsperson. Adults have similar options. Check the schedule for evening mountain-music concerts and Sunday gospel singing. The program runs from April through early November. The park is a mile north of Mountain View on Spur **382** off Hwys. 5, 9, and 14. Call 800/264-3655 or 870/269-3851.

Rock City Gardens *(1400 Mockingbird La. 706/820-2531):* These 14 acres of rock gardens atop Lookout Mountain offer a nice respite from indoor attractions. Try getting through the narrow opening between the big boulders of **Fat Man's Squeeze,** and take little kids to **Fairyland Caverns** and **Mother Goose Village.** At **Lovers' Leap,** you can see a panorama of seven states.

Ruby Falls *(Rte. 4, Scenic Hwy., Lookout Mountain. 423/821-2544):* Signs seemingly everywhere in the area tell you to see this "wonder," but after all the hype, we were unimpressed by the 145-foot waterfall inside **Lookout Mountain Caverns.** If your kids have never been in a cavern, however, you might consider giving them the opportunity to see this one.

Hunter Museum of Art *(10 Bluff View. 423/267-0968):* This museum is noted for its comprehensive collection of American art. Kids also like the building in which it is housed—a classic 1904 Southern mansion. The **Bluff View Art District** is an enclave of galleries, restaurants, and small museums.

Augusta Heritage Center
Elkins

For five weeks in July and August, Appalachian and other traditional arts, music, crafts, dances, and folklife take center stage at **Augusta Heritage Center** at Davis & Elkins College. These summer sessions are popular with families. Parents and kids 8 through 12 take separate classes but enjoy meals, dances, and concerts together. (Teens between 13 and 17 may enroll in an adult class with the instructor's approval.) Participants stay in the college's dorms, most of which sleep two adults, with floor space for young kids in sleeping bags.

Learn dulcimer playing, storytelling, flat-foot dancing, quilting, basketry, and carving. Take banjo, fiddle, or piano lessons. Try hornsmithing—etching designs on animal horns—or stonemasonry, twig furniture construction, lacemaking, and spinning. The five-week session includes more than 200 classes, workshops, concerts, and folklife programs. Most classes meet four to six hours a day.

The center offers theme weeks with single-topic classes and a guest artist each day. Examples include Cajun/Creole Week, Guitar Week, Blues Week, Swing Week, Irish Week, Bluegrass Week, Old Time Week, and Spring Dulcimer Week.

In **Folk Arts for Kids,** children complete week-long programs in art, music, and dance. They also take nature walks, learn creative writing, and visit with guest musicians, dancers, and storytellers. During Cajun/Creole Week, children focus on Louisiana, Quebec, France, and other places where French is spoken. They also dance, play games, hear stories, and take part in a Cajun Mardi Gras. The second week focuses on sharing tales through theater and improvisation, creating animal sculptures, building African slit drums and bamboo kazoos, and playing noncompetitive games. The third week explores traditional crafts, customs, folklore, dances, and the music of Ireland. The fourth week takes kids on an imaginary trip through Quebec, where they learn traditional dances and how to play the spoons. The fifth week features customs, crafts, and music from several parts of the world.

TIPS: The Augusta Heritage Center hosts the **Augusta Festival** on August 11-13.

BASICS: **Augusta Heritage Center** *(100 Campus Dr. 304/637-1209. www.augusta heritage.com).* For weeks 1 to 4, adults pay $325 for room and board (6 nights, 17 meals). Week 5 is $335 per adult (7 nights, 19 meals). For children in the same room, it's $108 a week for ages 8 to 13 and $163 a week for ages 14 to 17. Tuition is $325 to $355; **Folk Art for Kids** is $285 to $305. Some classes have a materials fee (adults about $45, kids $20 to $25). For an additional fee, rooms with private baths are available at the on-campus Graceland Inn and Conference Center *(800/624-3157 or 304/637-1600. www.wvweb.com/graceland).*

NORTHEAST

Llama Trekking
Bethel

If you can imagine taking a hike with Big Bird, you'll understand the appeal of llama trekking. Not only are these gentle creatures great companions, they'll also carry your gear—a trait that makes them particularly endearing.

Our three-day hiking adventure began with a crash training course at the **Telemark Inn** in Bethel. Guide and inn owner Steve Crone—who, by the way, is great with children—showed us some easy moves with the rope lead to get the animals to go, stop, and turn. Even the shy 5-year-old in our group proudly mastered the commands. Llama trekking is a great confidence-builder for kids.

It's also an easy camping alternative for families, especially those with young children or independent teens—or even grandparents who want to join the expedition. The guides pitched the tents, cooked and served the meals, and woke us in the morning with hot towels and fresh coffee. Instead of beef jerky, baked beans, and other basic camp fare, we dined on fish and chicken grilled on portable stoves. Despite these civilized touches, our trek took us satisfyingly deep into the forest. From our base camp, we hiked to waterfalls and scenic lookouts; we also observed a variety of wildlife, including a moose drinking from a pond.

For noncampers interested in varying their backcountry activities, Crone also offers multisport, lodge-based trips. The three- and five-day packages combine llama trekking, mountain biking, hiking, and canoeing around Bethel, Maine, and in nearby New Hampshire's **White Mountain National Forest.** At the end of the day, you return to the simple but comfortable Telemark Inn. The inn has only five rooms, which makes for smaller, more intimate groups.

Itineraries include canoeing on Umbagog Lake, mountain biking through the forest, and hiking to waterfalls, ponds, and the top of Tyler Mountain. Excursions range from 3 to 6 miles a day. Among the added attractions are birds of prey, beaver dams, moose—and spectacular views. To keep children interested, Crone punctuates each day with snack breaks and dips in swimming holes. At night the group gathers around the campfire for storytelling and stargazing.

In winter Crone turns his 360-acre property—which sits at the base of Caribou Mountain surrounded by the White Mountain National Forest—into a cross-country ski center featuring 12.5 miles (20 km) of groomed trails. Here you can also

Page 195: A skier and huskies hook up for a day of dog-joring at the Telemark Inn in Bethel.

 WILDLIFE ENCOUNTER    CULTURAL EXPLORATION   LEARNING ESCAPE

SUNDAY RIVER SKI RESORT

For those families that enjoy downhill skiing, consider a visit to **Sunday River Ski Resort** near the Telemark Inn. One of the largest ski resorts in the East, Sunday River has a great beginners' area as well as challenging slopes for intermediate and advanced skiers—and snowboarders too. The resort also offers ski instruction for various levels. If you need child care, Sunday River provides good nursery and day-care services for children 6 weeks to 6 years old.

Among Sunday River's special kids programs, **Tiny Turns** gets 3-year-olds started with one hour of private ski instruction. **SKIwee,** for the 4- to 6-year-old crowd, combines morning or afternoon ski lessons with snow play. **Mogul Meisters** gets 7- to 12-year-olds on the slopes for a full day of supervised runs and instruction. For those interested in snowboarding, **MINIrider** offers lessons for kids ages 6 and older. Teen activities include **Vertical Reality.** During school vacations, intermediate and advanced skiers enjoy power-packed skiing and parties at night. Snowboarders can sign up for the **Black and Blue Crew** program, offering the same challenging terrain and teen-centered nights. There are also adult classes and private lessons for all levels.

Tips: Kids 5 and under ski free. Ask about special ski packages *(Sun.-Thurs.).*

Basics: The season at **Sunday River Ski Resort** *(Bethel. 207/824-3000. Midweek $47, weekends $49. www.sundayriver. com)* runs from October to May. For information about lodging and reservations, call 800/543-2754.

---

try dog-joring—basically cross-country skiing while a dog on a tether pulls you along. The inn will provide a trained husky, or you can bring your own pooch (with permission) for mushing lessons. Other winter activities include snowshoeing and ice-skating on frozen ponds.

Trail use is restricted to inn guests and no more than 15 additional skiers a day by advance reservation. Thus, you're guaranteed a true wilderness experience. If you prefer downhill skiing, **Sunday River Ski Resort** is only 15 miles away.

TIPS: It gets quite dark here at night. The surrounding dense woods completely block out moonlight and the Telemark Inn cuts the generator-fired electricity at midnight. If your kids (or you) are scared of the dark, bring along industrial-strength flashlights and plenty of batteries. Also, the five-room inn has just two bathrooms, so be prepared to share with your fellow guests.

BASICS: A 3-day camping and llama trek with the **Telemark Inn** *(207/836-2703. www.TelemarkInn.com)* costs $475 per adult and $350 per child. Rates for a 3-day, 3-night package with lodging are $425 for adults and $285 for children 14 and under. A 5-day, 5-night package is $625 per adult and $450 per child. Call for information about dog-joring and custom 7-day packages.

From Bethel's Telemark Inn, trekkers and sure-footed llamas traverse Caribou Mountain in Maine.

Sierra Club Family Trips

For die-hard urbanites and would-be naturephobes, **Sierra Club Family Trips** offer a kinder, gentler introduction to the world of nature and the joys of camping. Experienced naturalists not only point out the flora and fauna but also teach you how to set up a tent and cook over an open fire.

Among Sierra Club's 28 trips nationwide, Northeastern options include the **Acadia Park Family Base Camp.** Visitors explore the spectacular coastal area of Acadia National Park, and hike up Mount Cadillac. For an extra fee, you can try canoeing, sea kayaking, or bicycling. The **Thousand Islands Family Adventure** features the lovely lakes and islands of upstate New York. Activities include hiking in the Adirondacks, canoeing, biking, and horseback riding. Lighthouses and cranberry bogs color the **Cape Cod Family Adventure,** which offers beachcombing, fishing, clamming, and whale watching.

TIPS: If California is in your future travel plans, note that Sierra Club offers a **Just for Grandparents and Grandchildren** trip. Participants are based at Clair Tappaan Lodge in Tahoe Forest in the Sierras. Children must be at least 5 years old.

BASICS: Sierra Club Outings *(85 Second St., San Francisco. 415/977-5522. www. sierraclub.org/outings/national).* **Acadia Park Family Base Camp** *(offered once per year, usually in June)* is $595 per adult, $495 per child. **Thousand Islands Family Adventure** *(once per year, usually in July)* is $630 per adult, $530 per child. **Cape Cod Family Adventure** *(usually in August)* is $475 per adult, $365 per child.

Shelburne Museum

Dubbed "New England's Smithsonian," this museum consists of 37 exhibit buildings that sprawl over 45 acres. Dedicated to American folk art, artifacts, and architecture, the **Shelburne Museum's** unusual exhibits—among them a historic steamboat, an authentic lighthouse, a train station, a locomotive, a railcar, and a covered bridge—are guaranteed to grab even the most skeptical family members. A visit here makes history real.

From the deck of the *Ticonderoga,* Lake Champlain's last operating side-wheel passenger steamer, your children can experience how it felt to cross the lake during the days of steamboat travel. A walk through the *Grand Isle,* an elegant 1890 railcar oufitted with mahogany paneling, brass fixtures, and plush seating, will show you the lavish luxury of Gilded Age railway travel. And a tour of the 1871 *Colchester Reef Lighthouse* and related exhibits will bring alive the history of navigation on Lake Champlain and the dangers faced by those who braved its waters.

Most of the Shelburne's exhibit buildings are interesting period pieces in themselves. Like the *Ticonderoga,* the *Grand Isle,* and the *Colchester Reef Lighthouse,* many of the structures here represent various times and places in the American landscape, with specific connections to Vermont as well. The **A. Tuckaway General Store,** for example, was built in 1840 and stood originally in nearby Shelburne Center. The store is featured as it would have looked then, complete with cracker barrels, pot-bellied stove, cider jugs, mailboxes, and a chessboard set up for the locals. The two cells in the 1890 **Castleton Jail** offer a favorite photo opportunity for children, who like to pose behind the iron doors, as well as in the reconstructed pillory and stocks outside.

Other favorite exhibits here include the carriage-filled horseshoe barn. The wagons, sleighs, and coaches delight children, as does the early fire-fighting equipment— horse carts, ladder wagon, and pump station—displayed in the **Shaker Shed,** a structure built in the Shaker community of Canterbury, New Hampshire, around 1840 and then transplanted.

Outside the **Circus Building,** kids can take a spin on an old-fashioned carousel. Inside is a 500-foot-long miniature circus complete with horses, lions, cowgirls, and cowboys. Nearby stand 40 life-size carousel figures carved by the Gustav Dentzel Carousel Company of Philadelphia.

Older children might enjoy the cigar-store figures found in the **Stagecoach Inn,** along with the colorful weather vanes crafted to resemble roosters, whales, fish, and other objects.

If you are visiting with younger children, stop by the **Owl's Cottage.** This family-oriented center offers lots of hands-on activities that parents and children can do together. In July and August, regularly scheduled events include workshops in stenciling and writing with feather quills. These sessions also teach hoops and other

A young visitor masters the milking way at Shelburne Farms, near Shelburne Museum.

vintage games, and provide colonial frocks and breeches for dressing up. Young readers peruse books on early American life.

Look for the Shelburne's newest exhibit, **The Fabulous '50s: Welcome Home to Post-War Vermont,** which presents a typical house that might have belonged to a World War II veteran, his pregnant wife, and their child. Your kids will be entertained by the era's inimitable furnishings, not to mention its distinctive sounds—specifically, that good old rock 'n' roll music. This could be just the place for an introduction to the "King" himself—Elvis.

TIPS: If you have young children along, take time to visit **Alyssia's Play Garden.**
The Shelburne is developing a family guide to the museum. The guide will feature a treasure hunt through the exhibits and other children's activities.

With preschoolers and young grade-schoolers, consider a visit to nearby **Shelburne Farms** (*1611 Harbor Rd. 802/985-8686. Mid-May–mid-Oct. 9 a.m.-5 p.m., walking trails 10 a.m.-4 p.m.; adm. fee*), a 1,000-acre farm with plenty of beautiful Lake Champlain frontage. Among the activities here, you can ride the tractor-drawn hay wagon to the barn and to the **Children's Farmyard.** There are goats, rabbits, and pigs to pet, along with special programs that teach kids how to perform such farm tasks as milking cows (above) and grooming horses. Bring a lunch and enjoy a picnic in the pastoral surroundings.

BASICS: **Shelburne Museum** (*US 7, Shelburne. 802/985-3346. Closed Jan.-March; adm. fee*)

Boston Children's Museum

One of the country's first museums for kids, the **Boston Children's Museum** is unquestionably one of the best. This sprawling and sumptuous facility is a monument to the power of curiosity and creativity. In room after room, children romp, crawl, touch, blow bubbles, flip switches, paint—and pretend.

The museum's exhibits are designed to be age appropriate for toddlers to teens. For example, **Teen Tokyo** introduces American youths to their Japanese peers. They can listen to songs by various Japanese rock groups and browse through popular Japanese comic books. At **Playspace**, tots 4 and younger can build with blocks, climb in cars, explore shapes, and more. **Kidstage**, geared for little ones ages 2 to 6, features short plays in which the children often participate. Young grade-schoolers like **Boats Afloat**, where they can launch tugs, barges, and other water toys. And just in case a storm is brewing, kids can don yellow slickers and life jackets and board the *Minnow*—a real boat.

Construction Zone! lets kids act out the "Big Dig"—Boston's in-progress underground highway system. The two-story exhibit area features an iron-workers' steel walk and life-size Bobcats. Sporting hard hats, kids drive toy bulldozers, dump trucks, and cement trucks. They can also wield kid-size jackhammers, operate cranes, and construct tunnels and bridges.

Children can clamber all over **The New Balance Climb**, a huge, hands-on sculpture bristling with towers and tubes. At **Arthur's World,** based on the popular book and television show, kids can play in the family kitchen, crawl into tents in the **Backyard Sleepover,** and even watch themselves on television.

We're Still Here introduces the Wampanoag Indians, a Massachusetts tribe. A *wetu,* or wigwam, shows how these Native Americans lived long ago. For contrast, the exhibit also features a local Wampanoag girl who describes her modern house. Kids are invited to touch, by appointment, the collection of authentic artifacts that includes drums, hides, headgear, and baskets.

The museum's popular **family overnights** feature a craft demonstration, a live performance, after-hours exploring—and, best of all, a sleepover in one of the museum's exhibit areas, including Arthur's World backyard tents.

TIPS: It can be difficult to keep tabs on your kids as they bounce from display to display. Discuss in advance what to do if members of your party get separated.

BASICS: Boston Children's Museum *(300 Congress St. 617/426-8855. www. bostonkids.org. 10 a.m.-5 p.m., Fri. 10 a.m.-9 p.m. Adults $7, children 2-15 $6)*

Right: Dressed for the part, a junior hard hat operates a Bobcat at the Boston Children's Museum.

Museum of Science Boston

If there is one attraction in Boston that captivates both parents and children, this is it. With more than 450 exhibits—most of them quite good—you can easily spend hours here. If your time is limited, skip the dioramas of mounted birds, which are dull compared with the engaging hands-on exhibits.

Science Park, for example, lets kids of all ages explore the science of play. You can ride a seesaw to learn about fulcrums or swing alongside your child and see how weight influences movement. Joggers can clock their pace along a track equipped with timed lights.

At the **Light House,** an exhibit about optics, light, and color, kids can enjoy a game of Optical Pinball, which uses mirrors to reflect light, while they learn about the color spectrum.

The **Theater of Electricity** stages simulated lightning bolts on giant metal domes above the audience. Thrilling but loud, the realistic effects can frighten small children, so warn them in advance. At the quieter **Seeing Is Deceiving** exhibit, kids discover how and why the brain plays tricks on its owner. Demonstrations ask—and answer—such questions as "Why do we see colors in spinning black-and-white images?" They also show how to discover your blind spot—a blank field in your vision that the brain disregards.

At the **Discovery Center** kids can dig for fossils, measure themselves against an 18-foot-long python skeleton, and get an up-close prairie-dog's-eye view through a domed window in the middle of the animals' simulated habitat. A special area designed especially for preschoolers features a water-activity center outfitted with boats and a Fantasy Tower for easy climbing. Even infants have their own stimulating spot, outfitted with mirrors and touch objects—all placed conveniently at a baby's eye level.

There is an additional admission charge to visit the **Charles Hayden Planetarium** and the state-of-the-art 3-D **Mugar Omni Theater,** but the experience is well worth the cost. Restricted to children ages 5 and older, the Omni features a state-of-the-art digital sound system, wraparound screens, and angled seats. The collective effect can be somewhat stomach-churning.

TIPS: The Boston science museum is mobbed on weekends and holidays, and Omni tickets sell out quickly. A wise strategy is to buy tickets a day in advance. Tickets can be purchased by credit card over the phone, but you will have to pay a handling fee.

BASICS: Museum of Science *(Science Park Boston. 617/723-2500. www.mos.org. July 5-Labor Day: Sat.-Thurs. 9 a.m.-7 p.m., Fri. 9 a.m.-9 p.m. Rest of year: Sat.-Thurs. 9 a.m.-5 p.m., Fri. 9 a.m.-9 p.m. Adults $10, children 3-11 $7)*

MORE BOSTON BREWINGS

Boston Tea Party Ship and Museum *(Congress St. Bridge. 617/338-1773. March-late Nov.; adults $8, children 4-12 $7):* On December 16, 1773, a band of patriots disguised as Indians climbed aboard the *Beaver,* a British brigantine, and tossed hundreds of crates of tea into Boston Harbor, setting the stage for the Revolutionary War. On the *Beaver II*—a working replica of the original Boston Tea Party ship—young visitors can replay this historic event. Under the guidance of costumed interpreters, children gleefully heave crates of "tea" into the harbor, then haul them back on board with block and tackle. The audiovisual presentation, however, fails to thrill schoolkids who haven't yet studied this chapter in history. If you plan to tour belowdecks, be prepared for exceedingly cramped quarters—virtually impossible to negotiate with a stroller.

Quincy Market and Faneuil Hall Marketplace *(Congress and State Sts. 617/523-1300):* Not long after the end of the Revolutionary War, three massive buildings were constructed near the Boston Harbor wharves to accommodate the burgeoning shipping trade. Today, these buildings—along with a few new ones—make up the colorful cluster of shops, restaurants, and snack carts collectively known as **Faneuil Hall Marketplace.** Of special interest to children are the street performers who frequent the area and assorted kid-oriented theme stores. This is a perfect place to let your teenagers roam while you stroll or rest with the young ones. You might even be able to squeeze in a quick tour of historic **Faneuil Hall,** built in 1742, where patriots hotly debated the independence issue.

Plimoth Plantation
Plymouth

The year is always 1627 at this memorable living history museum. Situated on a breathtaking stretch of coast a few miles from Plymouth (and 42 miles southeast of Boston), **Plimoth Plantation** transports you back in time. Smoke rises from the chimneys of thatch-roofed cottages, goats and chickens roam the unpaved streets, sparks fly from the blacksmith's anvil, and "settlers" like Myles Standish wander about in period dress—and character. The costumed actors converse in charmingly authentic, 17th-century dialect. They unshakably maintain a historic point of view, no matter how hard you try to make them break character with references to contemporary life, language, or events.

The **Irreconcilable Differences** gallery imaginatively presents the conflicting viewpoints of the colonists and of the Native Americans through the "voices" of real people and their personal responses to difficult circumstances. At **Hobbamock's Homesite,** a 17th-century Wampanoag Indian dwelling, you can talk with descendants of the tribe, who also serve as site guides.

EAST COAST AQUARIUMS

If you haven't been to an aquarium lately, you may be surprised to find far more than lonely fish in little glass boxes. These days wall-size tanks and live kelp forests share exhibit space with boa constrictors, river otters, and penguins. The concept behind today's aquariums—and zoos, for that matter—is to create a realistic context for creatures by showing them in their shared habitats.

NEW ENGLAND AQUARIUM, BOSTON, MA

Small compared to some, the **New England Aquarium** has no whales jumping through fiery hoops or harmonica-playing porpoises. The focus is on natural presentation—and it is done well.

Outside the entrance, a tank full of friendly harbor seals perform for onlookers. If you've ever wanted to touch a sea star or rub elbows with a manta ray, hands-on exhibits ringing the first level let you do just that. A pool in the center of the hall is home to a colony of penguins.

A massive glass column rises dramatically from the pool. This tank, which holds 187,000 gallons of saltwater, is filled with colorful corals and other creatures. Follow the surrounding spiral staircase up and around and you'll come nose to nose with sharks, sea turtles, eels, and dazzling tropical fish.

Check out the **Aquarium Medical Center,** an E.R. for aquatic creatures. A glass wall lets visitors watch experts minister to ailing animals, from a battle-scarred piranha to a shell-shocked turtle.

Outside the main building, a new theater called **Unforgettable Boston** will show an interactive sightseeing tour of the city. Kids can also play "Storm over Stellwagen," a wall-size video game about Stellwagen Bank, a major feeding ground for whales located 26 miles off the coast.

Across the street, **Sounds of the Sea** illustrates that the world under the sea is anything but silent. Kids can press buttons to hear damselfish clicking, toadfish popping, and humpback whales singing and grinding. This small, well-conceived gallery also asks—and answers—common questions.

Be sure to catch the sea lion show, featured five times a day on the **Discovery,** a floating pavilion adjacent to the aquarium.

Tips: Kids love feeding time in the central tank. The scuba diver has been known to upstage even the ever popular sharks. Check the schedule for daily times.

Basics: **New England Aquarium** *(Central Wharf, Boston. 617/973-5200. www. neaq.org. Adults $12.50, children 3-11 $6.50)*

MYSTIC AQUARIUM, MYSTIC, CT

Having recently completed a $52-million renovation, the **Mystic Aquarium** is now home to more than 4,000 marine creatures. The aquarium's 24 exhibits are designed to convey the idea that the ocean consists of "islands of life."

Mystic is home to the **Institute for Exploration,** a research center founded by oceanographer Robert Ballard, who also discovered the wreck of the *Titanic.*

The centerpiece of the renovated aquarium is **Alaskan Coast**—a one-acre outdoor exhibit that is the new home for Mystic's beluga whales and harbor seals.

Mystic offers a rare opportunity to see a massive Steller sea lion, while seals and black-footed penguins await in the aquarium's **Pribilof Islands** complex.

Shore life is the theme at **Where Rivers Meet the Sea.** Exhibits feature sea horses, green crabs, silversides, and mudskippers. Jellyfish float in the **Upwelling Zone** gallery, where you learn how bottom nutrients feed

Kids and puffins see eye to eye at the National Aquarium in Baltimore.

surface animals. The **Kids' Cave** offers a great underwater view.

The **Challenge of the Deep** demonstrates how robots are used to find objects in the deep sea, while Atlantic bottlenose dolphins are the main attraction at the **World of the Dolphin** theater.

In the summertime, the Mystic aquarium sponsors educational outings. Naturalists lead families on beach walks and introduce preschoolers to activities such as seining. Older children and their families can sign up for day programs aboard the *Peter W. Anderson*, a U.S. Navy gunboat converted to a marine laboratory vessel.

Tips: Take in the dolphin show in midvisit to give everyone a rest from walking.

Basics: **Mystic Aquarium** *(55 Coogan Blvd. [exit 90 off I-95]. 860/572-5955. www. mysticaquarium.org. Adults $15, kids $10)*

NATIONAL AQUARIUM, BALTIMORE, MD Explore the **Amazon River Forest** at the **National Aquarium,** the star of Baltimore's **Inner Harbor.** This newest exhibit shows how cycles of flood and drought created this unique environment. The "river" teems with piranha, stingrays, and tetra, while the banks conceal dwarf caimans, a giant anaconda, poison dart frogs, turtles, and tropical birds.

The lush **South American Rain Forest** features parrots, sloths, and other exotics. **Maryland Mountains to the Sea** features the state's waterways, from mountain streams to the Chesapeake Bay. Here you'll see the likes of bullfrogs and blue crabs.

Popular with kids are the **Open Ocean Tank's** shark exhibit and **Wings Under Water,** one of the world's largest ray displays. Another favorite stop is the dolphin show at the **Marine Mammal Pavilion.**

Special family programs include **Breakfast with the Dolphins** and **Behind-the-Scenes** tours to see how the animals' food is prepared and how filtration tanks work.

Tips: To avoid long lines, get here early or purchase advance tickets through Ticketmaster *(410/481-7328).*

Basics: **National Aquarium** *(Pier 3, 501 E. Pratt St., Baltimore. 410/576-3800. www.aqua.org)*

Check the summer schedule for special family programs. It's a great chance to learn to play 17th-century games such as stool pool or ninepin.

TIPS: Unless you have preschoolers, who tend to lose interest more quickly, plan to spend at least half a day at Plimoth. The **Wampanoag Indian Annual Conference** takes place during one of the last two weekends in September. You'll see wonderful costumes and special performances of Native Americans songs, dances, and storytelling. Plimoth Plantation also operates a week-long day camp *($225)* for children ages 8 to 12 and 13 to 16. Six different sessions are offered from July 10 to August 1; for details, call 508/746-1622, ext. 8238.

BASICS: **Plimoth Plantation** *(137 Warren Ave. 508/746-1622. April-Dec. 1, 9 a.m.-5 p.m.; adults $16, children $9)*

MORE PLYMOUTH PASTIMES

Plymouth Rock. There is indeed a Plymouth Rock. It sits unimpressively under a pillared portico on the banks of Plymouth Harbor. If it doesn't move you, don't worry; most visitors have the same reaction. Just be glad you aren't charged admission.

Mayflower II (State Pier. 508/746-1622. April-Dec. 1, 9 a.m.-5 p.m.; adults $6.50, children $4): This full-scale replica of the ship that carried 100 passengers to the New World is docked near Plymouth Rock. A crew of costumed actors re-creates the original landing of December 26, 1620, and the story of the survivors who established the first permanent European settlement at Plimoth Plantation. It's a fun stop for visitors 5 years old and up.

Plymouth National Wax Museum *(16 Carver St. 508/746-6468. March-Nov. 9 a.m.-5 p.m.; adults $6, children 5-12 $2.75):* The museum's 180 lifelike figures show in 26 scenes the events that led to the Pilgrims' departure from England. Lights and sound effects will entertain even the preschoolers. And who knows?—you might just learn a few new things about the Separatist movement and the *Mayflower.*

Children's Museum of Plymouth *(46 Main St. 508/747-1234. Adm. fee)* Geared to a younger crowd (ages 3 to 6) than most children's museums, this institution encourages creative, hands-on learning. Little ones can explore the inside of a bisected fire truck, shop at a child-size grocery store, board a fishing boat, and much more.

Pilgrim Hall Museum *(75 Court St. 508/746-1620. www.pilgrimhall.org. Feb.-Dec. 9:30 a.m.-4:30 p.m.; adults $5, children 5-17 $3, family admission $14):* Best for older children, the exhibits here include Pilgrim artifacts such as Myles Standish's sword and the cradle of the first English child born in New England, plus portraits and decorative objects. Visitors 5 years old and up can join in a scheduled **Treasure Hunt,** the goal of which is to match pictures of artifacts with items on display in the museum.

Mashantucket Pequot Museum

In 1637, colonial forces massacred hundreds of Mashantucket Pequots in order to seize their land. Only a handful of the Indians survived by hiding in nearby cedar swamps. The tribe's numbers dwindled over the centuries as did the members' sense of cultural pride. All that changed in 1992, when the Mashantucket Pequots—now recognized as a sovereign nation—opened the **Foxwoods Resort Casino.** This popular casino annually provides the state of Connecticut 25 percent of its overall slot revenues—a minimum of $100 million per year. Since 1993, Foxwoods has contributed $1 billion to the state's coffers.

Situated on tribal land near the casino, the **Mashantucket Pequot Museum** preserves the Pequots' history and cultural traditions in a 308,000-square-foot facility. Begin your visit by descending through a simulated glacier (complete with blasts of frigid air) to a series of dioramas depicting prehistoric Pequot life. The museum's centerpiece is a 22,000-square-foot re-creation of a 17th-century Pequot village.

Although the museum is a worthy destination for families, Foxwoods Resort Casino decidedly is not. It may have video games, shops, and restaurants, but the casino and the hotels offer no child care, and the gaming rooms are off limits to those under the age of 21.

TIPS: If you want to gamble, the **Mohegan Sun** casino *(888/226-7711),* located in nearby Unasville and operated by the Mohican tribe, offers **Kids Quest.** This supervised child-care program is for children ages 4 to 12.

BASICS: Mashantucket Pequot Museum and Research Center *(110 Pequot Trail. 860/396-6800)*

LIFE IN CHANTEY TOWN

Mystic Seaport *(75 Greenmanville Ave. 888/973-2767 or 860/572-5315. April–mid-Oct. 9 a.m.-5 p.m., rest of year 10 a.m.-4 p.m.):* "Thar she blows. . . !" Echoes of the days of sail fill the air at Mystic Seaport. This living history maritime museum re-creates 19th-century Mystic—at that time a bustling whaling and shipbuilding port. In addition to exploring a historic whaling barque and listening to rollicking sea chanteys, you can visit the **Children's Museum.** Here kids can swab decks and haul cargo, making them appreciate the tamer chores back home. In 2000, Mystic plans to complete a replica of the *Amistad,* the ship on which captive Africans rebelled en route to America in 1839. When its construction is completed, the ship will set sail to tour the country.

American Museum of Natural History, New York

This museum goes to great lengths for an exhibit. Consider the 25-foot-long giant squid that commands the **Hall of Biodiversity:** Once a denizen of the deep off the New Zealand coast, it was caught by a commercial fisherman in 1998, purchased by the New Zealand Institute of Water and Atmospheric Research, then offered to the **American Museum of Natural History (AMNH)** as a gift. On June 8 of that year, a refrigerator truck delivered the 250-pound squid to a New Zealand airport for shipment to the United States. During the squid's layover in Los Angeles, however, it was bumped from its scheduled flight because of its weight. Upon finally arriving in New York, the giant calamary sailed through customs (it was classified as seafood) and was delivered to the AMNH, where you can view it today.

When the museum opened in 1869, it contained a few hundred mounted birds and a handful of mammals. In the years since then, the AMNH has added to its collection an array of dinosaur skeletons and fossils (including a 57-million-year-old horse skeleton), an enormous diorama replicating a section of the Central African Republic's rain forest, and a 1,300-year-old giant sequoia.

The AMNH also offers a series of **Children's Workshops.** These half- and full-day programs are held on Sundays *(adm. fee)* throughout the year. Activities relate to the museum's collection and might include films, tours, making puppets, clay sculpting, science experiments, and learning about different animals or peoples.

In the **Discovery Room** *(open the last weekend of each month except Sept.),* kids ages 5 and older in the company of an adult can touch specimens and explore **Discovery Boxes** that relate to natural science and anthropology. The **Alexander M. White Natural Science Center** lets children learn about the plants, animals, and geology of New York City. Throughout the year, **Family Drop-In Programs** feature activities such as guided tours, interactive computer sessions, and crafts.

The museum's newest feature—the **Frederick Phineas and Sandra Priest Rose Center for Earth and Space**—is a 333,500-square-foot exhibition and research facility. This $210-million center houses the new **Hayden Planetarium,** the **Lewis B. and Dorothy Cullman Hall of the Universe,** and the **Davis S. and Ruth L. Gottesman Hall of Planet Earth.** The Rose Center's dazzling centerpiece is an 87-foot sphere that "floats" within a glass cube.

The **Hall of Planet Earth (HoPE)** focuses on how the planet works. You will learn about its geologic history and the latest theories about the origins of life on Earth as well as the possibilities of life elsewhere in the universe. (*Our Dynamic Planet,* an earth-science activity guide for 7- to 10-year olds, is a terrific resource to use while touring HoPE; it's available free of charge at the museum entrance.) At the center of the hall hangs the **Dynamic Earth Globe.** Eight feet in diameter, it

A giant blue whale dwarfs the Hall of Ocean Life at the American Museum of Natural History.

contains a unique internal projection system that generates a stunning view of Earth from outer space. Children can watch as clouds, vegetation, and oceans appear on Earth's surface, then disappear as the planet rotates. The **Event Earth Wall** is an electronic bulletin that broadcasts updates on global natural events such as earthquakes and volcanic eruptions. HoPE also displays geological models that suggest all the continents were a single landmass millions of years ago, while a touch cart holds rock samples to compare and contrast.

The Cullman Hall of the Universe examines how the universe evolved, how atoms were created, and where the matter for life may have come from. Displays and videos show how gravity works and why black holes warp time and space. Videos also depict colliding galaxies and a star exploding into a supernova. And children can touch the Willamette Meteorite, a 15.5-ton piece of space debris.

At the **Space Theater** in the Hayden Planetarium, virtual-reality technology makes viewers feel as if they are flying through space. At the **Big Bang Theater,** a spectacular sound-and-light show simulates the birth of the universe.

Although the new Rose Center gets all the attention, don't overlook the museum's many other fascinating halls. In **Mammals and Their Extinct Relatives,** for instance, kids can see the world's largest exhibit of fossils—including the head and trunk of

"Effie," a baby woolly mammoth, as well as the giant skeletons of a *Tyrannosaurus rex* and an *Apatosaurus*. They can also stroke the imposing nose horn of a *Triceratops*, flip through charts to see how dinosaurs moved, and walk through the skeleton of a *Barosaurus*.

In the **Hall of Biodiversity**, visitors are invited to walk through a replicated African rain forest and take a virtual tour of nine distinct ecosystems. Rock hounds will enjoy **Gems and Minerals**, which displays one of the largest pieces of crystallized gold ever found.

TIPS: It would take a week to see everything in the museum. To focus your visit, check out the museum's website before you go.

Lines at the Hayden Planetarium's Space Theater can be long, so you may want to begin there.

The website for the Hall of Planet Earth *(www.amnh.org/rose/hope)* is a great place for budding earth scientists. They'll find answers to such posers as how scientists "read" rocks and what causes climates to change.

BASICS: **American Museum of Natural History** *(Central Park W. at 79th St. 212/769-5100. www.amnh.org)*

Children's Museum of Manhattan

Designed for kids ages 2 through 10, the **Children's Museum of Manhattan** **(CMOM)** features interactive exhibits that make learning fun. In **Body Odyssey**, for example, young visitors can explore the human body from the "inside"—by sliding through the interior of a bone and emerging as a red or white blood cell, crawling through a layered piece of skin, and ogling a three-gallon bagful of dead skin (the amount you shed in a month). Kids relate to the exhibit that explains—in their language—why people "burp" and "fart" and what constitutes "snot."

There are plenty of special programs to choose from. On weekends and school holidays, CMOM stages performances by dancers, musicians, actors, and puppeteers. In summer the museum features a jazz program on Wednesdays and Broadway performers on Thursdays. Kids are encouraged to participate in many of the performances. At the **Russell Berrie Art Studio,** children participate in workshops such as finger painting and sculpting. (Sign up at the main information desk.) And throughout the day, there's storytelling in the **Helena Rubenstein Literacy Center.** In fact, at any given time there are more than 20 workshops—from sing-alongs to games to crafts—going on somewhere in the museum.

At **WordPlay**, infants, toddlers, and children up to 4 years of age are enticed to learn and use words through activities based on current research in brain and language development. For infants, there's **Baby Babble**, a sensory-rich exhibit with a mirrored wall, textures to touch, and animal sounds. **Explorer's Park** leads toddlers along a path marked with simple words that describe their various actions. As she crawls under a bridge, your toddler will see the word "under"—and, it is hoped, make the connection.

Apartment ABC features a child-size apartment where kids can plan menus with their parents or order take-out food. They can dress up in a squirrel costume and climb **Chatterbug Tree**, or pretend they are sorting and sending mail at the **Post Office Pickup**. An especially wonderful exhibit, **Reader's Pond** is padded from floor to ceiling with stuffed animals. You can curl up next to your kids and read them stories.

Seuss! invites kids into the zany and delightful world of Dr. Seuss. Here, they can visit the messed-up house from *The Cat in the Hat* and climb aboard the cleanup machine. They can also crawl into the Fun-in-a-Box and find Thing One and Thing Two, or take a bumpy ride on Sam-I-Am's boat. Seuss! closes in August 2000. It will be replaced by **Good Grief**, featuring characters from Charles Schulz's *Peanuts* comic strip. The new exhibit will focus on teaching children skills for resolving conflict without resorting to violence. Just for fun, kids will be able to stretch out on top of Snoopy's doghouse and visit Woodstock's nest.

The **Time Warner Media Center**, designed for children ages 7 and older, is staffed by adolescents who have been trained at CMOM. The action here involves performing in front of the camera as well as behind it. Kids get to handle actual sound and camera equipment, read the news from a TelePrompter, and participate in topical, on-camera panel discussions. For any child interested in the news business, this is a terrific opportunity to see how it all works.

TIPS: CMOM contains five floors of activity-rich exhibits. It's best to select a few stops rather than try to see it all. Get here early so you can sign up for the day's workshops at the Information Desk.

BASICS: Children's Museum of Manhattan *(Tisch Building, 212 W. 83rd St. 212/ 721-1234. www.CMOM.org)*

Bronx Zoo (International Wildlife Conservation Park)

At the **Bronx Zoo**—otherwise known as **International Wildlife Conservation Park**—you could easily spend your entire visit doing things like tunneling beneath **Prairie Dog Town** and visiting eye-to-eye with its residents through a plastic bubble. Or climbing a rope "spiderweb," petting a llama, trying on a tortoise shell, sampling a skunk scent, or sporting "fox ears" to hear what that animal hears. But then you'd miss out on all the other treats at the country's largest urban zoo. It feels anything but urban, though. Situated on 265 wooded acres, the park presents animals in natural environments rather than in cages. It's easy to forget you're in the heart of the Bronx, just across the river from Manhattan.

You can't see everything in one day. If possible, check the zoo's website in advance to plan your visit. The website also has information about classes and special activities for families and children. A great way to start your visit is with a 15-minute **Skyfari** ride. This aerial tramway gives you a wonderful overview of the zoo park.

The park's newest exhibit, **Congo Gorilla Forest,** is the largest African rain forest ever re-created. It spans 6.5 acres and is home to 75 species, including 22 lowland gorillas. Along with providing an opportunity to see these gorillas in a natural habitat, the exhibit helps visitors understand how wildlife conservation can be accomplished. Interactive learning bays teach visitors about the rain forest's flora and fauna, and allow kids to compare their weight and hand size with those of a gorilla. Among the various environments here, you walk through a colobus monkey forest and a Mbuti camp and encounter a giant fallen ceiba (kapok) tree, spotting rare okapi en route. Along the **Rain Forest Trail,** families are encouraged to assume the role of field biologists and search for trailside animal signs—a gorilla nest, a termite mound, a tree that's been scraped by an elephant, or a fish partially eaten by an otter.

A unique feature of this exhibit is that kids can choose how their admission fee will be used for conservation. Choices include animal research, cross-cultural communication, or wildlands conservation.

The **Bengali Express** monorail takes you through **Wild Asia.** The wide-open spaces in this area showcase native Asian species, such as rhino, Siberian tigers, elephants, gaur (large wild oxen), and a variety of deer. The advantage here is that you might catch a herd of deer on the run; the disadvantage, of course, is that sometimes the animals are too far away to appreciate. Wild Asia closes during the winter and in inclement weather.

JungleWorld, on the other hand, guarantees an up-close view of gibbons, tapirs, fruit bats, and crocodiles. This indoor exhibit is widely recognized as one of the best in the world. Another fun stop is the **World of Darkness,** where bats, leopard cats, porcupines, and naked mole-rats have adapted to reversed cycles of night and day. The result: Visitors get a rare opportunity to observe these creatures' nocturnal habits.

A camel ride is always a fun way to end a visit to the Bronx Zoo, but you can opt to go anytime during the day. It's a safe adventure for kids and a great photo opportunity for parents.

Among the zoo's special programs, **Educational Adventures** offers visitors various opportunities to go behind the scenes. Those who sign up for **Breakfast in the Congo**—it's held in the **Congo Gorilla Forest** area—will receive a Congo Safari Kit with useful information and games related to gorillas and the rain forest, including Congo Bingo and Gorilla Tic-Tac-Toe. You'll also get to eat breakfast in the treetops overlooking the forest and its residents. **Mommy and Me** invites mothers and children ages 5 to 10 to build a bird nest together and teaches participants how animal and bird mothers take care of their young.

Family Overnight Safaris, held on weekends in May and June, include a picnic dinner, a sing-along, and nighttime visits with intriguing zoo occupants such as Noah the Boa. Both Educational Adventures and Family Overnight Safaris require advance registration. For information about fees and reservations, call the Education Department *(718/220-6854)* or check out the zoo's website *(www.wcs.org).*

Seasonal events include the **Spring Extravaganza,** a fun celebration of spring—and a great introduction to life at the zoo—for families with children 3 to 7. Kids can join in races, paint eggs, and crawl through a rabbit burrow. **Holiday Lights,** with thousands of lights blazing and more than 50 animal sculptures illuminated from late November to early January, is a dazzling holiday treat for all ages.

TIPS: More than 300 animals were born at the zoo in 1998; check the website *(www.wcs.org)* for updates, as well as photos of new animal babies. See the zoo map for animal-feeding times and a list of the best photo spots.

The **Lakeside Café** (outdoor seating for 600) is closed for renovation until 2001. Alternatively, try the **African Market,** the **Flamingo Pub,** or the **Zoo Terrace.**

If you get lost, pull out your map and look for the nearest Directional Sign Post. Each post has an animal, along with a location number that corresponds to a number on the zoo map grid.

BASICS: **The Bronx Zoo** *(Fordham Rd. and Bronx River Pkwy. 718/367-1010. www.wcs.org. Adm. fee).* Bengali Express, Skyfari, the Children's Zoo, the Zoo Shuttle, and camel rides are all closed November through April.

MORE NEW YORK CITY NUGGETS

The Intrepid **Sea-Air-Space Museum** *(Pier 86, W. 46th St. and 12th Ave. 212/245-0072. Adm. fee):* Originally used during World War II, this 900-foot-long aircraft carrier now displays historic aircraft, a U.S. Army armored tank, and the only nuclear missile submarine in the world that is accessible to the public.

Metropolitan Museum of Art *(Central Park at 5th Ave. and 82nd St. 212/535-7710. www.metmuseum.org. Sun. and Tues.-Thur. 9:30 a.m.-5:30 p.m.; Fri.-Sat. 9:30 a.m.-9 p.m.; closed Mon.; adults $10, children $5):* So enormous is this collection that it's best to customize your visit. Perennial kid favorites include the **Egyptian** exhibit, the **Hall of Armor,** and the **African** collection. Let your kids wander and browse.

National Museum of the American Indian *(1 Bowling Green. 212/668-6624. www.si.edu/nmai. Fri.-Wed. 10 a.m.-5 p.m., Thurs. 10 a.m.-8 p.m.):* Part of the Smithsonian Institution, this small but interesting collection is thoughtfully displayed within a broad context. Special programs include **Harvest Ceremony,** a unique Thanksgiving story told from the Native American perspective.

Residents of Prairie Dog Town size up visitors under the observation bubble at the Bronx Zoo.

Journeys into American Indian Territory, Catskills

Under a starry sky in a clearing surrounded by towering pines, we listened to the chanting of an ancient Taino prayer of thanks and blessing on all who had gathered there. The Taino leader, a native of Puerto Rico, had painted his face with yellow and black streaks. Backlit by the fire, he glowed with an inner flame as his song pierced the night. Even the squirmy 5-year-olds fell quiet in the presence of some ancient spiritual power.

The campfire gathering was part of a weekend workshop on Native American culture sponsored by **Journeys into American Indian Territory.** The program features members of the Cheyenne, Abenaki, Mohawk, Taino, and other tribes. They teach participants ritual dances, lead interpretive walks to explain the use of medicinal herbs, and demonstrate flute carving. They also share creation legends, heroic tales, and a Native American perspective on history. "People have a chance to learn firsthand from Native Americans about significant events, rituals, and how their culture survives," explained our group leader, anthropologist Robert Vetter.

The workshops take place at a woodsy, creekside conference center in upstate

New York's Catskill Mountains, about a 20-minute drive from Kingston. The mood is laid back. Most of the time, we met outdoors under the shade of an open-air pavilion. Although the program is not oriented toward families, Vetter welcomes them. Kids learn to play Native American games, including a fast-paced combination of stickball and baseball. They also go on nature hikes and participate in children's workshops, where they craft rain sticks and dream catchers, sew moccasins, and listen to Native American stories.

The children are free to drift in and out of adult seminars, which for us included a talk by Moses Starr, a Cheyenne from Oklahoma. In addition to delivering a lecture on Cheyenne culture, he taught us how to step dance and led the group—interested children included—in a circle dance of friendship to welcome us to the conference.

The conference center's accommodations are adequate but basic. You stay in a camp-style lodge with 10 bunk beds to a room (bring your own bedding and towels). Men and women have separate sleeping quarters and bathrooms. A few rooms may be available for families to stay together. The food is okay. There's the standard fare of salads, hamburgers, and tacos, plus a few traditional Native American items such as fry bread and corn soup.

In addition to the New York weekend, Vetter runs extended trips to various Native American lands. On these trips, participants ages 10 and older are granted unusual access to reservations in Montana and elsewhere in the West. Vetter also arranges homestays with Native American families. These range from a bed and breakfast overnight to an extended cultural odyssey accompanied by a member of the tribe.

TIPS: The dorm mattresses smelled musty and the rooms moldy (there is no air-conditioning). Deterred by allergies and the prospect of sleeping 20 to a room, we opted to pay a bit extra for an inexpensive hotel stay in nearby Kingston.

BASICS: Journeys into American Indian Territory *(Westhampton Beach, NY. 800/ 458-2632 or 516/878-8655. www.indianjourneys.com)*

Cornell Adult University
Ithaca

Have you ever wished you could go to college with your kids? **Cornell Adult University** offers you the chance. You can register for full-day week-long courses, then meet over lunch or dinner to talk about your day. Adults may choose from a broad range of classes in ornithology, photography, archaeology, ballroom dancing, television production, cooking, and more.

Your children enjoy their own options based on age. Three- to five-year-olds can join **Li'l Bears** for a morning of theme-oriented activities. Sample subjects include peoples of the world, places, foods, and games. For kids ages 7 and 8, **Flying High** offers programs such as fun with birds, balloons, and airplanes. Preteens from 9 to 12 years might explore writing, science, or the outdoors with intensive courses in rock climbing, rappelling, windsurfing, and sailing. Teenagers from 13 to 16 can choose a class in windsurfing, sailing, acting, photography, debate, or cooking in the morning, then spend the afternoon swimming, hiking, or visiting various academic departments on campus.

Families can stay in dormitories or opt for nearby off-campus lodging.

TIPS: Most dorm rooms are small but comfortably accommodate two adults. If you have kids under age 8, you can squeeze them in with you or install them in a neighboring room. Kids 8 and older stay with their peers in another dorm, where they are supervised by counselors. If you want your children in the same room with you, it's best to book lodging in town. Note that not all dorm rooms are air-conditioned.

BASICS: Cornell Adult University *(626 Thurston Ave., Ithaca 14850. 607/255-6260. www.cau.cornell.edu or www.sce.cornell.edu/CAU).* Dorm rooms start at $890 (includes tuition and meals), hotel rooms at $975 (50 percent discount for the second child in a family). Prices for children are $340 to $490, with a 50 percent discount for the second child. Rates include tuition, room, and meals.

Chautauqua Institution

The **Chautauqua Institution** was born in 1874 as a summer training camp for Sunday-school teachers. Today this charming Victorian community functions as a nondenominational educational center. For nine stimulating weeks out of the year—from the end of June through August—Chautauqua offers more than 400 classes in every subject imaginable. It also serves as a performing arts center for ballet, theater, and the symphony.

If your kids regard summer school as a form of torture, Chautauqua will surely alter that perception. In fact, they'll probably find it hard to choose from the exciting options. Depending on your children's ages, you can sign up for fun family workshops such as intergenerational tap dancing, family folk dancing, photography, or jewelry making.

Chautauqua also offers separate programs for children and for adults. While you fill your schedule with seminars in writing, philosophy, foreign languages, watercolor painting, antique selling, yoga, or line dancing, your kids can enroll in programs designed especially for them. These might include drawing and painting classes, advanced web surfing and design, computer programming, or balloon sculpting. A theater-arts workshop teaches kids the basics of directing, playwriting, and set design for their own productions. For the technically minded, a new robotics class gets kids building their favorite machines.

Children's School, which operates on weekdays, occupies little ones ages 3 to 5 with crafts, nature hikes, and storytelling. **Group One,** a full-day program for children entering first grade, adds swimming instruction and more outdoor games. For children ages 6 to 15, the **Boys and Girls' Club** is essentially a day camp that offers sailing, swimming, field games, nature study, and music, as well as art and crafts.

Every Tuesday night there's family entertainment by singers, musicians, puppeteers, or storytellers. These sessions are included in the gate fee, which entitles visitors to twice-daily lectures as well as to evening performances of symphony, theater, or ballet. Fees for classes are separate.

Throughout the summer, Chautauqua runs lecture series by prominent speakers. Subjects cover history, science, education, economics, religion, international affairs, psychology, and more. There's something for everyone in each season's lecture schedule, which might, for example, include: "A World in Transition: Events That Shaped Our Tomorrows," "Education: New Goals for the Knowledge Era," "Business and Ethics: Human Values in a World Economy," "World Peace without Religious Peace?," "Identity, Alienation, and the Human Psyche," "International Affairs: The Balance of Global Powers," and "Chautauqua Oratory: The Impact of Eloquence."

Besides classes, this lovely lakeside community offers swimming, boating, golf, and tennis. The 750-acre campus is laced with bike paths. The grounds are also lovely for strolling. Chautauqua is located in southwestern New York State, about 60 miles southwest of Buffalo and 35 miles east of Erie, Pennsylvania.

TIPS: Families will be most comfortable renting an apartment or a vacation house. Make your reservations as early as possible. The family classes are listed in the Special Studies Catalog, which is available in April.

BASICS: Chautauqua Institution *(P.O. Box 28, Chautauqua. 800/836-2787 or 716/357-6200. www.chautauqua-inst.org).* Gate fees for adults range from $37 per day to $190 per week; for children 13 to 17, $95 per week; children 12 and under get in free. Class fees for children and adults range from $50 to $75. Contact Chautauqua for a complete list of fees, reservations, and other information.

Lodging and meals are extra. The **Athenaeum** *(800/821-1881),* the only hotel on the property, charges from $217 to $317 for two people per day, including three meals. Additionally, the Chautauqua Institution itself manages some apartments and houses on the grounds. Weekly rentals range from about $85 for a room to about $2,800 (that's no typo) for a spacious house on the lake. For information and reservations, call 716/357-6250.

Philadelphia Zoo

These days at the **Philadelphia Zoo,** you can try on a gorilla-size shirt, use radio telemetry to track animals, observe lemurs leaping through branches overhead, listen to animals communicating through microphones, and view lowland gorillas through glass walls. It's all available at the **PECO Primate Reserve,** a state-of-the-art exhibit showcasing 11 primate species. The exhibit represents the first phase of a $24-million renovation of America's oldest zoo, which was established in 1874 in Fairmount Park.

Another highlight here is the **Amphibian and Reptile House.** Refurbished in 1998, the new structure contains more than 87 species, including snakes, lizards, turtles, alligators, and frogs. Kids are particularly impressed by the king cobra—one of the world's largest venomous snakes. A thunderstorm complete with lightning adds a touch of real drama to the **Florida Everglades** habitat, which houses alligators and crocodiles.

At the delightfully named **Rainbow Landing,** an aviary that is open May through September, you'll meet the resident lorikeets. These vividly colored birds eat right out of your hand. Kids love the routine of holding a cup of nectar, which usually entices the birds to hover above it. There's more hand-feeding at **Wings of Paradise,** a bird exhibit that features red louries, parrots, cockatoos, and other exotic Solomon Islands species. The new **Bunny Village** at the **Children's Zoo** contains Himalayan rabbits that live in fanciful little houses. Also here are docile goats and lambs to pet, as well as ponies to ride. Another new zoo attraction is the **swanboat ride** on the lake.

Night Flight and **Safari Nights** offer kids an opportunity to camp out at the zoo and enjoy some quality time with the animals. Night Flight *(Oct.-June)* participants enjoy an educational workshop at the interactive **Treehouse** (shown opposite), have dinner, and visit the animals in the evening. On Safari Nights, you sleep in the Children's Zoo and are treated to an early-morning zoo tour.

TIPS: Book the popular Night Flight about two months in advance.

BASICS: The **Philadelphia Zoo** *(215/243-1100. www.philadelphiazoo.org)* is located at 3400 W. Girard Ave.

MORE PHILADELPHIA PHUN

U. S. Mint *(5th and Arch Sts. 215/408-0114):* Visitors can watch as molten metal is cooled, rolled into sheets, and punched into blank coins, which are then engraved. In summer, the Mint is open on Saturdays as well as during the week.

Franklin Institute Science Museum and Mandell Center *(20th St. and Benjamin*

At the Philadelphia Zoo, a four-story hollow fiberglass tree invites visitors to explore inside.

Franklin Pkwy. 215/448-1208. www.fi.edu): Among the kid-pleasing exhibits at this science center are a "walk-through" heart, a user-friendly guide to the Internet, and a planetarium.

Independence National Historical Park *(3rd and Chestnut Sts. 215/597-8974. www.nps.gov/inde):* All the buildings in this 37-acre park relate to America's first steps toward independence. Sites include **Independence Hall,** where the Declaration of Independence was drafted and signed; the **Liberty Bell;** and **Congress Hall,** where Congress met from 1790 to 1800. Pick up a map at the **Visitor Center.**

Philadelphia Museum of Art *(26th St. and The Parkway. 215/763-8100. www. philamuseum.org. Tues.-Sun. 10 a.m.-5 p.m., Wed. 10 a.m.-8:45 p.m., closed Mon.; adults $8, children $5, Sun. free until 1 p.m.):* The nation's third largest art museum contains a wide range of fine art as well as period furnishings. Highlights include works by 19th-century Philadelphia painter Thomas Eakins.

Penn's Landing *(Columbus Blvd. between Lombard and Market Sts. www. pennslandingcorp.com):* Here on the Delaware River, you can board historic ships and visit the **Independent Seaport Museum** *(215/925-5439. Adults $5, children 5 to 12 $2.50).* The **Family Entertainment Center,** opening in 2001, will contain two ice rinks, an IMAX theater, and shops.

Sesame Place *(Oxford Valley Rd., Langhorne. 215/757-1100. www.sesameplace. com. May 31-Oct. 23, $31.95 per person):* This 10-acre theme park features Big Bird and other characters from the television series.

Pocono Environmental Education Center

Learn about birds of prey, reptiles, and plants at a **Pocono Environmental Educational Center** (PEEC) family getaway. The center lies in the **Delaware Water Gap Recreational Area,** 20 miles southwest of the point where the borders of Pennsylvania, New York, and New Jersey come together. Led by guides, families explore the world of nature. These moderately priced weekend retreats are offered year-round, making it easy for families to enjoy canoeing, hiking, birding, and other activities.

Togetherness is the concept here. Parents and kids can track animals, hunt fossils, canoe on a pond, hike to a waterfall, or try their hands at seining. There's also quiet time if you want to make a dream catcher, dip candles, or do other crafts. In the evening, square dancing and storytelling take place around a campfire. On night hikes, guests learn to listen for owls and wood frogs, and how to spot deer. Guides also teach participants about the constellations and how to find the North Star.

Families stay in rustic heated cabins with bunk beds (bring your own towels and bedding) and no kitchens. Meals, included in the price, are taken at a central dining hall. The program is open to all ages, but children 5 to 10 will likely get the most out of it. Older kids may get bored with the easy hikes and simple activities.

TIPS: At certain times of the year, PEEC hosts special Elderhostel programs for grandparents and grandchildren.

BASICS: **Pocono Environmental Educational Center** *(Dingmans Ferry. 570/828-9693. www.peec.org)*

The National Zoo

How do orangutans think? What does a Sumatran tiger look like in the flesh? What does the skull of a *Tyrannosaurus rex* feel like? And who lives in the rain forests of the Amazon? To find out the answers to these and many other questions, head for Washington's **National Zoological Park,** a terrific place for children to glimpse some of the world's most intriguing mammals, reptiles, birds, and invertebrates.

The National Zoo works hard to make its exhibits accessible and understandable to children. In January 2000, for example, the facility added a new exhibit, **How Do You Zoo?,** designed to let 5- to 10-year-olds take on—and act out—the duties of three zoo professionals: animal keeper, commissary worker, and veterinarian. In the exhibit's **Animal Keepers** area, for example, kids learn all about the life-and-death tasks that make the job of zookeeper such a weighty responsibility. In addition to keeping careful daily records of the animals' behavior, the keeper has to know what type of food to feed each animal, how to embed a microchip for identification beneath the animals' skin, and how to "life trap" any animal that requires medical attention.

The **Commissary Workers** area shows children how to order food and use it to prepare a specific diet for each animal. In the **Veterinarians** area, kids can observe animals in the zoo's Intensive Care Unit, learn how to read an x-ray, and use a stethoscope to listen to the "heartbeats" of plush animals. How Do You Zoo? is open each afternoon during the school year—classes use it in the mornings—and all day in the summer.

Further distinguishing the National Zoo is the diversity of its collection. In June 1999, three Sumatran tiger cubs joined the zoo's inhabitants. The cubs, which can be seen view daily from 11:00 a.m. to 2:00 p.m., will remain at the zoo until the end of 2000.

Both the **Invertebrate Exhibit** and the **Reptile Discovery Center** feature low sight lines designed to let children look straight into the tanks. There they will discover how sea stars, sponges, and giant crabs move about and eat; how leaf-cutter ants farm the fungus on which they thrive; and how big the Komodo dragon—the world's largest lizard—grows to be. If your kids think that watching a snake devour a live mouse or other rodent is "awesome" rather than "gross," get a copy of the feeding schedule from the Visitor Center or one of the kiosks scattered around the grounds. In warmer months, bees, hummingbirds, and butterflies swarm the **Pollinarium.**

At **Tiger Tracks** (part of the **Great Cats** exhibit), kids can compare their own development with that of a tiger cub by matching how quickly both species grow, and what types of food each eats. From the *machon*—a hunting platform that overhangs the moat—children get an unobstructed view of the big cats. As the children

walk along, interactive displays let them feel a bronze cast of a tiger's tongue, push a button to hear a tiger roar, and compare the size of their hands with a tiger's paw. The **Predators Cove** is the place to hold a life-size cast of a *Tyrannosaurus rex* skull in your hands; the **Tiger Kid's Stop** is a shady oasis.

The **Think Tank** is an unusually innovative undertaking. Here visitors can watch scientists communicate with orangutans through the medium of a computer-generated symbolic language. **Amazonia,** the zoo's re-creation of a tropical river and rain forest, contains 350 plant species, titi and Goeldi's monkeys, a sloth, and poison-dart frogs. In the adjacent **Amazonia Science Gallery** (geared to children 4 and older), kids can examine insect parts under microscopes and use interactive computer programs to find out more about the rain forest.

TIPS: The National Zoo, part of the Smithsonian Institution's collection of museums, features members' nights and dinner-with-the-animals programs. These after-hours events, typically held in summer, are great times to visit: The temperatures are cooler, the crowds thinner, the animals more active.

BASICS: **The National Zoo** *(3001 Connecticut Ave. NW. 202/673-4800. www.si.edu/natzoo* or *www.fonz.org)* makes its schedule of animal demonstrations and feeding times available at the Visitor Center and at information booths throughout the park.

National Museum of American History

Like the United States itself, the collection at the National Museum of American History is diverse. Everything pivotal to the country's development is here, from the hulking locomotives that pulled the nation into economic prosperity in the 19th century to the totems that defined popular culture in the 20th, such as Archie Bunker's chair from the television show *All in the Family.*

On three floors presenting more than three million touchstones of everyday life from the American past, you can see the flag that inspired the poem that became the "Star-Spangled Banner," the compass used on the Lewis and Clark expedition, and the ruby slippers from the movie *The Wizard of Oz.* After listening to a radio announcement by First Lady Eleanor Roosevelt and making a pilgrimage to the lunch counter that inaugurated the antisegregation sit-ins, relax with an ice-cream sundae—a real one, that is—in an old-fashioned ice-cream parlor.

Not to be missed are the free interactive programs for children. At the **Hands-On Science Center,** for instance, children and parents can perform chemistry exper-

Left: A visitor feeds a carrot to a young elephant at the National Zoo.

iments together. Other available activities include measuring radioactive hot spots, discovering the chemical properties of common household items, and measuring distances with a laser. After watching conservators work on the Star-Spangled Banner, kids can carry out experiments on the same sorts of materials as those used in the flag.

The **Hands-On History Room** shows children how kids of a distant era did the impossible—that is, managed to entertain themselves in the absence of video games: Mechanical piggy banks, high-wheeled bicycles, and other 19th-century diversions are on display here. Visitors can also learn how to send a message by telegraph, harness a mule, say "Hello" in Cherokee, and work a cotton gin. If you get caught up in the moment, there are even clothes to try on from different eras in history.

OurStory is a series of family programs that brings history to life through exhibits, storytelling, music, dance, and arts and crafts. Each program kicks off with the author of a children's book reading excerpts from his or her work, then discussing them with the children. This is followed by a book-related hands-on activity that may include making anything from a Japanese kite to a Puerto Rican carnival mask. Participants also go home with age-appropriate booklets containing suggestions for books, websites, and hands-on activities. OurStory topics have included the Underground Railroad, Iroquois traditions, trains, Chinese-American music and crafts, and the Star-Spangled Banner.

Speaking of which, the **Star-Spangled Banner**—an $18-million conservation project—will open in 2002 with an exhibit of the flag that flew over Fort McHenry in 1814. The storied banner, bearing 15 stars and stripes, is 30 feet high and 34 feet wide; made of English wool bunting with cotton stars and backed by Irish linen, it weighs 150 pounds. As the preservation goes forward, visitors can watch the conservators at work in a specially designed laboratory.

Road Transportation is a veritable traffic jam of horse-drawn carriages (including one from 1770), antique cars, bicycles, and motorcycles—including the customized 1972 Harley-Davidson that Evel Knievel used for various stunts. Near **Railroad Hall** stands the *John Bull;* built in 1841, this locomotive is the oldest in operating condition. Pride of place in the **American Maritime Enterprise** exhibit is given to a power plant from the 1804 ship *Little Juliana,* while the **American Industrial Revolution** shows off a re-creation of the Crystal Palace—the site of the 1851 World's Fair in London, at which American technology won international recognition.

In **Information Age**, kids hear what *Superman* sounded like when it was a mere radio broadcast. They can also watch episodes of *Captain Kangaroo,* a children's program from the early days of television. **Science in American Life** features a laboratory from the early 1900s, a kitchen and living room from the 1950s, and—soberingly—a fallout shelter from the 1960s.

Ceremonial Court—a facsimile of the White House Executive Mansion—includes original furnishings, presidential memorabilia from Woodrow Wilson's golf bag to Jimmy Carter's hymnal, and White House china. Another exhibit traces the evolution of the role of first lady from Martha Washington to Hillary Clinton.

Test-tube buddies: A supervised science experiment at the Museum of American History

TIPS: To learn more about the Star-Spangled Banner preservation project, check out its website: www.americanhistory.si.edu/ssb. In addition to the ice-cream parlor (which serves lunch as well as dessert), the museum has a large cafeteria serving hot and cold meals; you'll find it on the lower level, opposite the bookstore. Befitting the museum's mission, even the cafeteria walls tell a story: They are graced with period photographs of people from all walks of life sitting down to a meal.

Before you visit the American History Museum in the flesh, make a cyber visit there by clicking on the "Not Just for Kids" page of the museum's website *(www.americanhistory.si.edu)*. The exhibits are presented in alphabetical order, so click on "Q" if quilts are your quirk, or enter "E" to enlighten yourself on the museum's ensemble of engines. (You might even print out the Web pages and bring them along as a homegrown guide.) Once you reach the museum, stop by the Information Desk for the four free family guides: Two of these are exhibit-specific and geared to younger children, while the other two are overviews aimed at older kids. All four are printed in both English and Spanish.

BASICS: The **National Museum of American History** *(14th St. and Constitution Ave. NW. 202/357-2700. www.si.americanhistory.si.edu. 10:00 a.m.-5:30 p.m.; closed Dec. 25)* often extends its summer hours; contact museum for details. For the **Hands-On Science Center** *(Tues.-Fri. 12:30-5:00 p.m., Sat.-Sun. 10:00 a.m.-5:00 p.m., closed Mon. and holidays)* and the **Hands-On History Room** *(Tues.-Sun. noon-3:00 p.m.)*, children under 13 must be accompanied by an adult; no kids under 5. Tickets available on a first-come, first-served basis (in busy periods, these may be timed tickets). **OurStory** *(202/633-6752. Reservations req.)* is usually held the third Saturday of the month at 10:30 a.m. and 1:00 p.m.; call to confirm times.

National Museum of Natural History

Since he was installed in 1959, the African bull elephant that dominates the Rotunda entrance of the **National Museum of Natural History (NMNH)** has symbolized the museum's mission to present the wonders and the history of the natural world. Stuffed to the eaves with such national treasures as dinosaur skeletons, the Hope Diamond, and a rock from Mars, Washington's Natural History Museum is one of the most popular stopovers in a city known for its captivating display halls.

Being family-friendly is a major goal of the NMNH: Discovery carts are located throughout the museum, while special areas have been set aside for family activities designed to enhance the visitor experience.

In the **Discovery Room,** opened in 1973 as the first of its kind in a natural history museum, families will find an inventive mix of activities and learning tools related to anthropology, biology, geology, and paleontology. Parents are encouraged to join their children in using the discovery boxes to learn about these fields. In an anthropology box, for example, you might find African jewelry made from such natural materials as wood, shell, fish bone, and myrrh. Seasonings and parts of plants could be in a biology box; children are challenged to smell each item and then try to match the seasoning to its plant. You can feel the different types of lava contained in the geology box, or handle the sharks' teeth that come out of the paleontology boxes. The Discovery Room also has a small library of children's books related to exhibits in the museum.

Bugs rule at the popular **O. Orkin Insect Zoo,** where you can peer inside an active beehive, crawl through a termite mound, or get a close look at two poisonous spiders, the brown recluse and the black widow. At various times during the day, you can observe the tarantula eating her favorite food: live crickets. In the tropical rain forest area, leaf-cutter ants march to an authentic sound track. Docents are on hand to offer caterpillars, hissing cockroaches, and other critters to touch and hold.

Even blasé kids get wide-eyed at their first glimpse of the 45.5-carat Hope diamond in the **Janet Annenberg Hooker Hall of Geology, Gems, and Minerals.** Other items in the collection make it not just international but extraterrestrial: In addition to touching rocks from both the moon and Mars, kids can view the Tucson meteorite, once part of an asteroid 4.6 billion years old—the commonly accepted geologic age of Earth itself.

The **Dinosaur Hall** is a well laid out display of reconstructed dinosaur skeletons, among them a full-size model of a *Tyrannosaurus rex* skeleton. Illustrations flesh out the skeletons, show how each dinosaur interacted with its fellow reptiles, and portray the foods they might have eaten. At the **FossiLab,** visitors can watch scientists in the act of preparing fossils.

Samurai armor and Chinese writing instruments are showcased in **Asian and Pacific Cultures,** which also presents tools used by Aborigines and an Easter Island statue that was believed to evoke the spirits of the deceased.

The museum's **African Voices** exhibit, opened in December 1999, examines the past and present of that continent, including the African diaspora and its impact on the cultures of Brazil and the Caribbean. A time line traces Africa's history from the beginnings of humanity through the ancient empires of Egypt to the triumph of such influential modern leaders as Nelson Mandela.

The **Butterfly Garden** on the museum's east side (across 9th Street from the **National Gallery's Sculpture Garden**) makes a nice stop in late summer and early fall, when the insects emerge from their chrysalises (moths, as your kids probably know, come out of cocoons). Thanks to informative plaques placed throughout the garden, children can put names to the beautiful creatures fluttering around them.

The **Samuel C. Johnson Theater** shows IMAX films (in both 2-D and 3-D) throughout the day.

TIPS: Check out the museum's website *(www.nmnh.si.edu)* for updates on current exhibits and schedules for both the Discovery Room and the Johnson Theater. With the museum in the throes of updating many displays, the website can help you avoid those maddening signs that say "Closed for renovation."

BASICS: National Museum of Natural History *(Constitution Ave. at 10th St. NW. 202/357-2700 or [in Spanish] 202/633-9126. www.nmnh.si.edu).* The **Discovery Room** is open afternoons only during the school year, but all day long in summer and on school holidays.

National Air and Space Museum

The **National Air and Space Museum** explores the miracle of flight with a galactic lineup of aircraft and space vehicles. Its interactive exhibits let kids touch a moon rock and walk through a replica of *Skylab,* the space station that re-entered Earth's atmosphere and rained debris on Australia in 1979. These and other attractions, combined with the museum's first-run IMAX films, draw more than nine million visitors a year, making the Air and Space Museum the most popular of the Smithsonian's 16 museums and galleries.

Families walk through the front doors and into an aerospace reliquary: Suspended from the ceiling of the **Milestones of Flight** gallery are the Wright brothers' 1903 *Flyer,* Charles Lindbergh's *Spirit of St. Louis,* John Glenn's Mercury 7 (the United States' first manned orbital spacecraft), and the command module from the Apollo 11 mission. Even NASA's notorious bureaucratese is faithfully preserved here: The moon rock, which you can touch, is termed a "lunar sample."

Before visiting the other galleries, obtain a museum map from the Information Desk in the south lobby (you'll find the desk beneath *Voyager,* the first aircraft to circle the globe without stopping or refueling). Type a special interest—World War I air battles, for example, or Latino-American participation in the space program—into an information kiosk to find out what the museum has to offer on that topic.

In **How Things Fly,** kids discover what they would weigh on other planets in our solar system (the scale accommodates wheelchairs). They can also climb into the cockpit of a Cessna 150 and manipulate its controls, or help their parents operate a supersonic wind tunnel that generates visible shock waves. Using an interactive computer, visitors work with wing shapes to learn about lift and drag; cranking a dummy astronaut into the air becomes a lesson in weightlessness. Storytelling, demonstrations of "touchables," paper-airplane contests, and videos are all staged throughout the day. At the **Visitor Resource Center,** children can pick up special handouts about the gallery's exhibits or take part in science activities that answer such questions as "Is air really there?"

In **Space Race,** kids enjoy learning how Skylab's three-person crew coexisted in space for up to three months at a time; expect young visitors to be inordinately fascinated by the collapsible shower and the Waste Management Compartment. On display in **Lunar Exploration Vehicles** is a model of the largest astronomical instrument in orbit, the Hubble Space Telescope. **Looking at Earth** contains a range of surveillance aircraft—everything from a deHavilland DH-4, used for mapping and surveying during the First World War, to the Lockheed U-2 that photographed Russian missile sites in Cuba in 1962. Although the U.S.S. *Smithsonian* referred to in **Sea-Air Operations** is purely fictitious, the gallery's Douglas Dauntless dive-bomber and Grumman F4F Wildcat played very real roles in the battle of the Pacific during World War II.

Where Next, Columbus? examines the problems that must be overcome before humanity can traverse the vast distances separating us from potentially habitable planets. The exhibit features a futuristic Martian terrain, a hydroponic greenhouse (one where plants grow in water without soil), and three films shown on a continuous basis.

To discover the present extent of our knowledge about what lies beyond Earth, visit the **Albert Einstein Planetarium.** Simulations of 9,000 stars—as well as our own sun, moon, and five neighboring planets—are projected onto the planetarium's 70-foot-diameter overhead dome. Every afternoon, the planetarium hosts a free informal presentation about the current night sky.

Downstairs in the **Samuel P. Langley Theater,** take in an award-winning IMAX film such as *Mission to Mir*—a 40-minute tour of Russia's space station, filmed in space by astronauts—or *To Fly,* in which you viscerally experience what it's like to hang-glide off the coast of Hawaii, soar in a hot-air balloon over Niagara Falls, or blast into space aboard a Saturn rocket. The museum's Space Fiction film series offers views of and from space, including Earth glimpsed from the cargo bay of the space shuttle.

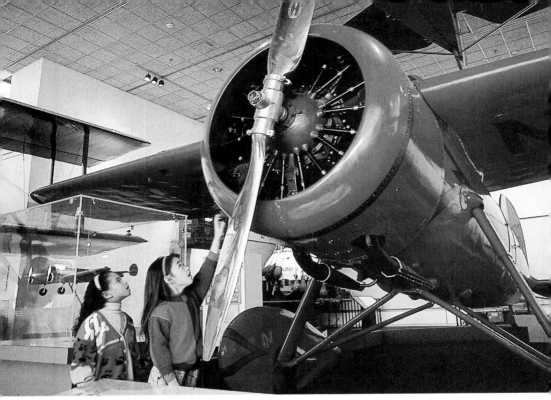

Future aviators inspect a copy of Amelia Earhart's Lockheed Vega at the Air and Space Museum.

TIPS: The museum gift shop sells "astronaut ice cream"—a freeze-dried concoction that is actually served in space—and military dog tags (go to the booth tucked under the escalator on the first floor to stamp your name on the tags).

BASICS: The **National Air and Space Museum** *(202/357-2700. www.nasm.si.edu)*, located at Independence Ave. between 4th St. and 7th St. SW., is open daily from 9:45 a.m. to 5:30 p.m. *(closed Dec. 25).* Take the Metro to L'Enfant Plaza.

MORE CAPITAL IDEAS

National Postal Museum *(2 Massachusetts Ave. NE. 202/357-2700. www.si.edu/ postal):* Located off the Mall on Capitol Hill near Union Station, this museum employs some surprisingly engaging exhibits to trace the development of the U.S. Postal Service. Visitors can find out about the Pony Express, climb aboard a stagecoach to hear piped-in sounds of the period, and discover how stamps are printed. Don't miss the display in the main atrium dedicated to Owney, the Postal Service's unofficial mascot from 1888 to 1897. The personable mutt accompanied postal workers and their mail bags to destinations all across the country—as well as to exotic locales in Africa, Asia, and Europe.

Capital Children's Museum *(800 3rd St. NE. 202/675-4120. www.ccm.org):* Also located on Capitol Hill, this museum is likely to be a hit with younger children. Preschoolers can shop in a Mexican village or listen to tales at the **Storyteller The-**

Brave news world: The News Zipper encircles the News Globe at the Newseum in Arlington.

ater. In the **City Room,** they get to watch puppet shows or slide down a fire pole. Children 6 and older create cartoons at the **Animation** exhibit, adding sounds and using blue-screen technology to star in their own creations. Older kids mix concoctions of a different sort—and analyze their effects—at the **CMA Chemical Science Center.** Kids can also envelop themselves in a life-size bubble, navigate a room-size maze, and make a virtual visit to Japan that includes drinking tea, trying on kimonos in a tatami room, and hopping aboard a mock bullet train.

U.S. Holocaust Memorial Museum *(100 Raoul Wallenberg Pl. SW. 202/488-0400. www.ushmm.org):* This facility presents the story of the Holocaust from Hitler's rise to power (and the American reaction to it) to the atrocities of the concentration camps, relocation, and the end of World War II. Because of the heart-wrenching subject matter and the use of actual artifacts—some of which are explicit photos and first-person accounts by survivors—the museum recommends the main exhibit for adults and children 11 years and older. A more age-appropriate exhibit to visit with children 8 and older is **Remember The Children, Daniel's Story.** In this fictional but representational tale, Daniel, having lost his home life with his parents and sister, is interned in a ghetto and then a concentration camp. Ultimately, he survives the war.

TIPS: Because of the museum's popularity, timed same-day tickets are distributed on a first-come, first-served basis starting at 10 a.m.; to get one, you'll have to line up much earlier than that. Advance tickets can also be purchased for a nominal charge from Tickets.com *(800/400-9373).*

> ## GOVERNMENTAL WASHINGTON
>
> Want to be a VIP in a city dripping with them? VIP tickets, available by contacting your senator or representative months in advance, guarantee entry to such bastions of bureaucracy as the **U.S. Capitol** *(202/225-6827),* **White House** *(202/737-8292),* **Federal Bureau of Investigation** *(202/ 324-3447),* and **Bureau of Engraving and Printing** *(202/ 874-3188).* The number of tickets allotted to each congressional office is limited.

Newseum *(1101 Wilson Boulevard, Arlington. 888/639-7386 or 703/284-3544. www.newseum.org):* This site, the only hands-on museum dedicated to news, invites kids to make choices about the day's top news stories, ponder ethical dilemmas faced by reporters, and watch the production of an actual TV-news show. In the park next door, young visitors can view icons of the fight for freedom: a piece of the Berlin Wall, for example, or a kayak used by Cuban refugees to reach the United States.

Atlantic Kayak

When Captain John Smith mapped the Potomac River in 1608, he noted several Indian villages along the shore, including the camp of the Piscataway Indian Nation. Nearly 400 years later, you can take a sunset paddle along **Piscataway Creek**—the Potomac River tributary that flows through the former tribal grounds—and feel the centuries slip away. On a guided 2½-hour tour with **Atlantic Kayak,** typical sights include a beaver lodge, the ramparts of Fort Washington, and Mount Vernon, George Washington's plantation.

This trip, like many of those offered by Atlantic Kayak, combines soft adventure with history and scenery. Interested paddlers can learn, for example, how "finger creeks" flowing into the Chesapeake Bay formed an essential element in the region's development. On the tour titled **Georgetown: Bridges from Below**, kayakers paddle under Key Bridge and Memorial Bridge, then around wooded Roosevelt Island; along the way, a historian from the Octagon Museum details Georgetown's evolution as a port. The Piscataway and Georgetown tours, covering only about 2 miles, are among the easiest of Atlantic Kayak's trips.

The **Haunted River Tour**, a Halloween tradition, follows the same route around Georgetown and Roosevelt Island but takes place at night. As you glide through the moonlight listening to ghost stories about the capital region, you may be surprised to hear that Francis Scott Key supposedly haunts his former mansion near the Potomac River.

Meanwhile, the Three Sisters—a trio of treacherous rocks jutting from the water upriver of Key Bridge—are said to carry their own centuries-old curse:

After a fierce battle between two Indian tribes living on opposite sides of the river, three warriors from the Virginia side paddled out to the three small islands to fish; there they were slaughtered by their still-vigilant enemies. That night, the widows vowed to cross the river, woo their husbands' murderers, and feed them poisoned food. All the canoes had been burned in the recent warfare, however, so the three women tried to cross the tricky current on makeshift rafts. Alas, the hastily fashioned floats went under, taking their riders down with them. The chief of the Virginia band, weary of the fighting and dying, put a curse on that stretch of the Potomac: No one, he decreed, would ever be able to cross there in safety. And that is why, local lore has it, all subsequent proposals for a bridge spanning the rocks have failed.

Additional day trips take paddlers along the waterfront of Old Town Alexandria; through Pohick Bay to Gunston Hall, home of Thomas Jefferson's "ghost-writer," statesman George Mason; down the Patuxent River to see osprey nests and learn the British invasion route of 1814; through the marshes and back bays of the Chesapeake; and along the Wye River on Maryland's Eastern Shore.

Feast on the Bay, a three-day trip in May along the Delaware shore, focuses on the cycle of horseshoe crabs and hungry shorebirds. Kayakers paddle the St. Jones River in Delaware Bay to reach the beaches where thousands of horseshoe crabs come ashore to lay their eggs. As they do, the sky overhead fills with the raucous squawks of shorebirds hoping to feed on the newly laid eggs. Other multi-day trips venture farther afield: to the Georgia sea islands, to the Everglades, and even to the U.S. Virgin Islands (where snorkeling and sailing round out the kayaking).

TIPS: The two-person kayak is extremely stable, making it ideal for a paddling team of one adult and one child. For a unique view of the capital fireworks, sign up for a July 4th outing.

BASICS: Atlantic Kayak *(1201 N. Royal St., Alexandria, Va. 800/297-0066 or 703/838-9072. www.atlantickayak.com)* charges about $40 per person for a typical 2½-hour paddle. Minimum age for Piscataway, Georgetown, and Halloween trips: 5. Minimum age for day trips and Feast on the Bay: 8.

RUSSIA

ARCTIC OCEAN

ALASKA

Beaufort Sea

Viscount Melville
Sound

Beechey
Island

U.S.
CANADA

• Dawson

YUKON
TERRITORY

Great
Bear
Lake

NORTHWEST

TERRITORIES

NUNAVUT

⊛ Whitehorse

Great Slave
Lake

⊛ Yellowknife

Queen
Charlotte
Islands

• Prince
Rupert

'KSAN HISTORICAL
□ VILLAGE AND MUSEUM

GWAII HAANAS
NATIONAL PARK RESERVE
AND HAIDA HERTIAGE SITE

BRITISH

COLUMBIA

Churchill
•

ALBERTA

SASKATCHEWAN

MANITOBA

ROBSON BIGHT
ECOLOGICAL RESERVE □

Quadra Island

Edmonton ⊛

PRINCE
ALBERT
NAT. PARK

COWICHAN NATIVE VILLAGE

□ Squamish
River Valley

BANFF
NAT.
PARK

ROYAL TYRRELL
MUSEUM OF
□ PALAEONTOLOGY

Cedar L.

Lake
Winnipeg

PACIFIC RIM
NATIONAL PARK

□ • Vancouver

Calgary
•

• Saskatoon

Lake
Winnipegosis

PACIFIC

Victoria ⊛

Brooks □ DINOSAUR
• PROV. PARK

RIDING MT.
NAT. PARK

NARCISSE SNAKE
DEN AREA
□

CANADA
U.S.

• Fort Macleod

Regina ⊛

L.
Manitoba

□ OAK HAMMOCK MARSH

OCEAN

WASH.

EASTEND FOSSIL □
RESEARCH STATION

Wood
Mountain

• Willow Bunch

Winnipeg ⊛

MONTANA

NORTH
DAKOTA

IDAHO

MINN.

WIS

ICELAND

G R E E N L A N D
(Denmark)

Baffin
Bay

Devon I.

ncaster Sound

Davis Strait

Baffin Island

AUYUITTUQ
NATIONAL PARK
RESERVE

Cumberland Sound

Iqaluit ⊛
QAUMMAARVIIT □
Kimmirut •

Southampton
Island

H u d s o n   S t r a i t

← Walrus Island

L a b r a d o r
S e a

Hudson
Bay

NEWFOUNDLAND AND LABRADOR

St. John's ⊛
← Cape Spear

Cape St. Mary's

Q U E B E C

ONTARIO

Les Escoumins •

Tadoussac •

St. Lawrence

PRINCE
EDWARD
ISLAND

Cape Breton
Island

• Louisbourg

Wendake •
Québec ⊛

NEW
BRUNSWICK

Charlottetown ⊛

ALGONQUIN
PROV. PARK

KING'S
LANDING ⊛

Fredericton ⊛

NOVA SCOTIA

under Bay

SLEEPING GIANT
PROV. PARK

ake Superior

FINLAYSON POINT
PROV. PARK

Manitoulin I. □

South River •

Huntsville ⊛

PIKWAKANAGAN

Laval •
Hull • Montréal ⊛

M.E.

NEW
BRUNSWICK
MUSEUM

Bay of Fundy

Halifax ⊛

A T L A N T I C

O C E A N

□ UPPER CANADA
VILLAGE

VT. N.H.

⊛ Ottawa

Midland •
• Bancroft

Lake
Huron

MICHIGAN

Lake Michigan

Toronto ⊛

L. Ontario

N.Y.

Ohsweken •

Lake Erie

PT. PELEE □
NAT. PARK

OHIO

P A.

□ Point of Interest

0 ———————— 500 mi

0 ———————— 500 km

Whale-watching in Canada

Watching one of earth's largest creatures burst from the water in front of you and plunge back into the deep is an experience you and your children will long remember. With more than 30 species of whales living in or traveling through Canadian waters, the country is prime whale-watching terrain.

But where are the best spots? Although the Atlantic, Pacific, and Arctic Oceans offer unsurpassed opportunities to see these giant marine mammals swimming and breaching, many experts claim that the best vantage point for families is near **Tadoussac**, a two- to three-hour drive northeast of Québec City. There, icy salt water carried up the St. Lawrence River from the Atlantic Ocean meets warm fresh water flowing out of the Saguenay fjord. As the two currents mix, they give rise to a rich harvest of plankton, krill, and capelin that draws eight species of whales each summer and fall. The **Saguenay-St. Laurent Marine Park** *(418/235-4703)*, encompassing both the fjord and the St. Lawrence estuary, was established in 1998 to protect this fragile ecosystem.

If you've been on a whale-watching excursion before, you may find this ocean trip different. For starters, children don't have to spend an hour on a boat before they see their first whale. On our cruise with **Croisières 2001**, for example, it was only a matter of minutes before two black minkes rose out of the water and a fin whale approached a nearby Zodiac motorized raft. Second, the relative calmness of the St. Lawrence River eliminates the danger of seasickness caused by ocean swells.

Naturalist Sebastian Boulianne, who has been leading expeditions for Croisières 2001 for six years, estimates the chance of seeing a whale here at "about 99.9 percent. Even if we don't see them because it's foggy, we can hear them." The whales arrive on a staggered schedule between May and October. In August, families may be lucky enough to spot a rare blue whale—at 98 feet and 140 tons, the largest animal on earth. When a blue whale breathes, its blowhole is so large and powerful that you can actually smell the creature's fish breath.

We also saw a playful pod of adult and baby belugas. About 1,000 of the small white whales reproduce in these waters and stay in the St. Lawrence year-round. The others—finback whales (the world's second longest creature), minkes, humpbacks, and blue whales—are here mostly from May to November, when they probably head for the North Atlantic (their precise destination remains a mystery). Atlantic white-sided dolphins occasionally travel to Tadoussac from the Gulf of St. Lawrence; endangered right whales have also made their way here from the Atlantic.

From May to mid-October, whale-watching boats leave daily from the **Baie-Sainte-Catherine** wharf or from the town of Tadoussac. A free ferryboat connects

On page 235: In the town of la Baleine, northern Quebec, a boy finds warmth inside an igloo.

 WILDLIFE ENCOUNTER    CULTURAL EXPLORATION    LEARNING ESCAPE

the two communities; the ride takes about eight minutes and is available 24 hours a day. Most companies offer cruises of varying length, and it's a fair bet they all provide commentary, a snack bar, and an on-board naturalist to identify whales and answer questions. Adventurous teens will love the outings on smaller Zodiac craft, which are more maneuverable. Younger children must ride on larger boats.

On another cruise—this one with **Croisières AML**—half a dozen minkes and a couple of finbacks were cavorting beside our boat within the first 30 minutes. We spotted about 20 whales all told, as well as a few gray seals and some harbor porpoises. Some children sat by the ship's rails, binoculars in hand, and waited patiently for the leviathans to show themselves. Others gathered around naturalist Agathe Poitras to get a closer look at the baleine plates she had brought along. "Feel them," she encouraged the kids, and they gingerly stroked the grill-like mouth plates, which certain whales use to filter food and water.

To learn more about whales, sea life, and local tides, families can visit a host of nearby interpretive centers. Handle sea stars, sea urchins, and anemones at the **Centre écologique de Port-au-Saumon** *(418/434-2209)* in Saint-Fidèle; discover at the **Maison des Dunes** *(418/235-4238)* how the towering sand dunes of Tadoussac were formed; or watch a drama on krill (seriously!) at the **Pointe-Noire Interpretation and Observation Centre** *(418/237-4383)* in Baie-Sainte-Catherine. A visit to the **Marine Mammal Interpretation Centre** *(near Tadoussac marina; 418/235-4701),* which offers films, slide shows, and hands-on exhibits, is a whale of a good time.

TIPS: Do not ask the pilot of a Zodiac to speed toward a whale. According to Canada's whale-watching code of ethics, boats cannot change speed or direction within 1,300 feet (400 m) of a whale; abrupt changes of speed stress the creatures. If a whale comes within 650 feet (200 m) of the craft, the pilot must shift into neutral. Most Zodiac operators follow these rules, says naturalist Sebastian Boulianne of Croisières 2001: "If a whale wants to give a kiss to the boat, it's his choice."

Conditions on the water are changeable. Bring a sweater, raincoat, and hat.

BASICS: Prices vary according to company, type of boat, and length of trip. For a four-hour trip, expect to pay about $40 (CN) for adults and $25 (CN) for children under 12. Here are some family-friendly companies:

Croisières AML *(800/463-1292 or 418/237-4274 in season; 800/563-4643 year-round. www.croisieresaml.com):* The larger boats have a cafeteria on board.

Croisières 2001 Inc. *(800/694-5489 or 418/659-5220):* A three-hour cruise aboard the 175-passenger *Katmar* catamaran includes a journey into the Saguenay Fjord. TV monitors connected to an underwater video camera show the Saguenay's thriving marine life.

Famille Dufour Cruises *(800/463-5250 or 418/692-0222. www.familledufour. com):* Naturalists lead cruises aboard a choice of vessels: the single-hull *Famille Dufour* (491 passengers), the catamaran *M/V Famille Dufour 2* (340 passengers), the schooner *Marie Clarisse* (100 passengers), or the Zodiac-style *Tadoussac 3* (48 passengers). Some packages include lodging at Dufour family properties.

MORE WHALE-WATCHING IN CANADA

NEWFOUNDLAND: Twenty-two species of whales—including humpback, fin, sperm, and minke—hug the Newfoundland coast. **Cape Spear,** North America's eastern-most point, boasts the world's largest concentration of humpback whales. Dozens of operators offer tours that include trips to **Witless Bay Ecological Reserve,** home to some of the largest bird colonies on the continent. Cape Spear is also one of the few places where icebergs can be viewed from shore. These 10,000-year-old mountains of freshwater, calved from glaciers in Greenland and the Arctic, glide past during late spring and early summer's whale-watching season. **Newfoundland Tourism** *(800/563-6353 or 709/729-2830. www.gov.nf.ca/tourism)*

NOVA SCOTIA: Plankton-rich waters make this province a prime whale-watching venue. Finback, humpback, pilot, and minke whales are common from June to mid-October. You may also spot rare right whales, porpoises, seals, bald eagles, and puffins. Tours depart from **Brier** and **Tiverton Islands.** Charters operate in the Bay of Fundy, the Gulf of St. Lawrence off Cape Breton Island, and along the Eastern Shore and South Shore. **Nova Scotia Tourism** *(800/565-0000 or 904/425-5781. nsvisit@fox.nstn.ca. www.explore.gov.ca)*

NEW BRUNSWICK: The **Bay of Fundy's** superlatively high tides have created tremendous feeding grounds for whales. Twice a day, 100 billion tons of seawater pulse into the shore, nearly equaling the 24-hour flow of all the world's rivers. Excursions setting out from Grand Manan Island, just off the eastern tip of Maine, often spot humpbacks, right whales, sei whales, minkes, and finbacks—not to mention gray seals, harbor seals, white-sided dolphins, and harbor porpoises. **Seaview Adventures** *(506/662-3211)* has a touch tank on board and an underwater camera. The **New Brunswick Museum** *(506/643-2300. Adm. fee),* on the waterfront of mainland town St. Andrews, features life-size whale models. **Tourism New Brunswick** *(800/561-0123. www.tourismnbcanada. com/web/ or www.nbfundy.com)*

BRITISH COLUMBIA: About 19 pods comprising a total of 330 resident orcas, or killer whales, make the waters off Canada's west coast their personal playground. Another 200 transients (as they are called to distinguish them from residents) roam the coast from Alaska to California. Possibly the best place to spot both kinds is near **Robson Bight Ecological Reserve** *(250/949-2815)* on Johnstone Strait, off the northeast coast of Vancouver Island. The World Wildlife Federation rates the reserve one of the top three whale-watching destinations in the world. Boats are prohibited inside the reserve, but from its borders you are almost sure to see orcas spouting, tail-slapping, breaching, and spyhopping—that is, looking out of the water. Guided tours depart from the Vancouver Island communities of Alert Bay, Telegraph Cove, Port Hardy, Port McNeill, and Sayward.

At **Pacific Rim National Reserve** *(250/726-7721)* on Vancouver Island, some 24,000 gray whales travel along British Columbia's west coast from February to April, heading north on their annual migration from Baja California to the Bering Sea. They pass by again in September and October, heading south. Wickaninnish Centre has some excellent displays on this extraordinary cetacean odyssey. Charters and tours depart from Vancouver and North

A blue whale, world's largest mammal, surfaces in the St. Lawrence River near Les Escoumins.

Vancouver, as well as from Tofino and Ucluelet on Vancouver Island.

About 30 pods of orcas live year-round in the waters between British Columbia and Washington State. The orcas, as well as Dall's porpoises, can often be spotted from the decks of ferries traveling the Inside Passage. **Stubbs Island Charters** *(800/665-3066, 250/928-3117, or 250/928-3185)* operates out of Telegraph Cove, one of the best viewing spots.

Other good vantage points include Victoria on Vancouver Island (tours leave from the Inner Harbour) and the remote Queen Charlotte Islands, where you can see humpback whales in February (the herring-spawning season). In spring and summer, look for Pacific gray whales, orcas, and the occasional blue whale or fin whale. Contact **Super, Natural British Columbia** *(800/663-6000)* or **Tourism British Columbia** *(800/435-5622)*

Stubbs Island Charters *(800/665-3066 or 250/928-3185. www.stubbs-island.com)* in Johnstone Strait has 60-foot boats that hold up to 48 people on a four-hour trip. Bring your own snacks or lunch if you don't want to buy the cookies, fruit, and drinks that are sold on board.

From Tofino, try **Chinook Charters** *(250/725-3431. www.chinookcharters.com)*; they operate a range of watercraft—including Zodiacs and a 32-foot cruiser with a heated inside cabin—on two-hour trips.

Festivals: The Pacific Rim Whale Festival, featuring children's programs, a parade, and nature tours, is held mid-March to April in Tofino and Ucluelet.

Book: *Killer Whales* by John Ford, Graeme Ellis, and Kenneth Balcomb (1999).

Fortress of Louisbourg
Cape Breton Island

"Gentlemen of quality are allowed to wear their swords," the guard told us, "but under no circumstances may English-speaking visitors make maps of the fortifications."

With that warning, we passed through the gates—and into the 18th-century French pageantry of Nova Scotia's **Fortress of Louisbourg**. The massive stone redoubt, 25 miles south of Sydney on Cape Breton Island, was built because of fish. In the 1700s, French fishermen caught massive amounts of cod in the Atlantic waters to the east, then landed at Louisbourg to salt and dry their catch. Louisbourg, a natural harbor, became one of the busiest ports in North America—not to mention a French toehold in the New World, hence the defense works. In 1745 the French lost the site to the British, who destroyed it lest it fall back into enemy hands.

For two centuries after that, the fortress was little more than ruins. Then, in the late 1950s, the Canadian government restored the fort. Today the property is the largest historical reconstruction in North America. Fifty buildings have been rehabbed, along with mammoth stone fortifications, gates, and wharves. Yet tourists easily miss the fortress, because it is so remote. For sheer grandeur of architecture and ocean scenery, however, we found the detour well worth the drive.

At Louisbourg it is forever 1744—the year before the British siege. To foster an 18th-century ambience, cars are parked out of sight, behind the visitor center. Everyone is then bused to **Des Roches House** outside the **Dauphin Gate,** where the guard waits ready with his warning to "foreigners."

The guided walking tour (about 90 minutes) gave us a good grounding in the history of the site. Afterward we wandered on our own, running into reenactors who played their roles with relish: "I may be full of rum," cried a drunken soldier to the gendarme trying to arrest him, "but *you're* full of something else!"

In the **Guardhouse,** we found out that the soldier had been driven to drink by the hardships of the day. Monthly pay was so low—about the cost of a bottle of wine—that the soldiers resorted to backbreaking work to supplement their earnings. (The stone walls around us were evidence of their labor.)

Rations were worse than the food in a contemporary school cafeteria. Children shudder as a soldier explains how he scavenged codfish heads from the beach, then boiled them in a pot for dinner. Every four days, each soldier received a single six-pound loaf of bread from the **King's Bakery.** Inside the same building today, visitors can buy their own loaf of rye or whole-wheat bread fresh from the wood-fired ovens.

The soldiers' spartan existence stands in stark contrast to the gracious stone residence of the **Ordonnateur,** or chief civil administrator. Peek inside the drawing room—bedizened with polished armoires, gilt clocks, and thick carpets—and you just might see a gentlewoman in pearls dancing the minuet to a harpsichord.

At the **Children's Interpretive Centre** in the Rodrigue House (no. 22 on the site map), children aged 4 to 10 can enjoy (for an extra fee) a two-hour supervised program of arts, crafts, costumes, games, and a puppet show. Kids may also visit the **King's Bastion**—a fort within a fortress—in time to witness the cannon firing. The model ships hanging in the windows of the **Chapelle St. Louis** would have been brought by fishermen grateful for the sea's bounty.

There's enough here to warrant a full day's visit, so plan to eat on site. We enjoyed lunch at the **Hotel de la Marine**, its rustic tables set only with pewter spoons (diners of the day carried their own knives, and forks were just for gentlefolk). The menu, heavy on meat pies, hearty soups, and sausages, fits the period. So do the drinks; you can order a hot buttered rum, but don't ask for ice in your water. If you're partial to a complete set of cutlery, take a stab at **L'Epée Royale**. The **Civilian Bakery** sells snacks and desserts.

Using an early appliance at Louisbourg fortress

TIPS: Bring everything you'll need for the day before leaving the parking lot; once you reach the fortress, it's a long trip back to the car. Marine weather being fickle, pack a windbreaker. All-terrain wheelchairs are available at the visitors' center.

BASICS: Fortress of Louisbourg National Historic Site, about 25 miles south of Sydney on Hwy. 22. *(902/733-2280. www.fortress.uccb.ns.ca/parks. Outdoor walking tours May-late Oct.; full services June-mid-Oct.; adm. fee)*

MORE LOUISBOURG ATTRACTIONS

Kennington Cove is an excellent oceanside picnic area, roughly 12.5 miles south of the fortress on a dirt road. Swim from the sandy beach if you can handle the waves and cold water. Seals are sometimes seen off shore, as are bald eagles.

Originally part of a movie set re-creating 17th-century Plymouth, England, the **Louisbourg Playhouse** *(11 Aberdeen Street. 902/733-2996)* is an Elizabethan-style theater in the modern town of Louisbourg. The stage often hosts the Cape Breton Musicians. **Tourism Cape Breton Island** *(800/565-9464)*

King's Landing Historical Settlement

King's Landing is one of Canada's best living-history museums, bringing extraordinary detail to its portrayal of the settlement of New Brunswick. Located on the banks of the St. John River, the bucolic museum village re-creates the life of 19th-century pioneers in buildings dating from 1790 to 1910.

Some might say that New Brunswick was born in discontent: Among the early settlers were 30,000 American refugees from the Revolutionary War—Tory Loyalists who fled the fledgling nation for safe haven in the British colony of New Brunswick. Later on, they were joined by a wave of immigrants from Britain and Europe. In 1867—the year that Canada became a nation—New Brunswick was one of the founding provinces.

The size of the King's Landing collection—70 historic buildings housing 70,000 artifacts—is matched by the spirit of its warm, open staff. "We encourage kids to touch old tools or sit on the back of an ox," says project executive Lynn Thornton. Among the costumed staff are children who enjoy meeting visiting youngsters, engaging them in a game of hoop roll or persuading them to join in a hayride. This interaction alone makes King's Landing a rewarding experience for young families.

Children ages 9 to 14 learn 19th-century social history the old-fashioned way: They *live* it. The **Visiting Cousins Program** is a five-day summer sleepover camp that brings children from across North America to work, play, and study on-site. Dressed in period clothes typical of rural New Brunswick, youngsters tackle authentic tasks: They card wool, churn butter, milk cows, make lye-and-tallow soap, and cook fudge in an open kettle over the fire. Before long, children raised on microwaved dinners are avidly stirring pots of steaming chicken soup and baking fresh bread in wood-fired stoves. Every camper attends the one-room school, where lessons are written in chalk on slates and children who talk out of turn wear dunce caps.

The cousins program is so popular that children may take part in it only once. For 12- to 15-year-old "graduates," there is the **Family Kin Program,** which gives them a chance to work alongside craftsmen as apprentices. The older campers learn cooperage, carpentry, or another trade. Dormitory-style accommodations are provided for both the kin and cousins programs.

Even grandparents get into the act. They have their own residential camp—a five-day **Elderhostel** program in September—that investigates the agricultural revolution, herbal medicine, and 19th-century fashions.

Not to be left out, parents can take a **Day Adventure** workshop, offered twice daily, in which King's Landing artisans give hands-on instruction in processing wool, caning chairs, brewing herbal medicines, and making rag rugs. Our favorite is the

A cart called a *sloven* leaves Joslin Farm at King's Landing Historical Settlement, New Brunswick.

Edible Adventure, a cooking class where rye griddle cakes and gingerbread are cooked in an open hearth, then eaten.

There's so much to see at this 120-acre site that even a casual visit will take the better part of a day. Kids can get a vivid idea of the settlers' varied lives by comparing the rough life depicted in the Irish immigrants' cabin with the relative luxury of the 1850 **Huestis House,** replete with maids' quarters.

There is even evidence of some 19th-century upward mobility: Daniel Moorehouse, a Loyalist and New Englander who fought for the British in the Queen's Rangers, received 500 acres of prime New Brunswick farmland in gratitude for his service to the crown. The land prospered: In 1812, Moorehouse built a Georgian house and furnished it with classic Loyalist trappings—among them a tall case clock once owned by Benedict Arnold. It all makes for a fascinating exercise in historical relativism: One country's loyalist is another's traitor.

TIPS: Visitors can enjoy a traditional lunch at the **King's Head Inn,** a rural posthouse where candles and lanterns light the dining rooms and the menu features a Ploughman's Lunch, New Brunswick salmon chowder with warm biscuits, and Queensbury apple dumplings.

BASICS: King's Landing Historical Settlement *(Trans-Canada 2, W of Fredericton. 506/363-4999. www.kingslanding.nb.ca. June-mid-Oct.; adm. fee)* Visiting Cousins and **Family Kin Programs** cost $320 (CN), including food, lodging, and 24-hour supervision for five days. Applications are available from the King's Landing Education Office *(20 King's Landing Service Road, King's Landing, New Brunswick. E6K 3W3).* The **Elderhostel** program costs $580 (CN) for five days. Adult **Day Adventures** cost $50 (CN) and must be booked before 3 p.m. the previous day.

For more living-history learning vacations, consider **Upper Canada Village** and **Black Creek Pioneer Village** (page 266).

French Immersion
Québec City

Simply to set foot in **Québec City** is a learning experience for most families. The town is not only cosmopolitan—95 percent of the population speaks French every day—but historic; within its walls, kids can absorb 400 years of history by strolling the narrow, cobbled streets of the **Upper Town** (Haute-Ville) or **Lower Town** (Basse-Ville).

Perched on high cliffs overlooking the St. Lawrence River, Québec is the only walled city north of Mexico. Kids accustomed to nothing older than the nearest megamall will enjoy walking down the oldest shopping street in North America. From the city's well-preserved stone ramparts, they can imagine they are colonists of New France repelling an attack by the English in 1759, or an attack by American troops under Benedict Arnold on New Year's Eve in 1775. Their parents, meanwhile, can pretend to be vacationing in Paris.

Start your visit to the city with the **Québec Expérience** *(418/694-4000. www.quebecexperience.com. Mid-May–mid-Oct.; adm. fee)*, a multimedia show just off the art-filled rue du Trésor in Upper Town. Small children may be alarmed by the production's mix of cannon fire, collapsing bridges, and giant figures that loom up to narrate the history of Québec. Older kids love the holographic effects—especially the "real" waterfall splashing onto the stage.

For a more thorough history, visit **National Battlefields Park** *(418/648-4071. Closed Mon. Labor Day–mid-May)*. Inside the Interpretation Center, children slip on headphones (a natural motion for them) and wander through sound-and-light shows *(adm. fee)*. Every Canadian schoolchild knows the story of the 1759 battle between the French and the British on the Plains of Abraham. The leaders of both sides—British general James Wolfe and French field marshal Marquis Louis Joseph de Montcalm de Saint-Véran—were killed that night, sealing the fate of North America. If Montcalm had repulsed the English troops and moved on to conquer parts of New England for France, many Americans might be speaking French today.

If you tour the 240-acre urban park in summer, don't be surprised to meet Generals Montcalm and Wolfe themselves, wandering about to interact with visitors. At the **Discovery Pavilion** *(835 Wilfrid Laurier Ave. 418/649-6157)*, families can sign up to ride Abraham's Bus with Abraham Martin, the legendary farmer who lent his name to part of the park.

For a less structured visit, let the kids clamber on the cannon, hike the park's nature trails, or take in a summer-evening concert (they're free). In winter, when hundreds of twinkling lights illuminate the park, rent cross-country skis and traverse the five family trails, or take a sleigh ride over the snow. Ski rentals: **Friends of the Plains** *(390 Avenue de Bernieres. 418/648-4050, 649-6476, or 648-2586)*

YEAR-ROUND FUN

Québec City Summer Festival. During the July festival, performing artists, clowns, and musicians take over the streets for spontaneous fun. More than 600 performances from as many as 25 different countries take place on stages, street corners, and in parks. Special children's activities include a circus camp on the Plains of Abraham, where kids can learn to juggle or fly on a trapeze. To attend the evening performances, buy a flashing button that gives access; at $8 (CN) per person, with children 12 and under free, it's a family bargain. *(418/523-4540. www.festival-ete-Quebec.qc.ca)*

Québec Winter Carnival. If your town got 135 inches of snow every winter, you'd put on the world's largest winter festival, too! For three weekends from late January to mid-February, a jolly *bonhomme* (snowman) leads parades of floats accompanied by music. Kids will seek out the ice palace, the International Snow Sculpture Show, and an Igloo Village. At Children's Place, they can glide down an ice slide. *(418/626-3716 or www.carnaval.qc.ca)*

That star-shaped, nearly hidden fortress bordering National Battlefields Park is the **Citadel** *(Cote de la Citadelle. 418/694-2815. Apr.-Oct.; adm. fee)*. A regimental brass band accompanies the **Changing of the Guard** daily at 10 a.m. *(late June-early Sept.)* and the **Beating of the Retreat** daily at 7 p.m. *(July-Aug. Wed.-Sat.)*.

The fortification is still an active military base for the Royal 22nd, a French-speaking regiment of the Canadian Forces, so families must tour the Citadel with a guide. Tours leave every 15 minutes. Although the objects collected in the small **Museum of the Royal 22nd Regiment** *(mid-March-mid-Oct.; by reservation only in winter)* look somewhat dated, you'll want to show your children the letter that English general Wolfe wrote to his mother on the eve of battle; he signed it, "Your affectionate and obedient son."

Located in the west corner of the old walled city, **Artillery Park** *(418/648-4205. mid-June-Labor Day)* housed both French soldiers and a British garrison. Reenactors give kids a glimpse of their lives: The soldiers slept on hard dormitory beds while the officers sipped tea and scarfed down scones in the elegant Dauphine Redoubt. If your kids are joiners, they can dress up in period togs too. Look for bread being baked in the outdoor ovens on Sunday. Young girls may want to visit Les Dames de Soie, a doll workshop and museum on the grounds .

Expose your children to street theater on **Terrasse Dufferin,** the mime-infested boardwalk that stretches along the upper cliff overlooking the river. Afterward, wander through the posh lobby of the **Château Frontenac** *(418/692-3861),* the castle-like hotel where Roosevelt and Churchill met in August 1943 to discuss the Normandy invasion.

In the costume room of the family-friendly **Musée de la Civilisation** *(85 rue Dalhousie. 418/643-2158. Closed Mon.; adm. fee),* both children and adults can dress

The Terrasse Dufferin—Quebec's street-theater mecca—leads to the Château Frontenac.

up like clowns, jugglers, or lion tamers and play the part. You'll also find interactive exhibits on architectural space, as well as an impressive array of First Nations artifacts (check out the 2,800-year-old necklace, made of copper from Lake Superior). If you've never seen a tree turned into a canoe, watch master builder Cesar Newasnish do precisely that on the video playing near an enormous birchbark rabaska. On weekends, kids can attend workshops (in French only) in which they examine Inuit objects such as sealskin gloves and a cradleboard to hold a baby. Afterward, wander through the Lower Town, then picnic at the small, leafy **UNESCO Park;** small children can blow off steam on the rope climber.

TIPS: The Upper Town (site of the Citadel and the Château Frontenac) is linked to the historic Lower Town by 11 steep staircases with names such as Break-Your-

Neck Stairs (Casse-Cou Escalier) and Sailor's Leap (du Sault-au-Matelot). These stairways, combined with Québec's uneven sidewalks and cobbled streets, make it difficult for strollers. Travel between the Upper and Lower Towns by funicular, about $1.25 (CN) per ride. The funicular's main entrance is in the **Louis-Jolliet House,** in the heart of Old Québec near **Place Royale.** The upper entrance is on the boardwalk of the Dufferin Terrasse.

BASICS: Québec City is about a 2.5-hour drive east of Montreal. **Greater Québec Area Tourism and Convention Bureau** *(835 Ave. Wilfrid Laurier, Québec, G1R 2L3. 418/649-2608 or 800/363-7777. www.quebecregion.com)*

For a different and dramatic way to approach the city—especially during the autumn color season in late September and early October—take a cruise ship from a city on the east coast of the U.S. and dock in Québec. At least three family-friendly lines have summer and fall sailings to Canada from New York: **Carnival Cruise Lines** *(800/227-6482. www.carnival.com),* **Norwegian Cruise Lines** *(800/327-7030. www.ncl.com),* and the **Big Red Boat II** *(800/990-7770. www.premier.com).*

Traditional Huron Site Wendake

Just 15 minutes north of Québec City is Wendake, the location of the Huron-Wendat village of **Onhoua Chetek8e.** Surrounded by woods and decorated with birch, cedar, maple, and stone, the village seems as if it has been here since the Huron arrived hundreds of years ago; in reality, it was built in 1988.

The sound of drumming and the scent of burning cedar logs greet your arrival at the high palisades of the entrance gate. Indeed, a stay here can be a trip down sensory lane. Families will smell the pine boughs used to smoke meat and fish, taste hot pumpkin soup or buffalo stew, and feel the furs of coyote, bears, and moose placed on sleeping lofts.

Because the reserve is small–just 1 square mile (about 2.5 sq km)–it can feel crowded with visitors. Still, families absorb a great deal in a short time. You'll find out why some snowshoes are round and others narrow (they're tailored to the terrain), learn how to play traditional games, and make your own beaded jewelry in a workshop. The guided tours keep things at a child's level, telling native legends or revealing the Huron cure for the common cold: kidneys from a beaver.

TIPS: The figure "8" symbolizes the "ouh" sound. At **Nek8barre,** an on-site restaurant, sample traditional dishes: buffalo pie, bison soup, and trout cooked in clay.

BASICS: **Onhoua Chetek8e,** Traditional Huron Site *(575 Stanislas-Kosca St., Wendake. 888/255-8857 or 418/842-4308. www.huron-wendat.qc.ca)*

Biodome
Montréal

Kids' lids flutter when they learn they're going to visit a museum about ecosystems. Tell them they're going to watch 9,000 creatures at play in four different habitats, however, and they react with wide-eyed wonder.

At the **Biodome**, Montréal's most popular attraction, kids can follow the Wall-to-Wall Tour Guide given out at the front desk. Try to spot the porcupine sleeping in a leafy tree, or the tiny poison-arrow tree frogs camouflaged in the rain forest. Along the paths, bilingual plaques offer information simple enough for third graders to read. Why is that two-toed sloth colored green? Because microscopic green algae grow in its fur. (Symbionts not parasites, the algae lend the two-toed sloth its protective camouflage.)

A blast of hot air and steaming mist, a trickling waterfall, and squawks from hundreds of tropical birds announce that you have entered the **Rain Forest.** This is the domain of black Goeldi's marmosets, as well as golden lion tamarins such as the pair shown on the opposite page.

Cooler weather prevails in the **Laurentian Forest** of hardwoods, evergreens, and songbirds. For kids *and* adults, the highlight here is the working beaver dam. An underwater window brings visitors nose to nose with a large, sleek beaver busily collecting sticks. Glance at the closed-circuit TV and you see the beaver inside its den, neatly stacking its newly gathered sticks like firewood.

The **St. Lawrence Marine Ecosystem** features an underwater observatory filled with 2.5 million liters of "sea water" and about 30 species of fish. Divers put on feeding shows in the tank three times a week, luring the sea creatures near the viewing windows.

The fourth ecosystem replicates the **Arctic of the North Pole** and the **Antarctic of the South Pole.** In penguin colonies enclosed by plexiglass barriers, some birds molt, others breed or nest (we saw one penguin couple take turns incubating an egg), and still others simply hang out on rock shelves.

Don't miss the **Naturalia Discovery Room,** tucked away in the basement. You won't find any "Don't Touch" signs here—children are encouraged to stroke the silky fur of a beaver, feel the jagged teeth of a shark, and peer through a microscope at the spines of a sea urchin. They can also handle bird feathers, reptile eggs, and tortoise shells. The overall atmosphere is welcoming; still, kids under 6 must be accompanied by an adult.

TIPS: As visitors move from room to room, the temperature fluctuates from 56°F to 88°F (about 4°C to 28°C), so dress in layers. Ask questions of the nature interpreters (the people wearing pith helmets). Arrive in time to witness a penguin feeding (feeding times vary; contact museum for schedule). To see the beaver at work, visit in the late afternoon when he awakens hungry from his nap. You can also

Golden lion tamarins at the Rain Forest exhibit in Montréal's Biodome

catch a daily bat feeding at the **Bat Cavern;** again, feeding times vary, so contact the museum to find out the day's schedule.

Gift-shop favorites include posters, books, and other nature items. Grab a snack at La Brise cafeteria or Le Bistro café, or bring a picnic to enjoy in the gardens. All public spaces are accessible by wheelchairs and strollers. A free shuttle bus runs every 15 to 30 minutes, linking the Biodome with the Insectarium and the Montréal Botanical Gardens.

The St. Lawrence Marine Ecosystem inside the Biodome

BASICS: Biodome de Montréal *(4777 av. Pierre-De-Coubertin. 514/868-3000. Adults $9.50 [CN], seniors and students $7 [CN], ages 6-17 $4.50 [CN]).* The Nature Package includes admission to the Insectarium and Biodome: adults $15.25 (CN), seniors and students $11.25 (CN), ages 6-17 $7.75 (CN).

The Insectarium
Montréal

Sautéed crickets for dinner. Chocolate-covered grasshoppers for dessert. Each year, the Montréal **Insectarium** offers these unique treats to visitors for a three-week period in February or March. That's when chefs from Québec's Tourism and Hotel Institute serve up 100,000 mealworms, 60,000 crickets, 10,000 locusts, 10,000 honeybees, and 5,000 silkworm pupae. And why not? Insects, a common food source in many parts of the world, are packed with vitamins, minerals, and protein.

The museum—an insect-shaped building in a corner of **Montréal's Botanical Gardens**—is renowned for its collection of 160,000 insects, both dead and alive. The museum's displays manage to fascinate and repel at the same time. Visitors can watch a giraffe weevil stretch out its neck, stare down a large live spider, or try to find another creature here as ugly as the Madagascar hissing cockroach. Between May and September, butterflies by the hundreds flit about in the **Butterfly House** next to the Insectarium.

THE MONTRÉAL BOTANICAL GARDENS
(JARDIN BOTANIQUE DE MONTRÉAL)

Smack-dab in the middle of the city, the 180-acre **Montréal Botanical Gardens** *(4101 rue Sherbrook est. 514/872-1400. www.ville.montreal.qc.ca/jardin/jardin.htm. Adm. fee)* is one of the most beautiful—and biggest—gardens in the world. It features 10 exhibition greenhouses, 30 themed gardens, the largest Chinese garden outside Asia, a peaceful Japanese garden and pavilion, and the **Insectarium.**

At the **Tree House,** kids can embark on a tree-naming scavenger hunt called the Big Rally. In late summer at the **Butterfly House,** children help tag and release monarch butterflies for the long migration to Mexico. From the middle of September to late October, hundreds of silk lanterns transform the Chinese garden into a nighttime fairyland. In winter, families can ski through the grounds.

Check out the live specimens in the scorpion colony. At the exhibit of a working beehive, you can observe bees returning to the hive with pollen-laden abdomen sacs, or try to spot the queen bee (it's marked with a painted spot). There are also hundreds of mounted specimens, plus educational exhibits on such mesmerizing critters as the silkworm and praying mantis.

Interactive displays encourage kids to create their own flying critters via computer. The digital displays also invite children to examine the furlike scales of a cicada, or compare their own jumping ability with that of a flea. Most popular is the Goliath birdeater tarantula; this spider, indigenous to Guyana, rears up on its hind legs when angry or threatened. Pregnant mothers may find solace in the giant waterbug pair: The female lays her eggs on the back of her mate, who carries them until they hatch.

To celebrate its 10th anniversary in 2000, the Montreal Insectarium is setting up special activities. Its entomologists are also helping to establish similar institutions worldwide. These include an insectarium in Shanghai, a butterfly house in the Adirondacks, an insectarium in Newfoundland, and similar efforts in Hong Kong and Taipei. "Insects live all around us," says André Payette of the museum's educational services. "It's useful for us to know about them."

Although you can't buy insects at the museum gift shop, you can pick up a souvenir of butterfly barrettes, a plush ladybug toy, or even a tasty mealworm lollipop.

TIPS: The museum operates a free service at the information counter that should captivate budding bug collectors. From 10 a.m. to noon and from 1 p.m. to 4 p.m. Monday through Friday, staff members are on hand to identify unknown insect species and to answer questions about any bug a child has found. Specimens should be presented in a see-through plastic box. Although the Insectarium lacks a cafeteria or snack bar, there is one on the site of the Botanical Gardens. Alternatively, families can picnic at the Maisonneuve Park just beside the museum. Avoid visiting during the early part of June, when the Insectarium is infested with school groups.

BASICS: The Insectarium *(Jardin Botanique de Montréal. 4101 rue Sherbrooke est. 514/872-1400. www.ville.montreal.qc.ca/insectarium. Adm. fee)*

Cosmodome & Space Camp Laval

The Cosmodome, in the city of Laval just north of Montreal, is devoted to space science. The building houses Canada's only **Space Camp** for kids, as well as the interactive **Space Science Centre Museum.** The value of a visit here lies in giving children a different perspective on the space program—that of other participating countries besides the United States.

The Space Camp offers kids ages 9 to 14 (and their parents) a range of options, from introductory sessions that last an afternoon to two-day weekend sleepovers. You can ride a skateboard to figure out Newton's laws, taste foods you would eat in space, or pick up moon rocks while bouncing around in zero gravity. In one of the five simulators, try performing the same upside-down maneuver that Neil Armstrong executed during the Gemini 8 mission.

The Space Camp boasts a full-scale replica of the *Endeavour* **Space Shuttle.** Kids don space suits and helmets, then climb into the cockpit to experience a launch—via video screen, that is. Suddenly, the video link to Mission Control is cut, the rocket boosters roar, and for a second it feels as if you just might take off.

As the mission proceeds, parents man the control room while kids serve as pilots or scientists (the latter conduct multimillion-dollar space experiments). After a rough day in space, children spend the night under reflective space blankets in an eight-bunk dormitory named for a Russian mission.

In the Space Science Centre Museum next door, start with the multimedia production **Reach for the Stars,** which replicates the thrill of space exploration. For realism, a three-story moving platform lifts and tilts the audience; participation is limited to those six and older. Other displays in the museum include rockets from Japan and Russia, and a moon rock brought back by the Apollo 15 astronauts.

BASICS: The Cosmodome *(2150 Autoroute des Laurentides, Laval. 450/978-3600. www.cosmodome.org).* **Space Camp** costs (all in Canadian dollars): half-day programs $20 for adults, $15 for children; one-day programs $38 for adults, $28 for children; weekend sessions $225 for one adult and one child. Week-long Space Camp summer sessions (ages 9-15) cost $675, meals included. *(800/565-2267 or 450/978-3516)* For **U.S. space camps,** check listings under Florida and Alabama.

Excursions in the Ottawa Area

Leave it to the world's second coldest capital (Ulan Bator is first) to stage the continent's largest winter festival. Each February, **Winterlude** *(800/465-1867 or 613/239-5000. www.capcan.ca)* attracts about 750,000 people to Ottawa, where they glide the world's largest skating rink (a canal 4.7 miles/7.5 km long), gaze at ice sculptures, and gambol in the snow. If you don't skate, you can hire someone to push you across the ice in one of the red sleighs for rent along the canal. For three weekends running, kids are treated to fireworks on Parliament Hill and their own ice-and-snow playground at Jacques Cartier Park in Hull. The second best thing about this friendly festival is the Beaver Tail pastries—deep-fried dough concoctions sprinkled with sugar and cinnamon or lemon juice. The best thing is that almost every event is free.

The **Canadian Museum of Civilization,** an architectural marvel perched on the banks of the Ottawa River in Hull, Québec, is Canada's largest and most popular museum. Families approaching the place from the Ottawa side of the river will get a great view of the unusual curves and layers of its buildings. Architect Douglas Cardinal, of Blackfoot descent, designed the museum to reflect the nation's geography. The curved and textured building represents the Canadian Shield. The flat plaza in between stands for the prairies. The domed building conveys the Canadian glaciers, its tall, thin windows evoking waterfalls and ice.

Cardinal's inspiration for the **Grand Hall** came from the myth of the Raven's magic canoe, which can shrink to the size of a pine needle or expand to hold the entire universe. The ceiling arcs in the shape of a canoe; sinuous posts between the glass suggest canoe paddles; wavy lines simulate rivers and sheltered bays that harbor native villages to this day. There are no 90-degree angles in the building's architecture because they are thought to harbor bad spirits.

It all makes for a majestic showcase featuring three totem poles and six homes of Pacific Northwest native peoples. Just as they do on the west coast of British Columbia, the dwellings face the "water"—that is, the polished-tile floor—with the "rain forest" (actually the world's largest screened print) at their back door.

On weekends and all through the summer, guides open up touch carts so kids can handle a bear's tooth, pat eagle feathers, or feel a whale's rib (Pacific Northwest Indians used the rib as a tool to strip bark from cedar trees). Explanations are age appropriate: "They didn't have cotton to make jeans," explains a guide, "but they did have cedar, so they used cedar strips to make clothes." Some of the darker houses display masks that may frighten very young children. Older kids will be drawn to the **Dig**—an eerily fascinating reconstruction of an archaeological site.

The Canadian Museum of Civilization boasts its own theater company, the Dra-

mamuse actors, who bring 1,000 years of history to life. While the shantytown cook stirs pork and beans in a caldron, the innkeeper announces the news of the day and a Mrs. Gordon spouts off about her teenage daughter. These characterizations are set to an appropriate soundtrack—the squawking of gulls, the creaking of wood in a Basque whaling ship, the hammering of hobnails in the cobbler's workshop—that enhance the historical authenticity of the scene.

The exhibits on Canada's settlement paint a vivid picture of everything from the Vikings to immigration in the west to northern outposts such as the Wildcat Café. There's an enviable gross-out factor, too: Dioramas show a pioneer giving birth in a prairie tent, a dying sailor whose ship got trapped in the ice; and a fisherman standing in buckets at a whaling station to ward off "Black Leg" arthritis.

Younger children should hit the **Canadian Children's Museum** inside. Kids pick up a passport at the entrance, then travel the world getting it stamped at each destination. Along the way, they might board a Pakistani bus, listen to a Nigerian folktale, or explore a North African market. In summer, kids can let loose in the **Adventure World** playground outdoors, which gives them a chance to play a giant game of checkers or board the tugboat once pictured on Canada's one-dollar bill. Picnic tables and play space are also available on the riverbanks behind the museum.

TIPS: *This Week at the Museum* (from the information desk) lists tours, temporary exhibits, performance times for interactive characters, and film times. To avoid crowds, visit on Saturday mornings. No adm. fee Sundays if you arrive before noon.

BASICS: Canadian Museum of Civilization *(100 Laurier St., Hull, Québec. 819/776-7000. www.civilization.ca. Closed Mon. mid-Oct.-April; adm. fee).* **Children's Museum** *(819/776-7001. Adm. fee)*

MORE OTTAWA MUSEUMS

Canada's capital is a city of museums, with galleries devoted to aviation, money, stamps, and even the black horses of the Royal Canadian Mounted Police. Here are two of the most popular museums for families:

Canadian Museum of Nature: Dinosaurs and live insects—not to mention a rare Arctic aquarium and animals such as a polar bear—keep kids riveted as they tour this natural-history museum. *(240 McLeod St. at the corner of Metcalfe St. 800/263-4433 or 613/566-4700. www.nature.ca. Adm fee.)*

Museum of Science & Technology: Kids love walking through the crooked kitchen, exploring steam locomotives, and trying their hand at the Virtual Voyages Simulator. For young stargazers, there are Discover the Universe telescope evenings and weekend astronomy workshops. *(1867 St. Laurent Blvd. at Lancaster Rd. 613/991-3044. www.science-tech.nmstc.ca. Adm. fee)*

Left: A skeleton crew enjoys a group sleepover at the Canadian Museum of Nature in Ottawa.

Anishinabe Experience
Golden Lake

Set amid the rugged greenery of eastern Ontario's Ottawa Valley about two hours west of Ottawa, Pikwakanagan on Golden Lake is a small First Nations reserve where Linda Sarazin has developed a program to share her culture with visitors from around the world. We arrived on a summer afternoon, uncertain what to expect, but before long my daughter and Linda were making bannock dough and drinking cedar tea in the café next to Linda's home. Bannock—a biscuitlike staple—is rolled in balls and cooked to crispy perfection in a deep fryer. It figures prominently on the menu at **Pikwakanagan,** which straddles cultures with such offerings as "Golden Lake steak on a bun"—in reality, slices of fried baloney on bannock.

Modern-day life on the reserve plays as much a part in Linda's program as do traditional Algonquin practices. Overnight guests are made comfortable in canvas-covered tipis, which are easier to maintain than classic Algonquin bark-covered wigwams. You can choose a tipi in the woods or, as we preferred, one closer to the road, with flush toilets and showers nearby. Ours was close enough to Golden Lake to attract a leopard frog—or Omagaki, as we learned to call it.

We assembled our mattresses from freshly cut evergreen boughs: spruce on the bottom and fragrant cedar on top, with twigs tucked underneath as a cushion. Sleeping bags and pillows completed the bedding. At night, Linda's husband, Mervin, lit a small fire in the tipi to drive off insects (the smoke escaped through an opening in the top). With plenty of room to stand up and a fire close by, this was truly comfortable camping.

Over the course of an afternoon and a morning, we made dream catchers while talking about the symbolism of the circle, which recurs in a ring of tipi poles, in dances, and in the medicine wheel. In the **Heritage Centre,** we watched birch bark being fashioned into drinking cups, moose calls, canoes, and baskets decorated with porcupine quills.

The center's curator showed us a pair of wooden sticks that are used to harvest wild rice; while one person paddles the canoe, the other uses the sticks to draw the stalks over the canoe and tap the grains loose. Wild rice is still harvested locally—as are many other wild plants, which are dried at the Heritage Centre for use in salves, soaps, teas, and medicines.

Linda also arranged for us to visit Stanley Sarazin, who continues to make traditional bark canoes, stitched with spruce roots and sealed with pitch over ribs of cedar. It's getting harder and harder, Stanley explained, to find birch trees large enough to provide the 16-foot length of bark he needs.

Visitors who come during **powwow** time—the third weekend in August—can experience the joy of a traditional celebration with drumming, dancing, lots of food, and a strong sense of community.

WHAT'S IN A NAME?

The Algonquin people obtained their present-day name from their neighbors to the east, who called them the Algoumequin—"the people who dance." The French heard that label as "Algonquin." The Algonquin also refer to themselves as the Anishinabe, a word that translates as "real men born of this land." Before European contact, their territory extended from the Montréal area through the Ottawa Valley and as far west as North Bay. Settlement and lumbering have transformed that landscape. Today the Anishinabe live in a handful of reserves—the Canadian term for "reservation"—in Ontario and Québec. These include Pikwakanagan on Golden Lake, a community of 1,600 people. An additional nine Algonquin communities are located in the province of Québec.

TIPS: Follow powwow etiquette. Refer to the dancer's traditional clothes as "regalia," not "costumes." Do not take photos without asking permission.

BASICS: **Anishinabe Experience** *(1528 Mishomis Inamo, Golden Lake off Hwy. 60. 800/897-0235 or 613/625-2579. www.anishexp.com).* Two-day, one-night, all-inclusive package *(May-Oct., by reservation):* adults $240 (CN), children 12 and under $175 (CN).

Rockhound Gemboree Bancroft

Mineral collectors from around the world gather at the annual **Rockhound Gemboree** in August in Bancroft, Ontario, three hours north of Toronto. About 50 dealers and 15,000 visitors come not only to view the outstanding mineral collections but to collect rock samples at about 30 field sites under the guidance of trained geologists.

One of the most popular sites is **Bear Lake.** Here, collectors search for apatite, feldspar, hornblende, and titanite in waist-deep trenches dug in the forest floor. The **Quadeville** area has rose quartz; **Faraday Hill** has pyrite and uraninite; the **York River** region has cinnamon-colored garnets. Experienced collectors show up with safety goggles, shovels, and rock chisels, but beginners can use an ordinary garden trowel to rake the rubble for fragments of apatite.

TIPS: The indispensable *Mineral Collecting Guidebook,* available at the Bancroft Chamber of Commerce in the old railway station costs only $10 (CN) if purchased from the chamber.

MORE POWWOWS

First Nations celebrate their culture and community with powwows. Drumming and dancing—often for prize money—are the focus of the celebrations. Each dance has its own regalia: shawls and jingle dresses for the women, traditional buckskin for the male grass dancers or fancy dress embellished with feathers for athletic youths. Vendors sell traditional foods such as corn soup and bannock with jam, along with crafts such as beaded earrings, dream catchers, and moosehide moccasins. Here are some of Canada's biggest powwows:

Buffalo Days Powwow and Tipi Vil- lage *(Head-Smashed-In Buffalo Jump, Fort Macleod, Alberta. 403/553-2731. 3rd weekend in July);*

Six Nations Champion of Champions Powwow *(Ohsweken, Ontario. 519/445-4391. Late July);*

Wikwemikong Annual Competition Powwow *(Manitoulin Island, Ontario. 705/859-2385. Aug. civic holiday);*

Canadian Aboriginal Festival *(Skydome, Toronto. 519/751-0040. Late Nov./early Dec.)* With an annual attendance of roughly 200,000, this is the largest powwow in Canada.

BASICS: Bancroft Rockhound Gemboree *(888/443-9999 or 613/332-1513).* The Chamber of Commerce offers tours given by experts. These same experts lead the Gemboree during the four days before Canada's legal holidays in August.

Wolf Howl
Algonquin Park

Ontario's oldest provincial park (and, at nearly 2 million acres, one of its largest), **Algonquin Provincial Park** is legendary for the opportunities it affords to see and hear wildlife, particularly moose and wolves. The park can be sampled two ways: Drive and hike from Highway 60, or access the remote lakes by canoe or rugged hike. We love both experiences.

Families with small kids may find it best to travel Highway 60 across the southern part of the park. From mid-May to early June, especially in early morning, the road offers excellent chances to spot moose from your car. After subsisting on twigs all winter—and with sodium-rich plants such as water lilies and milfoil not yet in bloom—the moose develop a salt craving that draws them to low-lying roadside areas; here they can lap up the road salt that runs off with the spring meltwater.

Oddly enough, your chances of spotting a moose in Algonquin park may be better thanks to logging, which is still allowed here. The tree-cutting fosters the growth of shrubs on which moose often feed.

Bull moose browsing in Algonquin Park

Algonquin is also famous for its wolves. The park has its own species, the red wolf, which is somewhat smaller than the gray or timber wolf. You'll find it surprisingly easy to commune with these symbols of the wild on an August **wolf howl.** The event originated in the late 1950s, when researchers found that the easiest way to locate the animals was to imitate their howls, then pinpoint the response. August is the best month for a wolf howl: The pups, left behind during the hunt, readily howl back at a decent imitation of their calls.

Guided wolf howls are usually held Thursday nights in August. After a quick introduction to wolf biology at the outdoor theater, visitors join a convoy of cars heading for a spot where wolves were heard the night before. The cars are parked by the side of the road, and everyone gets out as quietly as possible. A park ranger howls, then waits for a response. On roughly two evenings out of three, the wolves howl back.

TIPS: Be alert at road signs indicating "moose crossing," especially at night and especially in May and June. Fill your gas tank before heading out on a wolf howl— it could be a long drive.

BASICS: Algonquin Provincial Park *(Hwy. 60 between Whitney and Dwight, approx. 3 hrs. N of Toronto. 613/637-2828. Reduced services Nov.-March; day-use fee per car $10 (camping fee is additional).* Public wolf howls are held on Thursdays in August when a pack can be located. Call ahead to confirm.

MORE WILDLIFE-WATCHING: ALGONQUIN PARK

The park's 1,500 miles (2,400 km) of marked canoe routes allow serious paddlers to head out for weeks at a time. Inexperienced canoeists may want to contact one of several outfitters in the area, listed below:

Pow-Wow Wilderness Trips: Proprietor and guide Steve Sanna customizes weekend trips to a family's interests, from watching wildlife to simply finding a good swimming hole. He provides canoes, food, and van transportation from Toronto. In the wild, he has been known to fry milkweed fritters for breakfast and brew birch-bark tea.
   BASICS: Pow-Wow Wilderness Trips *(5580 Sheppard Ave. E., 6505 Scarborough. 416/754-9998. www.pathcom.com/~powow)* Two-night, 3-day inclusive trips cost $239 (CN); children 12 and under half-price, no minimum age.

Grandview Inn: This modern condominium resort, 25 miles west of Algonquin's west gate, offers a rich line-up of ecotourism outings. For ease and accessibility, we recommend the moose-watching excursion to **Hailstrom Creek Bog.** Moose-watchers ride inflatable Zodiac rafts piloted by guides.
   BASICS: Grandview Inn *(Hwy. 60, E of Huntsville. 800/461-4454 or 705/789-4417)* Day-long moose-watching trips cost $70 (CN), including lunch. Priority booking goes to resort guests. Room rates start at $80 per person, double occupancy. Children under 18 stay free, but pay for meals.

Voyageur Quest Log Cabin Lodge: Located outside Algonquin Provincial Park near the village of South River (three to four hours north of Toronto), Voyageur Quest offers many guided outdoor excursions: hiking in search of edible wild plants, learning to canoe, howling for wolves, and spotting moose on sunrise canoe trips. Winter activities include dogsledding and snowshoeing. The two-story log building has six guest rooms with rustic comforts—propane lights, woodstoves, cold running water.
   BASICS: Voyageur Quest Log Cabin Lodge *(599 Millwood Rd., Toronto. 416/486-3605. www.voyageurquest.com)* Summer packages start at $225 (CN), winter packages at $395 (CN). Children under 13 are half-price with two adults.

Haliburton Forest Wolf Centre: A pack of timber wolves occupy a forested enclosure at the 15-acre Haliburton Forest Wolf Centre, a private wildlife management area. Here visitors can watch wild animals in as natural a setting as possible. The windows of the indoor observation area are made of one-way glass, keeping visitors out of sight—and encouraging the wolves to display their natural behavior. In summer, pups play around an older wolf, sometimes biting its muzzle to trigger regurgitation (the partially digested food helps wean the pups). Outdoor microphones allow visitors to hear the pups' squeaks and howls. Displays of wolf mythology will interest older children, while youngsters may enjoy feeling the wolf pelt and skull on the touch table. Because the wolves' enclosure is so large, a sighting cannot be guaranteed; still, the odds are better than 75 percent.

BASICS: **Haliburton Forest Wolf Centre** *(Kennisis Lake Rd./County Rd. 7. 705/754-9653. Open daily late May–mid-Oct., Fri.-Sun. rest of the year; adults $7, children 7-17 $4)* lies 12 miles (20 km) north of West Guilford, 1 hr. S of Algonquin Park. Wolf howls are held on Thursday evenings in July and August.

Huron Reenactment
Midland

From the French court of Louis XIV to the virgin forests of Huronia, Jesuit missionaries linked two widely different cultures at **Sainte-Marie Among the Hurons,** a 17th-century Jesuit mission where priests lived among their Huron converts. The site's crude wooden buildings have been carefully reconstructed to depict life in 1648. Volunteer craftsmen re-create the labors of a shoemaker, surgeon, master builder, and blacksmith (the latter fashions nails, hinges, knife blades, and awls in his forge).

Although copper pots and iron fish hooks helped promote Christianity, the cultural exchange went both ways. The Hurons were expert farmers, and their corn and squash soon became staples of the Jesuit diet (as visitors see when they explore the cookhouse and gardens).

The Huron influence also emerges in the **Church of St. Joseph,** which was probably adapted to accommodate Huron spirituality. There is no wooden floor to separate the Huron from the earth, nor is there a sacristy; such a space might seem too secretive.

While Europeans lived in Norman-style log buildings, the Hurons preferred their traditional dwellings. In a 50-foot longhouse pierced by a few thin beams of sunlight, a Huron reenactor tells how her people are dying from smallpox, measles, and influenza (the three diseases reduced the population from 30,000 in 1635 to 12,000 in 1649).

Our favorite activity at Sainte-Marie is to watch the reenactment of an arriving canoe flotilla. In addition to unloading supplies, it delivers a flurry of news about Iroquois attacks on Huron villages.

BASICS: **Sainte-Marie Among the Hurons** *(Hwy. 12, just E of Midland, 2 hrs. N of Toronto. 705/526-7838. www.saintemarieamongthehurons.on.ca. Early April–mid-Oct. Adults $9.75, seniors and students $6.25, five and under free)*

Voyageur Adventure
Thunder Bay

Paddling massive birch-bark canoes and dancing to old fiddle tunes, visitors live the life of fur-trade voyageurs at **Old Fort William,** about 40 miles north of the Ontario border. The fort is a reconstruction of the trading post as it looked in 1815, when the fur trade was at its height. In an era when proper gentlemen wore top hats made of fur, beaver pelts became a prized commodity, and fortunes were made in the quest for them. Not surprisingly, intense rivalries developed for access to the best trapping grounds.

One such competition broke out between the Hudson's Bay Company and an upstart from Montreal, the North West Company. At Fort William—midpoint of the fur-trade route—the North West Company established a strategic base. European trade goods arrived here from the east; from the west, transported by French-Canadian voyageurs in 24- and 36-foot (7.3- and 11-m) canoes, came the pelts of beavers that had been trapped by First Nations and Métis Indians.

As a result, the fort was both a literal and cultural crossroads, a place where diverse peoples met, traded, and celebrated. First Nations and Métis trappers taught newcomers how to build birch-bark canoes for navigating southern Ontario's myriad inland waterways. This social interaction is faithfully depicted at the present-day site, opened in 1973 on the Kaministiquia River at Thunder Bay.

To relive the fur-trade atmosphere yourself, consider a **Voyageur Overnight Adventure.** These two-day, one-night paddling expeditions begin with each participant's donning period garb. For men, that means one of two costumes: either the voyageur's shirt, trousers, coat, and tuque (hat), or the gentlemanly attire of a company clerk, complete with cravat. Women dress in traditional native garments—long skirt, leggings, and moccasins. Children can wear whatever they like, but most opt for voyageur togs.

After learning a few songs in French, the group paddles down the Kaministiquia River in a voyageur brigade for about 45 minutes. Two hundred years ago, the voyageurs paddled from dawn to dusk; during portages, each man was responsible for hauling two 90-pound packs stuffed with beaver pelts. The brigade then returns to Fort William, where families work alongside artisans. You might join the tinsmith to craft a nutmeg grater, help the canoe maker fashion a birch-bark basket, or pack furs into compact, canvas-covered bundles for easy shipping.

Once the fort closes to daytime visitors, overnight voyageurs stay behind to learn gambling games and dances. Food is traditional—beef stew, wild rice, Labrador tea—and so are the accommodations: Guests sleep in a voyageur tent near the river or on straw mattresses in the Guides' House. Less rugged arrangements with modern plumbing are also available.

Even if you decide against an overnight adventure, a day visit to the fort can be tremendous fun. Summer visitors walk into a frontier day in 1815 when a cannon announces the approach of a wilderness canoe party, its arrival marked by a festive spread of fresh bread, cheese, and rum. You need not be a natural-born reenactor to enjoy the fun; it's easy to pass an entire day watching such scenes as the arrest of the blacksmith for trading with the rival Hudson's Bay Company or a display of ax-throwing. The Old Fort William guides do a good job of re-creating tasks from the past—baking bread and milking cows, for example—but our favorite activities are those unique to the fur trade. You can watch reenactors build a 24-foot-long "north canoe" by sewing together birch bark with strands of spruce root, or see how furs were pressed in the Main Square for the voyage to Montréal.

The Ojibwa who lived near Old Fort William in 1815 played a key role. They sold materials they had gathered or made, including spruce gum, maple syrup, and sheets of birch bark. They traded their labor—the men building canoes, the women working in the kitchen—for credits at the company store.

The Ojibwa way of life is depicted in

VOYAGEUR CANOE TRIPS

Expand your fur-trade experience with an overnight voyageur canoe trip. Ecotourism specialists **Blue Loon Adventures** (RR #7, 4398 Hwy. 61, Thunder Bay, Ontario. 888/ 846-0066 or 807/ 964-2823. www. blueloon.baynet.net) offer a program that starts with the Voyageur Overnight Adventure in Old Fort William, then continues with a visit to the dramatic **Ouimet Canyon** and a nature hike in **Sleeping Giant Provincial Park**. Participants then pile into the 36-foot (11-m) canot du maître (master's canoe) to explore the dramatic scenery along the north shore of Lake Superior. Because tour lengths and activities are customized for clients, the cost of each trip varies. In general, expect to pay at least $950 (CN) for a five-day trip, with a six-person minimum. Blue Loon also offers a wide range of ecotourism packages: dogsledding, back-country horseback treks, and sea kayaking to the Slate Islands to observe woodland caribou.

a wigwam encampment on the outskirts of the fort. Youngsters will be fascinated to learn the details of their dress and the tactics they used to survive the harsh north-country winters. (Here's one: The Ojibwa added a second layer of bark inside the wigwam, then insulated it with moss for winter warmth.)

TIPS: Two restaurants—including a canteen that serves traditional beef stew, pea soup, and scones—make it easy to spend an entire day here with children. On Thursdays, you can extend your visit by staying for an evening **Voyageur Feast**—a multicourse dinner with entertainment provided by fur-trade characters in costume. Special events take place throughout the summer. Our favorites are the **Ojibwa Keeshigun Native Festival,** which celebrates native culture one weekend each year, and the **Great Rendezvous Festival** in mid-July, which brings together fur-trade reenactors from across North America.

BASICS: Old Fort William *(Off Hwy. 61, W of Thunder Bay. 807/473-2344. www.oldfortwilliam.on.ca. Mid-May–mid-Oct.; adm. fee)* **Voyageur Overnight Adventures,** suitable for children 10 and older, can be booked for one night *($185 CN)* or two *($255 CN).* **Voyageur Feasts,** held Thursdays in July and August, cost $27.50 (CN) and should be booked in advance.

MORE LIVING HISTORY IN ONTARIO

Upper Canada Village east of Morrisburg depicts life in an 1860s riverside community in Upper Canada (now Ontario). At the **Children's Activity Centre** *(open July and Aug.),* kids can try on historical costumes and play with period toys. The horse-drawn **Tow Scow,** a replica canalboat, ferries visitors through the site.

TIPS: Before walking the 40-acre site, familiarize yourself with the village by taking a wagon ride on the **Carry-All** (it's pulled by true Canadian breed horses). A **Time Travelers** summer camp lets children live at the village for five days.

BASICS: Upper Canada Village *(Hwy. 2. 800/437-2233 or 613/543-3704. www.parks.on.ca/uc.village. Mid-May–mid-Oct.; adm. fee)*

Families and visitors seeking a respite from Toronto's busy pace may want to check out **Black Creek Pioneer Village.** Plank sidewalks and dirt roads connect more than 35 historic buildings in which cooks and craftsmen ply their 19th-century skills. Don't miss the family-friendly stage productions.

BASICS: Black Creek Pioneer Village *(corner of Jane St. and Steeles Ave., NW Toronto. 416/736-1733. www.trca.on.ca. May-Jan.; adm. fee)*

Ontario Science Centre
Toronto

To-do list for a day at the **Ontario Science Centre:**
Steer an Olympic bobsled;
Ring the bells from an Asian temple;
Listen to a heart murmur;
Discover a new computer game on the Internet;
Visit a tropical rain forest.

Your kids might have their own list, too. At the Ontario Science Centre, mild-mannered adults have been seen furiously pedaling bicycles in a contest to generate horsepower, or excitedly navigating their way to the moon on a rocket chair.

Located in a wooded ravine in midtown Toronto, the center has served as a model for science museums around the world for more than 30 years. Its 13 halls house more than 800 hands-on exhibits. Also on-site: a planetarium, a star lab, an OM-

Right: Astral projection at the Ontario Science Centre in Toronto

NIMAX theater, an auditorium, and classrooms. Children can dive into a wide range of science activities, from animals and space to volcanoes and computers.

A day at the center can make your hair stand on end—literally. At one of the popular electricity workshops, kids and adults get hair-raising results by touching the safe but shocking Van de Graaff generator. At the **Timescape** exhibit, a computer morphs a five-year-old child over a period of 70 years, showing what she will look like as a senior citizen (scary!). Visitors can also step into a time chamber and try to guesstimate a minute.

The ravine containing the center also happens to be North America's largest urban wetland. Home to frogs, foxes, and even coyotes, it is laced by hiking trails, which kids can explore on their own or as part of a guided hike.

Back inside the building, an array of scheduled activities encourages children to "have a little fun with the gray matter." Among the offerings are workshops, lectures, field trips, and special events such as robot games, tracing family roots, and a Science for Girls week.

TIPS: The center can get crowded and noisy midday. To avoid school and camp groups, visit early in the morning or after 2 p.m.

BASICS: Ontario Science Centre *(770 Don Mills Rd. at Eglinton Ave. E., North York. 416/696-3127. www.osc.on.ca. 10 a.m.-5 p.m. Adults $10, children 13 to 17 $7, children 5 to 12 $6).* Allow about 20 minutes' driving time to reach the center from downtown Toronto.

Toronto Zoo

"Please leave all your worries behind," the tour guide instructed our group as the Toronto zoomobile carried us past a pair of pacing jaguars. We were headed for our overnight destination—a wooded clearing in the **Toronto Zoo's** new **African Savanna** exhibit. Built at a cost of $18 million, the exhibit reproduces the look and feel of Africa's Serengeti Plain. Reconstructed kopje rocks and termite mounds heighten the realism—as do the signs, which are printed in Swahili. Lizards perch on high rocks; below them, an anti-poaching truck sits at the ready.

As the bus bumped past ostriches, giraffes, and pink flamingos, we felt like characters in *The Lion King,* on our way to "exciting, exotic Africa." At the clearing we found a circle of tents, some log benches around a fire pit, and—thankfully—a washroom with flush toilets nearby. Each of the six families participating in this **Serengeti Bush Camp** had its own tent—an army-surplus canvas shelter with folding cots and a wood floor. Plain but comfortable, the tents featured screened windows front and back to admit the breeze, and almost enough room to stand.

An overnight at Serengeti Bush Camp takes you behind the scenes. Between 5 p.m., when the main zoo closes, and 9 a.m. the next morning, we met the zookeepers and watched them perform a pedicure on a four-ton elephant. Armed with flashlights, we took a night hike past the hyena pen and saw eyes flashing in the dark. We listened to African music, stroked a cheetah's fur, saw river hippos disappear underwater, and examined specimens in a field station that appeared to have been flown in directly from a Kenyan game park.

All that activity stoked some powerful appetites, so we fell upon the deep-fried cassava root and samosas with tamarind sauce. Before bed—er, cot—we roasted marshmallows over a fire kindled to keep "wild animals" at bay. Early next morning (6:30 a.m.), we rolled out for a hike that revealed wolves eating breakfast.

Getting close to the animals was the name of the game. The kids erupted in giggles when an elephant unleashed a torrent of urine. They beamed with awe when our group came nose to nose with a lion cub; named Simba, it is the long-awaited offspring of Nokanda and Rowdy. As one kid exclaimed, "I just love a happy ending."

TIPS: Bush-camp participants receive a free zoo pass, allowing campers to stay for the following day or return another time. Beware of the Canada-geese droppings (kids should wear shoes that can be cleaned easily). Strollers or wagons can be rented at the entrance. The Family Centre next to the African Pavillion has changing rooms and a nursing station. Don't miss the **Edge of Night** exhibit, which enables visitors to see nocturnal animals in the dark.

BASICS: The **Toronto Zoo** *(361A Old Finch Ave., Scarborough. 416/392-5929. www.torontozoo.com. Adm. fee)*, the world's fourth largest, houses 5,000 animals from 499 species and is laid out in six zoogeographic regions: Africa, Australasia, Eurasia, the Americas, Indo-Malaya, and Canada.

The zoo is in the northeastern section of Toronto, about a 30-minute drive from downtown. **Serengeti Bush Camp** *(416/392-5947. Reservations required)* overnights take place from May to October. The camp costs $90 (CN) for ages 12 and up, $80 (CN) for ages 6 to 12. Bring a sleeping bag, pillow, towel, hat, sunscreen, insect repellent, and flashlight.

Royal Ontario Museum

This Toronto institution is Canada's "treasure trove." In addition to historical displays—old silver, Egyptian mummies, ancient Chinese artifacts—visitors will find objects from the natural world such as dinosaur skeletons, rocks and minerals, and an authentic re-creation of a bat cave. A new biodiversity gallery even features live creatures. The emphasis is on the eclectic: An elegantly carved Korean buddha may sit just a staircase away from a northern Ontario moose.

With 30,000 objects on display in the **Royal Ontario Museum's** 39 galleries—and another four million in storage—don't expect to see everything in a single visit. Instead, concentrate on a few areas popular with kids, interspersed with some quiet

IN THE STEPS OF GREY OWL

The following adventure mentions sites in Manitoba and Saskatchewan as well as Ontario. Archie Belaney—a 17-year-old from Hastings, England—was so fascinated by Canada's native peoples that in 1906 he went to live with a band of Ojibwa on Bear Island in Lake Temagami. The Ojibwa named him Grey Owl or He Who Walks by Night.

For the next 33 years, wearing braids and buckskin (and claiming to be half Indian), Grey Owl wrote books about the importance of respecting the land. He even lectured the queen of England about the plight of the beaver.

Grey Owl, the film version of his life, premiered in 1999; it was directed by Richard Attenborough and starred Pierce Brosnan. Kids intrigued by Grey Owl's story may want to travel in his footsteps, sketched below. They can also check out one of the books he authored, which include the following:

> *The Men of the Last Frontier* (1931)
> *Pilgrims of the Wild* (1934; the autobiography of Grey Owl)
> *The Adventures of Sajo and Her Beaver People* (1935)
> *Tales of an Empty Cabin* (1936)
> *A Book of Grey Owl* (1995)

Adults can read all about this overlooked figure, too, in some of the following volumes:

> *Grey Owl: The Many Faces of Archie Belaney* by Jane Billinghurst and Donald Smith (1998)
> *From the Land of the Shadows: The Making of Grey Owl* by Donald B. Smith (1990)
> *Wilderness Man: The Strange Story of Grey Owl* by Lovat Dickson (1973)

TEMAGAMI, ONTARIO: Grey Owl learned how to paddle a canoe in Temagami, which is prime country for it. To ply the sparkling waters of Lake Temagami yourself, rent a canoe and paddles at tiny **Finlayson Point Provincial Park** *(888/668-7275. www.OntarioParks.com. Adm. fee)*. The small cabin museum displays the books that Grey Owl wrote and the kinds of animals he trapped, including otters, owls, and a lynx. In Temagami, families can also rent houseboats that sleep up to 10 people; prices start at $885 (CN) per week. Houseboat companies include **Leisure Island** *(705/569-3261)*, **Ketchun-eny Lodge** *(705/237-8952)*, **Lakeland Three Buoys Houseboat** *(705/569-3455)*, and **Canusa Vacations** *(705/237-8965)*.

RIDING MOUNTAIN NATIONAL PARK, MANITOBA: When Grey Owl served as the caretaker of park animals for Riding Mountain National Park *(800/707-8480 or 204/848-7275 or -7272. Adm. fee)* northwest of Winnipeg in 1931, he used the opportunity to establish a beaver colony. Today it is a mix of ecosystems (eastern deciduous forest, boreal forest, and prairie grass) supporting black bears, coyotes, fox, elk, moose, white-tailed deer, timber wolves, porcupines, and beavers. A bison herd thrives near Audy Lake. There is also an 11-mile (18 km) round-trip hike to Grey Owl's cabin.

At the visitor center *(204/848-7249. Mid-May-Oct.)* in Wasagaming, kids can sign up for the Junior Naturalist's Keepers of the Wild Program, which gives them a chance to sample aboriginal foods, take an outdoor adventure hike, or visit a den of black bears at night—all in the company of park interpreters, of course.

A solitary paddler glides down Carson Creek in Manitoba's Riding Mountain National Park.

PRINCE ALBERT NATIONAL PARK, SASKATCHEWAN: In 1932, authorities built Grey Owl a secluded—and unique—cabin on the shore of Lake Ajawaan in **Prince Albert National Park** *(306/663-4522. Adm. fee)*, a wilderness of 14,700 square miles (38,000 sq km) 155 miles (250 km) north of Saskatoon. One wall of the cabin was open to the lake; this allowed Grey Owl's pet beavers, Rawhide and Jelly Roll, to swim right up into the cabin. Teenagers who relish canoe trips will enjoy the adventure of paddling to the isolated cabin (a good day's paddle, with portages), where Grey Owl lived with his wife, Anahareo. **Weekender Tours** *(144 2nd Ave. N., Saskatoon. 877/663-2722)* organizes a four-day **Canoe Quest for Grey Owl.** The trip, suitable for adults or teens, costs $355 and includes equipment, meals, and return transportation from Saskatoon.

For a less-intense wilderness experience, check out the daily programs and films at the park nature center *(877/255-7267)*.

time in out-of-the-way rooms where you can leisurely examine that child-size suit of armor or rare Ming tomb (the only one on display in the Western world).

Hands-on Biodiversity, the newest permanent interactive gallery, lets children handle live specimens. The most popular animal is Bruce, an Australian skink, who periodically emerges from his hiding place to be stroked. At the touch tables, children can examine a velvety beaver pelt or a rough whale vertebra. There's a strong make-believe component, too: Try on the child-size wings of a Goliath birdwing butterfly, then flit over to inspect the active beehive.

In the **Egyptian Gallery** on the third floor, children file past the Tomb of Kitines—a full-scale replica of a 2nd-century burial chapel—and head straight for the mummy of Antjau. A wealthy landowner who died some 2,500 years ago, Antjau still has his hair and toenails intact. Behind him are some fascinating animal mummies, including cats, hawks, and a small gazelle.

For many children, the **Bat Cave** is the best. Modeled on the St. Clair cave in Jamaica, this reconstructed subterranean chamber abounds with bats—some 3,000 in all, 11 of them real (but no longer alive). As kids edge forward into the dimly lit space, where live-looking crickets perch on slimy walls, they are greeted by the exotic calls of tropical birds and the eerie screeching of bats.

At the hands-on **Discovery Gallery**, opened in 1999 for children ages five and older, kids cruise through a crystal cave, dig for dinosaur bones, and try on chainmail or hippie clothing. Children who are capable of quiet investigation should head to the back of the room, where they can reconstruct a skeleton or examine specimens under a microscope. Younger children will probably flock to **Franklin's World,** named after the turtle in a line of popular Canadian storybooks; here they can crawl into an igloo to do puzzles, or sit on a parent's lap in a rocking chair to hear a story.

TIPS: As soon as you arrive at the Royal Ontario Museum, head up to the second floor for timed tickets to the Discovery Gallery. The place fills up fast during school holidays, and is often overrun by school groups between 10 a.m. and noon on weekday mornings. Also, ask for a museum map at the front desk and look at it with your children to decide which galleries they want to see; a game plan can spell the difference between a stressful visit and a successful one.

Two other new family-oriented galleries at the museum offer interactive exhibits: The **Dynamic Earth Gallery of Earth Sciences** is on the main floor, while the **Hands-on Biodiversity Gallery** is on the second.

If the weather cooperates, consider a family picnic on the grassy lawns of the University of Toronto, just behind the museum. If not, pick up a deli sandwich in the ground-floor cafeteria, or check out the fourth-floor restaurant, called **JK at the ROM**—it's operated by Jamie Kennedy, one of Canada's top chefs.

BASICS: Royal Ontario Museum *(100 Queen's Park, Toronto. 416/586-8000. www.rom.on.ca. Adm. fee; free admission daily 5 p.m.-6 p.m. and Fri. 4:30 p.m.-9 p.m.)*

Watching Polar Bears Churchill

Every kid is familiar with the stuffed-toy version, but in Churchill, Manitoba, children can observe polar bears up close and in the wild. From early October to mid-November, 1,500 of the snowy white beasts congregate here, waiting for solid ice to form so they can strike out on their first seal hunt of the season. Having spent the summer eating little and roaming the shores of Hudson Bay to the south, the bears are hungry.

Getting to Churchill can be a challenge. No roads reach the remote grain-shipping community of 1,000, so visitors must fly in or arrive by rail. A flight from Winnipeg takes two hours. You can also drive seven hours from Winnipeg to Thompson, then take the train—a 10-hour trip—from there. For a railborne marathon, you can take the train all the way from Winnipeg to Churchill (35 hours).

The best way to view the bears is to take a tour on a special vehicle designed to travel over the tundra. Len Smith, designer of the "tundra buggy"—the original Arctic all-terrain vehicle—has operated **Tundra Buggy Tours** since 1980. (The other main operator with similar vehicles is **Great White Bear Tours**.)

Like the bears they are designed to spot, each tundra buggy is a lumbering behemoth. The body—a metal box outfitted with propane heater, toilet, and school-bus seats for 42 people—stands 16 feet above the ground on eight balloon tires. Sliding windows allow passengers to take photos from inside; an open deck at the back affords an even better look at the bears.

Expect survival, not comfort. A tundra buggy inches ponderously over the spongy, semifrozen ground, slowly climbing over rocks and through icy lagoons. Temperatures at this time of year average 15°F to 32°F (-9.4°C to 0°C), so dress warmly. Layers are a good idea: You'll be dashing from the snug inside to the frosty deck fairly often. The daylong tours start at 8 a.m. and last until 5 p.m.

Several hours often pass before a bear shows up on the scrubby landscape, but patience usually pays off: Kids delight in spotting a mother nursing her cubs or watching two males square off in a playful sparring match. Other polar bears, however, may hardly move. This adventure is therefore best for motivated kids age 10 and older who can tolerate a long ride with a few boring stretches.

Polar bears are fascinating but unpredictable and deadly. They weigh 700 to 1,300 pounds (320 to 590 kg), may stand more than 10 feet (3 m) tall, and can run 30 miles an hour (45 kph). In short, keep your arms inside the buggy and never feed the bears.

The buggy driver usually doubles as a guide. On a typical tour, nature books and binoculars are passed around and lunch is provided. Avid bear-watchers can stay in the **Tundra Buggy Lodge**, owned by Tundra Buggy Tours. Located right in

Polar-bear cubs and maternal cushion at Cape Churchill on Hudson Bay

bear territory, the lodge is a series of converted tundra buggies fitted out with bunk beds. Guests usually stay two or three nights, taking buggy tours by day. Although the lodge gets you closer to the action, increasing your bear-sighting opportunities, there's no place to go once you're in for the night. If close quarters aren't your style, book a motel in town. Either way, we recommend staying a few days to make sure you spot a bear.

TIPS: Accommodations are limited, so book at least six months in advance.

BASICS: Tundra Buggy Tours *(P.O. Box 662, Churchill. 204/ 675-2121)* Costs are $130 for adults and $95 for children under 13.

    Great White Bear Tours *(Box 91, Churchill. 800/765-8344 or 204/675-2781. www.cancom/gwbt/. gsbt@cancom.net)* Rates are $161(CN) for adults, $100 (CN) for children under 12. Along with vehicles that seat 30 to 40 people, Great White Bear runs special photo vehicles that seat eight to 12.

PACKAGES: The Great Canadian Travel Company *(273 Donald St., Winnipeg. 800/661-3830 or 204/949-0199. sales@gctc-mst.com)* Costs for a three-day trip, including round-trip flight from Winnipeg, accommodations, and tour, are about $1,500 (CN) per person. **Travel Manitoba** *(155 Carlton St., Winnipeg. 800/665-0040 or 204/945-3777)* and **Churchill Chamber of Commerce** *(General Delivery, Churchill. 888/389-2327. cccomm@cancom.net. www.cancom.net)*

MORE ATTRACTIONS IN CHURCHILL

The **Eskimo Museum** *(204/675-2030)* displays historic Inuit art since the 1930s. The collection includes shaman belts, thumb-size carvings of seal and walrus hunts, and carvings of Inuit acrobats. Most are fashioned from walrus tusk, soapstone, or caribou antler.

Parks Canada Visitor Reception Centre *(204/675-8863)* in the Bayport Plaza has exhibits reflecting the French-English rivalry for control of Hudson Bay and its resources during the the early years (1700s) of the fur trade.

Churchill Northern Studies Centre *(204/675-2307)* offers courses in Arctic ecology and survival, the northern lights, photography, and ornithology. In August, seven-day **Family Hostel** courses cover flowers, belugas, birds, and other wildlife. $1,800 (CN) for adults, $1,500 (CN) for teens, and $1,300 (CN) for kids 8 to 12.

The **indoor polar bear slide,** made by a local artist and installed in the Town Centre Complex, is a big hit with smaller children.

Summertime whales: More than 3,000 beluga whales move into the Churchill River in July and August. Sea North Tours offers whale watching. *(204/675-2195. seanorth@cancom.net)*

Museum of Man and Nature Winnipeg

One of Canada's finest interpretive museums (voted best indoor site in Manitoba by Attractions Canada in 1999), the **Manitoba Museum of Man and Nature** focuses on the relationships between people and their environment. Kid favorites are the animal-filled dioramas and a spooky re-creation of a British wharf before dawn, complete with replica of a 17th-century fur-trading ship.

The prairie city of Winnipeg is considered Canada's "gateway to the West." You'll therefore find scenes of Métis hunting buffalo across the Plains, as well as an authentic reconstruction of a Red River cart (its wheels were easy to remove so pioneers could float their possessions across water).

The province of Manitoba also reaches far up into the north, where polar bears hunt for seals on ice floes and the Inuit erect Inukshuk rock sculptures to point the way for travelers. Seven interpretive galleries—including the **Grasslands Gallery** and the **Arctic/Subarctic Gallery**—tell the story of the province's peoples and landscape.

Visitors to the museum are greeted by a lifelike diorama of a Métis hunter on horseback directing a stampede of wild-eyed buffalo. Herding buffalo toward a jump site was the traditional way of capturing a supermarket on hooves: Animals who fell into the pit were used for food, clothing, medicine, and trade.

WINNIPEG

Canada's coldest spot? Most of the populace apparently believes the site lies at the intersection of Portage and Main, in downtown Winnipeg.

Never mind the wind and wild weather you'll find there in wintertime, though; Winnipeg is a warm, family-friendly city. To combat its icy reputation, the city has declared itself "Canada's Christmas Capital." Every February, it hosts a winter-chasing celebration of the early fur traders, the colorful voyageurs. Whether your own visit falls in winter or summer, check out these family learning opportunities.

At the **Manitoba Children's Museum** (*The Kinsmen Bldg., 45 Forks Market Rd. 204/924-4000. Adm. fee*), kids will love climbing aboard a refurbished 1910 passenger car and a restored 1952 diesel engine. They can also walk into a beaver dam or watch themselves perform on television as weather forecasters. The museum is small enough not to overwhelm youngsters, but sufficiently varied to keep preteens busy. In the new sports section, for instance, you can perfect your slapshot to equal Wayne Gretzky's.

Co-designed by Frederick Law Olmsted, 393-acre (159-ha) **Assiniboine Park** (*Corydon Ave. at Shaftesbury Blvd., or by footbridge from Portage Ave. 204/ 986-6921*) contains a miniature passenger train, slides, picnic sites, a statue of Winnie the Pooh (the bear was named after Winnipeg), cycling paths, a duck pond, and the **Assiniboine Zoo** (*204/986-6921. Adm. fee*).

Teens with an artistic bent will appreciate the Leo Mol sculpture garden. The local artist has crafted bronze animals and other figures for clients around the world, among them the Pope.

Other dioramas in the museum show a 1,200-pound polar bear about to lunch on a ringed seal, a female moose and her calf browsing at sunset, and a herd of caribou picking its way along a high ridge formed by glacial meltwater. Swarms of summer mosquitoes—Winnipeg's claim to entomological fame—contrast with another gallery's display of snow, an object for which the Inuktuk language has dozens of words.

The museum also portrays family environments. An Inukshuk stands guard at the entrance to the Arctic/Subarctic gallery; a Cree family gathers food; a sod house shows the early dwelling of Mennonite immigrants, who settled in Manitoba in greater numbers than anywhere else in the world. An urban streetscape depicts Winnipeg—wooden sidewalks and all—during its rowdy heyday in the 1920s.

Perhaps most popular is the reproduction of the *Nonsuch*—a 50-foot (15-m) ketch that arrived at the museum after visiting ports in England, France, the U.S., and Canada. The original *Nonsuch* sailed into Hudson Bay in 1668 carrying explorer and fur trader Medard Chouart Sieur de Des Groseillers. This voyage led to the founding of the Hudson's Bay Company—still active in Canadian commerce three centuries later.

Kids walk cautiously into the huge, dimly lit *Nonsuch* gallery, a realistic rendering of a 17th-century English wharf. Wooden townhouses and the Boar Head's Tavern sit dockside; the sounds of swooping gulls echo overhead. Walk up onto the ship and you find yourself in the sailors' quarters. The tiny cabins are the perfect size for kids, who pretend they're sailing to the New World in search of adventure. A new gallery, scheduled to open in May 2000, showcases the Hudson's Bay Company Museum Collection.

TIPS: The museum complex houses the **Manitoba Planetarium** and the **Touch the Universe Science Centre,** offering nearly 100 hands-on exhibits relating to science, technology, art, and illusion. Consider purchasing an Adventure Value Pass; it will get you into the museum, the planetarium, and the science center for three days at a reduced price.

BASICS: **Manitoba Museum of Man and Nature** *(190 Rupert Ave., Winnipeg. 204/956-2830 or 204/943-3139. www.manitobamuseum.man. Closed Mon. Labor Day–mid-May; adm. fee)*

Bird-watching
Stonewall

Oak Hammock Marsh, a thriving wetland 16 miles north of Winnipeg, supports nearly 300 species of birds—not to mention muskrats, salamanders, insects, and a profusion of other wildlife. Aquarium tanks in the interpretive center encourage kids to feel a garter snake, pat a gray tiger salamander, and watch—*not* catch!—a snapping turtle. Interactive games let kids measure their own "wing span" against that of a turkey vulture or a blue-footed booby.

A remote-control camera installed in the marsh lets visitors watch what's going on out there from the shelter of the interpretive center. Far better, though, to walk the 20 miles of boardwalk trails, or rent a canoe and paddle through the marsh; bug nets, magnifying boxes, and life jackets are included in the $2-per-hour fee.

During the spring and fall flyovers, another breed of visitors flocks to the marsh. Up to 200,000 ducks, snow geese, Canada geese, and other waterfowl fly over Oak Hammock Marsh or touch down somewhere in its 22 square miles (36 sq km) of wetlands, so don't forget a camera and binoculars.

TIPS: On Mondays, children and grandparents get two-for-one admission. The center extends its hours during the spring and fall waterfowl migrations.

BASICS: **Oak Hammock Marsh** *(Jct. Hwy. 220 and Hwy. 67, near Stonewall. 800/665-3825 or 204/467-3300. www.ducks.ca. Adm. fee.)*

Snakes Alive:
Narcisse Snake Den Area

The world's highest concentration of snakes—tens of thousands of the creatures—live at the **Narcisse Snake Den Area.** Both the Manitoba Museum of
Man and Nature *(see page 275)* and the Oak Hammock Marsh Interpretive Centre *(see page 277)* offer tours of these famous snake pits, about two hours north
of Winnipeg.

Twice each year, thousands of red-sided garter snakes congregate at the surface
of their winter dens. The snakes are most active in late April or May, when the first
warm, sunny days of spring drive them from their dens to perform their frenzied
mating ritual. (Cracks in the limestone rock below the frost line make ideal hiber-
nation spots.) As each female emerges, she is vigorously pursued by a band of males
that entwine themselves around her; this writhing mass often rolls along the ground
or up a tree.

During this period, the preoccupied snakes are easy for visitors to approach.
Because the snakes do not bite, kids are allowed to pick them up—but not to take
them home. If snakes aren't your thing, watch the action from the viewing platform at each den site; you'll have to walk through snake terrain, however, to reach
these platforms.

After spending the summer in nearby marshes, the snakes return to their dens
in early September. As the daylight hours wane and cool weather arrives, the snakes
return to their limestone nooks and crannies. There they hibernate until the snow
melts.

Fall visits are best during warm, sunny days in September. The snakes are calm
and numerous, and you can enjoy the golden colors of the landscape.

Whatever the season, gravel walkways lead visitors through aspen forest and
open grasslands blooming with wildflowers. If you are quiet, you may spot white-
tailed deer or a sharp-tailed grouse. Interpreters are available on-site to provide
information and directions.

TIPS: A picnic area with tables, bathrooms, and drinking water is provided. If you
plan to do the nature walk, which extends more than two miles (3.2 km), have the
kids wear sturdy walking shoes and dress for the weather. You won't have to hike
the entire route to see snakes; two dens are close to the parking lot. Interpretive
services are available.

For an overnight side trip from Winnipeg, continue to Hecla Island Provincial
Park *(800/214-6497)* on Lake Winnipeg; here you will find a full-service campground and cabins, hiking trails and beach, and a resort/golf course *(800/267-6700)*.

BASICS: **Narcisse Snake Den Area** *(3 m N of Narcisse on Hwy. 17. 204/642-6078)*

Prairie Wagon Treks

A ribbon of covered wagons, flanked by outriders on horseback, slowly threads its way across the grasslands of Saskatchewan. As wooden wheels etch a shallow rut in the dirt, coyotes howl from a distant ridge, sage grouse flap like noisy angels rising from the brush, and a hawk cuts lazy circles overhead. A group of homesteaders in the 1890s? Nope—we're taking part in a modern summertime **wagon train** in the prairie province.

Our journey from Willow Bunch to Wood Mountain pulls us through seamless flatlands, rolling hills, and aspen forests. We share the range with mule deer and fox, pronghorn antelope and porcupines. We watch eagles swoop and dive for prey, spy nesting osprey and great blue herons, and sample pink flowering cactus and delicious saskatoon berries. At night, owls hoot to a star-filled sky.

History comes to life alongside the wildlife: Thanks to this unique form of time travel, children learn about teamsters, chuck wagons, and the hardships faced by early settlers. They also have a chance to see the landscape of legends. Some wagon trains roll through **Chief Sitting Bull's last refuge.** (After defeating Custer at Little Big Horn in 1876, Sitting Bull and 5,000 Sioux crossed the U.S.-Canada border into Saskatchewan.) Other trails lead to cliffside buffalo jumps where native hunters once killed bison by herding them over the top.

On our trek, we pass an old North West Mounted Police trail, a pioneer house, a weathered 1907 tombstone, and **Henry's Hideout**—a hollow where outlaws led by Butch Cassidy and Sam Kelly once corralled their stolen horses. Horse-loving children welcome the chance to help the teamsters feed the tired stock, to learn which part of a harness is a belly-band or a tug, and to trot in front of the wagons.

Kids were usually the first in line with their plates and tin mugs. Our cowboy fare ran to hearty steak and baked potatoes. Breads—and even strawberry shortcake—were baked in an outdoor oven. Sometimes we ate high on wagon seats, overlooking the horses and the sweeping grasslands; other meals were served around a crackling campfire. The after-dinner entertainment had a strong homemade strain, too; it included storytelling, cowboy poetry, and sing-alongs.

Outfitters, working ranches, and communities offer different trips. Be sure to match your frontier experience to the ages and abilities of your children. A community wagon train may be the least expensive way of riding back into the 19th century. Some of these, however, are huge—dozens of wagons and more than 200 riders may be involved. Sure, it's a great way to meet local families on vacation, but are you prepared to bring your own horse and feed—*and* do all your own cooking, camp setup, and animal care? If not, consider renting horses from a local stable.

Community wagon treks sometimes include contests. Competitors place an egg in a spoon, then try to ride to a designated spot without dropping it. Invariably, the egg falls and the rider dismounts to pick it (or its remnants) up. The horse then

Prairie schooners sail across a sea of grass in Saskatchewan.

promptly takes off, stranding the red-faced competitor and putting big grins on the spectators' faces. Longer community wagon treks may include local events such as a rodeo, powwow, barn dance, or simply a swim at the community pool.

Novice cowpokes and those who want assistance with the outdoor work should sign on with a ranch or adventure-tour operator that takes small groups on day or overnight treks. With **Blue Heron Nature Tours,** families ride in the wagon, taking turns sitting up front by the teamster; at night, they sleep in tents or under the stars. On an **Otter Basin Outfitters** trip, one or two families ride horses, while the chuck wagon carries the food, water, and supplies. Other caravans allow less experienced riders to enjoy short forays on horseback each day.

Most outfitters give guests the option of riding horses or riding in the wagon, but some companies let you switch back and forth between saddle and buckboard. Depending on the outfitter and the type of trip, you could cover just a few miles or tackle a good day's drive—about 30 miles (48 km).

Good weather, of course, is never guaranteed. Blues skies and sunshine are the hallmarks of a Saskatchewan summer, but they can be punctuated by massive thunderstorms and lightning strikes. On our wagon trek from Willow Bunch, for example, the perfect weather gave way one night to pelting rain; as our tent sides flapped furiously in the wind, the open-air sleepers ran for cover under the wagons.

Nor should you rule out the occasional surprise, be it a wildlife sighting or the discovery of some tipi rings or dinosaur bones. Our surprise came at the end of our wagon-train trek, when a young boy on horseback suddenly broke into "O Canada!", the national anthem. The prairie wind carried his hauntingly pure voice across the rippling grass. It was the defining moment of a quintessentially Canadian experience.

TIPS: It gets hot on the trail during the day, then turns chilly at night and into the early morning. Bring hat, sunscreen, insect repellent, layers of clothes, gloves, and—just in case—rain gear.

BASICS: The *Saskatchewan Vacation Guide* lists some of the outdoor adventure operators who offer trail and wagon rides across the province. The season runs from mid-May to mid-October. Contact **Tourism Saskatchewan** *(877/237-2273 or 306/787-9600. www.sasktourism.com)* for information on wagon trains. **Foam Lake Heritage Wagon Trek** *(306/272-3858)* operates a large-scale trek. Outfitters include **Blue Heron Nature Tours** *(306/823-4992)*, **Otter Basin Outfitters** *(306/478-2271)*, and **Manito Outfitters** *(306/826-5546)*.

Outfitter and ranch trips average $100 to $200 (CN) per day for adults and children; the price includes horse, meals, and tent accommodations. Large-scale wagon treks usually cost less than $100 (CN) per family for a weekend pass: Foam Lake Heritage Wagon Trek, for instance, runs about $15 per person. However, you must also factor in the cost of providing your own horses and camping equipment, as well as purchasing meals or contributing to a food kitty.

A ROUND-UP OF COWBOY EXPERIENCES

Outfitters and ranches also offer pack-mule trips, working-ranch vacations, and roping and barrel racing on horseback. Saskatchewan hosts about 50 rodeos— among them **Wood Mountain Rodeo,** the oldest in Canada, which was founded by the Mounties in 1890. For an events guide, contact **Tourism Saskatchewan's** website: www.sasktourism.com.

Wanuskewin Heritage Park
Saskatoon

Learn how the Cree hunted buffalo. Bake bannock (native bread) over an open fire. Hear the stories of elders. These activities can be pursued at **Wanuskewin Heritage Park**, a spiritual First Nations site on the west bank of the South Saskatchewan River, three miles north of Saskatoon. Generation upon generation of Northern Plains Indians came here to hunt, gather herbs, and escape the winter winds. Wanuskewin (pronounced Wah-nus-KAY-win) is a Cree word meaning "seeking peace of mind."

Today, visitors to this national historic site can relive the early life of the Plains people and experience a culture that dates back 12,000 years. As guests approach the visitor center, perched on the valley's edge, they walk along a buffalo-drive lane where bronze sculptures depict the hunt. In the indoor theater, a multimedia presentation shows the natural beauty of the area and explains the meaning of the site.

Outside, families can hike along five miles of scenic trails, including paths that lead to a rare boulder alignment called a medicine wheel. The University of Saskatchewan is excavating 19 pre-contact archaeological sites; some of the reconstructed encampments may be viewed from a distance. The high-ceilinged restaurant overlooking the Opimihaw Valley is the place to introduce kids to buffalo burgers, wild rice, and saskatoon-berry pie.

TIPS: From June to September, school and youth groups can stay overnight in a tipi village. Accommodations and breakfast start at $39 (CN) for adults, $20 (CN) for children, and $95 (CN) for a family (maximum 4 children). Packages including meals and interpretive programs are also available.

BASICS: Wanuskewin Heritage Park *(R.R. #4, Saskatoon. 800/665-4600 or 306/931-6767. Adm. fee)*

RCMP Training Academy
Regina

Red-jacketed, Stetson-hatted Mounties astride black thoroughbreds are well-known symbols of Canada. In TV programs such as *Due South* and *Sergeant Preston of the Yukon,* the Royal Canadian Mounted Police "always got their man."

Visitors to Regina, the capital of Saskatchewan, can learn the history of the RCMP, created in 1873 to maintain law and order in Canada's west. The 45-minute guided tour of the **RCMP Training Academy** features the computer lab of the Applied Police Sciences building, as well as a model town where cadets practice handling everything from vehicle checks to bank robberies.

During the summer, visit on a Tuesday evening to view the **Sunset Retreat.** It's a moving ceremony: As a choir sings traditional Canadian songs, cadets in red serge uniforms lower Canada's red-and-white flag for the night. On a weekday visit, don't miss the **Sergeant Major's Parade.**

The collections of the **RCMP Centennial Museum**—including a 1914 police office and jail cell—trace the history of the force from its origins to the present. Among its treasures: an ornate rifle case and tobacco pouch that Sitting Bull gave to Mounted Police Superintendent James M. Walsh.

DIGGING DINOSAURS

Ogle a T-Rex skeleton at the **Eastend Fossil Research Station** *(118 Maple Ave. S., Eastend. 306/295-4009. www.dinocountry.com)* in Frenchman River Valley. On half- or full-day excursions to a dino dig, kids use chisels, hammers, dental picks, and wire brushes to pry vertebrae and fossils from chunks of rock. Scheduled to open in July 2000, the new $3.1 million **T-Rex Centre** has interactive displays on area finds and prehistoric mammals. All this excitement is located on Hwy. 13, about 5 hours from Drumheller, 4.5 hours from Saskatoon, 4 hours from Regina, and 4 hours from Great Falls, Montana.

Kids love the story of the Mad Trapper of Rat River, a cunning fugitive who consistently eluded the Mounties. On display are his sawed-off shotgun, a pail with a bullet hole, and the Mad Trapper's snowshoes, which he wore backward to throw off pursuers.

There are also James Bond-style gadgets galore, including a radio-transmitter suitcase belonging to a German spy nabbed by the Mounties. Nero, a large black horse who taught parade maneuvers to countless other horses—*and* recruits—until his death in 1973, has been mounted one last time to appear in a display.

TIPS: In July and August, bring folding chairs or a blanket to avoid standing throughout the 45-minute Sunset Retreat ceremony (Tuesday evenings) and 20- to 30-minute Sergeant Major's Parade (Mon., Wed., Fri.) Call ahead to check performance times and find out about weather-related cancellations. RCMP souvenirs can be ordered through their website or by calling 877/526-0585.

BASICS: **RCMP Training Academy and Centennial Museum** *(Dewdney Ave. W., Regina. 306/780-5838. www.rcmpmuseum.com. Donation)* Tours run every hour on summer weekdays; one tour only on winter weekdays. Call in advance to confirm times.

For further information, contact **Tourism Regina** *(800/661-5099 or 306/789-5099. www.tourismregina.com)* or **Tourism Saskatchewan** *(877/237-2273 or 306/787-2300. www.sasktourism.com)*

Tracking Down Dinosaurs
Drumheller

Northeast of Calgary, Alberta, lies a stark and barren terrain filled with eerie rock formations. Early settlers dubbed the area "the badlands" because they found it to be unsuitable for farming; today, however, the territory is fertile ground for dinosaur hunters.

The first to find a dinosaur skeleton here was geologist Joseph Burr Tyrrell. Surveying the area's coal deposits in 1884, Tyrrell unexpectedly came face-to-face with a 70-million-year-old skull. The owner of the skull was initially named the Alberta Lizard; paleontologists have since labeled it *Albertosaurus*. About 24 feet (7.3 m) long, 9 feet (2.7 m) high at the hip, and weighing more than two tons, *Albertosaurus* was a carnivore that could chase down its prey at speeds up to 24 miles per hour (38.6 kph). When Tyrrell loaded the skeleton onto a cart for Calgary, he touched off the Great Canadian Dinosaur Rush. Paleontologists from around the world have discovered half a million fossil specimens in the badlands, as well as bones belonging to more than 20 species of dinosaurs.

Today, families can set out on the **Dinosaur Trail,** a 29-mile (46.6-km) loop through the Red Deer River Valley that starts and ends in Drumheller, 90 miles (145 km) northeast of Calgary. About 4 miles (6.4 km) from town is the **Royal Tyrrell Museum of Palaeontology,** known worldwide for its collection of complete dinosaur skeletons—more than 30 in all, some of them two stories tall. Lifelike dioramas include scenes of an *Albertosaurus* opportunistically scavenging the remains of *Centrosaurus.* If you want to handle an *Albertosaurus* tooth, a dinosaur eggshell, or a raptor's killer claw, watch for the blue "Bone Buggies" that volunteers wheel around the museum. You can even try your hand at assembling the foot of a T. Rex.

In summer, children get multiple chances to dig and work alongside professional paleontologists. Kids of all ages—and even adults—can join a guided two-hour **Dig Watch,** where interpreters lead you to a site and answer questions. Those 10 and up can take part in a **Day Dig,** learning to extract bones from rock and finding out how fossils reveal information. Young adults 18 and older can spend a week working side by side with some of Canada's top paleontologists, collecting fossils and data for the museum. For simple fun and games, youngsters 7 to 12 can sign up for a half-day **Vacation Day Camp.** An afternoon of group activities, crafts, and excavation at a simulated quarry near the museum provides a first taste of digging for dinosaurs.

At a weekend **Dinosaur Camp-In,** budding paleontologists ages 5 to 13 (and

Left: A paleontologist frees a *Tyrannosaurus rex*—the fossil, that is—at the Royal Tyrrell Museum.

their parents) can sleep beneath their favorite predator. Bring a sleeping bag to the Dinosaur Hall and get set for supper, games, and an indoor digging experience.

Layers of fossil-bearing rock underlie much of Alberta, so it's not unusual for individuals and amateur paleontologists to find fossils—even major ones. In 1996, for example, a seven-year-old boy walking his dog near Lethbridge discovered a mosasaur—a giant sea lizard with paddles instead of feet. In 1995, a Cochrane resident found the tiny jaws of *Aphronorus* embedded in rock above the Bow River west of Calgary. And in 1994, an eight-year-old stumbled across an ornithomimid trackway, made by ostrichlike dinosaurs in southwestern Alberta.

And if this happens to you? Photograph the fossil and fix its location on a map, but leave it buried. If a piece is lying free on the ground, bring it to the museum for future identification. According to the Historical Resources Act of 1978, all fossils found in the province belong to the government of Alberta.

TIPS: Summer in Alberta's badlands can be blistering, with daytime temperatures reaching 86°F to 100°F (30°C to 35°C). Cloudy or windy days can be cool, however, so come prepared for all types of weather. Badland hazards include sinkholes (unexpected openings in the ground), open mine shafts (from the region's coal-mining days), cactuses, and insects such as mosquitoes and sandflies. Warn kids to watch where they put their hands and feet—and stay away from mine ruins.

BASICS: The **Royal Tyrrell Museum of Palaeontology** *(P.O. Box 7500, Drumheller. 403/310-0000, 403/823-7707, or toll-free in Alberta only 888/440-4240. info@tyrrellmuseum.com. www.tyrrellmuseum.com. Closed Mon. mid-Oct.–mid-May; adm. fee)* is located in Midland Provincial Park, on the north side of the Red Deer River. **Dinosaur Camp-In:** Campers $40 (CN), chaperones $20 (CN); fee includes breakfast and admission to the museum the next day (adults may bring more than one child).

FOR FURTHER FOSSILS

About a two-hour drive from Drumheller lies **Dinosaur Provincial Park** *(403/378-4342. www.gov.ab.ca/env/parks/prov_parks/dinosaur. Adm. fee),* one of the world's best dinosaur viewing and collecting areas. Despite the presence of a campground and 28 square miles (72.5 sq km) of prairie and river habitat, this park is not for the frivolous fan: Much of it is inaccessible to visitors except via bus tour or guided hike. Most children do not relish a two-hour bus ride in midafternoon heat; the hikes cover rough terrain and can be two and a half hours long.

As the source of some of the world's richest fossil beds, however, Dinosaur Provincial Park is a World Heritage site, and visitors flock here to learn more. Kids will likely enjoy the summer afternoon presentations at the visitor center, where live theater takes on a dinosaur theme, and the **Fossil Safari** hike to a bone bed. A 15-minute bus ride takes you to the hiking spot and back again; expect to spend about an hour at the site. Roughly half the tickets for these events are earmarked for advance reservations, so call ahead or visit the park's website. At the **Royal**

Tyrrell Museum Field Station about a mile from the park entrance, you can watch staff members prepare fossils.

Dinosaur Provincial Park is 108 miles southeast of the Royal Tyrrell Museum and about half an hour's drive northeast of Brooks, Alberta.

Calgary Zoo

At the Calgary Zoo, more than 1,100 animals live in habitats replicating their wilderness environments. Canada's second largest zoo sits in an 80-acre (32.4-ha) park on a tree-shaded island, 15 minutes from downtown Calgary.

The big draws are the Sri Lankan elephants, the **"Canadian Wilds"** exhibit, and the zoo's lowland gorillas. Two favorites are Julia, a 30-year-old gorilla, and Jawara, her mischievous two-year-old son. Next to the gorilla enclosure is a low-slung rope apparatus with a swing, which invites children to clamber about like their lowland friends.

The undisputed star is Kamala, the artistic elephant. Aware that elephants in the wild often use sticks or rocks to scratch patterns in the sand, wildlife biologists at the zoo gave Kamala and two other elephants the opportunity to paint. The other two were uninterested, but Kamala took to it with enthusiasm. In two years, she progressed from using her trunk to rub watercolors over a piece of paper on the ground to painting with a basting brush on paper taped to the wall. Kamala now works on easel-mounted canvas, dipping her custom-made brushes in acrylic paint. Two or three times a week, visitors can watch the elephant paint for 10 to 20 minutes at a time. Easel, paints, and canvas are all laid out for Kamala, who then chooses whether or not to paint. Shaded benches provide comfortable seating while you watch. At special times, kids can also line up to feed the elephants.

Check out the "Canadian Wilds" exhibit for its introduction to the Canadian Rocky Mountains. A zoo naturalist points out differences between a grizzly bear and a black bear, and helps kids learn to distinguish a Dall's sheep from a bighorn sheep. Other zoo habitats include the reptile building, where children may spy a dwarf crocodile, and the African bushveld with its lions, zebras, ostriches, and crowned cranes.

In summer, sign up for a **Northern Night! Sleepover.** Bring your own sleeping bags and bed down (indoors) on the floor of the large mammal enclosure. Warthogs and a trio of Asiatic elephants are your companions on one side; giraffes peer down at you on the other. The sleepover includes a campfire supper followed by storytelling.

Young kids will also want to visit the **prehistoric park.** Although it is part of the zoo grounds, the park lies on the other side of the Bow River and must be accessed by a footbridge. Wander past re-creations of rust red hoodoos and exploding volcanoes, then look up into the eyes of realistic dinosaurs such as a *Styracosaurus,* a triceratops, a meat-eating *Tyrannosaurus rex,* and other lizards and reptiles that roamed Alberta's swamplands in prehistory.

Orangutan at the Calgary Zoo

TIPS: Families with toddlers may want to park in the west-entrance parking lot, off Memorial Drive by the river, because it is closer to both the big mammals and the primates.

BASICS: The Calgary Zoo, Botanical Garden and Prehistoric Park *(1300 Zoo Rd. 403/232-9300. www.calgaryzoo.ab.ca. Adm. fee).* **Northern Night! Sleepover** *($35 [CN] per night per person)*

Glenbow Museum
Calgary

The **Glenbow Museum** is renowned for its exhibits on the native peoples who first roamed the plains and foothills of Alberta, as well as the early settlers who followed. But there's much more to western Canada's largest museum than that. With three floors of exhibits displaying more than two million artifacts—not to mention a rich line-up of special events—the museum offers myriad ways to occupy young minds.

Head for the collection on **international warriors** on the fourth floor. Here a wall-size diorama depicts a scene from a 16th- century German courtyard, where a young squire takes a fencing lesson from a master. Other dioramas show vignettes of everyday life in a medieval castle: A knight, flamboyantly dressed in feathered hat and red-and-blue leggings, discusses his breastplate with the master armorer. The warrior collection features Japanese arms, including an exquisitely carved 17th-century rapier and the stylized O-Yorori armor worn by persons of high rank.

The museum's fourth floor also displays a Plains First Nations story robe. The Siksika, the Blood, and the Piegan painted their stories of battles, horse raids, and other daring exploits on tipi covers and bison robes. This hide by He Dog (Percy Creighton) records the activities of several well-known Blood leaders a century ago. On one panel, Blood warriors Calf Robe and Bird Rattle scout out an unguarded Crow encampment, then ride off with a stolen horse. Another panel tells the story of Sun Calf and his eight fellow warriors, who bravely fought off a band of 300 Crow for four days from a dugout in a hill. In coming years, the Glenbow Museum plans a major focus on the Blackfoot, the main aboriginal people who lived in the prairies around Calgary.

For rock hounds, the **Mineralogy Gallery** and its fluorescent rock display make a popular stop. Press a button to shine ultraviolet light on 40 or so seemingly ordinary rocks, transforming them into green, blue, pumpkin orange, and electric purple.

Head downstairs to the third floor for its chronicles of the Canadian West. The first thing you see is a large tipi of the Siksika Nation, with pictures of otters painted on the outside. The entrance flaps hang open, inviting kids to explore inside. Leaning against the tipi is a travois—a sleigh-like device that could be loaded with a family's possessions and dragged behind a horse.

In the **First Nations Gallery,** pause to examine the quilled-and-beaded moccasins made in the 1900s by the mother of John Wounded Horse, a Lakota Sioux from the Wood Mountain Reserve in Saskatchewan. The family are descendants of the followers of Sitting Bull, who sought refuge in Canada after defeating Gen. George Custer at the Battle of Little Bighorn in 1876. Kids also like the ornate Blackfeet shirt used for ceremonial occasions and decorated with dyed porcupine quills, human hair, paint, and feathers.

School-aged children inevitably gravitate to the **Canadian Pacific Railway Gallery,** where a waterfall cascades behind a large wooden model of the Stoney Creek trestle bridge with an old train on top. Peer into the gloom of the life-size snow shed—a replica of similar structures in the Rogers Pass—and you'll see two maintenance crewmen coming at you on a handcar.

Depending on your children's interest, you may want to skip the displays of ranching and early settlers, but don't miss **Growing Up and Away: Youth in Western Canada.** This exhibit shows what life was like for children growing up in the last 100 years. There's a beautifully beaded Sioux horse doll, a collection of dolls from 1810 to 1949, and a plush toy cow, circa 1940, wearing white plastic spats. Kids will also get a kick out of the gold quilted smoking jacket sewn entirely from silk cigar ribbons; it was brought from Odessa, Russia, to a Saskatchewan homestead in 1908.

In the fully staffed **Discovery Room,** hands-on activities are geared to the theme of the third floor's revolving exhibits. Kids are encouraged to experiment with printmaking blocks, acrylic paints, and graphite sticks as they experience artmaking at the turn of the last century. They can also create a door-size poster using giant stencils, sponges, paint, and other materials.

The Glenbow Museum hosts themed programs throughout the year. In **Native Voices,** for example, members of the native community discuss the origins of traditional First Nations weaponry and other subjects.

TIPS: At a **Family Fun** Saturday event, you can create your own monoprint, painted windsock, or other craft—it all depends on the day's theme. The museum café offers soups, salads, and sandwiches.

In 2001, the Glenbow will open its new **Blackfoot Gallery.** As a tie-in to those exhibits, the museum hopes to offer tours to the Nations of the Blackfoot Confederacy (the Siksika, the Blood, and the North and South Piegan).

BASICS: **Glenbow Museum, Art Gallery, and Library** *(130 9th Ave. S.E., Calgary. 403/268-4100. www.glenbow.org. Adm. fee)*

Buffalo Jump
Fort Macleod

Sleep in a tipi, eat buffalo burgers, and find out how Plains Indians drove bison over a 60-foot cliff more than 5,500 years ago. Not only is Head-Smashed-In Buffalo Jump believed to be the oldest such locale in the world, it is also designated a World Heritage site. At the seven-level interpretive center, built into sandstone cliffs, visitors learn about ceremonies, food gathering, and the family life of pre-contact Plains Indians. A topographical model re-creates the drive lanes that directed buffalo toward the jump, while a film reenacts a buffalo hunt. The center also features a reproduction of the archaeological dig at the base of the jump, where researchers have uncovered a 33-foot-deep kill site full of buffalo bones and projectile points. Outside, trails lead to the jump itself and the actual dig site.

TIPS: The best package is the two-night **Buffalo Trails,** available April through October. Greet your Blackfoot guide and settle into one of six dirt-floor tipis, equipped with only a central fire or stove. Visitors dine on buffalo burgers the first night, then listen to Blackfoot stories and legends. The next morning, a breakfast of fry bread and saskatoon jam precedes a five-hour hike to the archaeological dig and a second buffalo-jump site. The evening meal is buffalo stew and bannock, or bread. Other activities include learning how the First Nations lived off the land and taking a guided tour of the interpretive center.

BASICS: **Head-Smashed-In Buffalo Jump** *(403/553-2731. www.head-smashed-in.com. Adm. fee)* The cost of the Buffalo Trails package depends on the number of people in your party; a family of four pays $850 (CN), including meals, tipi use, and guide services. For camping only, the cost is $50 (CN) per tipi per night.

'Ksan Historical Village Hazelton

Cedar longhouses. Stately totem poles. Prized Chilkat robes, woven from cedar bark and white wool. Barbecued sockeye salmon. Traditional songs and dances performed by native people wearing ceremonial regalia. How many more reasons do you need to visit **'Ksan Historical Village and Museum?** This replicated Gitxsan village, overlooking the Skeena River near Hazelton in northern British Columbia, was built on the site of the ancient village of Gitanmaax. The award-winning re-creation brings to life the culture and heritage of the Gitxsan people, whose territory once covered more than 13,200 square miles (34,200 sq km) of northwestern British Columbia.

The Gitxsan people have lived in communities along the great fishing rivers of the Skeena, the Nass, and the Babine for more than 3,500 years. Long before European contact, the Gitxsan were using dip nets, scoop nets, rakes, traps, hooks, and timber-and-brush weirs—every major technique currently employed by commercial fishermen—to catch the salmon abounding in these waters. Some fished from canoes at night, using a torch to attract their quarry; indeed, Gitanmaax means "the people who fish by torchlight."

The modern-day Gitxsan—about 3,200 people living in the communities around Hazelton—are perhaps best known for their long legal battle for their land. In 1984, the Gitxsan and their neighbors, the Wet'suwet'en, went to court to protect their traditional territories from devastation by logging. Thirteen years later, the case resulted in a historic Supreme Court of Canada decision, known as the Delgamuukw Aboriginal Title case. The December 1997 decision, named for one of the chiefs who brought the case to court, rules that aboriginal title must be recognized as a distinct property right to land, capable of overriding all other interests—including logging.

Approach the village as the ancient Gitxsan did—that is, from the river—and you will notice that the entrance totems before the houses form a single, powerful line. A 45-minute guided tour of 'Ksan takes you to three main houses, each named for a main clan. Displayed in the cedar plank-and-beam **Frog House**—a longhouse that originally would have sheltered 60 people—are an old fishing weir (a sieve-like trap) and other tools and artifacts used in daily life before European contact. Here you'll learn how the Gitxsan made bentwood boxes and chests by steam-bending a single plank to form four sides. Challenge your children to spot every item made from cedar bark or spruce roots; they'll find sleeping mats, baskets, canoe cushions, room dividers, pot lids, and even shrouds for the deceased awaiting cremation.

In the **Fireweed House,** a guide displays the ceremonial regalia. Some headdresses were inlaid with abalone shells and featured a cylinder of sea-lion whiskers extending above a crown filled with eagle down. The traditional red, black, and blue "button blankets"—so called because they were studded with mother-of-pearl buttons—were worn like cloaks. Tanned-hide aprons and leggings might be fringed with puffin beaks (symbolizing wealth) or deer hooves (symbolizing power).

On selected Friday evenings in summer, the 'Ksan Performing Arts Group dons these items to enact a song-and-dance drama of life before European contact. Kids especially like "the Animal Kingdom," performed by Gitxsan children dressed as rabbits, porcupines, and other wild creatures.

The Wolf House, used for feasting, intrigues children with its unusual entryway: a doorway carved through a totem pole.

Although younger children will probably get antsy in the museum, it's still worth a look around. Put these items on your not-to-miss list: the 3,500-year-old stone club with carved bird's head; the shaman's regalia with bearclaw headdress; and the ceremonial chilkat robes, each requiring 18 months to complete.

The 'Ksan Museum also contains coppers—shield-like totems that were the most valuable objects a chief could own. If the chief's honor was attacked, he would publicly cut off a piece of his copper and hand it to the offender; it was then up to the offender to break off a larger copper—or face disgrace. A copper's value grew with the number of feasts at which it had been displayed. Some were worth 16,000 blankets.

TIPS: Try to visit on a Friday in July to mid-August, when the 'Ksan Performing Arts Group entertains. Book a tour for the afternoon, enjoy dinner, then attend the family show.

In the House of Eating (the restaurant), kids can sample a variety of traditional Gitxsan dishes—barbecued salmon, herring eggs, village soup—or opt for Western cuisine. The facility is open for dinner on Fridays before the song-and-dance performances, which begin at 8 p.m.

BASICS: The 'Ksan Historical Village and Museum *(Rte. 62, 3 miles/4.8 km N of New Hazelton. 250/842-5544 or 877/842-5518. www.ksan.org. Adm. fee)* Next to the 'Ksan interpretation site is a 65-unit RV campground *(250/842-5297)* operated by the Gitanmaax Band. The Sportsman's Kispiox Lodge *(250/842-6455)*, on the Kispiox River 17 miles from New Hazelton, has cabins and a good restaurant.

HELPING HANDS FOR HISTORY HOUNDS

Evidence of the ancient Gitxsan people and their neighbors, the Wet'suwet'en, can be found throughout the surrounding area. Stop at the Hazelton Travel InfoCentre and Museum *(250/842-6071)* to pick up a brochure and map describing the self-guided Hands of History Tour, a 70-mile loop drive that leads visitors past longhouses, distinctive churches, a salmon hatchery, Battle Hill National Historic Site, eight scenic native villages, and dozens of carved totems. Plaques and signposts along the way explain events and area legends.

Queen Charlotte Islands

The hauntingly beautiful **Queen Charlotte Islands**—also known as Haida Gwaii, or "islands of the people"—are a remote and rugged archipelago about 60 miles off the northwest coast of British Columbia. The woods are thick with giant Sitka spruce, western red cedar, and hemlock. Just offshore, orcas (killer whales) breach from the sea. Along the wild, windswept coast and in old-growth rain forests shrouded in mist, visitors may sense the spirit of the ancient Haida people, who have inhabited the Queen Charlotte Islands for more than 10,000 years. You can even meet **Haida Watchmen**—First Nations guardians and hosts—at several old village sites. (Ancient, intricately carved totems grace some of these locales.)

Of the 150 islands that make up the Queen Charlottes, the southern 138 are protected as the **Gwaii Haanas National Park Reserve and Haida Heritage Site.** Pending the resolution of the Haida's claim to ownership of the land, Gwaii Haanas is being comanaged by Parks Canada as a National Park Reserve and by the Council of the Haida Nation as a Haida Heritage Site.

If you're looking for an isolated national park or living-history site, this is it: Gwaii Haanas has no roads, accommodations, or services. Tourism is not only new but controlled; about 2,000 people are allowed to visit each year. Most arrive on a guided day trip or as part of a multiday boat tour run by a commercial operator. Visitors can stay overnight in Queen Charlotte City or Sandspit outside the park reserve.

With the Haida just starting to tap the economic potential of tourism, few of them currently operate trips. For now, the Haida Watchmen protect the ancient sites and provide basic information services. They are your links to the living Haida culture; your encounters with Haida Watchmen are likely to be spontaneous, informal, and genuine.

Traces of Haida occupation have been discovered in more than 500 places throughout Gwaii Haanas. At some old village sites, the remains of cedar longhouses and weather-beaten totem poles testify to centuries-old traditions. So rare are these sites that on the island of SGaang Gwaii the ancient Haida village of **Nan Sdins** was declared a World Heritage site in 1981. The village has 22 poles—many more than a century old, and all in various stages of "returning to the earth."

From an estimated population of 20,000 before European contact, the Haida numbers plummeted to fewer than 500 people by the middle of the 19th century. Though devastated by infectious diseases carried by Europeans, the Haida managed to survive and endure. Today, most live on large Graham Island (the northern half of the Queen Charlottes), where they blend traditional hunting and gathering with modern lifestyles and careers.

The backbone of Gwaii Haanas is the San Christoval Mountains, which run down the center of Moresby Island—the large, hatchet-shaped island south of Graham. The San Christovals plunge steeply into the Pacific Ocean on Moresby's west-

Mortuary poles carved in the mid-19th century still stand tall on the island of SGaang Gwaii.

ern shore, which also happens to be the wettest place in Canada; it rains here about two days out of every three. On the gentler eastern shore, lush with temperate rain forest, cedars tower over gardens of ferns.

Haida art reflects this close bond with the environment. From red and yellow cedar, the Haida craft cedar-bark clothing, weave baskets, carve canoes and household tools, and chip beams and planks for longhouses and totem poles. The Haida's extraordinary carvings of ravens, whales, eagles, and other creatures depict mythical relationships; they also evoke the Haida's spiritual heritage by recording historic and family events.

Frontal poles, placed before houses, chronicle a family's lineage. A memorial pole honors a deceased person whose remains have not been returned to Haida Gwaii for burial because the individual died far from home. Mortuary poles, erected for persons of high social standing, hold a bentwood box containing the remains of the deceased. The memorial and mortuary poles in the ancient village of Nan Sdins (above) are more than a century old.

Although most of the Haida population is now concentrated in two villages on Haida Gwaii, their ancestors' presence can be detected throughout the islands. Along with the poles that stand guard, Haida Watchmen live at village sites during the summer to protect the places where their ancestors were born and died. You will meet Haida Watchmen in **K'uuna** (formerly Skedans) on Louise Island; **T'aanuu** on the east side of T'aanuu Island; **Hlk'yah** (Windy Bay) on Lyell Island; **Hot Spring Island** (Gandle K'ir); and in Nan Sdins on SGaang Gwaii. Look for the classic Haida identifying symbol—three human figures, wearing high hats and facing in three directions—that graces the top or base of many Haida poles.

TIPS: Gwaii Haanas is wild and remote, and its waters are unpredictable; travel with an experienced guide or tour operator. Any such person or company must be licensed by the Archipelago Management Board in order to operate in Gwaii Haanas (see Anvil Cove Charters, below). Visitors traveling without a licensed tour operator must reserve in advance with Super, Natural BC (800/435-5622); they also have to register for and attend an orientation before entering Gwaii Haanas.

BASICS: The **Queen Charlotte Islands** *(250/559-8316. www.qcinfo.com)* and **Gwaii Haanas National Park Reserve and Haida Heritage Site** *(Box 37, Queen Charlotte, B.C. 250/559-8818. www.harbour.com/parkscan/gwaii)*

ISLAND WILDLIFE

Nicknamed "Canada's Galapagos" for their abundance of indigenous plants and animals, the Queen Charlotte Islands teem with wildlife. Along with larger cousins of both the North American black bear and the pine marten, the islands boast deer mouse, dusky shrew, and short-tailed weasel.

Marine mammals and seabirds flourish here as well. Watch for orcas, minke whales, and the occasional humpback. Every spring, Pacific gray whales migrate through island waters. The southern tip of the Queen Charlottes, near Cape St. James, is home to a large breeding colony of Steller sea lions. From May through August, an estimated 1.5 million seabirds nest along the Queen Charlottes' 15,000-mile shoreline; almost half of them roost in Gwaii Haanas. You'll see tufted and horned puffins, Peale's and peregrine falcons, and other raptors. And with the islands astraddle the Pacific flyway, dozens of species of migrating birds drop in on the lakes, rivers, and coves each spring and fall.

A SUPER NATURAL CRUISE

With **Anvil Cove Charters,** a 53-foot schooner serves as a base for hiking and sea kayaking the natural attractions of Gwaii Haanas.

Anvil Cove's six-day **Voyage of Discovery** is best for families with younger children; you spend more time on shore and less time kayaking or shipboard.

On the first day of the tour, guests cruise to the Haida village of K̲'uuna, where Haida Watchmen show totems and longhouse remains.

The tour's second day includes a sail past the rocks at Laseek Bay to view some of the 400 sea lions that inhabit the place, as well as a visit to Hlk'yah (Windy Bay), where a pair of longhouses were constructed to house the Haida who camped there in 1985 to protest the logging of Lyell Island. This is the site of a rare first-growth forest; one giant spruce tree is 13 feet (4 meters) in diameter.

Day 3 brings a cruise to Kunghit Island, southernmost isle in the Queen Charlotte chain, where seabirds by the thousand bob and feed in the water. Keep an eye peeled for puffins, distinguishable by their brilliant orange beaks and dramatic black-

and-white faces. At night, when the seabirds nest in burrows on the shores of the aits surrounding Kunghit Island, their twittering can be heard for miles.

The fourth day of the Anvil Cove tour offers an exploration of the ancient village Nan Sdins, where totems teeter in profusion and visitors can view the remains of Haida longhouses.

Day 5 features sea kayaking around Burnaby Narrows, where paddlers get a chance to explore the intertidal display of green sea cucumbers, pumpkin- and cranberry-colored sea stars, crabs, and sea anemones.

The sixth day is capped by a stop in the abandoned village of T'aanuu.

TIPS: The schooner *Anvil Cove* has room for eight guests. Because the menu features seafood, notify owner-operators Keith and Barb Rowsell (who often crew together as skipper and cook) if your children have allergies to same. Young Haida children will often hitch a ride on the *Anvil Cove* to visit family members living on other islands.

BASICS: **Anvil Cove Charters** *(250/559-8207. www.qcislands.net/anvilcove)* charges $1,500 (CN) per adult and $750 (CN) per child (under 12) for the six-day **Voyage of Discovery** tour. The schooner may also be chartered for custom trips.

Others licensed to operate in Gwaii Haanas are **Queen Charlotte Adventures** *(800/668-4288. www.qcislands.net/qciadven)* for day and multiday trips; **Moresby Explorers** *(800/806-7633)* for day trips out of Sandspit; and **Duen Sailing Adventures** *(888/922-8822. www.duenadventures.com)* for overnight sailing trips.

Bald Eagle Viewing
Brackendale

Here's your chance to float to a fly-in. Each winter between November and February, thousands of bald eagles from Alaska, the Yukon, British Columbia, and parts of the U.S. flock to the **Squamish River Valley** near Brackendale (about halfway between Vancouver and Whistler) to feed on spawned-out chum salmon. To witness this magnificent spectacle—believed to be the world's largest concentration of bald eagles—you can design your own day trip, or paddle down the Cheakamus and Squamish Rivers in the company of naturalist guides on a river-rafting trip organized by **Canadian Outback Adventures.**

In 1994, 3,701 bald eagles were counted in Brackendale, breaking the previous world record of 3,600 observed at the Chilkat Bald Eagle Preserve near Haines, Alaska. On a float down the Cheakamus River on Canadian Outback's 10-mile (6-km), two-hour trip, the view includes the Tantalus mountain range, the snowcapped pyramid of Mount Garibaldi, and wall-to-wall bald eagles. The birds perch in cottonwoods along the riverbanks; as many as 20 may crowd into a single tree. On an average trip, visitors spot 400 to 600 eagles.

It's a thrill to spy these majestic raptors and hear their high-pitched squawks at

Catch of the day: A bald eagle fishes for salmon in the waters off Vancouver Island.

close range, but action-oriented kids should be forewarned that bald eagles don't actually *do* much but sit and look imposing at this time of day. Although the average 14-pound bald eagle eats 10 percent of its weight each day, it tends to feed in the early morning or evening. If you're lucky, however, you may see the odd eagle hop onto the riverbank and drag a fish away.

TIPS: In early November, salmon spawn and swim upstream beside your raft. Come December, however, decaying salmon carcasses litter the riverbanks and gravel bars. For most people, the resulting fishy odor is more than offset by the increased number of eagles.

Prepare for cold, sometimes rainy weather. Dress warmly: Wear a jacket with hood, and don't forget hat and gloves.

BASICS: Canadian Outback Adventures *(657 Marine Drive, Suite 100, West Vancouver. 800/565-8735 or 604/921-7250. www.canadianoutback.com)* charges $149 (CN) per adult and $109 (CN) per child (12 and under) for its eagle-watching float trips, including transportation from Vancouver. There is no minimum age, but the operator's smallest life jacket generally suits two-year-olds.

Quadra Island

Take a hike in the forests of **Quadra Island,** and your kids will learn how the ancient Coast Salish people turned cedars, alders, and other vegetation into food, bowstrings, and longhouses. Go sea kayaking in the ocean nearby, and your children will discover how to spot a shell beach that holds the remains of an ancient village or rocks that were once used to trap fish. Two soft-adventure tour operators combine nature tours on Quadra Island with a wealth of information about the Coast Salish and Kwagiulth Nations.

Quadra Island, a 10-minute ferry ride from the town of Campbell River on Vancouver Island, is a tranquil refuge from urbanization. Channels and inlets crenellate the heavily forested shore, itself pockmarked by crystal-clear lakes. Two-thirds of the island is inaccessible by road, and its northeastern part is protected by **Main Lakes Chain Provincial Park.** With fewer than 4,000 residents and only a handful of businesses, Quadra Island offers a pace of life so laid-back it's almost reclining.

Originally inhabited by the Coast Salish people, Quadra Island came to be occupied by the Kwagiulth Nation in the mid-1800s. Today, about 200 of the We-Wai-Kai band of the Kwagiulth Nation continue to live in the village of Cape Mudge on Quadra's southern tip. The first nonnatives arrived in the late 1800s; they set up a logging camp in Granite Bay atop the midden of an old Coast Salish village.

Modern-day adventurer Bernard Eberlein operates **Coastal Spirits,** a personalized hiking and sea kayaking business. Tell him about your family and he'll recommend an appropriate hike somewhere on the island's 150 miles of trails. (The **Nugedzi Lake Trail,** for example—a round-trip of just over 4 miles (6.4 km)—is suitable for ages 9 and older.)

On a guided hike past 300-year-old hemlocks and cedars, Eberlein points out salmonberries, blackcurrants, and huckleberries—great kid snacks all. He relates how the First Nations turned alder bark into dye and converted cedar roots into bowstrings. Using the Socratic method, Eberlein leads children to understand how native people made waterproof clothes, and how canoe trees were felled without axes (hint: start by heating rocks). A highlight of any guided hike with Eberlein is the trailside tea he brews from pine needles, licorice-fern root, and huckleberry leaves collected along the way.

Complementing Coastal Spirits is **Spirit of the West,** its focus cultural history rather than nature. Jeanette Taylor, the guide on Spirit of the West's **"cultural history" sea-kayaking tours,** uses old photos and containers of ochre powder and salmon eggs (for painting pictographs on rocks) to bring the early Coast Salish people to life. Taylor—museum curator, island resident, author of a book on local First Nations history—accompanies visitors to historic sites all over Quadra Island. When families sign up, she often brings along her own son and daughter.

The **Granite Bay day trip** run by Spirit of the West is ideal for children as young as six—provided they can sit still in a kayak for 1-1/2 hours. Taylor leads guests to the height of land where Coast Salish families lived 400 years ago, then invites

FIRST NATIONS MUSEUMS

The **Kwagiulth Museum and Cultural Centre** *(P.O. Box 8, Quathiaski Cove. 250/285-3733. www.island.net/~kmccchin/. Daily June-Sept.; Tues.-Sat. Oct.-May)* in Cape Mudge on Quadra Island displays masks, headdresses, coppers, and other gifts and treasures exchanged during potlatch ceremonies. The lofty structure, designed along the lines of a traditional longhouse, also features turn-of-the-century photographs of Kwagiulth villages. The site's new **Artist and Carving Centre** exhibits totem poles and provides a venue for native artists.

Across the road are several **petroglyph boulders** from the Tsa-Kwa-Luten Lodge site; they were brought here for protection. Making rubbings of these original petroglyphs is prohibited, but the museum has fiberglass replicas that serve just as well. On Vancouver Island—a 10-minute ferry ride from Quadra Island—the **Museum at Campbell River** *(470 Island Hwy., Campbell River. 250/287-3103. www.island.net/~crm_chin)* offers an array of First Nations artifacts, art, and clothing. A **vintage logging truck** is the centerpiece of the museum's logging gallery. Don't miss the sound-and-light presentation of **The Treasures of Siwidi,** a native legend featuring masks and ceremonial regalia.

youngsters to scavenge for fool's gold (iron pyrite, a yellowish mineral compound) at the abandoned 1908 Lucky Jim Gold Mine. From Granite Bay, families can paddle double or single kayaks to a range of archaeological sites. At **Orchard Bay**—site of a large First Nations village in continuous use for hundreds of years—Taylor explains how early villagers turned trash into treasure: They tossed their empty clam shells out their front doors, eventually creating a 10-foot-high (3 m) midden that protected the village from enemy attack. At another site, Taylor hauls out her ochre powder, which children mix with salmon eggs to paint pictographs on rocks.

TIPS: Wear hiking boots or sturdy walking shoes, and be prepared for weather changes. Put rain gear and a dry shirt in your backpack in case of rain.

BASICS: Bernard Eberlein and his wife run **The Lodge,** a small but comfortable B&B *(1069 Topcliff Rd. 888/427-5557 or 250/285-2895. www.coastalspirits.bc.ca)* not far from **Rebecca Spit Provincial Park.** Each of the cabin's three bedrooms ($59 to $69 CN) has its own entrance and bathroom; one room boasts a kitchenette.

Tsa-Kwa-Luten Lodge *(P.O. Box 460, Quathiaski Cove. B.C. 800/665-7745 or 250/285-2042. www.capemudgeresort.bc.ca)*, owned by the Kwagiulth people, is a two-story, weather-beaten cedar lodge standing on a bluff overlooking the Discovery Passage. The basic accommodations (about $125 CN) include two-story loft rooms with three double beds and two-bedroom beach cabins with kitchenettes. No TVs. On selected summer evenings, a youth group performs traditional Kwagiulth songs and dances.

Guided day hikes with **Coastal Spirit** *(Box 630, Quathiaski Cove. 888/427-5557 or 250/285-2895. www.coastalspirits.bc.ca)* run about $80 (CN) per person. Ask about their tours that combine hiking, sea kayaking, and local history.

The **Granite Bay day trip** offered by **Spirit of the West** *(P.O. Box 569, Herlot Bay, B.C. 800/307-3982 or 250/285-2121. www.kayak-adventures.com)* costs $89 (CN) per person and includes lunch. Also available: a two-night **Pictographs & Petroglyphs** trip to neighboring Cortes Island.

Vancouver Aquarium Marine Science Centre

"Sleeping with the fishes" takes on a positive spin at the **Vancouver Aquarium Marine Science Centre,** where **whale sleepovers** featuring tours behind the scenes give children a chance to hear beluga creaks and squeals, walrus bongs, and narwhal squawks and toots.

"Regular" visits are possible, too. The aquarium's **North Pacific Gallery,** for example, showcases the sea creatures found along the coast of British Columbia. Just how prickly is a sea urchin? You'll find out as a naturalist introduces you to live touch pools.

Register in advance for **Animal Encounters**—staff-guided experiences that get kids close to critters. Older children are partial to the **Arctic Encounter:** Standing knee-deep in the beluga habitat—and wearing hip waders and "aqua socks" furnished by the aquarium—a family of up to six may touch and pet a beluga whale, or feed it herring, capelin, and squid. In the **B.C. Water Encounters,** youngsters and adults come fingertip-to-tentacle with a giant Pacific octopus and get extreme closeups of sea lions, sea otters, and elusive wolf eels.

In summer, the aquarium sponsors outdoor adventure vacations of its own in the Vancouver wilderness. These include rafting, hiking, and kayaking trips lasting one to several days; all are suitable for families. On the **Squamish River overnight adventure,** for instance, guests board rafts to descend the Upper Squamish River Valley, home to bears, deer, salmon, and seals. A team of naturalists and guides comes along for the float, helping visitors navigate the generally well-behaved white water and explaining details of the area's diverse ecosystem.

The **B.C. Hydro Salmon Stream Project** debuts in 2000, when hundreds of salmon will swim up and spawn along a demonstration stream running from Coal Harbor in Stanley Park to the aquarium. In 1998, more than 10,000 salmon fry were released into Coal Harbor, along with a pheromone—an organic hormone that will help the now adult salmon "scent" their way back to Stanley Park, where they complete their life cycle in the waters of the demonstration stream.

TIPS: Overlooking the beluga habitat, the aquarium's **Upstream Café** allows you

Taking the measure of a beluga whale at the Vancouver Aquarium Marine Science Centre

to watch whales and eat lunch at the same time. The aquarium is located in Stanley Park, a five-minute drive from downtown Vancouver. Stanley Park offers biking around its seawall, a water playground, a giant outdoor swimming pool, and a wading pool.

BASICS: **Vancouver Aquarium Marine Science Centre** (*Stanley Park. Information 604/659-3474, registration 604/659-3505. www.vanaqua.org. Adm. fee*)

For **A Sleepover with the Whales,** aquarium members pay $73 (CN) per adult and $64 (CN) per child (minimum age: 6 years); nonmembers pay $78 (CN) per adult and $72 (CN) per child. One-on-one **Animal Encounters** start at $54.95 (CN) and include gift certificates to the gift shop and café. Minimum age for **B.C. Water Encounter** is 6 years. Minimum age for **Arctic Encounter** is 8 years. Other encounters available. Admission to the aquarium is included in all prices quoted.

FOR FUTURE SCIENTISTS & ANTHROPOLOGISTS

Science World British Columbia (*1455 Quebec St., Vancouver. 604/443-7440. www.scienceworld.bc.ca*). Freeze your shadow, mix music digitally, create comic strips, and use electricity to make your hair stand on end at this hands-on center. **University of British Columbia Museum of Anthropology** (*6393 Northwest Marine Dr. 604/822-3825. www.moa.ubc.ca. Closed Mon.*). Worth a visit for its impressive collection of totem poles, including several placed outdoors next to Haida houses. Displays also include First Nations art and artifacts.

Royal B.C. Museum
Victoria

At the **Royal British Columbia Museum,** carefully re-created street scenes and landscapes—authentic down to their very sound effects—bring alive the natural history of British Columbia.

Especially effective is the **First Peoples Gallery** on the third floor. Here, native chants and a large cedar house lit by the warm glow of a "fire" make it easy for kids to imagine what life was like for British Columbia's earliest peoples. Don't be surprised if you hear normally nonchalant school-age boys describe the Nawalag-watsi—the Cave of Supernatural Power—as "freaky" or "scary." Peer into the dark cave to find out why: Inside, painted ceremonial masks stare back at visitors to a soundtrack of chanting and drums.

Elsewhere in the First Peoples Gallery are snowshoes, woven baskets, and black-and-white photographs of natives in canoes and ceremonial dress. Visitors will also discover a detailed diorama of an early Kootenay encampment, replete with scale models of tipis, horse corrals, and women cleaning buffalo skins. At the reconstructed pit house, which served as a winter home for natives in British Columbia's interior, kids learn the trick of digging a home into the ground; they also come to understand why snow-covered sod made such an effective form of early insulation. Access to the pit house was via a notched pole ladder through the smoke hole above the central fire.

In the **Maritime Gallery,** children walk the planks—of an old corridor from a wood-paneled ship, that is. There are models of early "cruise ships"—Hudson's Bay steamships and stern-wheelers—and kids will want to troop up the wooden gangplank of *Discovery,* a life-size replica of the three-masted naval sloop that was launched in 1789. Capt. George Vancouver sailed aboard the vessel for 15 years, using it to explore much of British Columbia's coastline. On board the sloop, the realism of the reconstructed captain's quarters is heightened by sounds of the sea and the creaking of ship's timbers.

Detailed dioramas depict the fur trade that flourished along the banks of the Stikine River in northern British Columbia during the 1830s. The museum's re-creation of B.C.'s gold-rush era (from 1849 to 1900) features a giant Cornish water wheel, circa 1862, which pumped water out of flooded mine shafts and hauled ore to the surface. The simulated fish cannery provides a commendably high gross-out factor when kids get a glimpse of benches wet with slabs of pink salmon. A model of the 1900 Britannia Cannery at Steveston reveals that environmentalism is no new vogue: As early as 1921, B.C. newspapers were warning that depleted stocks threatened the area's salmon-fishing industry.

The best exhibit on the second floor is a simulated submarine dive, the **Open Ocean,** to the bottom of the sea. The descent takes 30 minutes and moves through seven ocean layers, including some of utter inky blackness. It's all an exercise in

A sea-monster house-front painting and totem poles outside the Royal B.C. Museum in Victoria

"stealth education": As you ascend in a submarine elevator with portholes and video cameras highlighting the fish outside, kids learn all about the vampire squid and bioluminescent animals that roam the ocean floor, not to mention the salmon and other fish that are native to British Columbia.

As you might expect, the Royal British Columbia Museum's exhibit on local forests is excellent. Stroll past the mounted deer, moose, and bears in their natural forest setting, for example, and you'll feel the cold wind blowing through the spruce and cedars.

The museum's **National Geographic Theatre** shows IMAX films on whales, Egyptian treasures, and other wonders of the natural and ancient world.

TIPS: Start on the museum's most interesting floor—the third—and work your way down from there. On the second floor, don't miss the Open Ocean exhibit and its convincing re-creation of a voyage to the seafloor by submarine.

Before leaving the museum, check out the gift shop; its well-stocked selection of children's books includes volumes with punch-out totem poles, as well as Northwest Coast Indian coloring books.

BASICS: **Royal British Columbia Museum** *(675 Belleville St., Victoria. 888/447-7977 or 250/387-3701. www.rbcm.gov.bc.ca. Adm. fee)*

Cowichan Native Village Duncan

Everyone—even very young children—gets a chance to carve at the **Cowichan Native Village** in Duncan, an hour's drive from Victoria on Vancouver Island. Owned and operated by the **Cowichan tribes,** the 6-acre (2.4 ha) facility provides hands-on opportunities to experience the Cowichan culture.

The Cowichan tribes can trace their history back 5,000 years. Part of the Coast Salish Nation of southern B.C. and Upper Puget Sound in Washington state, the seven tribes that made up the Cowichan band lived in 13 villages along the Cowichan River in the tranquil Cowichan Valley (Cowichan means "warm land"). The tribe numbered about 6,000 at the time of its first contact with nonnative settlers.

The Cowichan River, one of Canada's five unspoiled "heritage rivers," teems with spawning salmon in winter. The salmon were a staple of Cowichan existence, as were deer, elk, and moose. Today, about 4,000 Cowichans—the largest aboriginal band in B.C.—live in nine reserves on 6,000 acres (2,430 ha) of the Cowichan Valley.

To see the village, meet your Cowichan guide at the outdoor fire pit beside the giant totem pole. The 40-minute tour usually starts with an explanation of how totem poles figured in Cowichan culture: Originally designed to represent family wealth and heritage, the poles later took on myriad other meanings. Most kids like the idea of house poles. If you feel grouchy when you leave home, touch the house pole out front; you'll feel good again upon your return.

The **Comeakin House,** built of western red cedar, is a gathering place modeled on a traditional longhouse. It was constructed for World Expo '86 in Vancouver, then dismantled and rebuilt in the village. The Comeakin House now hosts summer performances of Cowichan song and dance. Children enjoy rubbing the front door's carved salmon eggs as they leave, a gesture purported to bring good luck.

At the world's largest **carving house,** the chips fly as Cowichan master carvers transform chunks of red and yellow cedar into works of art. You may meet John Murphy, who specializes in carving animal figures on plaques and yellow-cedar doors; Jacob Joe, known for his house poles and entrance poles; or Simon Charlie, whose sculptures reside in museums and galleries around the world.

Make a point of stopping at the visitors' carving pole in the carving house, where a guide helps kids chisel cedar, then collect the fragrant shavings as souvenirs. Each year, visitors work on a new pole, which is touched up by a master carver at the end of the season. The large whale sculpture at the entrance to the village, for example, is a visitor carving.

If you like, cap off the guided tour by attending a multimedia slide presentation depicting Cowichan history from the early 1800s to the present. Be aware, however, that the show's thunderclaps and flashing strobe lights may frighten toddlers.

Perhaps the most fun for kids is the **Circle of Children.** In this longhouse oper-

Cowichan carver Francis Horne Jr. uses a carving blade to turn a cedar tree into a totem pole.

ated by native Cowichan students, parents can work side by side with their kids to paint wooden disks, decorate masks, or create "spirit rocks" by painting stones plucked from the Cowichan River. The resulting crafts are for the keeping.

TIPS: Visit the carving house, a showcase of high-quality artwork. Four carvers worked 16,000 hours to complete the 30-foot-long (9 m) diorama, carved in yellow cedar, that depicts eight hunters harpooning a California gray whale. In summer, Cowichan women spin wool on a loom and knit sweaters in the gift shop. Book in advance for the midday salmon barbecue and native performance in the Comeakin House.

BASICS: **Cowichan Native Village** *(200 Cowichan Way, Duncan. 877/746-8119 or 250/746-8119. www.cowichannativevillage.com. Adm fee)* The village is open for guided tours from early spring to late fall. The **Circle of Children** operates from June 1 to September 30.

TEEMING TOTEM POLES

Duncan, the "City of Totems," boasts a totem-pole population of more than 40. Since 1985, when Duncan began participating in the revival of this art form, the city's Totem Pole Project has attracted carvers from as far away as Québec and New Zealand. Follow the yellow footprints for a self-guided walking tour of the totems.

Panning for Gold
Dawson City

When George Carmack, Skookum Jim, and Dawson Charlie hit pay dirt at remote Rabbit Creek in the Yukon in 1896, they touched off a gold rush of legendary proportions. More than 100,000 prospectors from around the world raced to the Klondike to strike it rich. About one-third of the treasure seekers wound up in **Dawson City.** Within 10 years, this speck on the map had grown into a boom town of 30,000, the largest city north of Seattle and west of Winnipeg.

People still flock to Dawson City, but most of them are summer tourists intent on touring the goldfields. Indeed, on a warm summer day, when cruise-ship passengers arrive by the busload, it seems that Gold Rush fever never cooled.

Kids will be ecstatic to find they can still pan for gold on genuine mining claims. In another echo of life 100 years ago, Royal Canadian Mounted Police officers, sporting traditional red serge uniforms, patrol the streets all summer on horseback.

Start your own search for gold at the **Visitor Reception Centre.** At **Dredge #4,** about 15 minutes by car up Bonanza Creek Road, the whole family can pan for gold. **Gold City Tours** runs guided excursions with the promise of "Gold Guaranteed." **Eureka Gold Panning Adventures** offers prospecting and camping trips.

Eureka can accommodate groups of six in wood-framed wall tents along Hunker Creek, the Yukon's richest stream during the 1930s. Kids—especially those 10 to 14—love searching for gold. Owner Morris George shows how to handle a prospector's gold pan, spilling water and gravel but leaving the gold behind. The flakes you find won't finance the trip, but nothing beats the thrill of striking gold.

Teens forced to read *White Fang* or *Call of the Wild* in school may be interested in the bizarre saga of Jack London's cabin. London was a 21-year-old student when he arrived in the Yukon in 1897, questing for gold. He lived in a rough cabin about 75 miles south of Dawson City, where he found no gold—but plenty of rich characters for his books. In 1965, Yukon author Dick North hired a native guide to locate the cabin; London's signature on the back wall vouchsafed the structure's authenticity. Oddly enough, the timbers were then divvied up: Half were shipped north to Dawson City and made into a replica of the cabin there, while the other half traveled south to London's hometown of Oakland, California, where they became part of a replica that sits on the main square.

Another writer who called Dawson City home was Yukon bard Robert Service. At the vintage **Robert Service Cabin,** daily readings of his poems celebrate northern characters and their foibles.

TIPS: Dawson City celebrates Canada Day (July 1) with the **Annual Yukon Gold Panning** championships, which are open to children. Visitors can also get privy

Two rivers of ice converge to form Kaskawulsh Glacier in Kluane National Park, Yukon Territory.

to the fun at the **Klondike International Outhouse Race,** run early in September.

BASICS: Dawson *(Visitor Reception Centre, 867/993-5566. Mid-May–mid-Sept.)* can be reached from Whitehorse via the Klondike Highway. Allow about six hours for the drive in good weather. The truly adventurous may canoe the Yukon River from Whitehorse to Dawson, a 10- to 14-day trip. **Eureka Gold Panning Adventures** *(Box 33072, Whitehorse, YT. 867/633-6519. www.eurekagoldpanning.yk.ca)* runs **Wall Tent Camp** *(June–mid-Sept.),* a 45-minute drive from Dawson City. Overnights cost $60 (CN) for the first person, $15 (CN) for each additional. Gold panning costs $15 (CN) per hour or $60 (CN) per day.

THE GREAT GABFEST

Storytellers from around the world gather each June in Whitehorse, the capital of Yukon Territory, for the **Yukon International Storytelling Festival** *(P.O. Box 5029, Whitehorse, YT. 867/633-7550).* Huge tents blossom on the banks of the Yukon River as venues for stories, mime, dance, drama, crafts, and children's programs. The First Nations component features legends, drumming, song, and a special tent for the elders. It's a relaxed festival: Balloon artists and musicians stroll the grounds, and storytellers weave tales geared to children and adults.

Nunavut Cruise

Don't look for **Nunavut** (NOO-na-voot) in any atlas published before April 1, 1999. That's when the eastern part of the Northwest Territories became a new territory, a result of the largest aboriginal land-claim agreement in Canadian history. Nunavut—"our land" in the Inuit language—covers more than 770,000 square miles (2 million sq km), making it nearly one-fifth the size of Canada.

Nunavut is hard to reach but easy to appreciate. Visitors make the long trek here to gaze upon vast unspoiled landscapes, to experience Inuit culture up close, and to admire the territory's rich variety of birdlife and animal life.

As you might expect, airplane flights are expensive—and dependent on the weather. Other than roads within and around local communities, Nunavut's only paved road connecting two cities is a 13-mile (21 km) stretch in the Baffin Region. You can therefore cross Nunavut off your list of family driving destinations.

An easier and less expensive way to visit the territory is by cruise ship. **Marine Expeditions,** based in Toronto, offers expedition cruises aboard a fleet of former Russian research vessels. Arctic cruises, which include Nunavut, vary from year to year. Two typical routes are the Northwest Passage (sailing from Nanisivik, at the northern end of Baffin Island, to Greenland) and Churchill to Greenland (with stops at ports on southern Baffin Island and at islands across the mouth of Hudson Bay).

Don't expect a party ship with floor shows and one-armed bandits. The goal of these cruises is to discover the flora, fauna, and people of the region. The expedition experience is therefore best suited for older kids and teens who are interested in wildlife and Inuit culture—and who are inventive enough to amuse themselves on a ship filled mostly with adults. On each sailing, experts deliver shipboard lectures on the region's birds, mammals, wildflowers, and history. On our cruise, we learned all about glaciers, icebergs, and Inuit culture.

Ice, polar bears, and extreme weather cause last-minute changes in ports of call. The Russian captain and crew go out of their way to alter the ship's course to spot items of interest, such as whales. For shore explorations, they launch Zodiacs (motorized rubber rafts), weather permitting. Kids love zipping through the waves on the Zodiacs, bundled up—even in summer—against the wind and salt spray. On our cruise, we approached walruses basking on **Walrus Island,** then skirted the base of towering cliffs crowded with thick-billed murres. Some of the black-and-white birds guarded eggs; others leaped into the sea around us. In the course of several shore explorations during our cruise, passengers discovered a caribou skeleton and antlers, a human skull in an ancient tomb, and some walrus bones.

Although sighting certain species can never be guaranteed, Marine Expeditions cruises have turned up walruses, arctic foxes, polar bears, arctic wolves, arctic hares, and lemmings. The animals often take you by surprise; one day as we examined

Fortified with gun, snowshoes, and igloo, an Inuit hunter and his dog team end the day in Nunavut.

the remnants of an old Hudson Bay trading post, for example, a caribou herd suddenly thundered by. A talk on polar bears opened our eyes to the dangers of an encounter with this massive predator. To guarantee the safety of cruise-ship passengers, armed sentinels scout out each island along the way, making sure it is "bear free" before allowing passengers to disembark and walk around. **Lancaster Sound** is home to bearded seals, harp seals, walruses, beluga whales, and narwhals. At **Auyuittuk,** you're likely to spot whales and the occasional polar bear.

History comes alive at sites such as **Qaummaarviit,** where kids can see the semi-buried stone-and-sod houses occupied by the Thule ancestors of today's Inuit. At **Beechey Island,** passengers visit the graves of some of the doomed Franklin expedition members. During this 1845 attempt by Sir John Franklin to find the Northwest Passage, all 132 crewmen died after their ships became trapped in ice.

For kids, the highlight of a Nunavut cruise is the chance to meet Inuit children. At **Kimmirut** (Lake Harbour) on Meta Incognita Peninsula, nearly the entire town— 397 people—came out to greet us. The local children were especially excited, riding their bicycles out to the docks to help the crew pull in the Zodiacs. In the town's gym, Inuit teenagers demonstrated high-kicking and Arctic games that prize strength and endurance. Back on board, passengers took classes in the Inuktitut language.

TIPS: Dress in layers of warm, waterproof clothing—and don't forget hats and gloves. Backpacks leave hands free to handle binoculars and cameras. Knee-high rubber boots are essential for Zodiac "landings" (splashdowns, really).

BASICS: Marine Expeditions *(890 Yonge Street, 3rd Floor, Toronto. 800/263-9147 or 416/964-9069. info@marineex.com. www.marineex.com)* offers Arctic cruises that stop in Nunavut in July and August. Prices range from $1,945 to $4,795, with discounts of 25 percent for children 7 to 17 sharing a cabin with adults. Each vessel carries 120 passengers; book early. Only U.S. dollars are accepted on board.

FAMILY TRAVEL RESOURCES

THE INTERNET

Free lodging at resorts. Air fares so low you can afford to fly your parents and kids across the country. Impossibly low passages on cruise ships. All these are commonplace finds on the Internet, where travel is a hot commodity and websites lure the logged-on with deals and destinations. As you would in any retail environment, however, take time to window-shop this cyber mall before making any purchase: Compare prices, seek references, and check the fine print before buying.

More than 85 million travelers surfed the Internet as a prelude to travel in 1999, reports the Travel Industry Association of America (TIA). That degree of travel-related Web usage represented an increase of 190 percent over 1996. It also gave birth to a bevy of new travel sites. To help you cut through the data smog, here are some sites worthy of bookmarking by the family traveler:

JUST FOR FAMILIES

Family.go.com: Much of the content for family.go.com, a Disney site for parents, comes from sister publication *FamilyFun* magazine. Attuned to kids' needs, reporters for the site are accustomed to dissecting the children's programs offered by a popular resort, for example, or recommending how to pace a trek through spots as diverse as New York City and Yellowstone National Park.

You can search "TravelPlanner" (family.com's database) by location or by type of vacation. "Road-Tested Vacations" is a compilation of users' tips on trips, but you can't tell if the rates and write-ups retrieved by the search engine are timely or outdated. Family.go.com acquired **Babycenter.com**—a site aimed at parents of infants to three-year-olds—so some of its information targets this age group.

Family Travel Network: Part of America Online, the Family Travel Network (AOL keyword FTN) showcases destinations that it considers best suited for a family visit. These include resort pools, living history sites, kid-friendly cruises, dude ranches, and children's museums. The on-screen box labeled "Bargain Bonanza" offers deals on air fares, rental apartments in Europe, and resort packages; advice on family camping and city safaris appears in the site's "Family Vacation Guide." FTN, which boasts a wide range of family travel information, active message boards, and a variety of chats, is scheduled to debut as its own website in the spring of 2000; it will also continue as part of AOL.

Family Travel Forum (*www.familytravelforum.com*): This 12-page newsletter appears six times a year, both online and in print. It covers traveling with teens, experts' favorite resorts, top getaways for parents with tots, best family ski places, and other useful roundups—including a section in which experts pick their favorite resorts. Although the online version does not differ substantively from its hard-copy counterpart, it does confer a few benefits: You can search its database rather than your basement for back issues, and online subscribers can get staff responses to travel queries—Where's the best place to host a family reunion in southwestern Montana? What are some tolerable motels for kids between Houston and Boston?—that they submit via e-mail. *Family Travel Forum* costs $28 per year for the online component only, or $48 per year for both the electronic and paper versions. The price for a one-month online membership is $2.95.

Family Travel Times (*www.familytraveltimes.com*): Dorothy Jordon had been writing and producing her own bimonthly family travel newsletter for about 13 years when she replaced it with the launch of this website in April 1998. A free area offers planning advice for road trips, as well as reviews of recent travel books. For an annual subscription of $39, users gain access to the site's password-protected area, which offers six bimonthly issues containing firsthand reports on resorts, cruises, dude ranches, and other destinations.

IT'S A DEAL!

Best Fares (*www.bestfares.com*): Self-styled "bargain buckaroo" Tom Parsons chases down the cheapest airline, rail, cruise, and hotel rates for subscribers to this site. In the area titled "Snooze-You-Lose," even nonmembers get to lasso low air-fare deals. Parsons also gives subscribers the lowdown on travel scams, Net specials, and money-saving strategies. In the past, the site's senior-fares feature has listed air tickets available at discounts of up to 70 percent for travelers 62 and older—*and* their companions. Such budget stretchers are a great way to facilitate grandparent/grandchild togetherness. For an annual fee of $60, subscribers gain access to deal information online, as well as 12 monthly issues of *Best Fares* magazine.

1travel.com: The packed home page reflects this website's comprehensive approach to value vacations. To get the most from the site, scope out its deals rather than its destination information, which is composed by practitioners of the "bland brochure" school of travel writing. The buys on cruises, car rentals, resorts, vacation homes, and city trips in the United States and abroad, however—not to mention the low air fares—can be genuine finds. The "Fare Beater" feature often turns up prices even lower than those you located on the previous search of 1travel.com. To go lower still, try the site's "White Label" fares, but beware of the catch: Only general travel information is made available about any ticket before you buy it—and the purchase is nonrefundable. Weekly e-mails keep you informed of last-minute low fares.

Expedia.com: Developed by Microsoft, Expedia.com is a full-service travel site offering hotel and airline deals and vacation packages, as well as destination information, maps, and special deals on travel merchandise. "Travel News" offers updates on attractions for family, adventure, cruise, and business travelers. "World Guide" presents highlights of major cities around the globe, while "Best Places" posts features on various destinations. The insider advice from the "Travel Doc" contains useful tips for traveling while pregnant, traveling with kids, traveling with kids with earaches—you get the picture.

Airlines: Sign up for carriers' free weekly e-mails announcing discounted deals at the last minute. Most such missives are sent on Wednesday for travel the following weekend, and most come with restrictions. Don't bet the family trip on catching one of these; if the fare fits, however, grab it and go. **Air Canada** *(www.aircanada.ca);* **American Airlines** *(www.aa.com);* **Continental** *(www.continental.com);* **Delta** *(www.delta-air.com);* **Northwest** *(www.nwa.com);* **TWA** *(www.twa.com);* **United** *(www.ual.com);* **US Airways** *(www.usairways.com)*

Amtrak. To check train schedules and keep abreast of deals, board Amtrak's website at www.amtrak.com.

DESTINATION STATIONS

Kasbah: The Travel Search Engine *(www.kasbah.com)* responds to digital inquiries by marshaling links to books, hotels, local attractions, and related places. Though not exhaustive, such one-stop shopping makes a more than adequate beginning. A quest for information on Washington, D.C., for example, yielded connections to the *TimeOut* and *Rough Guides* series, the Smithsonian Institution museums, and a quirky list of obscure hotels. (Lodging may be the site's weak spot.)

Another drawback is the circuitous navigation, occasioned by the lack of an area devoted exclusively to family travel. To reach the Mining Company's kid-friendly travel site, for example, you must first search Kasbah for "family," then click on "looking up information on Kasbah." Kludgy.

Some nice touches for world travelers are the currency converter and the international weather forecasts.

Great Outdoor Recreation Pages *(www.gorp.com)* allows active families seeking soft adventure to find out what it feels like to sea kayak in Bermuda, mountain bike in Québec, or crawl through a cave in New Mexico. Rafting, hang gliding, archaeological digs, and hundreds of other outdoor activities are included. Although most of the entries are not aimed at families, the write-ups will nonetheless pique the interest of parents, teens, and twentysomethings. Features in the site's smallish family section range from how-tos (teaching kids to climb) to first-person travel narratives (taking kids to Tanzania in search of elephants and giraffes).

Though well written, most of the articles have not been broken into smaller chunks for easy reading; it's therefore strictly "scroll as you go."

GORP recently purchased **American Wilderness Experience** *(Boulder, Colorado. 800/444-0099 or 303/444-2622),* a clearinghouse for quality adventure vacations (with an emphasis on dude ranches). A number of AWE outfitters offer family trips. These include rafting in Texas, Montana, and Idaho; dogsledding in Minnesota; and llama trekking in Colorado.

More and more visitor centers are using the Web to list basic information and lodging contacts. In addition to checking these out, try strolling through **Sidewalks** *(www.sidewalk-citysearch.com).* Distinguished by its easy navigation and local flavor, the site lists sporting events, movies, and theater information for many cities throughout the United States.

GIMME SHELTER

Hotel Chains and Private Homes: The quality of websites maintained by hotel chains varies, but don't rule them out. Many post maps pinpointing their locations within a city, plus photographs of their rooms. A few also highlight special rates.

Family travelers may wish to browse the sites for **Hyatt** *(www.hyatt.com),* **Radisson** *(www.radisson.com),* and **Starwood** *(www.starwood.com),* which covers the **Westin, Sheraton,** and **W** properties. If you prefer the charm of independent hotels (many of them overseas), check out www.srs-world-hotels.com for its collection of 360 hotels in 65 countries.

For more hotel deals and lodging suggestions, visit www.hotelbook.com or www.all-hotels.com. Despite their huge inventories, neither site lists all the hotels in an area; they seem to stint on upscale lodgings in particular.

ResortQuest International *(www.resortquest.com):* A vacation home or condominium confers some obvious bonuses—more living space, lower food bills—on the traveling family. ResortQuest, a booking agent for 15,000 privately owned properties in U.S. vacation destinations, boasts an easy-to-navigate site that presents its lodgings by region (beach, island, mountain, or desert) as well as by recreation (golf, skiing, tennis, or fishing).

NATIVE AMERICAN INTERNET SITES

If you are researching further cultural explorations with Native American nations, the following two university-library sites are windfalls of information:

www1.pitt.edu/~lmitten/nations.html contains histories and links to many tribes' home pages assembled by **University of Pittsburgh** librarian Lisa Mitten.

cavern.uark.edu/libinfo/subject/NatAm.html is the product of the **University of Arkansas Libraries;**

it provides links to general Native American sites, as well as to some Native councils and reservations.

Native Web *(www.nativeweb.org)* offers information, news, and links to other sites relating to indigenous peoples around the world, particularly those in North and South America.

The **Alliance of Tribal Tourism Advocates** seeks to "support cultural integrity and traditional values in the development of tribal tourism." The alliance's website *(atta.indian.com)* features links to in-depth information about eight Native American nations. Most of the nations do not offer overnight facilities, but some have small museums and tours by special appointment. Particularly interesting is the Powhatan Renape Nation's repudiation of the Pocahontas myth.

FACT-FINDING

The Web has given adventure travelers a powerful shortcut to governmental information. The site maintained by the **National Park Service** *(www.nps.gov)*, for example, furnishes details on park highlights, activities, hours, and fees.

Wondering which inoculations are required for a visit to Mexico or Canada? Visit the website of the **Centers for Disease Control** *(www.cdc.gov)* to learn their requirements and recommendations for travel abroad. Worried that a political situation will interrupt your trip? Journey to the website of the **U.S. State Department** *(travel.state.gov)* to read the latest travel warnings and concerns. You can also check out the free summary releases made available by **Pinkerton Global Intelligence Services** on their site *(www.pinkertons.com)*, but Pinkerton's detailed travel reports can be costly.

For driving directions and maps, try **Mapquest** *(www.mapquest.com)* or **Maps on Us** *(www.MapsOnUs.com)*. To get a weather forecast for just about any adventure-vacation destination, click on the **Weather Channel** *(www.weather.com)*.

FAMILY-FRIENDLY TRAVEL COMPANIES

The following organizations have tailored a number of their trips to intergenerational travel. If you can't find an adventure that suits you on their website or in their catalogue, contact the company and ask it to customize one for you.

Backroads *(800/462-2848 or 510/527-1555. www.backroads.com)* offers a variety of bicycling, mountain biking, and hiking tours (as well as combos of all three) in the U.S., Canada, Europe, and other destinations. Many of these tours are suitable for parents and teens; a few of the trips are tailored to families with grade-schoolers. The Backroads trip through the San Juan Islands of Washington state suits kids of all ages. You can tow your toddler in a Burley trailer, or let beginning cyclists (ages 4 to 7) pedal a Piccolo trailercycle—a one-wheeled bike

hooked to the back of yours. Kids 7 and older bike on their own. Most family trips involve camping, but some are inn to inn.

Grandtravel *(800/247-7651 or 301/986-0790. www.grandtrvl.com)* offers domestic and international trips designed for grandparents traveling with grandchildren. The company simplifies this daunting task by organizing each vacation, arranging the transportation for it, and furnishing an escort who provides enrichment—and diversions—for the kids. Departures for two separate age groups—7 to 11 and 12 to 17—help ensure that grandchildren travel in the company of kids their own age. (For grandparents, the arrangement guarantees the presence of other adults.) Although Grandtravel itineraries are packed with activities, the trips are costly.

Outdoor Adventure River Specialists *(800/346-6277 or 209/736-4677. www.oars.com)* features a variety of raft trips on Western and Midwestern rivers, as well as on waterways in Canada, Mexico, and a few other international locations. Several departures each season are designated as appropriate for families; some are even pitched to mothers and daughters, fathers and sons, or fathers and daughters. The family trips include a Fun Director, who rallies the kids onshore with games and educational play. For flatwater trips, the minimum age is about 5; for mild whitewater, it's 7.

Rascals in Paradise *(800/872-7225)* specializes in family and small-group tours to the Caribbean, Mexico, and the South Pacific. When there are enough families, Rascals assigns an escort or nanny to help out with the kids.

River Odysseys West *(Coeur d'Alene, Idaho. 800/451-6034 or 208/765-0841. www.rowinc.com)* stages **Family Focus Salmon River Canyons** raft trips in which participants ride the rapids through rock-walled canyons and past grassy mountains topped with ponderosa pines. The Lower Salmon River—the last 53 miles of the watercourse—presents ideal whitewater conditions for families: sandy beaches for camping, water that is warm enough for swimming, and class II to III waves (exciting, but not difficult to run). An extra staff member is assigned to each Family Focus trip, ensuring that a leader is always available to engage the kids in nature talks or games. ROW also offers **Parent-Teen Focus trips** on the Salmon River.

Sierra Club Outings *(415/977-5522. www.sierraclub.org/outings/national)* offers a variety of camping, hiking, rafting, and lodge-based nature trips for families. Some adventures are geared to grandparents traveling with their grandchildren, to parents of toddlers, or to teenagers. The outings are affordable, well run, and low key.

INDEX

ILLUSTRATION CREDITS

ACKNOWLEDGMENTS

Many fine writers assisted with this book. I am grateful for the good judgments and fine writing of the following contributors to the Canadian section: Barb and Ron Kroll, Maureen Littlejohn, Janice Mucalov, Kate Pocock, and Betty Zyvatkauskas. I also appreciate the hard work of Diane Ney, who contributed to some of the U.S. sections.

DEDICATION

As always to my favorite traveling companions, Alissa, Matt, and David

ABOUT THE AUTHOR

Having written about family travel for more than 17 years, **Candyce H. Stapen**, Ph.D., is a pioneering expert in the subject. She is the author of eight previous travel books, among them the four-part series *Great Family Vacations*. Stapen also contributes to Expedia.com and AOL's Family Travel Network, and she reports on family travel for WUSA-TV, the CBS affiliate in Washington, D.C. Stapen's travel articles have appeared in newspapers, magazines, and websites, including *FamilyFun* magazine, *Vacations, The Washington Times, National Geographic Traveler, family.go.com, Parents, Good Housekeeping, USA Weekend. com,* and *Child.* In 1997, Stapen won the gold award of the Society of American Travel Writers' Lowell Thomas Travel Journalism Competition.

CREDITS

Text copyright © 2000 Candyce H. Stapen

Copyright © 2000 National Geographic Society

Published by
THE NATIONAL GEOGRAPHIC SOCIETY

John M. Fahey, Jr.
President and Chief Executive Officer

Gilbert M. Grosvenor
Chairman of the Board

Nina D. Hoffman
Senior Vice President

William R. Gray
Vice President and Director, Book Division

Elizabeth L. Newhouse
Director of Travel Publishing

Allan Fallow
Editor

Joan Wolbier
Art Director

Melissa Ryan
Illustrations Editor

Caroline Hickey
Senior Researcher

Carolinda E. Averitt,
Alison Kahn
Text Editors

Barbara Quarmby,
Lise Sajewski
Copy Editors

Josie Dean, Rebecca Mills,
Jane Sunderland,
Mark Waner
Editorial Researchers

Carl Mehler
Director of Maps

Mapping Specialists Ltd.,
Gregory Ugiansky
Map Research and Production

Meredith C. Wilcox
Illustrations Assistant

Lewis Bassford
Production Project Manager

Mark Wentling
Indexer

Composition for this book by the National Geographic Society Book Division. Printed and bound by R.R. Donnelley & Sons, Harrisonburg, VA. Color separations by North American Color, Portage, MI. Covers printed by Miken Inc., Cheektowaga, New York.

Library of Congress Cataloging-in-Publication Data

Stapen, Candyce H.
National Geographic guide to family adventure vacations : wildlife encounters, cultural explorations and learning escapes in the US and Canada / by Candyce H. Stapen.
p. cm.
Includes index.
ISBN 0-7922-7590-X
1. United States--Guidebooks. 2. Canada--Guidebooks. 3. Family recreation--United States--Guidebooks. 4. Family recreation--Canada--Guidebooks. I. Title: Guide to family adventure vacations. II. Title: Family adventure vacations. III. National Geographic Society (U.S.) IV. Title.

E158.S777 2000
917.104'648--dc21   99-462106
                                                                              CIP

Visit the Society's website at http://www.nationalgeographic.com